Litigation and Arbitration in EU Competition Law

Litigation and Arbitration in EU Competition Law

Edited by

Mel Marquis

Part-time Professor of Law, European University Institute, Italy

Roberto Cisotta

Lecturer and Adjunct Professor, LUMSA Free University, Italy

EE Edward Elgar PUBLISHING

Cheltenham, UK • Northampton, MA, USA

Published by
Edward Elgar Publishing Limited
The Lypiatts
15 Lansdown Road
Cheltenham
Glos GL50 2JA
UK

Edward Elgar Publishing, Inc.
William Pratt House
9 Dewey Court
Northampton
Massachusetts 01060
USA

A catalogue record for this book
is available from the British Library

Library of Congress Control Number: 2014954948

This book is available electronically in the **Elgar**online
Law subject collection
DOI 10.4337/9781783478866

MIX
Paper from
responsible sources
FSC® C013056

ISBN 978 1 78347 885 9 (cased)
ISBN 978 1 78347 886 6 (eBook)

Typeset by Columns Design XML Ltd, Reading
Printed and bound in Great Britain by T.J. International Ltd, Padstow

Contents

Contributors

Adelina Adinolfi	University of Florence
Laura Bergamini	Cleary Gottlieb Steen & Hamilton LLP, Rome
Giacomo Biagioni	University of Cagliari and Studio Pietrangeli, Rome
Gordon Blanke	International Arbitration Group, Baker & McKenzie/Habib Al Mulla, Dubai
Roberto Cisotta	LUMSA Free University of Rome
Daniele Gallo	LUISS Guido Carli University, Rome
Edoardo Gambaro	Studio Santa Maria, Milan
Alexandre Geulette	European Court of Justice, Luxembourg
Sonja Keske	Bundeskartellamt, Bonn
Mel Marquis	European University Institute, Florence and LUMSA Free University of Rome
Francesco Munari	University of Genoa and Munari Giudici Maniglio Panfili, Genoa
Renato Nazzini	King's College London and Labruna Mazziotti Segni, Milan
Lorenzo F. Pace	University of Molise and Studio Legale Pace, Rome
Kostandin Peci	Cleary Gottlieb Steen & Hamilton LLP, Rome
Sebastian Peyer	University of Leicester
Mario Siragusa	Cleary Gottlieb Steen & Hamilton LLP, Rome

Litigation and arbitration in EU competition law

Roberto Cisotta and Mel Marquis*

This book contains the proceedings from a conference on litigation and arbitration in EU competition law which we organized at LUMSA University in Rome on 8 November 2013. The motivation behind the conference arose from two principal considerations. First, in the last decade, the role of national courts in competition-related litigation has been significantly enhanced both *de jure* and *de facto*. This is linked, as is well known, to the effects of Regulation 1/2003,[1] which (among other things) empowered national courts to apply Article 101 TFEU in its entirety in appropriate cases. These effects, combined with those of key judgments of the European Court of Justice (ECJ) which have established an EU 'right to damages' as compensation for injury caused

---

* Roberto Cisotta is Lecturer and Adjunct Professor at LUMSA Free University of Rome. Mel Marquis is Part-time Professor of Law at the European University Institute in Florence and *Professore a contratto* at LUMSA. We would like to express our warm thanks to the contributors to this volume and to all who participated at the conference to which we refer in the main text. Most of the papers in this book were presented at the conference but they have been updated more recently. The conference was organized as part of the activities of the Research Working Group on 'The Charter of Fundamental Rights of the EU, the ECHR and the Fundamental Values of the Italian Constitution', which is chaired by Professors Monica Lugato, Eduardo Gianfrancesco and Chiara Favilli. We thank each of them, as well as Dean Angelo Rinella, for their gracious institutional support. Finally, we are deeply grateful to Cristina Montaldi and Kanako Nagao for their cheerful encouragement and patience.

[1] Council Regulation (EC) No 1/2003 of 16 December 2002 on the implementation of the rules on competition laid down in Articles 81 and 82 of the Treaty [2003] OJ L1/1.

by competition law infringements,[2] are significant factors giving national courts a central role in the application of EU competition law.

This shift in the institutional structure of competition law enforcement can only be reinforced by the new 'Damages Directive' of the European Parliament and of the Council Directive 2014/104/EU, which introduces a series of provisions governing certain aspects of private damages actions.[3] This instrument, which has been touted as 'democratizing' the enforcement of competition law,[4] is discussed in several of the chapters that follow.[5] Whether a democratization of enforcement (a concept not altogether clear) is to emerge in Europe remains to be seen. However, at least on certain parameters and in certain Member States (most visibly Germany, Netherlands and the UK but also, *inter alia*, Belgium and Spain) it is difficult to deny that Europe has been warming up to private litigation, descriptively and normatively, as a means of resolving disputes linked to competition law. Such litigation is not limited to actions aimed at securing compensation for past harm: they may relate, for example, to proceedings to obtain injunctions.[6] Nevertheless, in general it is damages actions that are receiving the most attention, and it is plainly important to examine the new EU Directive critically and to elaborate an early assessment.

Yet claims brought before courts for the purpose of obtaining damages or injunctive relief are only part of a broader range of controversies that must be decided by national courts in the field of EU competition law, including notably State aid cases, which are also discussed in the contributions to this volume. Expanding the focus, the authors herein also consider the position of individuals (natural and legal persons) and issues related to the judicial protection of their (substantive and procedural)

---

[2] See especially Case C-453/99 *Courage Ltd v Bernard Crehan v Courage Ltd and Others* [2001] ECR I-6297; Joined Cases C-295/04 to C-298/04 *Vincenzo Manfredi v Lloyd Adriatico Assicurazioni SpA* [2006] ECR I-6619.

[3] Directive of the European Parliament and of the Council. The Directive was signed into law in Strasbourg on 26 November 2014 following its adoption by the Council of Ministers on 10 November 2014 and by the Parliament on 17 April 2014. It entered into force in late December 2014 and must be transposed by the Member States by 27 December 2016.

[4] See Joaquín Almunia, 'Looking back at five years of competition enforcement in the EU', SPEECH/14/588 of 10 September 2014, at p. 4.

[5] For in-depth analysis of the Damages Directive, see also Mel Marquis and Giorgio Monti (eds), *Shaping Private Antitrust Enforcement in Europe* (Hart Publishing 2015, in preparation).

[6] See Barry Rodger (ed), *Competition Law Comparative Private Enforcement and Collective Redress across the EU* (Kluwer Law International 2014).

rights. This issue lies at the root of the current complex interaction between the work of the courts of the European Union and the national courts, in particular in the field of competition law. The matter would be trivialized if confined to a somewhat sentimental deference to be shown in particular to the European Convention on Human Rights, emphasized after the *Menarini* judgment,[7] and to the EU Charter of Fundamental Rights (CFREU). On the contrary, the issue of judicial protection has several concrete declinations, and it is capable of conditioning the substance of the rights of individuals and the possibilities of their effective enjoyment.

It is by examining this broader picture, extending across the range of issues just mentioned, that we endeavor to break ground with this contribution. We hope and expect this volume to function as a stimulus in this respect, encouraging more scientific efforts to shed further light on how EU competition law is implemented by courts deciding cases in different EU Member States. Our subject also encompasses the EU Courts themselves as part of our investigation, and touches on, for example, the explicit and implicit dialogues that take place between (especially) the ECJ and the courts of the Member States. Interactions between the latter courts and the European Commission in the field of competition law are also discussed.

The first objective is therefore to survey a variety of issues arising where competition law cases are litigated. These issues will be further specified below in our overview of the contributions that appear in the first two Parts of this book.

The second principal aim is to explore a set of issues where published research has been rather sparse and incomplete: the application of EU competition law by arbitrators. Arbitrators too have been affected in important ways by the 'modernization' of the enforcement of EU competition law. Indeed, the reformed framework that took effect in 2004, together with jurisprudence of the Court of Justice concerning the arbitrability of EU law issues, have made it more common for both practitioners and public enforcers to look to arbitration as a means of enforcing competition law or monitoring (enforcing) enforcement solutions.[8] The subject of arbitration is thus tied to our understanding of the

---

[7] *A Menarini Diagnostics SRL v Italy,* App no. 43509/08 (ECHR 27 September 2011).

[8] See Carl Baudenbacher and Imelda Higgins, 'Decentralization of EC Competition Law Enforcement and Arbitration', (2002) 8(3) Columbia Journal of European Law 1; Luís Silva Morais, 'Integrating Public and Private Enforcement of Competition Law in Europe: Legal Issues', in Philip Lowe and Mel Marquis

implementation of EU law by a complex and heterogeneous institutional apparatus. A well-known obstacle to complete research in this domain is the largely confidential nature, with some exceptions, of arbitral proceedings. Nevertheless, there is ample material to be explored, both in terms of what EU law permits and requires, and in terms of particular legal and institutional problems posed by commercial arbitration, including for example how it affects and is affected by the activities of public authorities enforcing EU competition law. In this respect, two legal circumstances, and their (at least apparently) opposite effects, make the relationships between EU competition law and arbitration a subject of particular interest for lawyers engaging with EU law. These circumstances are, first, the refusal by the Court of Justice to consider arbitrators and arbitral tribunals as 'courts or tribunals' capable of referring questions to the Court for a preliminary ruling under Article 267 TFEU; and second, the above-mentioned trend increasing the role of arbitration in the enforcement of EU competition law.

The latter developments suggest the following two conclusions. First, we must take note of the risk, absent appropriate mechanisms to ensure coherence, that the unity of EU competition law enforcement might be undermined. According to the Court's case law, where national courts are called on to review arbitral awards dealing with competition law issues, they must treat EU competition law as a matter of 'public policy', a mandate that may appear apt to achieve uniform enforcement. However, uncertainty remains as to the precise extent of the scrutiny to be applied

---

(eds), *European Competition Law Annual 2011: Integrating Public and Private Enforcement of Competition Law – Implications for Courts and Agencies* (Hart Publishing 2014) 109. The EU Damages Directive, which is, as explained in the main text, the most recent move towards a greater role for national courts, will also have a direct and indirect impact on arbitration. In particular, arbitrators may have to apply some of its provisions in proceedings before them, and they will have to consider the possible relevance of the Directive in the context of any subsequent review by national courts of the award they render at the end of those proceedings. See the abstract of Renato Nazzini's presentation, 'Arbitration of Competition Law Disputes and the New EU Directive on Antitrust Damages Actions', TILEC Seminar: Enforcement of competition law, 22 May 2014, <http://www.tilburguniversity.edu/upload/9e2d2ba8-29b2-4bb9-a08f-32d7416b7f73_TILEC%20Invitation.pdf> accessed 28 August 2014. Subject to boundaries set by arbitrators' circumscribed jurisdiction (deriving from both private autonomy and the untouchable sphere of public enforcers' competences) and by the extent of judicial review of awards (see in particular chapters 11 to 13 herein), the reflections on the Directive appearing in this book may thus be potentially relevant in the context of arbitral proceedings as well.

by courts exercising their powers of review. Moreover, when arbitral awards are not challenged before a court, the intransparency of the proceedings means that the uniform application of the law cannot even be assessed, let alone guaranteed. The second conclusion is that, despite the risks just described, arbitration is becoming a valued and even routine tool employed by economic actors, often with the encouragement of the public authorities responsible for enforcing competition law in the public interest. In light of the growing importance of arbitration in the field of competition law, we devote Part III of the book to this subject.

The three Parts to which we have already alluded are the following:

PART I PRIVATE ANTITRUST ENFORCEMENT AND JUDICIAL COHERENCE IN EUROPE

PART II LITIGATING ANTITRUST AND STATE AID ISSUES BEFORE THE COURTS OF THE EUROPEAN UNION AND THE COURTS OF THE MEMBER STATES

PART III EU COMPETITION LAW BEFORE ARBITRATORS

In the remainder of this introductory chapter we briefly preview the chapters included under each of the above heads.

PART I PRIVATE ANTITRUST ENFORCEMENT AND JUDICIAL COHERENCE IN EUROPE

Sebastian Peyer's chapter is called 'The Antitrust Damages Directive much ado about nothing?' This title telegraphs Peyer's critical conclusions, according to which the Directive may be expected to have only a limited impact and is deficient in light of its own ostensible *raison d'être* – the stimulation of private claims for damages arising from infringements of competition law. As Peyer argues, the Directive subtly eats its own tail by (i) imposing formidable barriers making it difficult for claimants to obtain evidence from competition authorities (for which compensation is made only partially in the form of rules on the probative value of final infringement decisions); and (ii) avoiding the issues that really matter, in other words, aggregation of small claims (collective redress[9]) and funding and cost issues (given that, in many Member States, cost rules chill the urge to take matters to court). If one continued down the line of Peyer's reasoning one might conceivably even ask if the Directive itself is compatible with the *effet utile* of the EU competition rules, although we doubt that such a radical position can be sustained.[10] Peyer, however, limits himself to observing that the Directive seems as effective as the proverbial damp squib: not only are its provisions weak; its objectives are fundamentally contradictory (ensuring full compensation for victims while at the same time 'coordinating' public and private enforcement) and its consequent identity crisis. But beyond Peyer's critical remarks, the chapter also serves, particularly in its third section, as a useful overview of the Directive's various provisions. In the following sections he then provides a critical review of three of the Directive's specific subjects: access to evidence; joint and several liability (and the significant limitations thereto); and the rules on the standing of indirect purchasers to bring claims (and their relationship to the provisions on the passing-on defense). The chapter concludes the burial of the Directive with its epitaph: 'unlikely to fulfil the promises it has made'.[11]

One may then add that the growing trend toward more frequent use of private means of antitrust enforcement in certain Member States (which

---

9 Peyer's remarks in his introduction make clear that he regards the Commission's Recommendation on Collective Redress as wholly inadequate. This view is consistent with the critique presented in the next chapter by Sonja Keske (see below).

10 In this regard, a pertinent benchmark would be the status quo. We agree with Peyer that at least some aspects of the Directive are weak, and may even prove ineffectual. However, on the whole (and appreciating that the Directive entails tradeoffs), it does not make damages claimants worse off than they are absent the Directive. Our views regarding the Directive and related issues have been published elsewhere. See Roberto Cisotta, 'Some Considerations on the Last Developments in Antitrust Damages Actions and Collective Redress in the European Union' (2014) 10(1) Competition Law Review 81 (and more recently, Cisotta, 'The Evolving Framework for Antitrust Damages Actions and Collective Redress in the European Union: a First Assessment', (2014) 28(3) Rivista del Commercio Internazionale 709); Mel Marquis, 'Perchance to Dream: Well Integrated Public and Private Antitrust Enforcement in the European Union', in Lowe and Marquis (eds), *Integrating Public and Private Enforcement*, cited above note 8, xiii et seq.

11 Page 46.

does not extend to compensation of ordinary small consumers) will not fundamentally be a consequence of the Directive as such but rather should be attributed, in large part, to the consciousness-raising discourse among stakeholders that ensued from the judgment in *Courage v Crehan*;[12] to the more complete powers of national courts post-'modernization' to apply Article 101 in particular; and perhaps also, in part, to a general evolution from bureaucratically-driven enforcement toward increasing reliance on 'legal' instruments, legal 'support structures',[13] and institutions.[14] Arguably, and while certain provisions of the Directive were pointedly contested by the EU's political institutions during the legislative process, the relatively anodyne nature of the legislation may partly explain its adoption at first reading.

Sonja Keske's chapter, 'Collective redress – (too) great expectations?', is partly prompted by and focuses on the Commission's 2013 Recommendation on common principles for injunctive and compensatory

---

[12] Cited above, note 2. It is perhaps needless to say, but reflections on the private enforcement of EEC/EC/EU antitrust law, and relevant antecedents in the case law (in other words, both Community and national case law), went much further back than *Courage*, with policy discussions dating back to the 1960s. (See, for example, H. van den Heuvel, 'Civil-Law Consequences of Violation of the Antitrust Provisions of the Rome Treaty' (1963) 12 American Journal of Competition Law 172, especially at 184–191 [correctly discerning that the ECJ's judgment in *Van Gend en Loos* tended to point by implication towards a conceptualization of the EEC antitrust rules whereby those rules were imbued with concerns not only of general interest but also of individual interest; van den Heuvel thus hints at page 188 that those rules have direct effect, and he perceives at page 193 that the discrepancies that would arise from the litigation of antitrust matters in a multi-state system with divergent civil law institutions would likely justify the adoption of a Regulation or Directive at EEC level to establish coherent governing principles]). Nevertheless, the run-up to *Courage*, and the judgment itself, effectively institutionalized the European private enforcement discourse in a manner not theretofore seen.

[13] On the trend in Europe towards greater legalism and juridification, with reference to the post-*Courage* private enforcement debate, see R. Daniel Kelemen, *Eurolegalism: The Transformation of Law and Regulation in the European Union* (Harvard University Press 2011) 171–174 and generally Chapter 5.

[14] Compare Simon Vande Walle, 'What Keeps Plaintiffs Away from the Court? An Analysis of Antitrust Litigation in Japan, Europe and the US', in Dimitri Vanoverbeke et al. (eds), *The Changing Role of Law in Japan – Empirical Studies in Culture, Society and Policy Making* (Edward Elgar 2014) 209 (making a roughly similar observation, in other words, one that attributes the 'turn' to private antitrust litigation in certain EU Member States to institutional reforms but also (rapidly) evolving cultural attitudes and other contextual factors).

collective redress mechanisms in the Member States concerning violations of rights granted under Union Law ('Recommendation').[15] According to Keske, who writes from a competition law perspective (although, as she notes, the Recommendation also covers other kinds of claims such as those arising from, for example, environmental law), if a collective redress system is to be successful it must encompass a sound combination of interdependent features, which in turn requires a firm understanding of the factors by which group litigation can succeed or fail. The first key factor in this context is the 'rational apathy' problem, that is to say, the disproportionate cost of seeking damages for an individual plaintiff compared to the relatively small amount of individual harm done. The damages caused – although significant in the aggregate – are 'scattered' among diffuse, rationally apathetic victims of wrongdoing, leading to coordination problems and leading, to the extent that public enforcement does not fill the void, to malfeasance with impunity, and unjust enrichment. In this light, a collective redress system has to find ways of rebalancing benefits and costs, including the costs of detecting the harm in the first place, and the costs of demonstrating damages and causation – not to mention the extra costs befalling the plaintiff if the suit should fail. As Keske points out, there is evidence, especially as far as competition law violations are concerned, that it is end-consumers who are most affected by rational apathy; yet even a 'good' collective redress mechanism is not always apt to overcome this kind of problem. A second key factor to be taken into account when establishing a collective redress system is procedural economy: although aggregated actions are not always possible because of potential conflicts of interest among plaintiffs (for example, conflicts between direct and indirect purchasers), proceedings which are brought against the same alleged infringers and which arise from the same facts tend to be best treated in a consolidated manner. In light of the foregoing perspectives, end-consumers stand to gain a great deal from an efficient, effective system of collective redress.

However, not all the EU-level instruments that ostensibly support damages actions and the underlying goal of compensation consistently pursue this objective. For example, Article 11 of the above-mentioned Damages Directive exempts small and medium enterprises (SME) from the general rule of joint liability, making them liable only to their own (direct and indirect) customers. This rule essentially forces customers of

---

[15] For her extensive commentary on collective redress that pre-dates the Recommendation, see Sonja Keske, *Group Litigation in European Competition Law: A Law and Economics Perspective* (Intersentia 2010).

other (non-SME) cartelists to sue their providers separately. Keske argues that, even where a Member State introduces collective redress mechanisms following the model proposed in the Recommendation, there will still be difficulties, in particular in the context of competition law. Access to evidence is an illustrative potential obstacle, in particular for end-consumers. Since they are unlikely to be able to obtain a case-worthy body of evidence independently, they are likely to act (if at all) only after a public enforcer has adopted an infringement decision. With the adoption of the Damages Directive, and especially Article 9 thereof, a court must recognize such a decision as either irrefutable evidence of the infringement (if the enforcer is an authority of the Member State in which that court sits) or as *prima facie* evidence of it (in the case of authorities of other Member States). Thus, it may be that end-consumers, in line with the explicit aims of the Commission, will be more inclined to bring follow-on actions than to bring stand-alone claims. But it has to be borne in mind that follow-on actions, despite their evidentiary advantages, are not guaranteed to be successful. Indeed, it may still prove difficult, under the applicable (national) rules, to demonstrate that all the other criteria which condition liability and recovery – in other words, those beyond the existence of the infringement – are satisfied. Moreover, with regard to collective redress, other problems may complicate the joining of forces of numerous claimants, perhaps above all where Member States conform to the opt-in system chosen by the Commission as the preferred mechanism for forming the group. For example, complications may arise from the need to identify victims, which can be costly and difficult. This leads to a consideration of costs, and to the related problem of raising the funds necessary to sustain an action and to hedge against the risk of defeat. The need for adequate funding relates both to the initial phase and to the proper litigation phase; together with the rules on entry into and exit from a collective action, the way funding rules are shaped can be a crucial determinant for the effectiveness of a collective redress system.

Keske's main point is that the rules proposed in the Recommendation, together with a series of factual, legal and cultural circumstances in the various Member States, have to be understood in the context of the role collective redress has played in the EU. Although, as Keske explains, there have been interesting experiments in Europe with collective redress in certain Member States, the litigation environment in Europe as a whole remains worlds apart from the experience recorded in the United States. The U.S. 'litigation culture' – meant in the positive sense of a thriving system of effective compensation, and not in the fear and loathing sense – probably cannot be expected to emerge in Europe in the foreseeable future, notwithstanding the trends toward more vibrant litigation in the Member States mentioned earlier. Coming to the final reflections in her chapter, Keske questions the trajectories the Commission has laid down by electing soft harmonization (as opposed to binding minimum standards) and by favoring a 'horizontal' approach, which rejects the promulgation of a more finely honed instrument governing competition law-related litigation only. Not unpersuasively, Keske intimates that renewed attention to the need for EU-level action can be expected following the Commission's assessment of the Member States' implementation of the Recommendation, a review scheduled to be carried out by late July 2017.

Adelina Adinolfi discusses 'Judicial dialogues and uniformity in the multi-level application of EU competition law'. Parts of this chapter pick up on themes seen in the chapters by Peyer and Keske, but the lens is widened to encompass a broader *tableau.* Adinolfi, taking Regulation 1/2003 as a pivotal frame of reference, provides extensive reflections on the complex relations between the ECJ and the courts of the Member States. But she also focuses on the relations between the national courts and the Commission, as these trans-institutional interactions are equally relevant to the principle of the uniform application of EU competition law. The richness of the chapter cannot be conveyed in a capsule summary but we cover its main lines here. The starting point is the re-designed application of EU competition law as conceived in the choices crystallized in the Regulation. Since the new design amplified the application by national courts and authorities of the EU competition rules, it also inherently raised the risk of fragmentation. In many ways, modernization has produced a profound convergence among enforcement cultures, in particular as concerns competition authorities in Europe; but the situation with regard to national courts is made more complex in part by a range of distinctive (and occasionally inconsistent) legal traditions and entrenched procedural rules, and in part by the principle of judicial independence. These elements and potential divergences across Member States do not imply judicial and institutional anarchy: national autonomy, in the form of traditions and even constitutional foundations, is ultimately subordinate to EU law principles such as, among others, effectiveness and equivalence. But 'negative integration' is no panacea and, without additional mechanisms, centrifugal forces would pose an existential threat to EU law in this field. The risks of Europe's new enforcement architecture were well appreciated, however, and several such compulsory and voluntary mechanisms have been established by the Regulation and by practice – supplemented by binding guidance provided via the preliminary reference procedure (per Article 267 TFEU). Adinolfi describes and evaluates the utility and application of these mechanisms in her chapter.

Following her introduction, the subsequent sections of Adinolfi's chapter address four themes: the role of national courts in pursuing the uniform enforcement of EU competition law; judicial enforcement of competition law and preliminary references; the means by which Regulation 1/2003 strives to maintain coherence among judicial decisions; and the Regulation's 'leftovers' from the perspective of the uniform enforcement of EU law. These themes underscore the tension between: (i) the uniformity principle, as expressed and promoted by, for example, the qualified 'unassailability' of Commission infringement decisions (deriving from the *Foto-Frost* and *Masterfoods* judgments[16] of the Court of Justice and from Article 16(1) of the Regulation); and (ii) judicial independence, which should not be compromised too much by the supranational character of Commission decisions or by the superior expertise of the Commission on questions of substantive competition law.

That tension may be exacerbated if, in addition to the inability of national courts to review Commission decisions, the Court of Justice itself shows the Commission too much deference. Here and elsewhere, Adinolfi's chapter serves as a bridge to the other chapters in this book (see chapters 4 and 5 by Geulette and Nazzini). On the other hand, the intensity of review by the EU Courts is becoming relatively more rigorous, at least with regard to fining decisions. More robust quality assurance at EU level could thus potentially enhance trust in Commission decisions. In any case, however, the 'unassailability' of Commission decisions is fundamentally without prejudice to the option (or obligation) of national courts to seek a preliminary ruling. There is no guarantee that the solicited guidance will always be lucid, wise and univocal, but the procedure is nevertheless crucial for maintaining workable coherence throughout the system.

In the fourth section of her chapter, Adinolfi discusses Article 15 of Regulation 1/2003, which together with the principle of sincere cooperation serves as a principal legal base for cooperation between national courts and the Commission in the field of antitrust (including, for example, requests for information or opinions from, and/or *amicus* interventions by, the Commission). Several points must be neglected here for reasons of space but one may note the 'dark' side of cooperation,

---

[16] Respectively, Case C-314/85 *Foto-Frost v Hauptzollamt Lübeck-Ost* [1987] ECR 4199; Case C-344/98 *Masterfoods Ltd v HB Ice Cream Ltd* [2000] ECR I-11369.

since cooperative mechanisms may be thinly veiled means of monitoring and 'controlling' national judges' activities – again reflecting the risks of destabilization that flow from 'modernization'. However, it has become increasingly evident that certain mechanisms established by Article 15 of the Regulation could function better than they do, particularly as concerns the obligation on Member States to furnish relevant judgments to the Commission. Poor compliance in this regard hampers the ability of the Commission, in appropriate circumstances, to file case observations with national appellate courts. Another point re-emerging here is that, as with the above-mentioned Article 16(1), there is some (potential) interplay between Article 15 and the preliminary reference procedure.

In the fifth section, Adinolfi discusses the Regulation's 'leftovers'. As powerful and incisive as the Regulation has been, it remains an invertebrate instrument, in particular from the perspective of the uniform application of competition law. The key point here is that constellations of procedural law often drive, and may potentially have more systemic consequences than, substantive outcomes; yet Regulation 1/2003 has neither the aim nor effect of aligning rules of national civil procedure. One might have predicted at the time of the Regulation's adoption that the EU's neofunctionalist instincts would eventually trigger a further incursion into the traditional spheres of the State, and in the coming years the nature and intensity of the next incursion(s), shaped partly by the priorities of a new Commission, will be hotly contested. A series of issues which may require (perhaps informal) attention, as Adinolfi points out, relate to arbitration. For example, where parties resolve disputes via arbitration, the cooperation mechanisms under Regulation 1/2003 are inapplicable; and, as noted earlier, the Court of Justice can only directly consider issues germane to the dispute if the award is challenged in national court and the court then refers questions to Luxembourg, a circuitous and contingent mechanism. Thus, while arbitration raises issues of great importance to the uniform application of EU competition law, EU law has hobbled itself, foreclosing paths to workable coherence. In underlining these issues, Adinolfi once again establishes links with other chapters of this book (see Part III). The same may be said with regard to her final remarks, which fall upon certain provisions of the EU's Damages Directive and the Commission's Recommendation on Collective Redress; the chapter thus ends where chapters 1 and 2 begin.

PART II LITIGATING ANTITRUST AND STATE AID ISSUES BEFORE THE COURTS OF THE EUROPEAN UNION AND THE COURTS OF THE MEMBER STATES

Section 1: Antitrust

Alexandre Geulette contributed a chapter on the 'Evaluation of evidence by the European Courts in competition cases'. Not so long ago, it was uncommon for this topic to be contemplated as a stand-alone object of discussion; but considering that so much turns on how evidence is reviewed by the EU Courts, it is easy to accept Geulette's claim that familiarity with the nuances of this subject are essential to litigation in Luxembourg. Beginning with a review of the burden of proof, the standard of proof and the standard(s) of review that apply in competition law cases, Geulette turns to his principal theme. In this context he discusses the jurisdiction of the General Court to establish the facts and to examine the evidence before it; the evidence adduced by the parties to the litigation; the 'rules of evidence', such as they are, that apply before the Courts; their holistic appreciation of the evidence, as opposed to a more narrow, piece-by-piece examination; and in some detail Geulette analyzes the probative value or credibility the Courts attach to various types of documents (admissions, corporate leniency statements, economic analyses, and so on) and the matrix of factors that may have an impact in that regard. One factor not explicitly mentioned but alluded to at the end of the chapter is the 'human' factor. As Geulette notes (though not in these words), besides the obvious fact that the expertise of the judges in Luxembourg is legal and generally not economic in nature, reactions to evidence are to some extent inevitably subjective; it is only in the realm of the ideal that perfect consistency across cases may be achieved – in the EU Court system or any other. Nevertheless, the trend toward more minute and explicit discussions in judgments of how the evidence has been treated in particular cases – and one must note the tradeoff in terms of efficiency and elegance – helps to advance that cause.

Renato Nazzini's chapter, 'The evolution of the "full jurisdiction" of the Union Courts in Article 101 and 102 matters', extends his previous work discussing, *de lege lata* and *de lege ferenda*, shifts toward increasingly intense judicial scrutiny (in other words, toward a more searching standard of 'correctness'), especially in connection with the *KME* case[17] decided in 2011 by the Court of Justice.[18] The principal aim of this new chapter is to evaluate the impact *KME* is having, and the impact it should be having, on the subsequent jurisprudence of the EU Courts. The chapter is helpfully summarized in Nazzini's 'Conclusions', on which we draw here. First, the significance of *KME* is confirmed. In light of that judgment, where the Commission has imposed a fine for an infringement of EU competition law, the Commission is not entitled to any (*de facto*) margin of discretion with respect to the manner in which it has set the fine.[19] This individualized decision-making, where the standard of correctness applies, should be distinguished from the manner in which the Commission formulates its general fining policy; in this different setting, the Commission executes its legitimate function as a policy maker and is not constrained by the principle of effective judicial protection. (The Courts remain free to invalidate the Commission's policy orientations if they are contrary to EU law as properly construed, but this is a separate issue that does not bear precisely on the proper standard of review.)

The second point is that the standard of correctness also applies to the Commission's evaluation of factual evidence unless that evaluation can be characterized as a complex economic or technical assessment, in which case the Courts show more self-restraint. As Nazzini argues, this standard of correctness applies (or should apply) not only as regards the

---

[17] Case C-272/09 P *KME Germany AG v Commission* [2011] ECR I-12789. See also Case C-386/10 P *Chalkor AE Epexergasias Metallon v Commission* [2011] ECR I-13085.

[18] See Renato Nazzini, 'Administrative Enforcement, Judicial Review and Fundamental Rights in EU Competition Law: A Contextual-functionalist Perspective' (2012) 49 Common Market Law Review 971.

[19] Going beyond the narrow matter of the setting of the fine, Nazzini adds that '[i]f any deference to the Commission's discretion in relation to the setting of the individual fine is inconsistent with the principle of effective judicial protection, it seems that the same approach should extend not only to the actual calculation of the fine, but also to the attribution of liability, reductions or increases in fines depending on cooperation or lack thereof, and any other issue of fact or law that is directly relevant to the imposition or the setting of the fine. However, on such matters the General Court is still wavering'. Page 134. By wavering, Nazzini means that the General Court's recent case law has not yet concretely come to terms with the principle that the Commission's margin of discretion, such as it is, cannot be a basis for dispensing with an in-depth review of both the law and the facts, and hence also of the Commission's assessments thereof (a principle which follows from *Chalkor*, cited above, note 17, para 62; and implicitly from *KME*, cited above, note 17, para 109).

relevance of the evidence *vis-à-vis* the fine but also logically as regards its relevance *vis-à-vis* the existence of an infringement of the law.[20]

Third, picking up on the subject of complex assessments, the continuing zone of deference which the Commission enjoys in this context is, in Nazzini's view, contrary to Article 47 of the CFREU.[21] On the one hand, the matter of complexity is resolved at first instance by an institution that is not itself impartial, despite the potentially decisive impact the complex matter may have with regard to grave legal and pecuniary consequences for a defendant; on the other hand, the Courts' limited review of that institution's choices imply that errors made regarding those potentially crucial issues will not adequately be rectified via the exercise of full jurisdiction.

In light of the foregoing descriptive and normative assessments, it may be hoped that further work in this area will encourage the adjustments needed to 'complete' the trend toward more robust quality and legitimacy control of Commission decisions by the EU Courts in Article 7 cases where fines are imposed under Article 23. In the quite different context of Article 9 cases – which this chapter is not designed to address – questions regarding such quality and legitimacy control remain unanswered, even if one may point to mechanisms that substitute in some measure for judicial scrutiny.

Lorenzo F. Pace contributed a chapter entitled '*Dura lex sed lex*: the parent-subsidiary relationship in EU antitrust law and the *AEG Telefunken* presumption – independence of the EU legal system, effectiveness of competition law and protection of fundamental rights'. Pace begins by briefly reviewing the evolution of fundamental rights protection in the context of the application of EU competition law, in respect of which the Court of Justice has played an enormous role. Although the fundamental rights discourse in the competition law context has ramped up in the last decade or so (as the 'war on cartels' expanded), Pace recalls that an early

---

20 This position seems to chime with arguments made elsewhere on more text-based grounds that the Court's unlimited jurisdiction should apply not just to the setting of the fine but also more broadly to the Commission's infringement decision whereby the fine is imposed. See Ian Forrester, 'A Bush in Need of Pruning: The Luxuriant Growth of "Light Judicial Review"', in Claus-Dieter Ehlermann and Mel Marquis (eds), *European Competition Law Annual 2009: The Evaluation of Evidence and its Judicial Review in Competition Cases* (Hart Publishing 2011) 407, 423 and 417–419.

21 The second sentence of Article 47 of the Charter provides that everyone is entitled to a fair and public hearing within a reasonable time by an impartial and independent tribunal.

judgment in which the Court acknowledged that fundamental rights were part of Community law – the *Nold* case[22] – was a competition case. Pace then recalls that already in the 1980s arguments were raised to the effect that the European system of competition law enforcement was contrary to Article 6 ECHR. It was then that the claim – seemingly ubiquitous nowadays – that the European institutional structure, in which investigative and decisional powers are both placed in the Commission's hands, is incompatible with the rights that must be guaranteed when undertakings may be exposed to quasi-criminal sanctions. More recently, in the era of the above-mentioned 'war on cartels' and of the Commission's weapons of financial destruction, fundamental rights arguments have become part and parcel of Europe's competition law 'conversation'. As Pace notes, Article 6(2) TEU, as amended by the Treaty of Lisbon, the binding nature of the CFREU, the *Menarini*[23] judgment of the European Court of Human Rights and other factors have all encouraged the development of fundamental rights-based claims before the EU Courts.

Passing to his main theme, which may be seen as a case study, Pace focuses on the issue of the imputation to parent companies of liability for the antitrust mischief of their subsidiaries.[24] As competition lawyers in Europe know, if a parent and its subsidiary constitute a single economic entity, the parent will be legally responsible for the subsidiary's infringements and will therefore be jointly and severally liable for payment of the fine imposed by the Commission. To secure this result, the Commission must demonstrate that the parent is not only capable of having 'decisive influence' on the subsidiary, but that it has also effectively exercised such influence. According to the presumption established in *AEG Telefunken*,[25] where the parent holds a 100 per cent (or close to a 100 per cent) shareholding in the subsidiary that violated the competition rules, the single economic entity doctrine will apply unless the parent rebuts that presumption by demonstrating that the subsidiary acts independently on the market. Pace considers the *AEG Telefunken* presumption to be a typical consequence of the autonomy of the EU legal order *vis-à-vis* those of the Member States. By the same token, it illustrates the

---

22 See Case 4-73 *J. Nold, Kohlen- und Baustoffgrosshandlung v Commission of the European Communities* [1974] ECR 491.

23 Cited above, note 7.

24 For a recent extended discussion of the subject, see Nada Ina Pauer, *The Single Economic Entity Doctrine and Corporate Group Responsibility in European Antitrust Law* (Wolters Kluwer 2014).

25 Case 107/82 *Allgemeine Elektrizitäts-Gesellschaft AEG-Telefunken AG v Commission* [1983] ECR 3151.

notoriously functional way in which the Treaty's competition rules are understood, and the occasional preoccupation that undertakings might exploit formalistic rules to elude or limit[26] their responsibilities under EU competition law.[27] While ensuring the effectiveness of the EU competition rules, the *AEG Telefunken* presumption has raised, especially since 2011, growing concerns with regard to its compatibility with fundamental principles of law: the presumption of innocence; the principle of 'personal' responsibility; and respect for the rights of defense. Although the Court of Justice has not responded to the latest revolts against the presumption by abolishing it, Pace explains how in its recent jurisprudence the Court has heightened the standards to which the Commission will be held. In particular, the Commission will be obliged to counter the arguments and evidence put forward by parent companies seeking to defeat the presumption. This measured but increasingly rigorous position taken by the Court is in our view laudable, and it provides an example of how fundamental rights protection can inject a dose of reasonableness and proportionality into the application of EU competition law – although in this regard there is more work to be done.

Francesco Munari contributes his thoughts on the 'Judicial assessment of anticompetitive behaviour in Italy'. In this chapter, Munari draws the picture of judicial enforcement of competition law in Italy by recalling, first, the historical circumstance that the only antitrust law that applied in Italy prior to 1990 was supranational, and stemmed from the Treaty of Rome. Second, following the adoption of Law No. 287/1990,

---

[26] It has to be borne in mind that the cap fixed at 10 per cent of worldwide turnover, if calculated solely by reference to the turnover of the subsidiary, would almost certainly reduce the amount of the fine compared to a fine that also reflects the turnover of the parent. The concern, of course, relates to the effectiveness of the Commission's enforcement actions (see also the following note).

[27] See Opinion of Advocate General Kokott in Case C-501/11 P *Schindler Holding Ltd and Others v Commission,* delivered 18 April 2013, EU:C:2013:248, para 66, to which Pace makes reference in his chapter. The relevant passage is worth quoting: 'In assessing an undertaking's *responsibility under antitrust law* [...] the crucial factor cannot be whether there is a "*corporate veil*" between the parent company and the subsidiary. What is important is economic reality, since competition law is guided not by technicalities, but by the actual conduct of undertakings on the market. In assessing, for the purposes of antitrust law, the effect on competition of an undertaking's conduct on the market it is irrelevant what legal constructs the natural or legal persons behind the undertaking have chosen to regulate their legal relationships'. (notes omitted; emphasis in the original text).

which introduced antitrust rules within the domestic legal order, the Italian system confers a special role upon the AGCM, in other words, the Italian competition authority. The AGCM's central role within the national system, together with a framework for private litigation that is shaped by the civil law tradition – with the absence of discovery and with structural difficulties in dealing with complex factual issues – has resulted in a typically limited role for Italian courts in adjudicating antitrust cases. Munari points out that it is these fundamental features of the Italian legal system, and not a supposed incapacity of Italian judges to apply substantive antitrust rules, which are the root cause of the historically stunted growth of private enforcement in Italy.

While administrative courts are vested with the power to review the legality of AGCM decisions, civil courts are mainly called on to hear private claims in follow-on actions. In the latter context, the decisions of the AGCM have traditionally had the value of privileged proof, and could be rebutted. The possibility of rebuttal was important since, as Munari pointedly stresses, it allowed for scrutiny with regard to the merits of such a decision and the respect for the procedural rights of the parties. Against this background, Munari raises some concern about Article 9 of the EU Damages Directive, a provision to which we referred earlier. Since, in damages actions before the Italian civil courts, Article 9 upgrades the AGCM's infringement decisions to proof that is incontrovertible (with a more cautious rule according other EU-NCA decisions at least *prima facie* probative value), a layer of control seems to have been removed (without prejudice to the preliminary reference procedure). Commenting on other rules contained in the Directive as well, Munari focuses on the special 'discovery' rules (see Articles 5 and 6), which are aimed at enhancing the powers of courts to grant disclosure orders. Here Munari argues that the introduction of these more liberal rules might lead to discrimination in the Italian legal order against tort victims in areas other than competition law.

With regard to the concrete approach of the Italian courts, Munari observes that, despite some encouraging statements by the Consiglio di Stato (the Italian Supreme Administrative Court) that clearly overturn the traditional rule limiting judicial scrutiny of AGCM decisions to 'extrinsic review' (in other words, review limited to logical errors), the extent of that scrutiny in practice – in particular concerning the AGCM's determination of the 'relevant market' – remains unsatisfying. This is especially true as concerns the concept of 'technical discretion', a sphere of untouchable evaluations granted to the AGCM due to its technical expertise and the impartiality to which it is bound by law.

A further subject covered in this chapter, which again illustrates the AGCM's special status, relates to Article 21-*bis* of Law 287/1990, a provision which was added to the Law in late 2011, and whose constitutionality has already been upheld by an Italian administrative court. Remarkably and controversially, Article 21-*bis* empowers the AGCM to challenge the acts, decrees and regulations of its sister administrative authorities on the ground that they infringe competition rules. The provision is recognized both judicially and by Munari as an 'extreme' remedy, which is to say that litigation should be resorted to only where advocacy and consultations fail. Munari raises doubts as to the use of this provision by the AGCM where a parallel challenge against the same administrative act has already been brought by a private party, and he questions whether such actions are consistent with the intent of the legislator. In any case, he points out, national courts are empowered by a long-standing EU jurisprudence to disapply acts by national authorities that are incompatible with provisions of EU law and to entertain challenges to state measures on the basis of, for example, Article 106 in conjunction with Article 102. Thus, if any added value is to be contributed by the AGCM where a challenge has already been launched by a private party, it would be in a form analogous to *amicus* interventions under Article 15(3) of Regulation 1/2003 (providing for written and, with judicial leave, oral submissions by national competition authorities). Munari suggests that 'such a conception may contribute to an organic system of decentralized antitrust enforcement, and may ensure that, in certain Member States such as Italy, this enforcement does not become unbalanced compared to the situation of other Member States'.[28] He proceeds to propose an interpretation of Article 21-*bis* which more clearly makes the AGCM an agent of an EU-oriented application of competition law, in line with its role within the system of EU competition law enforcement and in line with the abundant corpus of substantive principles established in the EU jurisprudence. Such principles, as Munari points out, do not only impose constraints on public activities; they also recognize legitimate spheres of action – for example, where services of general economic interest are concerned. His final observation extrapolates from the nature of the Article 21-*bis* procedure and comes full circle: since the AGCM is now an interested 'party' in institutional litigation against other public authorities, it should also be considered a party in all cases where the administrative courts review the AGCM's own decisions. The courts should thus be able to scrutinize those

[28] Page 178.

decisions free of restraint. From this perspective, maintaining an anomalous zone of deference where, for example, the AGCM's 'technical discretion' is concerned, is even more unsustainable.

Section 2: State Aid

Daniele Gallo's chapter, 'Services of general economic interest and state aid in EU law: the challenges for the Court of Justice after the "Almunia Package"', was written mainly with the EU Courts in mind, but the subject matter may be of interest to national courts as well. In his introduction, Gallo suggests that the financing of Services of General Economic Interest (SGEIs) is a topic through which one may explore, on the one hand, the dialectical relations between the EU institutions, political and judicial, and on the other hand the eternal tension between State and market. Gallo reviews the *Altmark* and post-*Altmark* (Monti Package) background before providing, in the third section of his chapter, a detailed description of the Almunia Package that was issued in late 2011 and took effect in April 2012.[29] In the fourth section, he turns to the 'quest for legal certainty' and discusses what he regards as the principal challenges which the Almunia Package (in other words, the Commission's Framework Communication and Decision) poses for the Court of Justice. These relate to certain concepts or passages appearing in the Package that are not entirely clear, such as 'efficiency', or how the benefits that accrue from an SGEI mission are to be defined, or the modalities of the consultation referred to in the Communication, or the role of tendering procedures in assigning SGEIs, and so on. As is usually the case in the field of state aid, the choices made on these issues at the legal stage of adjudication may well display traces of, and feed back into, the underlying politics of eurofederalism.

Edoardo Gambaro's chapter is entitled '*Locus standi* of natural and legal persons before the European Courts in State aid cases'. It is in some respects a counterpart to the chapter written by Mario Siragusa and Kostandin Peci, which concerns State aid actions brought before national courts, such as challenges to national recovery measures.[30] With regard to the EU Courts, the dilemma relating to *locus standi* in the field of State aid is clear enough due to the fact that addressees of State aid decisions

---

[29] For another recent assessment, see Marianne Dony, 'Les règles régissant le financement public des services d'intérêt économique général après la réforme de 2011', (2014/1) Cahiers de Droit Européen 97.

[30] See p. 224 et seq. The chapter by Siragusa and Peci is summarized below.

are Member States and not undertakings. Thus, in order to challenge the Commission's State aid decisions before the EU Courts, actual or potential aid recipients or, as the case may be, competitors of actual or potential aid recipients, must first in principle demonstrate that they are directly and individually concerned by the decision in question, and that they have a present interest in bringing such proceedings.[31] Such is the lot of 'non-privileged' applicants, although they may qualify as 'interested parties' within the meaning of the Procedural Regulation. Gambaro leads the reader on a tour of terrain which an abundant jurisprudence has hewn into a complex and still-evolving topography, covering, for example, the potential difficulty of showing individual concern in scenarios involving aid schemes (unless a recovery order has been adopted) or where the applicant is a rival of an aid recipient (where outcomes depend in part on whether the appeal follows a preliminary examination of the aid under Article 108(3) TFEU or the formal investigation under Article 108(2)). Gambaro also reviews the criticisms (for example, based on unequal treatment) that have been raised against the prevailing jurisprudence in these areas.

Finally, he provides remarks concerning the possibility of challenging regulatory acts under the 'recast' Article 263(4) TFEU (specifically, the final limb thereof). Although this intriguing provision deviates from the *Plaumann* straitjacket by allowing challenges of non-legislative acts of general application, it raises its own obstacle by precluding such challenges against acts that entail implementing measures. As it is often easy to envisage implementing measures following State aid decisions, it is perhaps unsurprising that Article 263(4) has not thus far led to a significant liberalization of the rules on standing in this context.[32]

[31] Theoretically, if in a particular case a State aid decision can be characterized as a 'regulatory act' of direct concern that does not entail implementing measures then, by way of exception, the formidable '*Plaumann*' approach to individual concern may be bypassed. However, as noted below, this possibility has not led to concrete results.

[32] In some contexts, therefore, the apparent attempt by the authors of the draft Constitutional Treaty and later the Treaty of Lisbon to massage the notoriously strict approach to 'direct and individual concern' by removing the requirement of individual concern in the case of regulatory acts proves somewhat illusory. For another recent analysis, see Denis Waelbroeck and Thomas Bombois, 'Des requérants "privilégiés" et des autres … A propos de l'arrêt *Inuit* et de l'exigence de protection juridictionnelle effective des particuliers en droit européen', (2014/1) Cahiers de Droit Européen 21. As Waelbroeck and Bombois observe, the Court of Justice has consistently failed to apply either a teleological or a systematic interpretation to Article 263 TFEU as far as the

However, as Gambaro points out, there remain a few untested factual scenarios in which implementing measures would be unnecessary. Accordingly, there is still some limited scope for enhanced access to the closely guarded citadel of the EU Courts.

Mario Siragusa and **Kostandin Peci** contributed a chapter entitled 'State aid cases before national judges', and as noted earlier they pick up the State aid theme addressed by Edoardo Gambaro but do so from the different perspective of actions litigated at national level. The chapter is divided into three main sections. In the first section, Siragusa and Peci review the basic outlines of State aid procedure and the nuanced mandate of national courts in this field of law (including, for example, the questions of whether a measure constitutes State aid, whether aid is new or 'existing', whether the standstill obligation under Article 108(3) TFEU and Article 2 of the Procedural Regulation has been breached and if so what remedies apply, and so on). In the second section the authors discuss scenarios where claims that the State aid rules have been infringed are 'sword-like', such as where the rival of an aid beneficiary alleges the aid was granted contrary to the standstill obligation, or where the rival attempts to sustain a *Francovich*-style claim for damages against a Member State that has granted aid unlawfully. The authors also consider the possibility of damages claims lodged against a recipient of unlawfully granted aid; in this context, understandably, no action lies as a strict matter of *EU* law, although a Member State may be potentially compelled to allow such a claim under *national* law by the EU law principle of equivalence. In Italy, if a recipient of unlawful aid derived benefits from the aid (which is not difficult to imagine), it may be possible for a rival to seek damages on grounds of unfair competition under Article 2598 of the Italian Civil Code.

The final section of the chapter concerns actions that are 'shield-like'. Can a Commission decision finding aid to be unlawful be challenged before national courts? Axiomatically, by dint of a *jurisprudence constante* to which we referred earlier, under EU law national courts have no competence to find Union acts to be invalid, nor thus do they have

---

locus standi of non-privileged applicants to challenge acts of general application is concerned. Having assessed the Court's persistently wooden approach in the light of Articles 6 and 14 ECHR, they conclude that 'on ne peut que constater que les modalités d'accès aux juges compétents pour examiner la validité d'un acte législatif de l'Union qu'il s'agisse du Tribunal ou de la Cour, soulèvent d'importantes réserves au regard tant du droit au recours effectif, que du principe d'égalité. L'arrêt commenté [*Inuit*] n'examine toutefois pas, malheureusement, ces questions'. Ibid. at 72–73.

competence to follow the logical civil consequences of such invalidity. Nevertheless, as Siragusa and Peci observe, the Court of Justice does allow national courts, as a matter of effective judicial protection, to entertain applications for interim measures suspending the recovery of aid, and to grant such measures under certain circumstances. Such proceedings would normally be brought in parallel with an action under Article 263 TFEU before the General Court on the basis of direct and individual concern. The authors query whether a national court suspecting the Commission decision to be invalid must send a preliminary reference to the ECJ in such circumstances, and they sensibly suggest that no such obligation applies. Aside from the other considerations they raise, the jurisprudence that seemed to impose such a duty preceded the establishment of the Court of First Instance, and thus hardly seems decisive.

PART III EU COMPETITION LAW BEFORE ARBITRATORS

Roberto Cisotta authored the opening chapter of Part III, entitled 'Some considerations on arbitrability of competition law disputes and powers and duties of arbitrators in applying EU competition law'. Cisotta suggests that the problem of defining the limits to the application of national procedural rules lies at the root of both strands of case law of the Court of Justice, in other words, its judgments concerning EU competition law enforcement through arbitration and its judgments on antitrust damages actions. Therefore, these two lines of private enforcement of competition law are characterized by the interplay of national procedural rules – which, as far as arbitration is concerned, define the attitude of the national legal order toward this 'private dispute settlement system', with the statement in *Eco Swiss* to the effect that EU competition law must be treated by national judges as part of public policy[33] – and the need for a uniform application of EU competition law. On the one hand, national judges have to juggle these two different – and often contrasting – forces, in line with the emerging trend toward increased responsibilities of national judges in the context of the private enforcement of EU competition law.[34] On the other hand, arbitrators have to take due account of EU competition law in order to render awards which are

[33] Case C-126/97 *Eco Swiss China Time Ltd v Benetton International NV* [1999] ECR I-3055 paras 36–40 and 44–47.

[34] See Cisotta, cited above, note 10.

unlikely to encounter difficulties in the context of a possible review before the courts of an EU Member State, but as already mentioned they do not have the possibility to resort to the preliminary ruling procedure.[35] This legal framework governs the relationship between public and private enforcement when EU competition law issues are at stake in a dispute to be settled by an arbitrator or an arbitral tribunal. The framework entails that: with regard to the arbitrability of EU competition law issues, limits have to be set with a view to respecting the exclusive competences of public enforcers; and with regard to arbitrators hearing disputes where such issues may arise, they should stand ready to consider whether those issues are relevant, and to competently rule on them. Cisotta observes that, by setting this framework, the Court of Justice has implicitly overcome an old traditional *méfiance* toward arbitrators' capability of dealing with complex factual issues and applying competition law.[36] Moreover, the Commission as well as the EU Courts have started to appreciate arbitration as an effective tool to enforce competition law, in particular in the field of merger control.[37]

Gordon Blanke considers 'The interaction between arbitration and public enforcement: clash or harmony?'. As the title suggests, Blanke in this chapter discusses the interaction between arbitration and the public enforcement of EU competition law. The argument put forward is that, given the absence of formally accepted practice and firm regulatory guidance regarding the forms of coordination and cooperation between arbitration institutions and public competition authorities, resort must be had to the fundamentals of EU law, in combination with the duty of arbitrators to render an enforceable award. This dynamic equilibrium, it is suggested, provides a means of avoiding clashes. In this regard, Blanke highlights three particularly significant elements in the context of the arbitration of EU competition law issues. The first is what Blanke calls

---

[35] See Case 102/81 *Nordsee Deutsche Hochseefischerei GmbH v Reederei Mond Hochseefischerei Nordstern AG & Co. KG and Reederei Friedrich Busse Hochseefischerei Nordstern AG & Co. KG* [1982] ECR 1095, paras 10–12.

[36] Around 15 years before the arbitrability of competition law issues was implicitly recognized in *Eco Swiss*, the U.S. Supreme Court had endorsed arbitrability as a matter of U.S. law in *Mitsubishi Motors Corp. v Soler Chrysler – Plymouth Inc.*, 473 U.S. 614 (1985). A similar orientation had also already emerged in German courts. See Gordon Blanke, 'EU Competition Arbitration', in Luis Ortiz Blanco (ed), *EU Competition Procedure* (Oxford University Press 2013) 1075, 1082.

[37] See in particular Case T-158/00 *Arbeitsgemeinschaft der öffentlich-rechtlichen Rundfunkanstalten der Bundesrepublik Deutschland (ARD) v Commission* [2003] ECR II-3825, paras 203, 211–212, 295, 297 and 352.

the *supranational imperative*. It stems from some of the fundamental principles of EU law, in other words, the direct effect of key EU provisions, the primacy of EU law, the (reciprocal) duty of sincere cooperation between the EU institutions and national authorities, the principle of State liability for breaches of EU law, including those caused by national courts, and the role of the Commission as a guardian of the Treaties, especially in the field of EU competition law. The complex system of obligations that emerges, together with the prohibition against the use of contractual autonomy as a means to elude EU law, implies, sensibly enough, that arbitration cannot be used to circumvent the application of EU competition law. As Blanke suggests, if arbitral proceedings are in fact a sham, the arbitrator granting the award (who arguably qualifies as an 'undertaking') may bear legal responsibility as either a participant in, or a facilitator of, unlawful conduct under EU competition law. For their part, national authorities may also be exposed to State liability if they have in some way facilitated the enforcement of the suspect award.

The second element to which Blanke refers is the duty of the arbitrator to render an enforceable award. To survive public policy control, in line with the jurisprudence of the Court of Justice, and in particular the *Eco Swiss* judgment,[38] the arbitrator must in the course of her duties respect EU competition law. In practical terms this duty also applies, as Blanke underlines, when the seat of the arbitration is outside the EU, if it is likely that enforcement of the award will be sought in an EU jurisdiction, and if the anticompetitive effects in question may reverberate appreciably within the internal market (in other words, if the criteria of the 'effects doctrine' are satisfied).

The third element concerns the will of the parties that may be engaged in arbitration to ensure the interaction between the arbitral proceedings and the public enforcement of EU competition law, with a view to complying with the requirements of the law and obtaining an enforceable award. Explicit commitments to that effect are often incorporated within arbitration agreements, as in the case of arbitration commitments in the context of EU merger review[39] or in connection with commitments under

[38] Cited above, note 33.

[39] See Council Regulation (EC) No 139/2004 of 20 January 2004 on the control of concentrations between undertakings [2004] OJ L24/1.

Article 9 of Regulation 1/2003.[40] In Blanke's view, such explicit indications as to the will of the parties provide a stronger basis for compliance with EU law than reliance upon 'legitimate expectations', in other words, upon the implicit will of the parties, as has been proposed in legal scholarship.

Therefore, all the forms of coordination and cooperation examined in this chapter – which sometimes consist of informal and non-compulsory arrangements in the context of arbitration proceedings – find their structural basis in the intertwined legal framework just described. Of course, arbitral tribunals are not directly bound by the same rules to which national courts are subject, in particular in their capacity as '*juges communs du droit communautaire*'. Still, they must always strive to render an enforceable award; and they must maintain their power to evaluate autonomously every point in law not covered by an EU law act capable of having direct or indirect relevance within the arbitration proceeding, while also providing an *extra ordinem* forum for the litigation of claims which would be inadmissible before the EU Courts.

Giacomo Biagioni's chapter concerns the 'Review by national courts of arbitral awards dealing with EU competition law'. In it, he first clarifies that the extent of the review to be conducted by national judges is wider under procedures for setting aside arbitral awards than under those for recognizing and enforcing them in accordance with the 1958 New York Convention. When the validity of an award is challenged and annulled, the annulment may have relevance in all other countries, which is not the case when a court declines to recognize and enforce an award. However, no significant differences emerge in the case law regarding the two different types of procedures. To analyze the emerging trends regarding the review of awards dealing with EU competition law, Biagioni then refers back to the *Eco Swiss* judgment of the Court of Justice,[41] which establishes that EU competition law is part of the national public policy that has to be taken into account by a court reviewing an arbitral award. As he recalls, the Court acknowledged that this public policy scrutiny was not unconditional – in other words, that it may be restricted in scope and subject to time constraints for the sake of legal certainty. Nevertheless, the Court makes it clear that the breach of EU competition law properly belongs to the exceptions enshrined in the 1958 New York Convention. While these exceptions are mostly of a

[40] See Council Regulation (EC) No 1/2003 of 16 December 2002 on the implementation of the rules on competition laid down in Articles 81 and 82 of the Treaty [2003] OJ L1/1.

[41] Cited above, note 33.

procedural nature, national courts have generally confined themselves to annulling awards only on substantive grounds, including most importantly and commonly the claim that they violate public policy. (Biagioni nevertheless also discusses possible procedural claims that may be raised in the final section of his chapter.) Therefore, since they lack the power to review an award on the merits – in line with the scheme of Article 34 of the UNCITRAL Model Law on International Commercial Arbitration – national courts rely mainly on public policy to review arbitral awards that raise competition law issues.

Biagioni also discusses the special case of the English courts. He queries whether the relevant concept of public policy in this context should be the (broader) domestic concept of public policy or the concept of international public policy. On the basis of the current case practice, and in line with the reference by the Court of Justice to Article V.2 of the 1958 New York Convention in *Eco Swiss*, Biagioni demonstrates that it is the concept of international public policy that is relevant. Nevertheless, where a court action is filed in order to have an award set aside, and where the award is 'domestic' (for example, because it is reviewed in the same country where the arbitration took place), the court may resort, on the basis of the New York Convention, to domestic public policy, and may thus determine the award's compatibility with EU competition law. In jurisdictions where 'international' arbitral awards (and Biagioni notes the need for greater certainty in defining when an award can be so qualified, particularly where EU competition policy is concerned) are not 'protected' by national rules which ensure (as those of France do) that review is to be conducted only by reference to international public policy, there is a risk that national courts may engage in more searching scrutiny on the basis of wider-ranging domestic public policy. A tension thus emerges between, on the one hand, the widely accepted goal of achieving rapid 'finality' via the arbitration of disputes and, on the other hand, the legal principles (driven by the Court of Justice and by EU law itself) of effective and uniform application of EU competition law. The fact that it is the 'minimalist' approach (whereby only blatant breaches of EU competition law may justify the annulment of an arbitral award) that prevails among national courts can be seen as being connected to the application of international public policy. Nonetheless, Biagioni underlines that the actual extent of the powers national courts may exercise under this approach is far from clear.

Laura Bergamini provides an 'Analysis of recent competition cases decided by arbitrators'. In this chapter, Bergamini discusses two cases that illustrate the relationships between arbitral proceedings (both strictly private and State-investor arbitration) and EU competition law enforcement by the European Commission. The two cases are *Reti Televisive Italiane v Sky Italia*[42] and *Electrabel v Hungary.*[43] The first case, an arbitration administered by the ICC, is so far the only reported merger remedy arbitration where an award has been rendered. The second case is an investment treaty arbitration under the International Centre for Settlement of Investment Disputes (ICSID) system, where Hungary resorted to EU competition law by way of exception in order to justify actions allegedly in breach of its obligations as regards foreign investments. Skipping over the case analysis, we can draw on the chapter's concluding section for a summary of the emerging trends. First of all, with regard to the tribunals in question, each of them: (i) understood its power to interpret EU law in general as including the power to interpret Commission decisions; (ii) resorted to EU law, as opposed to domestic or international law, when interpreting those decisions; (iii) interpreted the Commission's decisions as a whole, and without establishing relations with other provisions of EU law (even those the Commission had applied); (iv) did not defer to the Commission's own interpretation of its decisions, let alone consider that such an interpretation could bind the tribunal itself; and (v) reviewed the correctness of the Commission's decisions in light of EU law. The autonomous character of these tribunals' interpretation of EU law may be broadly acceptable, bearing in mind the exclusion of arbitrators from the possibility of seeking preliminary rulings, although some doubts might be raised regarding the unwillingness of the arbitral tribunals to engage in a proper systematic interpretation of EU law.[44]

---

[42] ICC Case No. 16974/FM/GZ, *Reti Televisive Italiane v Sky Italia*, Award, 17 February 2012.

[43] ICSID Case No. ARB/07/19, *Electrabel* S.A. *v The Republic of Hungary*, Decision on jurisdiction, applicable law and liability, 30 November 2012, available at <http://italaw.com>.

[44] It seems likely, particularly in light of para 40 of *Eco Swiss* (cited above, note 33), that an effective application of EU competition law principles generally presupposes a systematic interpretation of the competition rules, whereas interpreting those rules in a decontextualized fashion could raise problems of coherence. Indeed, since the Court of Justice itself generally applies systematic interpretation when considering the proper construction of the competition rules, this method is arguably a necessary (though not sufficient) condition for the uniform application of EU law – a core concern of the Court in *Eco Swiss* and a hallmark of the Court's jurisprudence as a whole. By the same logic we submit that arbitrators will generally be expected to carry out systematic interpretation regardless of whether an award is later reviewed by a national court, although the

As for the Commission, although in the ICSID arbitration it was allowed to intervene as *amicus curiae* upon its own request, it preferred to remain formally extraneous to the remedy arbitration. One may note that some of the most recent merger remedy packages explicitly reserve to the Commission ample rights to intervene in any subsequent arbitration proceedings. It would therefore be erroneous to conclude that the Commission is likely to limit its participation in proceedings to investment arbitrations only.

absence of judicial review will necessarily imply limited means of controlling compliance. See again para 40 of *Eco Swiss* (uniform interpretation of any EU provision required 'irrespective of the circumstances' in which the provision is to be applied).

PART I

Private antitrust enforcement and judicial coherence in Europe

1. The Antitrust Damages Directive – much ado about nothing?

Sebastian Peyer*

ABSTRACT

This chapter examines some of the key features of the EU Directive on antitrust damages actions. The Damages Directive aims to ensure effective private enforcement by facilitating claims in the courts of the EU Member States. However, the proposed measures do not address pressing issues such as claim aggregation or the funding of claims. Instead, the Directive introduces complex rules regarding access to information and joint and several liability. The new EU framework for antitrust damages actions is incoherent and unlikely to create the envisaged level playing field.

INTRODUCTION

Shakespeare's 'Much Ado About Nothing' elegantly combines comedy with more serious politics and embarrassment. The new EU Directive on Antitrust Damages that introduces measures to facilitate and balance damages actions in the EU Member States also joins these elements but rather less gracefully. Many of the provisions of the Directive are the result of a polemical and political process that lasted for more than a decade. The product is a mix of provisions, and not the coherent rules one had hoped for. Unlike Shakespeare's comedy, the Directive lacks any comical value, as it is soon to be translated into national law in 28 Member States.[1] In this chapter, I will look closely at the key features of

* Lecturer in Law at the University of Leicester.

[1] Directive of the European Parliament and of the Council on certain rules governing actions for damages under national law for infringements of the competition law provisions of the Member States and of the European Union,

the reform of antitrust damages actions in the EU. As I will suggest, the new framework for EU damages actions is a seesaw between the two antithetical goals of the Directive: compensation and the coordination of enforcement.

THE GOALS OF THE DIRECTIVE

Article 1(1) of the Directive seeks to ensure more effective private enforcement actions by strengthening the right to compensation. Article 1(1) reflects the jurisprudence of the Court of Justice of the European Union (CJEU). The CJEU created an EU right to competition damages in its *Courage* and *Manfredi* judgments.[2] According to these judgments, every individual should be able to claim compensation for loss caused by the breach of EU competition rules in the courts of the Member States. The Court also explained that:

> In the absence of Community rules governing the matter, it is for the domestic legal system of each Member State to designate the courts and tribunals having jurisdiction and to lay down the detailed procedural rules governing actions for safeguarding rights which individuals derive directly from Community law, provided that such rules are not less favourable than those governing similar domestic actions (principle of equivalence) and that they do not render practically impossible or excessively difficult the exercise of rights conferred by Community law (principle of effectiveness) […].[3]

According to Article 1(2), the Directive also aims at coordinating effective public and private enforcement. Recital 6 clarifies that coordination refers to the interaction of public and private enforcement and its regulation, especially regarding access to information. In the context of the Directive, this means implementing safeguards to protect law enforcement by competition authorities in general, and to protect leniency programmes in particular.[4]

Over the past 15 years, the European Commission has subscribed to the popular view that private antitrust enforcement in the EU Member

---

adopted by the Parliament on 17 April 2014 and by the EU Council of Ministers on 10 November 2014 ('Damages Directive').

[2] Case C-453/99 *Courage Ltd v Bernard Crehan* [2001] ECR I-6297; Case C-295/04 *Vincenzo Manfredi v Lloyd Adriatico Assicurazioni SpA* [2006] ECR I-6619.

[3] *Manfredi,* cited previous note, para 62.

[4] See Section IV below.

States is underdeveloped and that claimants face considerable obstacles when pursuing antitrust damages claims in the courts.[5] The Commission and other policy makers have measured the effectiveness of private antitrust enforcement in the number of successful damages claims.[6] Consequently, compensation was declared to be one of the goals of this reform. In more recent years, beginning with the Commission's White Paper, the compensation objective has been complemented by the objective of coordination of public and private enforcement.[7] This coordination aim is to be understood as a countervailing force to compensation, especially when private enforcement interferes with public enforcement activities. The proposition that these two enforcement modes can interfere with each other is not new, but the problems posed by private actions in Europe have become particularly obvious in recent years. Firms that sue or are planning to sue for compensation have begun to ask for access to information that is or was in the hands of the competition authorities, thus interfering with leniency programmes and settlement procedures.[8] Both agencies and firms that submit evidence to the authorities clearly consider that this material should be treated as confidential and should not be disclosed to potential claimants. Hence, the new objective of coordinating public and private enforcement was introduced.[9]

This 'interaction' problem typically occurs in follow-on litigation, in other words, litigation running in parallel with public investigations or initiated after a decision has been adopted; it does not affect all antitrust damages litigation. One interpretation of the coordination objective is that national laws should refrain from encouraging follow-on actions.

---

[5] See the Commission's earlier consultations: European Commission, 'Green Paper – Damages Actions for Breach of the EC Antitrust Rules', COM(2005) 672 final (19 December 2005); European Commission, 'White Paper on Damages Actions for Breach of the EC Antitrust Rules', COM(2008) 165 final (2 April 2008).

[6] European Commission, 'Antitrust: Commission proposal for Directive to facilitate damages claims by victims of antitrust violations – frequently asked questions' (MEMO/14/310 of 17 April 2014); White Paper (cited previous note), at page 2. For a critical view of this benchmark, see Sebastian Peyer, 'Private Antitrust Litigation in Germany from 2005 to 2007: Empirical Evidence' (2012) 8 Journal of Competition Law and Economics 331.

[7] See Recital 6 of the Damages Directive.

[8] Case C-536/11 *Bundeswettbewerbsbehörde v Donau Chemie AG*, 6 June 2013, EU:C:2013:366; Case C-365/12 P *Commission v EnBW Energie Baden-Württemberg AG*, 27 February 2014, EU:C:2014:112.

[9] White Paper (cited above note 5), at page 3; Damages Directive, Article 1(1).

Such actions are more likely to interfere with investigations if, for example, potential claimants request information from the authority. The rules proposed in the Directive partly support this reading, as they do not facilitate follow-on actions as far as access to information is concerned but they do encourage stand-alone damages claims.[10] If the Damages Directive indeed places limits on follow-on claims, then the two main aims of the Directive are mutually inconsistent.[11] The compensation objective means fostering private actions, while the coordination objective demands restrictions on private claimants. The objective of effective compensation cannot be achieved without compromising the coordination objective, and *vice versa*. The effective coordination of public and private enforcement may thus be a euphemism for curtailing private enforcement when it interferes with agency activity. Overall, the two objectives are contradictory and have obscured the scope of the Directive. Its unclear scope, in turn, bears on several provisions.

KEY FEATURES OF THE DAMAGES DIRECTIVE

Before discussing certain aspects of the Directive in more detail in the following subsections, I will outline the general features contained in the Damages Directive. As will become obvious in this section, the Directive does not create a complete or coherent framework for damages actions in the Member States. It only addresses selected issues while avoiding politically sensitive and important problems: class litigation and litigation funding. Chapter I of the Directive states the scope of the Directive and provides some definitions in Article 2. Article 3 incorporates the *Manfredi* and *Courage* jurisprudence of the CJEU, articulating the right to compensation.[12] Full compensation is achieved if the position of an injured individual is restored as if the infringement had not taken place. The Member States must ensure that a successful compensation claim includes redress for actual loss, loss of profits and the payment of interest.[13]

---

[10] Articles 6 and 7 of the Damages Directive. Article 9 declares final (domestic) infringement decisions of a competition authority to be binding in private disputes, thus supporting follow-on litigation. Article 9 is discussed later in this chapter.

[11] In a recent press release, the Commission stresses the lack of follow-on damages actions. See MEMO/14/310 (cited above, note 6).

[12] The *Courage* and *Manfredi* judgments are cited above, note 2.

[13] Article 3(2) of the Directive.

Chapter II of the Directive deals exclusively with disclosure and access to information. Article 5 introduces disclosure of evidence in competition law damages proceedings in the courts of the EU Member States. The Directive then proposes, in Articles 7 and 8, a stricter test for disclosure of evidence that is included in the file of a competition authority. This narrower test limits the disclosure of information from competition authorities and excludes access to leniency statements and settlement submissions from general disclosure.

Chapter III of the Directive concerns three different issues. Article 9 declares final infringement decisions of competition authorities or review courts regarding EU and national competition law as binding (in the sense that a national court is precluded from adopting decisions running counter to such final decisions) and irrefutably established. This "binding" effect is limited to national decisions but foreign decisions are to be given the status of *prima facie* evidence, pursuant to Article 9(2). Article 10 regulates limitation periods. The minimum statutory period must be no less than five years from the time the infringement has ceased and the claimant knows or should reasonably have known about the infringement. In follow-on actions, the period of limitations must be suspended for the duration of a public investigation (Article 10(4)). In Article 11(1), the Directive requires the Member States to ensure that joint and several liability applies to companies that have jointly breached competition law. The principle of joint and several liability is relaxed, however, for small- and medium-sized enterprises and for leniency applicants that have been granted immunity.[14] The exemption from joint and several liability does not apply to repeat offenders and ring leaders. Article 11 also limits contribution from an immunity recipient to its co-infringers so that the contribution does not exceed the harm it caused to its direct and indirect purchasers or providers.[15]

Articles 12 and 13 of Chapter IV of the Directive recognize the passing-on defence. Specifically, Member States must allow a defendant to show that the claimant did not actually suffer harm because the overcharge was passed on to the next level in the supply chain. Articles 14 and 15 of Chapter IV give indirect purchasers standing to sue. Every individual, independent of its position in the supply chain as direct or indirect purchaser, has the right to claim compensation.[16] In this regard, the Directive facilitates the proof that part of the overcharge was passed

---

[14] Article 11(2)(a) and (b) and Article 11(4).

[15] Article 11(4).

[16] Article 14(1).

on to indirect purchasers by introducing a *de facto* presumption of passing-on in follow-on damages cases.[17] Defendants can rebut this presumption.

Finally, Article 17(1) of the Directive (Chapter V) allows courts to estimate the harm caused by competition law infringements where the available evidence does not permit a precise quantification of damages. Article 17(2) creates a presumption that the infringement caused harm but it does not provide any specificity with regard to the magnitude of the harm. In Chapter VI, out-of-court settlements are encouraged by providing for a suspension of the period of limitations (Article 18(1)) and for a limitation of the joint and several liability principle for settling defendants (Article 19).

Many of these rules relate to specific aspects of damages claims while others, such as the disclosure of information, are rather broad and will have a wide impact on the civil law systems in many Member States. In the next subsections, I will explore access to evidence issues, direct and indirect purchaser standing, and the rules of joint and several liability in more detail.

ACCESS TO EVIDENCE

Articles 5 to 8 of the Damages Directive deal extensively with access to information in antitrust damages actions. Article 5 encourages compensation claims by introducing disclosure of evidence in all antitrust damages actions in the courts of the Member States. The Member States must ensure that their courts are empowered to grant access to documents that are held by the defendants or third parties if the access-seeking party can reasonably justify why access is needed. In deciding on whether to grant a disclosure order, a court must use a proportionality test to weigh the interests in favour of and against disclosure. The court should consider the supporting material that underpins the access request, the scope and cost of disclosure, and whether the evidence that is to be disclosed contains confidential information.[18] The Directive incorporates the recent jurisprudence of the Court of Justice and allows claimants to specify categories of documents to facilitate the disclosure procedure.[19]

Where the relevant conditions are satisfied, disclosure is available both to claimants bringing a damages claim independent of any investigation

---

17 Article 14(2).

18 Article 5(3).

19 See *Donau Chemie* and *EnBW Energie*, each cited above, note 8.

by a public authority (stand-alone action) and to claimants pursuing a legal action for compensation that does relate to a public investigation (follow-on claim). Follow-on claimants can benefit from an ongoing or terminated agency case by requesting access to the agency's records. However, Article 6 of the Directive, which is largely driven by the objective of enforcement coordination, imposes strict limitations on the national courts regarding the disclosure of material included in the files of competition authorities. Article 7 extends the protection of information that has been acquired from the agency and is now in the hands of third parties or the defendants.

Article 6(6) 'blacklists' leniency and settlement submissions. These categories of documents enjoy 'absolute' protection from disclosure and cannot be revealed to access-seeking parties at any time (without prejudice to the possible application of Regulation 1049/2001, the 'Transparency Regulation', which could apply only in very narrow circumstances, if at all). Article 6(5) establishes a temporary blacklist. This closed category includes: (i) information that was specifically prepared for the proceedings of a competition authority; (ii) information the competition authority has drawn up and sent to the parties; and (iii) withdrawn settlement submissions. These types of materials are protected from disclosure requests until the competition authority has adopted a decision or otherwise terminated the proceedings. Moreover, requests for access to documents held by competition authorities are subject to a much stricter proportionality test. This stricter test for evidence in the possession of competition authorities applies to both non-blacklisted documents (which essentially means pre-existing documents) as well as temporarily blacklisted documents after the embargo period has expired.

The Directive's rules on the disclosure of evidence mark a turning point for many civil law jurisdictions. Unlike common law systems, civil law jurisdictions work with rebuttable presumptions and shift the burden of proof to encourage the production of evidence. A disclosure regime, such as that now imposed by the Directive, is alien to most civil law jurisdictions. This begs the question of whether a Directive specifically aimed at antitrust damages actions for the violation of EU competition law is the right instrument to initiate a potential reform of civil procedure in the Member States. The implications of these provisions in the Directive are far-reaching and should have been part of a more general Directive applicable to other areas of civil litigation as well. Theoretically, Member States could choose to apply these rules to 'EU' damages actions only ('EU' actions here meaning claims either based exclusively on EU competition law or where EU law and national law are applied by the court in parallel pursuant to Regulation 1/2003 on the ground that trade between Member States may be affected[20]), but it is more likely that they will allow disclosure in damages actions arising purely under national competition law as well and, possibly, they may even extend disclosure to other types of claims. For this reason it is problematic to use a narrowly focused Directive to reform civil litigation in the Member States.[21]

The provisions on access to documents also reflect the contradictory goals of the Directive. Article 5 creates a right to access and encourages disclosure, while Articles 6 and 7 limit access to agency information. The Directive discourages the use of crucial information held by the competition authorities and thus also discourages the bringing of follow-on claims. Follow-on claims will have to rely on the binding effect of final infringement decisions by the relevant national competition authority.[22] However, the new framework does provide incentives to bring standalone claims, in other words, legal actions that are unrelated to agency investigations. Antitrust damages actions are more often than not follow-on cases, in other words, they are typically cases that are brought after the competition authority has unearthed potential evidence about wrongdoing or launched an investigation.[23] In a deterrence model, follow-on actions increase the fine that is imposed on culpable firms but they do not increase the detection rate a great deal, as they rely on known infringements.[24] On the other hand, follow-on actions create multiple issues regarding access to information contained in the files of competition authorities. Restricting access to information in follow-on actions reduces the incentives to bring such actions. The claim-encouraging binding effect of agency decisions in Article 9 is probably outweighed by the lack of information about the harm caused. This silent change of policy is to be welcomed, given that follow-on actions are an expensive

---

20 It follows from Article 4 and Recital 10 of the Damages Directive that the terms of the Directive apply to both purely EU law claims and combined EU law-and-national law claims.

21 A similar point is raised in Chapter 7 of this book.

22 Article 9 of the Directive.

23 Peyer, 'Private Antitrust Litigation in Germany from 2005 to 2007', cited above, note 6; Barry J. Rodger, 'UK Competition Law and Private Litigation' in Barry J. Rodger (ed), *Ten Years of UK Competition Law Reform* (Dundee University Press 2010) 53.

24 For a different view on private damages actions, see Robert Lande and Joshua Davis, 'Benefits From Private Antitrust Enforcement: An Analysis of Forty Cases' (2008) 42 University of San Francisco Law Review 879. The basic deterrence model is explained by Gary Becker, 'Crime and Punishment: An Economic Approach' (1968) 76(2) Journal of Political Economy 169.

means to compensate victims. Redress schemes – such as, for example, those proposed in the UK – could be a more cost-efficient solution to promote the compensation of victims.[25]

LIABILITY ISSUES

The Directive also addresses liability issues relating to multiple defendants, making them jointly and several liable. The suggested framework is complex due to the designated exceptions; and it demonstrates once more the conflict between the compensation objective and the goal of coordinating public and private enforcement.

Article 11(1) holds co-infringers jointly and several liable, in other words, any defendant is liable for the whole amount of damage caused by the other co-infringing firms. The potential claimant is given a choice to sue one, some, or all infringers for the total amount of the loss that the claimant has suffered from the joint infringement. However, Article 11(2) deviates from the principle of joint and several liability. First of all, a small- or medium-sized company is only liable for the damage it has done to its direct and indirect purchasers if this firm has a market share of less than 5 per cent and if '[...] the application of the normal rules of joint and several liability would irretrievably jeopardize its economic viability and cause its assets to lose all their value'.[26] Ringleaders, repeat offenders or firms that have coerced others into participating in the illegal conduct cannot benefit from this exception.[27] Neither the reasoning behind this exemption nor the wording of the rule is very clear. The exemption undermines the deterrence effect of potential damages actions for small- and medium-sized companies. It will also make litigation more complicated, as claimants do not know whether the exemption rule will apply to the defendant. Claimants will have to find out during the litigation process whether a small company can be held liable for the whole amount of loss. It may therefore reduce the incentives to sue small companies if the claimant thinks it is plausible that the defendant will not be liable for all the harm; and it may thus increase the risk and length of

[25] The UK Consumer Rights Bill, which contains proposals regarding alternative dispute resolution, is currently being considered in Parliament.

[26] Article 11(2)(b) of the Directive.

[27] Ibid.

legal proceedings. Whether that really matters in practice where, for example, most cartel members are being sued anyway, remains to be seen.[28]

Second, joint and several liability (and contribution) is further restricted in cases where the defendant receives full immunity from fines. Somewhat confusingly, Article 11(4)(a) states that immunity recipients shall be jointly and severally liable to their direct and indirect purchasers. This actually means that there is no joint and several liability for this category of defendants. The joint and several liability principle *extends* the liability of the defendant: it implies that he is responsible not only for harm caused by the defendant himself but also for harm his co-infringers have caused to the claimant. Article 11(4) states the opposite by limiting liability to the directly caused damage. Consequently, immunity recipients benefit from an exemption from joint and several liability. Immunity recipients will only be liable for other than directly caused harm if claimants are not able to receive full compensation from the other infringers (Article 11(4)(b)).

Third, settling defendants benefit from a similar exemption pursuant to Article 19(1). The claimant cannot sue a defendant that has settled with the claimant for the damage that was caused by other co-infringers. However, if the claimant is not able to recover from the remaining defendants, he will be able to sue the settling defendant for the remaining damage. Co-infringers cannot ask for contribution from defendants who have settled.

The rules governing joint and several liability make for a complicated arrangement and drawn-out litigation. A claimant has to sue all companies concerned other than the immunity recipient and/or settling defendant to find out if they can obtain full redress for the harm caused by other infringers. If compensation cannot be achieved, the claimant must then sue the immunity recipient or settling defendant. The potentially long period a claimant must wait to ascertain exactly which companies are the proper defendants reduces legal certainty for all parties. It furthermore decreases the number of potential defendants if, for example, a larger cartel consists of: two or three medium-sized companies which may potentially benefit from the liability limitation explained above; a settling defendant; or a leniency applicant that has

[28] See, for example, *National Grid Electricity Transmission Plc v ABB Ltd and others* [2012] EWCA 869 (*National Grid II*).

been granted immunity from fines. All of these potential defendants would benefit from one or another limitation, thus complicating the litigation.

Furthermore, the reasoning behind the exemption for immunity recipients is weak. The Damages Directive states that immunity recipients (in other words, first-in leniency applicants) mitigate the harm that could have been caused to claimants by revealing the breach of competition law. Their exposed position potentially makes them preferential targets for civil litigation.[29] It is not clear why firms that have already received a discount of up to 100 per cent of the administrative fine should receive a second discount. Firms considering whether to blow the whistle will engage in a cost-benefit analysis before submitting evidence to the authority. Such firms are very likely to take exposure to civil liability into account. It is arguable that immunity recipients do not deserve protection from both administrative fines and damages claims. U.S. antitrust litigation shows that joint and several liability can be applied without a right of contribution, which to some extent facilitates the framework. According to Baker, contribution should be based on one simple and comprehensive formula.[30] Neither the rules on joint and several liability nor the contribution rules are simple in the EU's new antitrust damages framework. Maybe the Directive should have followed the U.S. approach or, even better, it should perhaps have waited and regulated this issue for civil litigation in general. The current framework may need to be adjusted soon and, in the meantime, it is likely to lead to satellite litigation in the courts of the Member States.

ISSUES RELATED TO STANDING TO BRING CLAIMS

The final comment to be made here deals with the standing arrangements and the passing-on defence that are outlined in Articles 12 to 15 of the Directive. Article 12 grants both direct and indirect purchasers the right to sue for damages. More importantly, Article 14(2) creates a presumption that harm was passed on to indirect purchasers if: (a) the defendant has committed an infringement; (b) the infringement resulted in an overcharge for the direct purchaser; and (c) the claimant shows that he has purchased affected goods or services. The claimant will have few

---

[29] Recital 38.

[30] Donald I. Baker, 'Revisiting History – What Have We Learned About Private Antitrust Enforcement that We Would Recommend to Others' (2004) 16(4) Loyola Consumer Law Review 379, 388.

difficulties proving (a) and (c), especially in follow-on cases where the affected products and services are named and the infringement is made public. It will be more difficult to convince the courts that the infringement resulted in an overcharge for the direct purchaser. This information is not normally in the defendant's domain, so the claimant has to rely on the competition authority or on disclosure of information from the direct purchaser. Depending on the interpretation of this rule, it may work as a *de facto* presumption of passing-on or as a serious barrier to litigation. In the spirit of the Directive, it is more likely that the courts will opt for a claimant-friendly approach.

The presumption of passing-on of harm may conflict with the passing-on defence which is allowed pursuant to Article 13. With the passing-on defence the defendant can show that the claimant has not suffered any damage because the overcharge has been passed on to the next level in the supply chain.[31] This becomes interesting in cases where not all but only a certain percentage of the overcharge is affected. Assuming that the defendant is sued by both a direct and indirect purchaser, the defendant is likely to invoke the passing-on defence against the direct purchaser. He must therefore show that the claimant levied the overcharge on the indirect purchaser.[32] At the same time, to defend himself against the claim of the indirect purchaser the defendant must rebut the *de facto* presumption and show that the claimant has suffered no harm. From an evidentiary point of view, the defendant is in a comparatively poor position to substantiate both the passing-on defence and the rebuttal of the passing-on presumption. A direct purchaser is in a much better position to shed some light on the issue. The Damages Directive takes this into account by stressing that the defendant may request reasonable disclosure from the claimant.[33] However, additional disclosure requests raise the costs of litigation and may work as a disincentive for potential claimants. Furthermore, if the (direct purchaser and indirect purchaser) claims against the defendant are joined, he has to prove contradictory points in court. The proposed rule is awkward and complicated. It should be replaced by a presumption or estimation of the harm that is passed on to the next level of the supply chain.

[31] The passing-on problem also poses difficulties for the calculation of harm. See Oxera and a multi-jurisdictional team of lawyers led by Dr Assimakis Komninos, 'Quantifying Antitrust Damages – Towards Non-binding Guidance for Courts (Study prepared for the European Commission)' (Luxembourg, 2009).

[32] Article 13 of the Directive.

[33] Ibid.

Like the contribution rules, the provisions on standing and the passing-on defence lack coherence and will lead to drawn-out litigation (or early settlements). Even the authors of the Directive acknowledge that this may be too complicated. Article 15 grants national courts discretion to avoid instances of multiple liability, or no liability, due to the rules expressed in Articles 12 to 14.

CONCLUSIONS

The Damages Directive sends mixed signals to potential damages claimants. On the one hand, it introduces sensible rules such as, for example, the binding and *prima facie* effect of agency decisions in follow-on litigation. On the other hand, it has adopted complex rules with regards to liability, standing and access to information. Some provisions signal clear support for private antitrust damages actions, whereas others point to the protection of public enforcement. The Articles of the Directive reflect contradicting objectives and the protracted legislative process. Unfortunately, the Directive fails to create a coherent framework for damages claims in the national courts.[34] Nor does it address the real issues for victims who have suffered losses from anticompetitive conduct: the provisions in the Directive do not introduce or harmonize tools to aggregate small individual claims (a subject covered in the next chapter of this book). The Directive also avoids the hot topic of litigation funding. If the assumption that underpins the reform holds true – not enough damages claims are being brought – then the Directive misses the target. None of the provisions reduces costs or helps claimants to overcome the cost problem for small claims. Especially regarding small individual losses, victims often deliberately forego compensation because it is rational to do so when the costs of litigation outweigh the potential benefits. To increase the number of claims in the courts (and again, assuming that this is a good policy goal), funding should be liberalized and claim aggregation be allowed. No rational consumer will sue for a loss of several Euros if he faces hundreds of thousands of Euros in legal expenses. These damages actions will only be brought if a representative can aggregate them.

Overall, the Directive lacks coherence, and it is not always clear why certain aspects are regulated while others are not even mentioned. The policy makers should have been clearer about the real goal of the

[34] The authors of the Damages Directive unconvincingly claim that uneven rules lead to uneven enforcement. See Recital 7.

Directive: the protection of public enforcement where it overlaps with private actions. At the moment, the Directive pursues two goals: compensation and coordination. This has caused some confusion and has led to conflicting provisions. The drawn out genesis of this Directive was underpinned by unsound assumptions, and the Commission's approach to private actions has suffered from a change of objectives during the process. Consequently, the Directive got stuck half-way between a sound common-law class-action litigation system and a civil law system of antitrust litigation.

The Directive is unlikely to fulfil the promises it has made. In many Member States, the courts and legislators are ahead of the Directive, either introducing class actions already[35] or planning to do so in the near future.[36] Some issues regulated in the Directive had already been settled at national level but may now have to be dealt with again, such as, for example, problems regarding access to information.[37] Overall, the Directive is unlikely to encourage more claims because it does not lower the cost for litigation but instead creates expensive and ineffective means to achieve the compensation objective.

---

[35] See, for example, Part 23a of the Danish Administration of Justice Act; Article 140 *bis* of the Italian Consumer Code; and the Dutch class action regime under Article 3:305a BW.

[36] See the UK Consumer Rights Bill.

[37] With regard to access to leniency materials held by a competition authority (in this case the European Commission), the UK High Court applied the CJEU's *Pfleiderer* test in *National Grid II*, cited above, note 28 (granting limited access). (That test was established in Case C-360/09 *Pfleiderer AG v Bundeskartellamt* [2011] ECR I-5161; see also *Donau Chemie*, cited above, note 8.) For German law, see Higher Regional Court of Hamm, decision of 23 November 2013 (1 VAs 116/13) (allowing the requesting court to access case files, including leniency applications).

2. Collective redress – (too) great expectations?

Sonja Keske*

ABSTRACT

This chapter considers issues related to collective redress for harm suffered as a consequence of competition law infringements. The chapter examines both the European Commission's Recommendation on Collective Redress of June 2013 and relevant national practice in Europe. The theoretical elements behind the need for collective redress are discussed, and the likely impact of the Recommendation is questioned on various grounds. It is found that collective redress as envisaged may have an impact in a subset of cases, in other words, where individual damages are large enough to motivate victims to opt in or to initiate collective actions themselves (but not so large as to limit the benefits to be gained from sharing costs and risks due to the additional costs of collective proceedings and, in the case of opting in, due to the loss of control over the litigation). In other cases, especially where damages are relatively small, it is unclear that the Recommendation, taking account of its own provisions but also in the light of other pertinent instruments such as the Damages Directive of 2014, is capable of stimulating collective actions for compensation. In order to craft the right combination of elements to stimulate adequate compensation claims, it is suggested that Member States should experiment with a range of solutions so that compared outcomes may serve as a basis for improved instruments a few years hence.

* Bundeskartellamt, Bonn. The views expressed in this chapter are those of the author and do not necessarily reflect the position of the Bundeskartellamt (German Federal Competition Authority).

INTRODUCTION

'The End for European Collective Actions – The European Parliament votes against',[1] as the headline read in a German newspaper in April 2014 when the Parliament approved the text of the EU Directive on 'certain rules governing actions for damages under national law for infringements of the competition law provisions of the Member States and of the European Union'.[2] However, the newspaper's farewell to the EU influence on group action mechanisms may have been a bit premature. It is true that the Directive does not contain rules on a collective redress mechanism, although that was discussed as an option. But the Commission's 'Recommendation on common principles for injunctive and compensatory collective redress mechanisms in the Member States concerning violations of rights granted under Union Law' does.[3] The Recommendation was also accompanied by a European Commission Communication, 'Towards a European Horizontal Framework for Collective Redress', which explains the Commission's position on a range of important issues.[4] Furthermore, the Recommendation foresees an assessment four years after publication of the Recommendation to evaluate the degree of implementation and to consider whether further action, including legislative measures, are necessary.[5]

The question of what likely effects can be expected from the Commission's Recommendation is the subject of this contribution. Academics and practitioners on both sides of the Atlantic have discussed the need for and the optimal design of collective or class actions – either in general or in the specific context of competition law – for a long time.[6] Based on insights gained from this research, the present chapter focuses on the

---

1 'Aus für europäische Sammelklagen – Das Europaparlament stimmt dagegen', *Frankfurter Allgemeine Zeitung* (Frankfurt, 19 April 2014) (author's translation).

2 Directive of the European Parliament and of the Council A7-0089/2 [2014] <http://www.europarl.europa.eu/sides/getDoc.do?pubRef= -//EP//NONSGML+AMD+A7-2014-0089+002-002+DOC+PDF+V0//EN>.

3 Commission Recommendation 2013/396/EU [2013] OJ L201/60.

4 Commission Communication COM (2013) 401 final [2013].

5 Recommendation, para 26 of the Preamble.

6 See, *inter alia*, Sonja E. Keske, *Group Litigation in European Competition Law: A Law and Economics Perspective* (Intersentia 2010); Samuel Issacharoff and Geoffrey P. Miller, 'Will Aggregate Litigation Come to Europe? ' (2009) 62 Vanderbilt Law Review 179; Andrea Renda et al., *Making antitrust damages actions more effective in the EU: welfare impact and potential scenarios* (2007) <http://ec.europa.eu/competition/antitrust/actionsdamages/documents.html> accessed 15

effects of group litigation mechanisms put forward in the Recommendation from a more case-based practical perspective. The actual effect of a collective litigation mechanism depends on a wide variety of factors, including: features of the collective action system itself (for example, whether the opt-in or opt-out rule is selected); features of the litigation process as a whole (for example, the existence and nature of discovery rules); and sometimes even factors beyond civil procedure rules. Here, however, the effects of a few selected features of the recommended collective redress mechanisms will be discussed, as far as possible, as a separate issue.

THE EUROPEAN COMMISSION'S RECOMMENDATION ON COLLECTIVE REDRESS

The key features of the collective redress mechanism the Commission proposes that the Member States adopt are the following: collective redress actions for damages as well as for injunctive relief (para 2); representative actions by *ex ante* or *ad hoc* certified non-profit entities as well as by public authorities for and in the name of two or more legal persons (paras 3.b and 4); collective actions by two or more harmed individuals themselves (para 3.a); opt-in principle for the constitution of the claimant party as general rule (para 21); opt-in and exit possibility of harmed individuals at any time before a final judgment or valid settlement (paras 22 and 23); allowing third-party funding but without percentage-based remuneration or 'excessive' interest (paras 16 and 32) and prohibiting contingency fees to a large extent (para 30); and encouragement of consensual or out-of-court settlements of compensation disputes (para 25).

GREAT EXPECTATIONS

With these features of the recommended collective redress mechanism, the Commission expects to 'facilitate access to justice, stop illegal

June 2014, at 271ff; Hans Micklitz and Astrid Stadler, 'The Development of Collective Legal Actions in Europe, Especially in German Civil Procedure' (2006) 17 European Business Law Review 1473; Hans-Bernd Schäfer, 'The Bundling of Similar Interests in Litigation' (2000) 9 European Journal of Law and Economics 183; Harry Kalven and Maurice Rosenfield, 'Contemporary Function of the Class Suit' (1941) 8 University of Chicago Law Review 684.

practices and enable injured parties to obtain compensation in mass harm situations'.[7] Finding it difficult to define the term 'justice' clearly enough in this setting to enable an evaluation of the degree to which this can be achieved, and noting also that stopping and punishing illegal practices is the core task of public enforcement,[8] the following considerations concern the impact of a collective redress mechanism on the ability of injured parties to obtain compensation (as opposed to deterrence or punishment) in competition law disputes.

Where individual damages are small compared to the individual costs of enforcing one's rights, collective redress is expected to reduce the financial burden on the individual and thereby encourage claims for compensation.[9] Therefore, one expected benefit of collective redress in competition law cases would be increased compensation of victims of competition law infringements that caused mass harm or small and widely dispersed damages. According to former Commission Vice-President Joaquín Almunia, the risk is that 'when the victims are consumers and small businesses, they would not go to court if their losses do not justify the costs of litigation and the uncertainty of the outcome'[10] unless they are provided with a collective redress mechanism. Even if that were not the case, if numerous victims 'go to court individually to seek compensation, [...] the court would be drowned under a flood of lawsuits and the costs would be huge for victims, defendants and society at large'.[11] The implementation of the Recommendation is therefore also expected to lead to procedural economy.

These benefits are discussed in more detail below, beginning with collective actions as a means to overcome a perceived problem of too little litigation due to mismatched potential costs and rewards for individuals in individual litigation – in economists' terms, this is called a problem of 'rational apathy'.[12]

---

7 Recommendation, para 1 of the main text.

8 See Recommendation, para 6 of the Preamble; Communication, at 10.

9 Recommendation, para 9 of the Preamble.

10 Joaquín Almunia, 'Common standards for group claims across the EU', SPEECH/10/554 of 15/10/2010 <http://europa.eu/rapid/press-release_SPEECH-10-554_de.htm?locale=en> accessed 15 July 2014.

11 Ibid.

12 Keske, *Group Litigation*, cited above, note 6, at 71f; Schäfer, 'The Bundling of Similar Interests', cited above, note 6, at 183f; Kalven and Rosenfield, 'Contemporary Function of the Class Suit', cited above, note 6, at 684f.

Rational Apathy

The most important expected benefit of collective action is the potential to overcome the perceived under-enforcement of rights due to rational apathy. This has been one of the main arguments for the Commission's intervention from the very 'beginning' in 2004, when the so-called Ashurst Study stated that private enforcement of competition law in the Member States was in a state of 'total underdevelopment'.[13]

The problem of rational apathy can appear in (at least) two different forms in cases where a number of individuals are harmed by the same illegal conduct (a 'mass harm situation', to use the Commission's term).[14] The individual may find that the costs of litigating claims are not justified by the quantum of damages, and he may therefore refrain from bringing suit even if that would stop the illegal conduct and thus provide benefits for others. Rational apathy may also play a role even prior to these considerations, especially in some complex competition law cases. The amount of damages to the individual may not even justify investing any efforts in monitoring prices and finding out whether there was any harm at all and/or the potential causes. In terms of deterrence considerations, rational apathy may thus lead to a low rate of detection.

To clarify these points, consider a price cartel operated by producers of a consumer good. A price-fixing cartel on the producer level could lead to higher prices for direct customers, which may or may not be able to pass (part of) these overcharges on to their customers in turn, who likewise may or may not be able to pass on (part of) their overcharges, and so on, until the distribution chain ends with the end-consumers. In such cases, damages can be widely dispersed and very small for the individual – especially for the end-consumer. A good example may be a case like the coffee roasters cartel fined by the Bundeskartellamt (the German Competition Authority) in 2009.[15] The companies in that case were found to have coordinated prices and to have agreed on price increases, leading to higher prices for their direct consumers (which were

---

[13] Denis Waelbroeck, Donald Slater and Gil Even-Shoshan, *Study on the conditions of claims for damages in case of infringement of EC competition rules* (Comparative Report, 2004) 1 <http://ec.europa.eu/competition/antitrust/actions damages/comparative_report_clean_en.pdf> accessed 15 July 2014.

[14] Recommendation, para 3.b of the main text.

[15] Bundeskartellamt, Case B11-18/08, Decision of 18 December 2009. See also the corresponding press release, <http://www.bundeskartellamt.de/SharedDocs/Meldung/EN/Pressemitteilungen/2009/21_12_2009_Kaffeer%C3%B6ster.html> accessed 15 July 2014.

mainly food retailers) and, potentially, also for end-consumers. Direct consumers (for example, large retail companies) probably have noticed these price changes, as the monitoring of prices can be considered part of their business activities. Individual overcharges to end-consumers, on the other hand, which reached up to 70 cents per package[16] and resulted in an average overcharge of €4.55 per year (assuming an average consumption in Germany of 6.5 kg of coffee per year)[17] may have been too small to be noticed for some or many consumers. Some individuals may not invest time or effort in monitoring such price changes, at least if the expected damages are too low to justify these investments. Many consumers thus probably remained unaware of the price changes until the Bundeskartellamt made its investigation public. Even then, some consumers may still not have made the connection between the behaviour of the coffee roasters and their own potential harm. At the same time, even if consumers at a larger scale noticed these price changes, the majority likely would not have been aware of the (potential) underlying cause until the public enforcement action was reported: price increases can have any number of causes (for example, the cost of input factors may rise) and it is very difficult to gather the relevant information to prove an illegal cartel agreement. The probability of detection (noticing the effect and having sufficient insight to have an idea about the causes) of such a cartel by individual end-consumers is therefore likely to be small.

Once the end-consumers knew about the price changes and their underlying cause (either of their own accord or through the media reports), the individual damages in many cases would likely have been too small to justify individual actions for damages due to the relatively high costs and risks of litigation.

In fact, empirical evidence on private litigation raising competition law issues in Germany suggests that hard core cartel cases, such as the coffee roasters cartel, represent only a minor fraction of all civil litigation cases (including follow-on actions, in other words, actions after a finding of infringement in a public enforcement action).[18] The most frequently

---

[16] Bundeskartellamt, Case summary B11-18/08, <http://www.bundeskartellamt.de/SharedDocs/Entscheidung/EN/Fallberichte/Kartellverbot/2009/B11-18-08.pdf?__blob=publicationFile&v=6> accessed 15 July 2014.

[17] Data taken from Statistica, <http://de.statista.com/statistik/daten/studie/199898/umfrage/konsum-von-kaffee-in-europa/> accessed 15 July 2014.

[18] See Sebastian Peyer, 'Myths and Untold Stories – Private Antitrust Enforcement in Germany' (1 July 2010) Centre for Competition Policy Working Paper No. 10–12 <http://ssrn.com/abstract=1672695> or <http://dx.doi.org/10.2139/ssrn.1672695> accessed 15 July 2014, at 61.

litigated disputes are refusal to deal cases, followed by cases involving (non-price) discrimination and excessive pricing.[19] Also, the vast majority of private competition litigation seems to be done by direct customers (companies), who are primarily litigating to obtain a declaration of nullity of contract clauses, followed by injunction or interim relief; while only 20 per cent of cases deal with pecuniary issues (damages and unjust enrichment cases).[20] The Bundeskartellamt was aware of close to 2,000 civil litigation cases concerning competition law in the years 2004–2012.[21] From these findings it seems that companies engaged in business-to-business litigation are generally quite able to achieve justice under existing civil law procedures in Germany. It may well be that the picture is similar in other countries.

Based on these insights, one could argue that the greatest need for a collective redress instrument enabling victims of competition law infringements to join forces and share litigation expenses could therefore relate specifically to claims for damages sustained by end-consumers – at least in Germany.

Procedural Economy

Economizing on court procedures can be important even where many victims have sufficient incentives to sue individually. For example, buying a travel package and then being stranded at the airport in a foreign country because the travel agency has become insolvent in the meantime is a quite obvious and noticeable cause of harm to the victims, as it is also a quite substantial harm. Detection is thus very likely. A larger number of the victims can also be instantly known to each other, and sitting at the airport together for hours may also facilitate communication between victims. In such cases, the initiation of multiple individual suits by each of the travellers in order to establish wrongdoing by the travel agency may be inefficient and might also entail the risk of conflicting judgments. For these reasons, many countries have already developed various mechanisms to handle these forms of mass claims –

[19] Ibid.

[20] Ibid., at 39ff and 46ff.

[21] Numbers taken from the biannual activity reports 2007/2008, 2009/2010 and 2011/2012 by the Bundeskartellamt as published in the Official Parliamentary Publication Journal. BT Drucks. 16/13500 [2009] 50; BT Drucks. 17/6640 [2011] 49; BT Drucks. 17/13675 [2013] 42.

these include, for example, joinder procedures or even test case procedures, as in Germany.[22]

Similarly, some competition law infringements can also harm a (limited) number of victims to a relatively substantial degree, so that the issues of whether harm is being caused, who is causing the harm and the amount of harm may be quite obvious to the victims, comparable to the travel package case above. A prime example would be a refusal to deal case, where one company or few companies – those no longer supplied by the infringing company – are directly harmed.

It is clear that the usefulness of a new mechanism supplementing those already well-established in the EU Member States corresponds to the (hypothetically) greater number of individual suits that would be brought in the absence of that mechanism. Furthermore, procedural economy may generally be increased where more individual claimants are included in a single group and where fewer claims are treated individually. For example, the Dutch collective settlement procedure deviates from the common principle of individual and full compensation in damages litigation, as the settlement is for a fixed amount from which victims will be reimbursed; victims are notified and given the opportunity to opt out only after the settlement is reached.[23]

In some cases, however, it may be necessary to have several groups of victims even if they were all harmed by the same cartel. Due to conflicting interests concerning the degree of passing-on, for example, indirect and direct purchasers probably could not be joined in one group. At the same time, the Damages Directive contains rules that exempt small and medium enterprises from the general rule of joint liability, making them liable only to their own (direct and indirect) customers,[24] so that customers of other cartel participants may have to bring separate collective actions against those other cartelists.

---

22 For an overview and description of such mechanisms in the United States, the United Kingdom and Germany, see Keske, *Group Litigation*, cited above, note 6, at 40ff and 193ff.

23 See Xandra E. Kramer, 'Enforcing mass settlements in the European Judicial Area: EU policy and the strange case of Dutch collective settlements (WCAM)', in Christopher Hodges and Astrid Stadler (eds), *Resolving Mass Disputes – ADR and Settlement of Mass Claims* (Edward Elgar, 2013) 74; Ianika Tzankova and Eric Tjong Tjin Tai, 'The Netherlands' (Focus on Collective Redress) <http://www.collectiveredress.org/collective-redress/reports/thenetherlands/thecollectivesettlement> accessed 15 July 2014.

24 Directive, Article 11.

ACTIONS FOR DAMAGES IN COMPETITION LAW CASES – REMAINING DIFFICULTIES

The Bundeskartellamt has, in the last decade, discovered and sanctioned a number of cartels in a large variety of sectors, including consumer goods such as confectionery,[25] frozen pizzas,[26] beer,[27] sugar[28] and coffee[29] as well as rail tracks,[30] cement[31] and insurance, which could be considered prime cases for collective damages actions.[32] However, a number of difficulties faced by potential plaintiffs are likely to remain significant despite the Directive and the collective redress mechanisms proposed in the Recommendation, even if the focus is on follow-on actions alone – which may be less complex in some respects but may by comparison yield slightly less overall benefit.

Stand-Alone Versus Follow-On Actions for Damages

The detection of competition law infringements, and in particular of cartel behaviours, is often very difficult, complex and time-intensive. This is true even for specialists in the field, such as competition authorities that generally have significant powers and competences

---

25 See Bundeskartellamt press release of 27 March 2013, <http://www.bundeskartellamt.de/SharedDocs/Meldung/EN/Pressemitteilungen/2013/27_03_2013_Hema.html> accessed 15 July 2014.

26 Ibid.

27 See Bundeskartellamt press release of 13 January 2014, <http://www.bundeskartellamt.de/SharedDocs/Meldung/EN/Pressemitteilungen/2014/13_01_2014_Fernsehbiere.html> accessed 15 July 2014.

28 See Bundeskartellamt press release of 18 February 2014, <http://www.bundeskartellamt.de/SharedDocs/Meldung/EN/Pressemitteilungen/2014/18_02_2014_Zucker.html> accessed 15 July 2014.

29 Bundeskartellamt, Case B11-18/08, decision of 18 December 2009, cited above, notes 15 and 16.

30 See Bundeskartellamt press release, <http://www.bundeskartellamt.de/SharedDocs/Meldung/EN/Pressemitteilungen/2013/11_07_2013_Moravia-Steel.html> accessed 15 July 2014.

31 See Bundeskartellamt press release, <http://www.bundeskartellamt.de/SharedDocs/Meldung/EN/Pressemitteilungen/2013/10_04_2013_BGH-Zement.html> accessed 15 July 2014.

32 Compare Bundeskartellamt, 'Ban on Cartels', <http://www.bundeskartellamt.de/EN/Banoncartels/banoncartels_node.html> accessed 15 July 2014

(including the power to conduct dawn raids).[33] This is why leniency programmes are perceived to be very – or even the most[34] – successful tools for discovering and prosecuting cartels.[35] With regard to private enforcement, the difficulty of proving the existence of an anticompetitive agreement can pose immense challenges; the discovery rules that apply in civil litigation can thus play an important role.[36]

The prospects of obtaining adequate initial proof to sustain a claim for damages may depend to some degree on whether there has already been a finding of infringement by a competition authority. The Directive contains a provision that makes prior infringement decisions of public authorities either binding on the courts (in the case of the authority of the Member State of that court) – a rule that is already contained in the German Act against Restraints of Competition[37] – or at least giving them the character of rebuttable, *prima facie* evidence of an infringement (in cases where the prior decision has been adopted by an authority of another Member State).

The European Commission's Memorandum on the draft Directive[38] makes it particularly clear that the focus of the Directive was always on follow-on actions in competition law cases. It seems unlikely that the collective redress mechanisms proposed in the Recommendation would be able to change that, despite the fact that increases in the detection rate (which would make it possible to bring more infringements to an end) could be considered an extremely valuable goal. Most actions for damages due to competition law infringements, and particularly cartel cases, will probably not be brought by individuals or associations as

---

[33] See the statements made and supporting material by the OECD, <http://www.oecd.org/daf/competition/exofficio-cartel-investigations.htm> accessed 15 July 2014 and <http://www.oecd.org/competition/cartels/> accessed 15 July 2014.

[34] Ibid.

[35] See also Scott D. Hammond, 'Cornerstones of an Effective Leniency Program', (Presentation at the ICN Workshop on Leniency Programs, Sydney, 22–23 November 2004), <http://www.usdoj.gov/atr/public/speeches/206611.pdf> accessed 15 July 2014, at 2–4; Wouter P.J. Wils, 'Leniency in Antitrust Enforcement: Theory and Practice', (2007) 30(1) World Competition 25, 40.

[36] See Renda et al., *Making antitrust damages actions more effective,* cited above, note 6, at 348ff.

[37] Directive, Article 9; and cf. Section 33(4) of the German Act against Restraints of Competition (*Gesetz gegen Wettbewerbsbeschränkungen*).

[38] See European Commission Memo of 17 April 2014, <http://europa.eu/rapid/press-release_MEMO-14-310_en.htm> accessed 15 July 2014.

stand-alone actions but rather will follow an investigation and a finding of an infringement by the competent public authority.

Establishment of the Group

In a follow-on case, an infringement has already been detected by a public enforcer. However, it may still be difficult for the (prospective) claimants in such a case to establish a group for the purpose of launching a collective action. Again, the coffee-roaster cartel example may help to clarify more general arguments. Assume the decision by the competent competition authority establishing illegal price-fixing by coffee roasters has become final and will be 'binding' on the court in a follow-on action, in the sense that the court is precluded from adopting any form of ruling that runs counter to that decision. As individual damages may be too small to justify individual suits, a collective action for damages could be considered. One possibility envisioned in the Recommendation could be for a consumer association, if *ex ante* or *ad hoc* certified in line with the Commission's text, to contact end-consumers, for example by writing a letter to their member base or publishing notices in the media, in order to find victims of the cartel. This would make it necessary to finance the up-front notification costs without a clear picture of how many victims may be found or whether enough victims would be willing to join the case in order to justify the representative action. Opt-in rates tend to be very low in general – participation rates are considerably larger in opt-out procedures.[39] And the willingness of notified victims to opt in to a legal procedure may still be limited from the outset in cases like the coffee-roasters cartel where, as explained earlier, prices increased by a maximum of only 70 cents per 500g of coffee purchased. To a certain degree, there may be rational apathy even with regard to participating in group litigation.

Even if there are a sufficient number of victims declaring their willingness to participate, the consumer association in the cartel example

---

[39] See Roger Van den Bergh, 'Private Enforcement of Competition Law and the Persisting Collective Action Problem', (2013) 1 Maastricht Journal of European and Comparative Law 12f; Sonja Keske and Roger Van den Bergh, 'Rechtsökonomische Aspekte der Sammelklage', in Matthias Casper et al. (eds), *Auf dem Weg zu einer europäischen SammelKlage?* (Sellier 2009) 25; Rachael Mulheron, 'Reform of collective redress in England and Wales – a perspective of need' (2007), <http://www.judiciary.gov.uk/wp-content/uploads/JCO/Documents/CJC/Publications/Other papers/reform-of-collective-redress.pdf> accessed 15 July 2014, at 154.

may find that a large number of those victims no longer have many or all the receipts showing their purchases during the duration of the cartel (which may have lasted for several years or even decades) by the time the representative action is started. Furthermore, not all receipts given to the customer by shops and businesses are necessarily detailed enough to allow a clear identification of the specific product that was bought. Other purchases may have been made during a special sales event by the retailer (for example, 'two-for-one' offers or coupons issued by the retailer) and may therefore be less clear-cut to prove damages. In the end, in cases like the coffee roasters example, the consumer association might come to the conclusion that it is not worthwhile to initiate (long, complex and costly) proceedings for the few consumers who (once found) would be willing to opt-in and provide sufficient proof to establish their amount of harm.

The same problems arise, maybe to an even larger degree, where a collective action is initiated by individual consumers and their lawyer(s). For the individual consumer, it may be more difficult and potentially more expensive to find and contact other potential victims. These (search and contact) costs would again have to be borne by the victim without knowing whether and how many other victims may want to opt in to the proceedings. An individual victim may therefore still have limited incentives to pursue such an action *ex ante* – especially when individual harm amounts only to a few Euro cents.

These issues relating to the difficulty of establishing the group will have direct effects on the entities when considering whether or not to initiate a group litigation procedure. Rules on the allocation of litigation costs in combination with the possibility to enter and leave a collective action at any time prior to final judgment can also influence the establishment of the group *ex ante* and the risk borne by the initiator. Rules on civil litigation costs establishing which costs have to be borne by whom can be very complex, and they have a large impact on the incentives to initiate collective proceedings. In Germany, for example, a proposal was made for a collective redress mechanism containing a regulation on cost division between the members of the group and the individual initiating the collective action.[40] This proposal contains a cap on the financial liability of those opting in and makes the initiator of the action liable for all remaining costs (including, under the applicable

---

[40] Official Parliamentary Publication Journal, BT Drucks. 18/1464 (2014) § 629, <http://dipbt.bundestag.de/dip21/btd/18/014/1801464.pdf> accessed 15 July 2014.

loser-pays principle, the costs of the other party to the proceeding).[41] This form of cost regulation might increase victims' willingness to opt into a collective action; however, if the initiator of the claim runs the risk, due to strategic opt-in and exit of other victims combined with rules on litigation costs, of being solely liable for at least some of the costs in the end, this may also deter the initiator in the first place. It should also be noted that, due to procedural safeguards designed to avoid unmeritorious suits, such as a verification stage establishing the admissibility of a given collective action, and other procedural steps relating to the establishment, management or dissolution of the group, the overall costs and risks of a trial in this context can be greater than in traditional individual litigation. Issues arising to the financing of litigation are discussed below.

Litigation to Recover Damages

Assuming a cartel has been detected and prosecuted by a public enforcer, and assuming the group of victims is successfully established in a follow-on collective action for damages, the subsequent steps in court may still be far from smooth sailing. Contrary to what seems to be a widespread general perception, not even the irrebuttable nature of a prior finding of infringement by the relevant national competition authority (or by the Commission) will make a victory for damages claimants a foregone conclusion. Plaintiffs (in Germany and surely also in many other Member States) would still need to establish at least a causal link between the illegal conduct and the resulting harm, as well as the amount of harm sustained.[42] As discussed above, each of these elements may pose significant difficulties.

Proof of causation, which is one of the two factors that surely will have to be established in order to obtain damages, probably – generally speaking – becomes more complex as the distance between plaintiffs and defendants grows. In cases such as the vacationers stranded at the airport due to the insolvency of the travel package provider, the distance between the infringer and the harmed victims may be relatively modest. By contrast, in cases like the coffee roasters cartel case, the distance may be greater, as there can be other entities making their own choices in between – such as the retailers buying the coffee from the coffee roasters and then selling it to the end-consumers. Despite the desirability of ensuring that injured parties recover full compensation, only widely

41 Ibid.

42 See, *inter alia*, Joachim Bornkamm, '§ 33 GWB' in Herman-Josef Bunte (ed), *Kartellrecht Kommentar* (Volume 1, 12th edn, Luchterhand 2014) para 169.

dispersed and relatively small damages are likely to accrue to the consumers most distant from the infringer, the end-consumers – precisely where collective redress may be of the most relevance.

Even if causation can be established, proving the amount of harm in competition law cases can often entail extremely complex analysis and may lead to extensive disputes, including debate over different economic models, types of analyses and expert testimonies. The Bundeskartellamt has had much experience in that regard since, until 2005, cartel fines had to be based on the cartel overcharge.[43] A very illustrative example would be the cement cartel case. The Bundeskartellamt conducted dawn raids and were approached by a leniency applicant in 2002, following which it fined the companies, based on the estimated overcharge, in 2002 and 2003.[44] Between 2003 and 2009, these fines were appealed before the court, requiring both sides to provide their assessments of the overcharges. In addition, an expert was appointed by the court to conduct its own analysis, to which both sides again had the opportunity to respond.[45] The cartel investigation by the Bundeskartellamt was completed relatively quickly, taking only about a year, but the subsequent debate on the estimation of the overcharges shows that establishing the amount of overcharge can be extremely complex – and hence costly to litigants on both sides of a dispute. The final court judgment in the cement cartel case was rendered in 2013.[46] Interestingly, there was also a (follow-on) private action for damages arising from the same circumstances.[47] The plaintiff in that action, Cartel Damages Claims S.A. (CDC), initially purchased the claims of 28 damaged companies and began preparing its

---

[43] See OECD, 'Roundtable on Quantification of Harm to Competition by National Courts and Competition Agencies', Country Contribution Germany (2011), <http://www.oecd.org/daf/competition/QuantificationofHarmtoCompetition2011.pdf> accessed 15 July 2014.

[44] See Bundeskartellamt press releases of 14 April 2003 and 29 June 2009, <http://www.bundeskartellamt.de/SharedDocs/Meldung/EN/Pressemitteilungen/2003/14_04_2003_Bu%C3%9Fgeld_Zementkartell_eng.html> accessed 15 July 2014; <http://www.bundeskartellamt.de/SharedDocs/Meldung/EN/Pressemitteilungen/2009/29_06_2009_OLG-Zement.html> accessed 15 July 2014.

[45] See Country Contribution Germany, cited above, note 43; Bundeskartellamt press releases of 14 April 2003 and 29 June 2009, cited below, note 46.

[46] See Bundeskartellamt press release of 10 April 2013, <http://www.bundeskartellamt.de/SharedDocs/Meldung/EN/Pressemitteilungen/2013/10_04_2013_BGH-Zement.html> accessed 15 July 2014.

[47] For the case description as well as links to the relevant court rulings on this case, see <http://www.carteldamageclaims.com/portfolios/cdc-german-cement-cartel/> accessed 15 July 2014.

case including a calculation of damages, already in 2002. In 2005, CDC then filed its action for damages before the German courts. In those proceedings, the assignment of the claims as such was ruled to be generally admissible; however, eight years later, the case was finally dismissed by the Regional Court of Düsseldorf in December 2013 on the ground that the transfer of claims in this case was contrary to public morality and therefore invalid. An appeal to the Higher Regional Court of Düsseldorf is pending as of this writing (July 2014).

Naturally, there are, and there will be, other competition law cases. Following the Bundeskartellamt's investigation and imposition of fines in the so-called 'rail track cartel',[48] the customer concerned, Deutsche Bahn AG, filed suit for damages in 2012.[49] According to statements by Deutsche Bahn AG, the financiers of the German railway network – the German Federal Government and State Governments – had assigned their claims to Deutsche Bahn AG.[50] Damages in cases such as these are invariably large, the victims are (more or less) direct contract partners of the infringers, and the necessary evidence to prove this business relationship is still at hand. The characteristics and challenges of such litigation between large businesses may therefore often be distinguished from some of the problems discussed above.

Putting aside the latter case, it seems that even a follow-on action for damages based on a prior finding of infringement cannot by any means be considered easy. The capacity to invoke a collective action mechanism does not reduce the burden of proof in every respect. Such a mechanism may only allow victims to share the costs of, for example, expert testimony establishing the amount of harm; indeed, it can add complexities to the procedure which result in additional costs and risks that do not exist in individual litigation. The certification stage of a collective action alone can take years of litigation.[51] And although settlements may

---

[48] See Bundeskartellamt press release of 11 July 2013, <http://www.bundeskartellamt.de/SharedDocs/Meldung/EN/Pressemitteilungen/2013/11_07_2013_Moravia-Steel.html> accessed 15 July 2014.

[49] See Ron Knox, 'Deutsche Bahn strikes settlement deal with ThyssenKrupp' (Global Competition Law Review, Europe, 20 November 2013), <http://globalcompetitionreview.com/news/article/34604/deutsche-bahn-strikes-settlement-deal-thyssenkrupp/> accessed 15 July 2014.

[50] See Deutsche Bahn AG press release of 20 November 2013, <http://www.deutschebahn.com/de/presse/presseinformationen/pi_k/5056524/h20131120.html> accessed 15 July 2014

[51] See, for example, the Swedish Case *Kraftkommission*, Court of Appeal for northern Norrland, 4 November 2011, T 154-10, *Kraftkommission*. For discussion, see Gustaf Sparrman and Linn Göransson, 'Sweden' in Paul G. Karlsgodt

help to reduce litigation costs by reducing the time spent on litigation, the price to be paid for settlements may be that victims receive less, potentially even considerably less, than their actual damages.[52] As a side note, there could also be other surprises in store for would-be plaintiffs. In Germany, for example, the Higher Regional Court of Munich dismissed an action for damages brought against a company by competitors claiming to be harmed by anticompetitive conduct. The court stated that, while the prior and valid decision of the Bundeskartellamt finding a competition law infringement was indeed 'binding' on the court, this did not extend to the market definition the Bundeskartellamt had applied, nor to the statement of the Bundeskartellamt that small competitors in particular (the plaintiffs in that case) were harmed by the offence.[53] Applying its own definition of the relevant market, the court found that the plaintiffs were not active on the same market where the illegal conduct had taken place, making it unlikely that they could have been harmed by that conduct.[54] Admittedly, such court decisions may not be the rule; but they serve as a reminder of the multitude of issues that can arise in an action seeking damages for competition law infringements. In summary, litigation in this context may remain costly and risky – and for this reason, financing and risk distribution mechanisms can play an important role.

The Financing of Litigation

All these considerations described above, which potential initiators of a collective action have to bear in mind, are closely linked to other problems that cannot be solved merely by introducing the Commission's proposed collective action mechanisms: those of funding and risk allocation.[55] Both an individual victim (and her lawyer) as well as certified

(ed), *World Class Actions: A Guide to Group and Representative Actions Around the Globe* (Oxford University Press 2012) 198, 207.

52 See, *inter alia*, Robert H. Lande 'The Proposed Damages Directive: The Real Lessons from the United States', (2014)(3) Nr. 2 Competition Policy International, Antitrust Chronicle 7, <https://www.competitionpolicyinternational.com/mar-14/> accessed 15 July 2014.

53 Oberlandesgericht München, Decision of 21 February 2013, Case U 5006/11 Kart.

54 Ibid., paras 91ff.

55 cf. Keske, *Group Litigation*, cited above, note 6, at 29f; Sonja Keske, Andrea Renda and Roger Van den Berg, 'Financing and Group Litigation', in Mark Tuil and Louis Visscher (eds), *New Trend in Financing Civil Litigation in Europe* (Edward Elgar 2010) 57ff.

non-profit organizations, like consumer associations, will have to pre-finance and – at least initially – bear the risk of losing the trial (including, under a loser-pays rule, the costs of the other parties). In specific circumstances, if the case is dismissed because the court finds it lacks merit, there may even be a risk of being counter-sued, for example, for reputational losses or for the hindrance of profitable business activities by the originally suspected companies. All these potential costs and risks can be quite substantial, and, depending on the applicable rules, they may have to be borne by the lead plaintiff or by the relevant consumer association.

These obstacles remain, and they are hardly diminished by the fact that, according to the Recommendation, contingency fees and punitive damages, which might otherwise provide incentives for lawyers and victims to incur the risk and initiate proceedings, are to be either prohibited or allowed only under very specific circumstances. It is also not foreseen that the certified non-profit organizations could receive financial incentives for themselves to take on such risks. As such, it seems that third-party funders, such as professional litigation funders, could be an option. Unfortunately, the Commission also wants to prohibit both a 'contingency reimbursement' as a percentage of the damages awarded to funders (unless additional regulatory safeguards apply) and 'excessive' interests on their – risky – investment.[56] At the same time, the Commission recommends that private funders should not in any way be able to influence the proceedings.[57] These recommendations are likely to significantly reduce the incentives of professional litigation funders to conduct such a business transaction. Legal insurance may also fail to really close the gap. Before-the-event legal insurance often does not cover all types of claims, which may include complex, risky and expensive competition law disputes. After-the-event insurance is often characterized by some form of contingency fee arrangement[58] – which according to the Recommendation should be either precluded or at least regulated.

Overall, it seems that there are a lot of obstacles faced by prospective plaintiffs that the foreseen collective redress mechanism (even in conjunction with the provisions of the Damages Directive) is still unable to overcome.

---

[56] Recommendation, paras 16 and 32 of the main text.

[57] Recommendation, para 16(a) of the main text.

[58] Willem H. van Boom, 'Financing Civil Litigation by the European Insurance Industry', in Tuil and Visscher (eds), *New Trend in Financing*, cited above, note 55, at 92, 99.

Experience with Collective Redress Mechanisms

These cautionary observations warning against an excessively optimistic view with regard to what the Commission's Recommendation may be able to achieve are supported by the experiences of some EU Member States.[59] For example, even the above-mentioned Dutch opt-out settlement procedure has not resulted in numerous cases: as of 2013, there were only six cases reported in the first eight years of the existence of this procedure.[60]

Sweden may provide a particularly fitting example, as the Swedish Group Proceeding[61] resembles the recommendation of the Commission in several important features, such as representation by a certified body, opt-in of victims and an admissibility stage at court (where the commonality of features of the individual cases to be included in the class action are assessed). The Group Proceeding Act entered into force on 1 January 2003.[62] In the preparatory works preceding the final Act it was estimated that more than ten collective redress cases would be brought per year, and thus expectations were high. However, six years later, only twelve group actions had been reported.[63] Many cases have reportedly been dismissed and others may have been settled before getting to the courts or abandoned for several reasons, including reasons of financial risk.[64] Cases in Sweden also often seem to have had a comparatively limited number of victims included in the action, sometimes in conjunction with significant individual damages.[65] A notable example was the group action

---

[59] For a discussion of the German and UK experiences, see Keske, *Group Litigation*, cited above, note 6, at 208ff.

[60] See Kramer, 'Enforcing mass settlements', cited above, note 23, at 74f; Tzankova and Tjong Tjin Tai, 'The Netherlands', cited above, note 23.

[61] Group Proceedings Act issued on 30 May 2002 (Lag om grupprättegang), <http://www.government.se/content/1/c6/02/77/67/bcbe1f4f.pdf> accessed 15 July 2014.

[62] Sparrman and Göransson, 'Sweden', cited above, note 51, at 198.

[63] Ibid. at 206.

[64] Annina H. Persson, 'Collective enforcement – European prospects in light of the Swedish experience', in Stefan Wrbka, Steven Van Uytsel and Mathias Siems (eds), *Collective Actions – Enhancing Access to Justice and Reconciling Multilayer Interests?* (Cambridge University Press 2012) 341, 350; Sparrman and Göransson, 'Sweden', cited above, note 51, at 206.

[65] Compare also the description of antitrust litigation in Finland in Hanna Laurila and Toni Kalliokoski, 'Developments in Finnish private antitrust litigation: Finland fast-forwards into the future?' (2014) 35 (11) European Competition Law Review 519.

against the Swedish University of Agricultural Sciences regarding gender discrimination, which was brought by 44 women.[66]

The United Kingdom had similar experiences with the Group Litigation Order and the representative follow-on action.[67] By 2008, after 18 years of its existence, there had been only 13 consumer-related cases.[68] Most of them concerned travel packages (for example, unsatisfactory holiday arrangements) or flight cases (a plane crash); others arose from alleged harm to health (McDonald's coffee was too hot; breast implants malfunctioned).[69] At first glance, many of these cases seem to have the features already discussed above: there were not too many harmed individuals, and the individual damages were not too small. However, the most often cited case relating to competition law was the one brought by the consumer association *Which?* as a follow-on representative action.[70] *Which?* was able to induce only a minor fraction of affected consumers to opt in to the action, and then it could only achieve a small degree of compensation for the class members – a fraction of the estimated actual damages. This led to the declaration by *Which?* that it would not again attempt to bring such a suit.[71] Many commentators criticized the then-available collective redress mechanism for several reasons, including the perceived negative effects of the opt-in solution and the excessively narrow definition of the requirement of 'the same interest' under the representative rule.[72] The Consumer Rights Bill being discussed in

66 Sparrman and Göransson, 'Sweden', cited above, note 51, at 207.

67 For a description of both mechanisms, see Geraint Howells, 'Evaluation of the effectiveness and efficiency of collective redress mechanisms in the European Union – Country Report United Kingdom', (2008), <http://ec.europa.eu/consumers/redress_cons/uk-country-report-final.pdf> accessed 15 July 2014, at 10; Keske, *Group Litigation*, cited above, note 6, at 208ff.

68 Howells, 'Country Report United Kingdom', cited above, note 67, at 10.

69 Ibid. at 11ff.

70 Competition Appeal Tribunal, *The Consumer Association v JJB Sports PLC*, Case nr 1078/7/9/07. For a description, see, *inter alia*, Keske, *Group Litigation*, cited above, note 6, at 226.

71 Christopher Cook, 'Private Enforcement of EU Competition Law in Member State Courts: Experience to date and the Path Ahead', (2008)(4) Nr. 2 Competition Policy International Journal 15.

72 Cf. Keske, *Group Litigation*, cited above, note 6, at 210f; Office of Fair Trading, 'OFT 916: Private actions in competition law: effective redress for consumers and business' (2009) 12; for a summary of reactions by commentators, see Howells, 'Country Report United Kingdom', cited above, note 67

Parliament as of this writing, now includes the possibility – in contrast with the Commission's Recommendation – of pursuing opt-out collective redress.[73]

CONCLUSION

The Commission has decided not to recommend a specific collective redress mechanism for competition law, but rather has taken a horizontal approach. The question remains whether such a 'one size fits all' approach is likely to work equally well in different areas of law and in different types of cases within a specific body of law – particularly competition law. The scheduled future assessment of developments four years after the adoption of the Recommendation may be read as a statement that the present soft harmonization experiment, if found to be inadequate, will be followed by 'hard' harmonization. It remains to be seen what the results of that assessment will be.

Whether or not many more collective redress cases in Europe can be expected rather depends on the definition of 'many'. Doubts that there will be hundreds of cases each year, even taking all the Member States together, may be well founded. Difficulties remain with regard to rational apathy, procedural economy, procedural requirements concerning standing and proof, costs and risks of litigation, and financing possibilities. Based on the considerations and experiences described above, it seems that collective redress mechanisms may be effective, useful and beneficial in a specific subset of cases – in other words, where individual damages are large enough to make victims motivated enough to opt in or even to initiate actions themselves, but not so large as to limit the benefits resulting from the possibility of sharing costs and risks due to the additional costs of collective proceedings and due to the loss of control over the proceeding for the individual victim.

At the same time, there may be other elements of a judicial system and features of private as well as procedural law (or even national culture) which may inhibit a large and sudden expansion of damages litigation. In order to gain more experience with collective redress mechanisms and factors outside these rules that may inhibit actions for damages, it would be useful if the Member States refrained from introducing exactly the same collective action mechanism. For example, those Member States

73 For information on the Draft Consumer Rights Bill, see <http://services.parliament.uk/bills/2013–14/consumerrights.html> accessed 15 July 2014.

that have gained, or are about to gain, experience with opt-out mechanisms could usefully still maintain these, as the Commission only asks for a justification for this deviation from the recommended practice. Furthermore, experience with contingency fees, third-party litigation funders, and potentially even punitive damages could also be vital to see whether different features of the collective redress mechanism could be further improved to better overcome remaining problems. Overall, legislators and governments should not jump the gun and fall prey to the proclamations of, for example, consumer associations to the effect that, due to numerous expected actions securing compensation for consumers in the future, they could now make specific (financial) demands. It might be advisable overall to gain more experience first, to learn from different variations on the collective action theme, and to amend the system(s) over time and in line with the particular national legal systems – and maybe even the particular national legal cultures.

3. Judicial dialogues and uniformity in the multi-level application of EU competition law

Adelina Adinolfi*

ABSTRACT

This chapter attempts a review regarding enforcement of EU competition law by national courts over the ten years of application of Regulation 1/2003. It seeks to determine whether the mechanisms set up by the Regulation in order to ensure uniformity in judicial enforcement of EU competition law were actually used by national courts, and possibly to ascertain whether they had a real impact in achieving the desired unity of application of antitrust law. The chapter argues that important divergences remain in the judicial enforcement of competition law, largely due to the wide margin of discretion at times conferred on national courts, and due to the differences of national procedural rules. The chapter also briefly considers some of the recent measures and proposals adopted by the Commission for the purpose of harmonizing the legislation of the Member States by which national institutions enforce EU law.

INTRODUCTION

When in 1999 the Commission proposed, in its White Paper on the modernization of competition law,[1] to abolish the centralized system for enforcing the Community's antitrust rules, it was self-evident that the new approach bore the risk of undermining the uniform application of competition law. After all, a centralized mechanism for the enforcement

* Professor of European Union Law, University of Florence.

[1] White paper on modernization of the rules implementing Articles 81 and 82 of the EC Treaty [1999] OJ C132/1.

of competition law based fundamentally on the primary role of the Commission, which had applied for nearly 40 years, was undoubtedly the most effective way to attain uniformity. However, this system of enforcement was quite eccentric, considering that, in other policy domains, EU law is normally enforced by national administrative authorities and domestic courts. In this regard it is also significant to consider that the Treaty of Rome did not require a centralized mechanism; it was in fact silent with regard to the way in which the competition rules were to be enforced.

One cannot deny that competition law is marked by very special features when compared with other legislative areas falling within the EU's competences. First, it requires complex technical skills and poses challenges with regard to enforcement by domestic courts and national authorities. One may recall furthermore that, when the Community was established, some Member States lacked a fully-fledged set of national competition rules and institutions. Thus, most national authorities were not well-equipped for ensuring the appropriate enforcement of the competition provisions of the Treaty. Moreover, in the context of competition law enforcement, the need for uniformity is generally perceived as stronger than it is in other domains of EU law: in short, competition policy aims, *inter alia*, to ensure that the impediments to intra-Community (now intra-Union) trade that are denied to the Member States under the Treaty are not replaced by new barriers raised by private undertakings. From this perspective, inadequate enforcement of the competition rules in a given Member State may not only yield advantages for an infringing undertaking on the national market, it may also have a significant effect on the EU's common market. Competition law is therefore plainly instrumental to the proper functioning of the common market, which is at the very core of the Union's objectives.[2]

However, during the long era in which a centralized system was in place, a wide body of decisions and rulings progressively shaped a true antitrust legal system for the Community. Several documents adopted by the Commission contributed to the enhanced effectiveness of the enforcement mechanism, and ultimately helped to guarantee compliance with the principle of legal certainty for the benefit of private persons and companies. Overall, antitrust law was clarified in the course of time, and its application has become fairly foreseeable for national authorities

[2] Anne-Marie Van den Bossche, 'EU Competition Law in 3D', in Inge Govaere, Erwan Lannon, Peter Van Elsuwege and Stanislas Adam (eds), *The European Union in the World. Essays in Honour of Marc Maresceau* (Brill 2013) 366, 379.

and courts, as the Commission properly emphasized in the above-mentioned White Paper of 1999.

On the other hand, the shortcomings of the old mechanism were well-known: first of all, the concrete risk that any proceeding pending before a national court could be easily stopped if a party applied for an exemption to the Commission, possibly with a merely dilatory purpose. The expected difficulties in maintaining a centralized system after the then-imminent enlargement of the Union in 2004 surely played a decisive role in helping to reach the political consensus required to adopt new legislation.

As a result, the reform process leading up to Council Regulation 1/2003 sought to counterbalance the need for decentralized enforcement with the establishment of some new mechanisms – either compulsory or voluntary – that aimed at maintaining uniformity. The Commission ultimately retained its leading role, and important constraints were imposed on national administrative authorities and courts. The pivotal role of the judiciary was strongly emphasized, but, as will be discussed below, the strict obligations imposed on national courts were combined with instruments favouring their 'dialogue' with the Commission in order to avoid any unacceptable encroachment on their discretionary powers.

After more than 10 years of application of the new system, an overall analysis may be attempted in order to assess the merits, defects and pitfalls of the multi-level system from the standpoint of the judicial application of EU antitrust law. The chapter thus seeks to determine whether the mechanisms set up to ensure uniformity in the judicial enforcement of EU competition law are actually used by national courts, and possibly to ascertain whether they have a real impact in preserving the desired unity of application of antitrust law.

THE ROLE OF NATIONAL COURTS IN PURSUING THE UNIFORM ENFORCEMENT OF EU COMPETITION LAW

The crucial role of the judiciary in the enforcement of competition rules in Europe was strongly emphasized by Regulation 1/2003. The Regulation recognizes that national courts have an essential part to play in applying those rules: when deciding disputes between individuals, they protect the subjective rights of private parties, but at the same time they contribute to the application of competition law under a public enforcement perspective.[3] Arguably, the strong support given by the Commission to the private enforcement of competition law was due to this double dimension of the new strategy. Of course, the stance of the Commission is not a new feature in EU law, as it may be easily framed according to the ECJ's reasoning in *Van Gend en Loos*: in a well-known paragraph of this judgment, the Court declared that 'the vigilance of individuals concerned to protect their rights amounts to an effective supervision in addition to the supervision entrusted by Articles 169 and 170 [now Articles 258–259 TFEU] to the diligence of the Commission and of the Member States' ([1963] ECR 1, 13).

The private enforcement of competition law is thus strongly supported and fostered by the Commission,[4] and by the case law of the ECJ. But although a growing number of private disputes may in itself enhance compliance with the rules of the Treaty, the real impact of private enforcement needs to be measured against the actual incentives private parties have in seeking judicial protection. Indeed, in the domain of

---

[3] See Recital 7 of the Regulation. The literature on this issue is very extensive; among the most recent studies, see Stefano Bastianon, *La Tutela Privata Antitrust: Italia, Unione Europea e Nord America* (Giuffrè 2012); Lorenzo F. Pace, 'The application of antitrust law by national courts: The influence of the "Private Enforcement Negative Harmonisation Framework" of the Court of Justice in the Italian experience', in Oliver Remien (ed), *Schadensersatz im Europaeischen Privat- und Wirtschaftsrecht* (Mohr Siebeck 2012) 99; Francesco Munari, 'Antitrust Enforcement After the Entry into Force of Regulation No. 1/2003: The Interplay between the Commission and the NCAs and the Need for an Enhanced Role of National Courts', in Bernardo Cortese (ed), *EU Competition Law: Between Public and Private Enforcement* (Wolters Kluwer 2014) 111; Lorenzo F. Pace, 'The Court of Justice['s] "Antitrust Enforcement Negative Harmonisation Framework" and the *CDC* and *Pfleiderer* Judgments: "Another Brick in the Wall"', in Cortese (ed), ibid., 241.

[4] See, for example, European Commission, Green Paper, Damages actions for breach of the EC Antitrust rules, COM(2005)672 final; European Commission, White Paper on Damages actions for breach of the EC antitrust rules, COM(2008)165 final; Proposal for a Directive of the European Parliament and of the Council on certain rules governing actions for damages under national law for infringements of the competition law provisions of the Member States and of the European Union, COM(2013) 404. The Council adopted the Directive on 10 November 2014, and as of this writing the Parliament is expected to sign it during its plenary session at the end of November. Other documents concerning the private enforcement of competition law and compensation for damages can be found at <http://ec.europa.eu/competition/antitrust/actionsdamages/documents.html> accessed 7 October 2014.

competition law, private parties' incentives to bring an action may be less strong than in other areas (such as, for example, non-discrimination or the free movement of persons),[5] and collective redress may be particularly difficult to obtain (see Chapter 2 of this book). Furthermore, access to justice is sometimes hampered by significant procedural constraints.[6]

Whilst the importance of the role of the judiciary in the enforcement of competition law was plainly acknowledged at the time of the reform in 2003, the identification of appropriate instruments to attain uniformity was necessarily a more challenging task with regard to national courts than it was with regard to administrative authorities.[7] In particular, the need to comply with the principle of judicial independence requires that national courts retain significant discretionary powers in reviewing any administrative decisions, including those adopted by the Commission.

The outcome was a two-fold strategy which is not free of some inconsistency: on the one hand, the discretionary powers of the national courts were substantially limited by imposing a strict obligation to comply with decisions already adopted by the Commission or even contemplated by it; on the other hand, the need for mutual cooperation and assistance was strongly emphasized, and a wide range of different devices were put at the disposal of domestic courts in order to achieve such cooperation. The Commission, in its 'Notice on the cooperation

---

[5] As observed in the Commission's Joint Information Note entitled 'Towards a Coherent European Approach to Collective Redress: Next Steps' (SEC(2010)1192), 'citizens and business are also often reluctant to initiate private lawsuits against unlawful practices, in particular if the individual loss is small in comparison to the cost of litigation' (para 4).

[6] See below. See also, *inter alia*, Assimakis Komninos, 'Public and Private Antitrust Enforcement in Europe: Complement or Overlap?', (2006) 3(1) Competition Law Review 5; Francesco Rossi Dal Pozzo and Bruno Nascimbene (eds), *Il Private Enforcement delle norme sulla concorrenza* (Giuffrè 2009); Zygimantas Juska, 'Obstacles in European Competition Law Enforcement: A Potential Solution from Collective Redress' (2014) 7(1) European Journal of Legal Studies 125; Roberto Cisotta, 'Some Considerations on the Last Developments on Antitrust Damages Actions and Collective Redress in the European Union' (2014) 10(1) Competition Law Review 81.

[7] The Commission is well aware of the need to adopt a particular approach with regard to judicial bodies, an approach that contrasts to the one that applies to administrative authorities. See Commission Staff Working Document, 'Ten Years of Antitrust Enforcement under Regulation 1/2003', accompanying the Communication from the Commission to the European Parliament and the Council, Ten Years of Antitrust Enforcement under Regulation 1/2003: Achievements and Future Perspectives, July 2014, para 244 (hereinafter: Staff Working Document, 'Ten Years of Antitrust Enforcement').

between the Commission and the courts of the EU Member States in the application of Articles 81 and 82 EC' (hereinafter the 'Notice on cooperation'),[8] has specified the procedures for and content of such mechanisms.

The most important expression of the first strand was enshrined in Articles 3 and 16 of Regulation 1/2003.

Under Article 16 of the Regulation, national courts cannot take decisions running counter to a decision already adopted by the Commission with regard to the case before them in a pending dispute. One may argue that this is simply a logical expression of the principle of primacy of EU law. Since national courts have to comply with a regulation or even with an unimplemented directive that produces direct effect, they must similarly conform to any decision that the Commission adopts when applying EU competition law. One might then easily object that, in this case, the decisions binding the national courts are adopted by an 'administrative' authority rather than by a legislator; however, under EU law the division of powers is still drawn according to principles that differ substantially from those that apply under national constitutional systems. The binding force of Commission decisions *vis-à-vis* domestic courts was clearly upheld by the ECJ in *Lucchini*,[9] where the Court explained that 'a national court which is called upon, within the exercise of its jurisdiction, to apply provisions of Community law is under a duty to give full effect to those provisions [...]' (para 61). In this well-known case, the provision at issue was a decision the Commission had adopted in the exercise of its exclusive power to assess the consistency of state aid measures with the common market.

The wording of Article 16 raised some doubts with regard to the kinds of decisions covered by the said obligation, given the wide range of different decisions that can be adopted by the Commission in the domain of competition law. As the ECJ clarified in *Toshiba*, Article 16(2) 'covers all conceivable decisions that the Commission may have adopted on the basis of Regulation No 1/2003'.[10] Thus, national courts must comply with any decision the Commission adopts within its competences when applying EU competition rules.

Under Article 16, the remarkable extent of the duty imposed on national courts is such that they 'must also avoid giving decisions which

---

[8] [2004] OJ C101/54, para 32.

[9] Case C-119/05 *Ministero dell'Industria, del Commercio e dell'Artigianato v Lucchini SpA* [2007] ECR I-6228.

[10] Case C-17/10 *Toshiba Corporation and Others v Úřad pro ochranu hospodářské soutěže*, 14 February 2012, EU:C:2012:72, para 87.

would conflict with a decision contemplated by the Commission in proceedings it has initiated'. Arguably, this solution resulted from a compromise between the need to ensure the primacy of EU law and the need to preserve the independence of the judiciary. An obligation to stay proceedings in order to wait for the Commission's decision would probably have been considered as impinging too much on the judiciary's discretionary powers. However, the position adopted by the ECJ in *Masterfoods* does entail a limited obligation to stay proceedings when the outcome of the dispute before the national court depends on the validity of the Commission's decision; in such a case, 'it follows from the obligation of sincere cooperation that the national court should, in order to avoid reaching a decision that runs counter to that of the Commission, stay its proceedings pending final judgment in the action for annulment by the Community Courts, unless it considers that, in the circumstances of the case, a reference to the Court of Justice for a preliminary ruling on the validity of the Commission decision is warranted'.[11] Referring a question for a preliminary ruling may appear to be a convenient means to avoid a significant delay when the decision to be adopted by the national court has to await the outcome of the annulment action; one could also consider that a further delay may occur when the ruling given by the General Court is appealed before the ECJ.

In any case, domestic courts may find that staying the proceedings is the most appropriate solution in order to avoid a supervening inconsistency. Yet national courts may opt to proceed with the case when the correct legal position is self-evident, as may occur where there is a steady practice followed by the Commission, or where the ECJ has already clarified the interpretation of the relevant provisions. This latter course is clearly exemplified by a decision adopted in 2011 by the Rotterdam District Court: the court rejected an interim application to stay its proceedings in a damages claim against Shell Corporation pending a judgment of the General Court. For its part, the General Court then dismissed Shell's action for annulment,[12] implying that the Rotterdam Court was not wrong in adopting its decision.

The obligation of national courts to comply with the Commission's antitrust decisions is also indirectly expressed by the provision laid down by Article 3 of the Regulation enshrining the so-called 'convergence' rule. Under this provision, national competition law may not lead to

---

[11] Case C-344/98 *Masterfoods Ltd v HB Ice Cream Ltd* [2000] ECR I-11369, para 57.

[12] Case T-38/07 *Shell Petroleum NV v Commission* [2011] ECR II-4383.

prohibit agreements, decisions by associations of undertakings or concerted practices which do not restrict competition within the meaning of the Treaty or which fulfil the conditions for an exemption. This implies a duty for national courts to discard or perhaps re-interpret any national antitrust provision that would lead to a result more rigorous than that required under EU law.

JUDICIAL ENFORCEMENT OF COMPETITION LAW AND THE PRELIMINARY REFERENCE PROCEDURE

A sort of escape hatch from the strict system of obligations imposed upon national courts is found in the preliminary reference procedure. Resort to this procedure gives national courts, *inter alia*, the opportunity to challenge the validity of a Commission decision. Article 16(1) of the Regulation clarifies that the obligation to comply with the decisions of the Commission 'is without prejudice to the rights and obligations under Article 234 of the Treaty [now Article 267 TFEU]'. This provision codifies the principle enunciated by the ECJ in *Masterfoods*, where the Court, despite its statement that national courts 'cannot take decisions running counter to that of the Commission' (para 52), specified that 'if a national court has doubts as to the validity or interpretation of an act of a Community institution it may, or must, in accordance with the second and third paragraphs of [Article 267], refer a question to the Court of Justice for a preliminary ruling' (para 54). Therefore, since the *Foto-Frost* principle prevents national courts from finding that an EU act is defective or void, the sole possibility for a national judge to take a decision running counter to a decision of the Commission is to seek a preliminary ruling by the ECJ. In other words, the lawfulness of any 'administrative' decision with which national courts must in principle comply may then be reviewed by the ECJ, thereby restoring the discretionary power of the judiciary and ultimately ensuring that the principles of the rule of law and the separation of powers, as reflected in the notion of 'legality', are respected.

However, in this perspective, the actual value of the ECJ's role in ensuring the legitimacy of the whole system depends on the nature of the review that the Court carries out. A mere summary review by the ECJ could hardly ensure suitable conditions for national courts to satisfy their role with regard to administrative decisions they are essentially compelled to enforce. In *Otis*,[13] the defendant in the main proceeding argued that the review carried out by the Court was insufficient because of the wide margin of discretion it allows the Commission in relation to matters of complex economic assessment. Consistently with other recent jurisprudence,[14] the ECJ explained that this margin 'does not mean that the EU courts must refrain from reviewing the Commission's interpretation of information of an economic nature' (para 59). Thus, one may infer that such review is considered by the Court to be appropriate in order to ensure respect for the principle of effective judicial protection. The remainder of the judgment in *Otis* contains (again, consistently with the trend in the ECJ's case law) a very detailed description of the method used to review the Commission's decisions. Arguably, this thorough reasoning is aimed at demonstrating that the Court's review involves in-depth scrutiny of both the law and the facts. Moreover, the Court emphasizes that, where the Commission imposes fines, the EU Courts have the power to substitute their own appraisal for that of the Commission.[15] The very detailed position given by the Court reveals that it is well aware of the decisive importance of its review in ensuring the legitimacy of the strict obligations imposed on national courts under Article 16 of the Regulation. Furthermore, as noted above, intensive scrutiny is needed to safeguard the right to obtain effective judicial protection, long recognized as a general principle of law and now enshrined in Article 47 of the Charter,[16] since a detailed review of any administrative decision is required to satisfy the requirements of that principle.[17]

---

[13] Case C-199/11 *Europese Gemeenschap v Otis NV and Others*, 6 November 2012, EU:C:2012:684.

[14] See further Chapters 4 and 5 of this book.

[15] See also Case C-386/10 P *Chalkor AE Epexergasias Metallon v Commission* [2011] ECR I-13085.

[16] See, for example, Bruno Nascimbene, 'Fair Trial and the right of defence in antitrust proceedings before the Commission. A need for reform?', in Marco Frigessi di Rattalma and Patrizia De Cesari (eds), *Nuove Sfide in tema di concorrenza e aiuti di Stato nell'Unione Europea* (Editoriale scientifica 2013) 125.

[17] The Court recently specified that 'the effectiveness of the judicial review guaranteed by Article 47 of the Charter also requires that the Courts of the European Union are to ensure that the decision, which affects the person or entity concerned individually, is taken on a sufficiently solid factual basis. That entails a verification of the allegations factored in the summary of reasons underpinning that decision, with the consequence that judicial review cannot be restricted to an assessment of the cogency in the abstract of the reasons relied on,

Further interpretative techniques used by the ECJ emphasize the pivotal role of national courts and the important margin of discretion they should enjoy. In particular, whenever the ECJ acknowledges the discretion and autonomy of national courts *vis-à-vis* the Commission it arguably takes into account the need to endorse the role played by those courts. Thus the Court held, *inter alia*, that it is for a national court to decide whether an agreement constitutes, within the meaning of Article 101 TFEU, an appreciable restriction of competition even if the outcome of this assessment is inconsistent with the non-binding threshold specified by the Commission in its *De minimis* Notice.[18] Overall, the non-binding nature of the Commission's Notices is strongly emphasized in the case law of the Court in order to clarify that national courts may deviate from them and develop their own appraisal.[19]

The aim of preserving the autonomy of national courts also seems to drive ECJ rulings which reaffirm that the preliminary reference procedure establishes a system of cooperation between courts, and which highlight its inherent nature as a system of judicial dialogue. This is well illustrated by the recent ruling in *Consiglio Nazionale dei Geologi*,[20] where the Court reaffirms that 'the system established by Article 267 TFEU with a view to ensuring that European Union law is interpreted uniformly throughout the Member States institutes direct cooperation between the Court of Justice and the national courts by means of a procedure which is completely independent of any initiative by the parties' (para 28).

---

but must concern whether those reasons, or, at the very least, one of those reasons, deemed sufficient in itself to support that decision, is substantiated'. Case-348/12 P *Council v Manufacturing Support & Procurement Kala Naft Co., Tehran,* 28 November 2013, EU:C:2013:776, para 73.

[18] Case C-226/11 *Expedia Inc. v Autorité de la Concurrence and Others*, 13 December 2012, EU:C:2012:795.

[19] Case C-360/09 *Pfleiderer AG v Bundeskartellamt* [2011] ECR I-5161, para 21; see also Cases C-189/02 P, C-202/02 P, C-205/02 P to Case C-208/02 P and C-213/02 P, *Dansk Rørindustri and Others v Commission* [2005] ECR I-5425, para 209; Case C-520/09 P, *Arkema SA v Commission* [2011] ECR I-8901, para 88; Case C-501/11 P, *Schindler Holding Ltd and Others v Commission,* 18 July 2013, EU:C:2013:522, para 51; Case C-557/12 *Kone AG and Others v ÖBB Infrastruktur AG*, 5 June 2014, EU:C:2014:1317, para 36.

[20] Case C-136/12 *Consiglio Nazionale dei Geologi v Autorità Garante Della Concorrenza e del Mercato*, 18 July 2013, EU:C:2013:489. See also Case C-210/06 *Cartesio Oktató és Szolgáltató bt* [2008] ECR I-9641, para 90; Case C-104/10 *Patrick Kelly v National University of Ireland* [2011] ECR I-6813, para 62.

However, the Court seems to be particularly demanding with regard to the admissibility of preliminary questions that concern EU competition law, as it states that 'the need for precision with regard to the factual and legislative context applies especially in the area of competition, which is characterized by complex factual and legal situations […]'.[21] This stance is justified by the frequent difficulty of the issues and ultimately by the need for the Court to have a clear picture in order to give an appropriate answer; yet it may sometimes impair the judicial dialogue envisaged by the Treaty. The two preliminary rulings adopted in the *Viacom* case are emblematic of this attitude. The reference submitted by an Italian court of first instance was held to be manifestly inadmissible in 2002 because of its lack of adequate information;[22] the national court then referred some fresh questions later in the same proceedings, and the Court in 2005[23] again declared the request to be partly inadmissible, referring to the same defect, a lack of adequate specifications. A relevant factor in that case may have been the fact that the referring court was an Italian *giudice di pace*, a sort of honorary judge who lacks specific expertise in the field of competition law.

In the light of this issue, one may first of all argue that in such cases the national court should first seek the support of the Commission relying on the cooperation mechanisms established by Regulation 1/2003 (see below). Furthermore, one might consider whether a new system of support could be made available to national courts when they draft their request for a preliminary ruling: in short, any judge who envisages a need to make such a request but is experiencing difficulties in the formulation of his/her reference could seek the assistance of a technical unit working in the framework of DG Competition. This could help the national court to clarify the legal and factual context, and could arguably prevent or reduce the incidence of decisions of non-admissibility of the reference (which may discourage the referring court and perhaps other courts from

---

[21] Case C-134/03 *Viacom Outdoor Srl v Giotto Immobiliare SARL* [2005] ECR I-1167, para 23. See also Case C-157/92 *Giorgio Domingo Banchero* [1993] ECR I-1085, para 5; Case C-176/96 *Jyri Lehtonen and Castors Canada Dry Namur-Braine ASBL v Fédération Royale Belge des Sociétés de Basket-ball ASBL (FRBSB)* [2000] ECR I-2681, para 22; Case C-116/00 *Claude Laguillaumie* [2000] ECR I-4979, para 19.

[22] Case C-190/02, *Viacom Outdoor Srl v Giotto Immobilier SARL* [2002] ECR I-8287.

[23] Case C-134/03, *Viacom Outdoor Srl v Giotto Immobilier SARL* [2005] ECR I-1167.

requesting preliminary rulings, to the detriment of the effective enforcement of EU law). Moreover, since competition law has many peculiar features, as carefully emphasized by the Court itself, the adoption of specific guidelines in the Court's jurisprudence can provide useful details to supplement the general Recommendation on the preliminary ruling procedure,[24] thus supporting and facilitating the tasks of the national courts.

VARIED MEANS UNDER REGULATION 1/2003 TO MAINTAIN UNIFORMITY WITH REGARD TO JUDICIAL DECISIONS

Walking the Line Between Cooperation and Control: An Overview

With a view to ensuring uniformity in the enforcement of competition law, Article 15 of Regulation 1/2003, which bears the heading 'cooperation with national courts', establishes the different means by which the Commission interacts with those courts. Actually, only some of these instruments may be described as part of a true cooperation-oriented system, whilst others rather appear directed at guiding the action of national courts or monitoring national judicial decisions in order to assess whether they are consistent with the obligations under the Regulation.

The power conferred upon national courts to request that the Commission transmit information in its possession or provide its opinion (Article 15(1)) plainly seeks to give support to the national courts when they consider issues of EU competition law. By contrast, there is no doubt that the obligation of the Member States to forward to the Commission a copy of any written judgments applying EU competition law (Article 15(2)) aims to facilitate a monitoring function attributed to the Commission by the Treaty.

Furthermore, a single instrument of cooperation may have a two-fold nature. This is the case with the intervention of the Commission when it submits written observations to national courts as *amicus curiae* (Article 15(3)). Under the Regulation, the Commission may act on its own motion 'where the coherent application' of the Treaty provisions so requires; the permission of the national court is required only if the Commission wishes to present oral observations in the proceedings. When the

---

[24] Recommendations to national courts and tribunals in relation to the initiation of preliminary ruling proceedings [2012] OJ C338/1

Commission submits written observations on its own motion or requests permission to present oral observations, its intervention clearly aims at guiding the national court in the adoption of its decision in order to avoid possible inconsistencies with EU law, and in particular, to avoid inconsistencies with the Commission's decisions. However, the intervention of the Commission may be advocated by private parties or solicited by the national court itself. In this latter case, of course, framing the Commission's intervention as assistance or cooperation is unproblematic.

Although neither the Commission's opinions nor its submissions as *amicus curiae* are binding on national courts, they may nevertheless have a significant impact on the judicial decision to be adopted. In that regard, national courts are likely to consider that a decision 'running counter' to the opinion expressed by the Commission may imply a high risk of violation of EU law; thus, when inclined to deviate from the Commission's position they may first prefer to seek the support of the ECJ by requesting a preliminary ruling.

Request for Information and Documents: The Thorny Issue of Disclosure

Cooperation instruments are basically identified by the Regulation in the power conferred upon national courts to seek information and opinions from the Commission. These instruments give expression to the general principle of sincere cooperation, which is now enshrined in Article 4(3) of the Treaty of the European Union. According to this principle, 'the Union and the Member States shall, in full mutual respect, assist each other in carrying out tasks which flow from the Treaties'. As the Court of Justice declared in *Inspecteur van de Belastingdienst v X BV*,[25] the cooperation mechanisms between the Commission, the national competition authorities and the courts of the Member States set up in Chapter IV of Regulation 1/2003 'is part of the general principle of sincere cooperation [...] which governs the relationships between the Member States and the Community institutions' (para 21). The mutual duty of sincere cooperation seems to take on its greatest importance when the judicial application of EU law is at stake. As the Court held in assessing the lawfulness of the refusal by the Commission to transmit certain documents to a national court, this 'duty of sincere cooperation imposed on Community institutions is of particular importance *vis-à-vis* the

[25] Case C-429/07 *Inspecteur van de Belastingdienst v X BV* [2009] ECR I-4833.

judicial authorities of the Member States, who are responsible for ensuring that Community law is applied and respected in the national legal system'.[26] The Regulation also confers on the Commission a limited power to request documents from national courts 'for the purpose of the preparation of their observations only'; this implies a mutual obligation to transmit documents which, under certain conditions, seems to put the Commission and the national courts on the same footing.

One should also mention the general duty of Member States to ensure effective legal protection in the fields of EU law, a duty now enshrined in Article 19(1) TEU. National courts, because of their nature as authorities of the Member States, are subject to that duty to ensure such protection. As the Court declared in *Donau Chemie*,[27] those courts, which are obliged to apply the rules of EU law in areas within their jurisdiction, 'must ensure that those rules take full effect and must protect the rights which they confer to individuals' (para 22).

Under Article 15(1) of the Regulation, 'courts of the Member States may ask the Commission to transmit to them information in its possession or its opinion on questions concerning the application of the Community [now EU] competition rules'. As specified in the Notice on cooperation, a national court may ask the Commission 'for documents in its possession or for information of a procedural nature to enable it to discover whether a certain case is pending before the Commission, whether the Commission has initiated a procedure or whether it has already taken a position'. A national court may also be interested in finding out when a Commission decision is likely to be taken in order to decide to stay the proceedings, or to decide whether interim measures need to be adopted.[28]

Limitations to the transmission of documents and information may be justified by reasons of confidentiality. In general, the Commission is bound by Article 339 TFEU, which prevents members, officials and other servants of the Commission from disclosing information covered by the obligation of professional secrecy. Striking a balance between the principle of sincere cooperation and the protection of professional secrets can sometimes be a difficult task. The Commission rules out an absolute

---

26 See Case C-2/88 *IMM Zwartveld and Others* [1990] ECR I-3365, para 18.

27 Case C-536/11 *Bundeswettbewerbsbehörde v Donau Chemie AG and Others,* 6 June 2013, EU:C:2013:366.

28 As the Commission states in its Staff Working Document, Ten Years of Antitrust Enforcement (cited above, note 7), 'this provision has most often been used by national courts to obtain information about the state of proceedings of cases investigated by the Commission' (para 245).

prohibition on providing national courts with information and documents covered by the obligation of professional secrecy. However, to avoid violating Article 339 TFEU, the Commission will transmit certain information and documents to a national court only when the court has offered a guarantee that it will protect the confidential information and business secrets;[29] although the Commission normally specifies those parts of the information which are covered by professional secrecy and which parts can be disclosed, this solution necessarily leaves some room to national courts, which will arguably decide on the basis of national law. The Commission tries to avoid national divergences and expects the national court to ensure that any disclosure order granted by it 'will provide a level of protection equivalent to that required by Article 339 TFEU, Article 28 of Regulation (EC) 1/2003 and Article 15(4) of Regulation (EC) 773/200'.[30] This actually invites national courts to rely on the standard established by EU law as a benchmark for the interpretation of national legislation; however, this approach may give rather loose guidelines to national courts because of the non-binding nature of the said benchmark and because of the wide margin of discretion that may be exercised in the interpretation of the relevant EU provisions.

Some uncertainties have arisen especially with regard to the disclosure of information given to the Commission by a company in connection with an application for leniency.[31] On the one hand, disclosure to a court could be valuable for, among other things, ascertaining the responsibility of other companies implicated in the relevant anticompetitive behaviour; on the other hand, the risk that confidential documents might be transmitted to national courts may possibly discourage companies from applying for leniency. The Notice on cooperation clearly attaches prevailing weight to this latter concern by establishing that 'the Commission will not transmit to national courts information voluntarily submitted by a leniency applicant without the consent of that applicant' (para 26).

In this regard, the ECJ seems to take quite a flexible approach. Under its case law, the duty of sincere cooperation implies that the Commission has to provide a national court with whatever information the court asks for, including information covered by professional secrecy. However, the

---

29 See the Notice on cooperation, paras 23–26.

30 Recent opinion given by the Commission on the disclosure of documents created in the course of an investigation: Commission Opinion of 5 May 2014, C(2014) 3066 final, *Morrison Supermarkets plc and Others v MasterCard Incorporated and Others*, para 19.

31 On the different solutions adopted by national courts, see Cisotta, 'Some Considerations', cited above, note 6.

core of the problem seems not to be the mere transmission of information and documents by the Commission to national courts, but rather the use to which national courts put those materials. The case law of the ECJ acknowledges the discretionary power of Member States with regard to disclosure of the information provided by the Commission; indeed, the Court has declared that, in the absence of EU rules on disclosure, it is for the Member States to establish and apply national rules on the right of access to documents relating to national proceedings, subject to the principles of effectiveness and equivalence. This approach is consistent with the well-established case law regarding national procedural autonomy, but it also implies the risk that possible divergences in domestic laws may produce an uneven protection of business secrets in different Member States.[32] In *Donau Chemie*,[33] the Court held that the effective application of EU competition law could be undermined if a generalized access to documents were recognized. Thus, the Court declared that national courts must carry out a balancing test, weighing up the reasons which justify disclosure and the reasons for protecting confidential information. In any case, in order 'not to jeopardise the investigatory powers of the Commission, national courts are asked to refrain from ordering disclosure where such disclosure could undermine an ongoing investigation concerning a suspected infringement of the EU competition rules'.[34] It is therefore up to the national courts to decide whether disclosure could undermine the effective application of antitrust law. In the leading case, *Pfleiderer*, the Court left room for discretion even with regard to information submitted to a national competition authority under a leniency programme; in this case too, the Court took the view that it was up to the national courts to weigh the respective interests in favour of, and against, disclosure of the information provided

[32] See below. For a comparative survey, see Kati Cseres, 'Comparing Laws in the Enforcement of EU and National Competition Laws' (2010) 3(1) European Journal of Legal Studies 7.

[33] *Donau Chemie*, cited above, note 27. See also Case 681/11 *Bundeswettbewerbsbehorde and Bundeskartellanwalt v Schenker & Co. AG and Others*, 18 June 2013, EU:C:2013:404. In *Schenker*, the Court held that a national competition authority may decide not to impose a fine on an undertaking that has participated in a national leniency programme. However, this decision can be made 'only in so far as the programme is implemented in such a way as not to undermine the requirement of effective and uniform application of Article 101 TFEU' (para 47).

[34] Commission Opinion in *Morrison Supermarkets plc*, cited above, note 30, para 17.

voluntarily by a leniency applicant.[35] The risk of this case-by-case approach is that it will produce results that are scarcely predictable by the interested undertakings (thus potentially discouraging their use of leniency instruments, as already suggested), and that it opens the way to divergent solutions in the Member States.

Requests for Commission Opinions

As indicated in a Report published recently by the Commission,[36] from 2004 until the end of 2013 the Commission provided 26 opinions, 12 of which were to Spanish courts, nine to Belgian courts, two to Lithuanian courts, two to Swedish courts and one to a Dutch court. The majority of the opinions were requested by first instance courts. The publication of the opinions is however conditional upon a decision by the requesting national court;[37] it is advisable to urge upon national courts the importance of consenting to publication, considering that the Commission's opinions may provide other national courts across Europe with useful guidelines.

The statistics above easily show that the power to seek opinions was not widely used by national courts in the nearly 10 years of application of Regulation 1/2003; moreover, almost half of the requests were presented by courts of a single Member State, namely, Spain. One may infer that national courts generally are well-equipped to apply EU competition law and therefore they do not need any support. However, one could equally maintain that the low number of requests reflects the scant knowledge among judges about these cooperation instruments by national courts; the specific training programmes co-financed by the Commission may have a useful impact in this respect.[38] Furthermore,

---

[35] *Pfleiderer*, cited above, note 19. On this case, see, for example, Ingrid Vandenborre, 'The Confidentiality of EU Commission Cartel Records in Civil Litigation: The Ball is in the EU Court' (2011) 32 European Competition Law Review 116.

[36] Staff Working Document, Ten Years of Antitrust Enforcement (cited above, note 7), para 246.

[37] During the reporting period, the Commission published only 13 opinions. Ibid.

[38] As stated in the Staff Working Document, Ten Years of Antitrust Enforcement (cited above, note 7), the 'Commission continuously endeavours to encourage the exchange of knowledge and practical experience in the enforcement of the competition rules. DG Competition's Grant Programme on the "Training of National Judges in EU Competition Law" provides practice-oriented training tailored to the needs of competition law judges in the Member States.

national courts may arguably be reluctant to seek assistance from an EU Institution whose nature is that of an administrative authority. A risk of misinformation or distrust might particularly affect some non-specialized courts, which are only occasionally required to enforce EU antitrust provisions.

As to the substance of the opinions, the core issue concerns the need for the Commission to give support to the national courts without substituting its own appraisals for theirs. The Notice on cooperation envisages a wide-ranging approach, specifying that 'national courts may ask the Commission for its opinion on economic, factual and legal matters' (para 27). One should note that the opinion that the Commission can be requested to provide is significantly different from the preliminary rulings adopted by the ECJ. First of all, the opinions given by the Commission do not bind national courts. However, it can be expected that national courts would most likely either: conform to the opinion provided in order to avoid the risk that an infringement proceeding might be started by the Commission; or, in case of doubt, refer a preliminary question to the ECJ. Furthermore, the opinions provided by the Commission may assist the national courts with regard to technical issues and to the appraisal of facts, whilst preliminary rulings may only interpret EU law and scrutinize the lawfulness of acts adopted by the Union, without assessing the facts of the case before the national court. Therefore, one may argue that the opinions given by the Commission and the preliminary rulings adopted by the ECJ are aimed at satisfying different needs of the national courts. They thus complement each other in giving national courts sound support in the application of competition law.

The request for an opinion from the Commission may trigger a sort of dialogue with the requesting court whenever the Commission deems that, in order to provide useful support, there is a need to obtain additional information from the requesting court.[39] The Commission will not hear the parties before formulating its opinion for the national court; this seems fully coherent with the technical nature of the opinions, and it helps to avoid the risk that the Commission could play a rather intrusive role in the national judicial proceedings. In principle, a national court should seek an opinion from the Commission only when it cannot find

This Programme enables hundreds of judges to be trained in EU competition law every year. In the last six years approximately 6000 judges have benefited from the programme' (para 252).

[39] As indicated in the Notice on cooperation, '[i]n order to enable the Commission to provide the national court with a useful opinion, it may request [further information from the national court]' (para 48).

guidance in EU legislation and case law;[40] however, under the Regulation the request for an opinion is not made conditional upon the lack of guidance in existing EU legislation or practice. Thus, a national court could decide to seek the support of the Commission even if it has not conducted thorough research into EU law and practice.

The content of the requested opinion is crucial with regard to the need to avoid inappropriate limitations on judicial discretion. In this regard, the Commission seems to favour a self-restrained attitude in order not to impinge on the discretionary power of national courts. The need to ensure the coherent application of antitrust provisions is also relevant in defining the substance of the observations submitted by the Commission. The Notice on cooperation specifies that the Commission will restrict its observations to an economic and legal analysis of the facts underlying the case pending before the national court. Thus, the Commission will limit itself to providing the national court with the 'factual information or the economic or legal clarification asked for, without considering the merits of the case pending before the national court' (para 29).

This cautious stance is well illustrated by an opinion given at the request of the Supreme Administrative Court of Lithuania.[41] At the outset, the Commission recalls that its opinions are not binding, and that only the Court of Justice is entitled to give a binding interpretation of the EU competition rules by way of a preliminary ruling. It then states that, when giving an opinion under Article 15(1) of Regulation 1/2003, it should limit itself to providing the national court with factual information, or economic or legal clarification, without considering the merits of the case pending before the court. Therefore, the Commission will refuse to answer a question aimed at assessing whether or not an agreement infringes Article 101 TFEU because, as it says pointedly, '[t]he Commission cannot substitute the analysis that the national court needs to make on the basis of the facts and information before it'.[42] Thus, since an assessment of the agreement in order to ascertain whether it

---

[40] 'When called upon to apply EC competition rules to a case pending before it, a national court may first seek guidance in the case law of the Community courts or in Commission regulations, decisions, notices and guidelines applying Articles 81 and 82 EC. Where these tools do not offer sufficient guidance, the national court may ask the Commission for its opinion on questions concerning the application of EC competition rules' (Notice on cooperation, para 27).

[41] Supreme Administrative Court of Lithuania, Case A502-337/2008, <http://ec.europa.eu/competition/court/opinion_2002_uab_en.pdf> accessed 4 September 2014.

[42] Ibid., para 48.

constitutes an infringement of the antitrust provisions 'appears to be related to merits of the case, the Commission will not make such assessment in this opinion'.[43]

Although this attitude is certainly consistent with the system of the sharing of competences established by the Regulation, such a sharp refusal to answer, or the provision of a loose reply, may seem somewhat frustrating to the national court. One can imagine that it may lead the court either to avoid seeking further support in the future, or possibly to refer a preliminary question to the ECJ.

Amicus Curiae Submissions

In the period examined, the Commission decided to participate as *amicus curiae* in national courts proceedings on 13 occasions and in eight different Member States (France, Belgium, Slovakia, Austria, the Netherlands, the UK, Ireland and Spain). Almost half of the interventions were made before courts of last resort (8); the others were made before appeal courts (3) and first instance courts (2).[44]

As a general remark, one may observe that the Commission mainly intervened in higher courts, and especially when the appealed decision seemed to be incorrect. This stance appears coherent with the aim to avoid violations of EU law, as pursued by Article 15 of the Regulation. However, it necessarily emphasizes the monitoring and intervention functions rather than the grant of support to national courts charged to apply EU competition law.

In this perspective, the Commission's intervention to prevent violations of EU law could be impaired in the absence of an obligation on Member States to inform the Commission with regard to the opening of any national proceeding implying the application of EU competition law; this obviously makes it difficult for the Commission to assess whether reasons of 'coherent application' of EU competition law would justify its intervention as *amicus curiae*. The Regulation requires Member States to forward to the Commission any judgment applying EU competition law,[45] but it does not require that the Commission be informed upon the *opening* of national judicial proceedings where EU law will be applied. In the Notice on cooperation it is observed that the transmission of

---

[43] Ibid., para 12.

[44] See Staff Working Document, Ten Years of Antitrust Enforcement (cited above, note 7), para 246. A further submission was made in 2014 in a proceeding before the Supreme Court of the United Kingdom.

[45] See below.

national judgments enables the Commission to become aware of cases for which it might be appropriate to submit observations where one of the parties lodges an appeal. The instrument is thus only relevant to the Commission when the judgment is appealed, which may explain in part why such interventions occurred mostly before appellate courts.

The Commission may be informed of the opening of a judicial proceeding by whatever means,[46] and in practice its interventions have sometimes been solicited (though the Regulation does not establish any procedure in this regard) by the national court itself, or possibly even by parties to the proceedings. Seeking the Commission's intervention as *amicus curiae* rather than simply requesting its opinion may imply for the national court the advantage of fostering a 'dialogue' with the Commission as the proceeding develops. The particular complexity of an issue, which may be due to a *lacuna* or to the need to apply an ambiguous or unclear provision, may be one reason why the national court would encourage an *amicus curiae* intervention. As an example one may just cite the case where the UK High Court sought the intervention of the Commission in a proceeding that concerned the difficult and hotly debated issue of the disclosure of leniency documents.[47]

As indicated in the 2009 Report on the functioning of Regulation 1/2003,[48] stakeholders have called on the Commission to put the *amicus* mechanism to greater use; according to the Report, the Commission deems that 'it should be reflected upon how this practice should further develop' (para 35). Ensuring that the Commission is properly informed about the judicial application of EU competition law at national level would certainly be crucial for the development of this practice. A useful means to that end could arguably be an obligation to inform the Commission about the opening of proceedings in which EU competition law is likely to be applied. Moreover, given that the obligation to forward national judgments applying EU competition law seems to be poorly

---

[46] For example, in *Inspecteur van de Belastingdienst v X BV*, cited above, note 25, the Commission intervened as *amicus curiae* after 'having been informed by the press and through the national competition authorities'.

[47] *National Grid Electricity Transmission Plc v ABB Ltd & ors* [2011] EWHC 1717 (Ch). The Commission specified in its *amicus* submission that its observations were submitted pursuant to Article 15(3) of Regulation 1/2003 and 'to the invitation issued by this Honourable Court [...]'.

[48] Communication from the Commission to the European Parliament and the Council – Report on the functioning of Regulation 1/2003 SEC(2009)574, COM/2009/206 final, para 35.

respected by most Member States,[49] it could be expedient to establish that such judgments must be forwarded directly to the Commission by the national courts; doing so could also strengthen the 'dialogue' between national courts and the Commission.

With regard to the Commission's power to submit written observations on its own motion, important clarifications were given by the ECJ in a preliminary ruling of 2009. In this case, the Commission notified the referring court, by letter of 15 March 2007, that it wished to intervene as *amicus curiae* pursuant Regulation No 1/2003 in a dispute concerning the tax deductibility of a fine imposed by the Commission for infringement of the EU antitrust rules.[50] The Commission also requested that any documents necessary for the assessment of the case be transmitted to it by the national court. The parties to the main proceedings contested the Commission's competence under Article 15(3) of Regulation No 1/2003 to submit, on its own initiative, written observations in proceedings which concerned fiscal law rather than the application of EU antitrust provisions. Thus, the national court, namely the Gerechtshof of Amsterdam, decided to make a preliminary reference to the ECJ questioning the scope of the power conferred to the Commission under Article 15.

The Court, emphasizing that the purpose of the power conferred to the Commission is to ensure the coherent application of antitrust law, declared that 'the option for the Commission, acting on its own initiative, to submit written observations to courts of the Member States is subject to the sole condition that the coherent application of Articles [101 or 102 TFEU] so requires' (para 30). That condition may be fulfilled 'even if the proceedings concerned do not pertain to issues relating to the application of Article [Article 101 or 102]' (ibid). The Court argued that, depending on the outcome of the case, the decision to be taken by the national court was capable of impairing the effectiveness of the penalties imposed by the Commission and 'therefore might compromise the coherent application of Articles [101 or 102]' (para 38). Thus, finding that the power to submit observations conferred upon the Commission fell, in the case at

[49] See below.

[50] See *Inspecteur van de Belastingdienst v X BV*, cited above, note 25, para 16). On the vexed issue of whether fines imposed by the Commission due to a violation of competition law are tax deductible for the undertakings fined, the Commission submitted two other *amicus* observations, one to the Amsterdam Court of Appeal (see Case 10/01358 *X B.V. v Inspecteur van de Belastingdienst*, 11 March 2010, upheld by the Dutch Supreme Court, 12 August 2011) and one to the Belgian Constitutional Court (Case 161/2012 *Tessenderlo Chemie v Belgische Staat*, 20 December 2012).

hand, within the scope of Article 15(3) of Regulation 1/2003, the Court in substance endorsed the wide discretion enjoyed by the Commission in assessing whether there is a risk that the coherent application of antitrust provisions may be impaired. This functional approach may be seen as giving some support to the idea that EU competition law may radiate effects even in areas not pertaining directly to that domain.

When the Commission submits observations as *amicus curiae*, this does not imply that the national court will necessarily abstain from sending a preliminary reference to the Court of Justice. Indeed, the position taken by the Commission may even strengthen the need to obtain clarification from the ECJ, a point well illustrated by a case decided by the Austrian Supreme Court. Here the Commission, intervening as *amicus curiae* at the request of the Supreme Court on 12 September 2011, maintained that a national court that finds a violation of EU competition law may, as an exceptional matter, decide at his discretion not to impose a fine on the undertakings found liable. The Austrian Supreme Court, doubting the Commission's point of view, decided on 5 December 2011 to refer a preliminary question to the Court of Justice; however, the ECJ in essence upheld the position taken by the Commission.[51]

For that matter, the Commission itself may occasionally suggest that a court make a preliminary reference. In a case before the *Cour d'appel* of Paris, the Commission recommended in its written observations that the court should refer a preliminary question to the ECJ 'if it had further doubts'. The dispute concerned a general prohibition of on-line sales imposed by the supplier on all distributors belonging to its network. The Commission maintained in its written observations that this amounted to a restriction to competition, and that no block exemption could apply. The national court decided to refer a preliminary question, and the Court confirmed the substance of the Commission's views, declaring that the situation at issue did not fall within the scope of the vertical agreements block exemption.[52]

In any case, a national court may decide to refer a preliminary question to the ECJ when it does not share the opinion expressed by the Commission in its written or oral observations. A court may arguably consider that it would not be prudent to deviate from the Commission's position without first seeking the support of the ECJ. Furthermore, since

---

[51] *Schenker*, cited above, note 33.

[52] Case C-439/09 *Pierre Fabre Dermo-Cosmétique SAS v Président de l'Autorité de la Concurrence and Ministre de l'Économie, de l'Industrie et de l'Emploi* [2011] ECR I-9419.

national courts of last resort are generally under an obligation to refer preliminary questions, the position adopted by the Commission as *amicus curiae* may be relevant in the sense that it might convince such a court to avoid a reference when it helps the court to conclude that the interpretation of the provision at issue in the given case is 'clear' within the meaning of the ECJ's *CILFIT* jurisprudence.[53]

The Commission's Monitoring of the Correct Application of EU Competition Law

Whilst the Commission no longer enjoys a quasi-exclusive power to enforce the EU competition rules, it still has the duty to monitor the effective application of those rules in the Member States. In order to facilitate this control, each Member State is required to forward to the Commission, without delay, a copy of any written judgment by its national courts in which EU competition law is applied (Article 15(2)). This provision aims not only to provide a means of control but also, as noted above, to enable the Commission to decide whether to intervene as *amicus curiae* in an appellate proceeding.

However, this obligation seems to be poorly respected by certain Member States. In the period examined, the Commission received about 370 judgments, primarily from Spain, Germany and France;[54] there are about 10 Member States that have not yet sent a single judgment to the Commission. The statistics are dramatic: in short, just one judgment was forwarded by Italy, and only six judgments were notified by the United Kingdom, whilst more than a hundred rulings were transmitted by Spain and about 90 were submitted by Germany. Considering that it seems unlikely that in some Member States the number of relevant judgments is so low in contrast to others, the perception that this obligation is not properly respected seems persuasive. In its 2009 Report on the functioning of Regulation 1/2003, the Commission regrets that this notification mechanism 'has not functioned optimally' (para 36).[55] A similar remark is expressed in the recent document on the enforcement of Regulation 1/2003,[56] where the Commission argues that the absence of feedback on

---

[53] Case 283/81 *Srl CILFIT and Lanificio di Gavardo SpA v Ministry of Health* [1982] ECR 3415.

[54] Staff Working Document, Ten Years of Antitrust Enforcement (cited above, note 7), para 247.

[55] Report on the functioning of Regulation 1/2003, cited above, note 48.

[56] Staff Working Document, Ten Years of Antitrust Enforcement (cited above, note 7).

judicial activity by some Member States and the overall small number of judgments that it received 'suggest that there are lapses in the cooperation mechanism that need to be corrected'; the Commission is thus 'considering options for resolving this problem' (para 247). In spite of this assessment, the Commission has not thus far launched any infringement proceedings on account of the Member States' non-compliance.

When the Commission detects that a violation has occurred because a national judgment disregards or misapplies EU law, it may initiate infringement proceedings against the Member State concerned. However, the Commission is likely to have a cautious attitude in order to avoid impinging on the constitutional principle of the separation of powers. There have in fact been a small number of infringement proceedings launched because a national court contravened EU law.[57] According to the principles established in the landmark judgment in *Köbler*,[58] a violation may give rise, under certain conditions, to an obligation on the Member State to compensate an aggrieved party for damages caused by the infringement of EU law.

One indicator with regard to the degree of compliance with EU competition law is that the Court of Justice has found no infringement in the last 10 years for violations concerning the enforcement of EU competition law (whilst one may find several infringement proceedings and judgments in related domains, such as state aids or tax law). This may be compared with different areas of EU law – environmental law, for instance – where the infringement rate is rather high.[59] In principle, the absence of infringement decisions basically reveals a satisfactory degree of compliance. However, this does not mean that there has been no infringement at all, since the Commission enjoys full discretion in deciding whether to start and pursue proceedings for the violation of EU law.

---

[57] See, for example, Case C-304/09 *Commission v Italy* [2010] ECR I-13903.

[58] Case C-224/01 *Gerhard Köbler v Republik Österreich* [2003] ECR I-10239.

[59] Report from the Commission, 30th annual report on monitoring the application of EU law, COM(2013)726 final.

THE LEFTOVERS OF REGULATION 1/2003 IN PURSUING A UNIFORM ENFORCEMENT OF EU COMPETITION LAW

Remaining Divergences in National Laws and their Effect on the Enforcement of EU Competition Law

As recalled above, the main purpose of Regulation 1/2003, since its provisions empowered national courts to apply the competition rules in full, was to maintain uniformity in the application of those rules. The devices for cooperation, assistance and monitoring laid down by the Regulation are all thus designed to contribute to the goal of uniformity. However, in the 10 years or so that the Regulation has been in force (as of this writing), important divergences in the enforcement of EU competition rules have emerged.

First of all, one should recall that the lack of access by arbitrators to the cooperation and assistance instruments of the Regulation remains an important shortcoming of the whole system, given that a rising number of commercial disputes (possibly implying the application of EU competition law) are decided on the basis of out-of-court redress, and given that some Member States adopt a restrictive approach with regard to judicial review of arbitral awards. (See Part III of this book.) Whilst Regulation 1/2003 does not preclude disputes involving the application of EU competition law from being arbitrated,[60] the Notice on cooperation specifies that, for the purpose of access to the mechanisms established under the Regulation, 'national courts' are only those courts and tribunals that are entitled to refer preliminary rulings. The notion of a 'court' therefore depends on the settled case law of the ECJ, which does not permit arbitrators to refer preliminary questions when they do not have

[60] Among an extensive literature, see Laurence Idot, 'Arbitration in Competition Law Disputes', in Ioannis Lianos and Ioannis Kokkoris (eds), *The Reform of EC Competition Law: New Challenges* (Kluwer 2010) 75; Matthieu. de Boisséson, 'Arbitrabilité et Droit de la Concurrence' in David Arias and Miguel Ángel Fernández-Ballesteros (eds), *Liber Amicorum Bernardo Cremades* (Kluwer 2010) 243; Luca Radicati Di Brozolo, 'Arbitration and Competition Law: The Position of the Courts and of Arbitrators' (2011) 27(1) *Arbitration International* 1; Assimakis Komninos, 'Arbitration and EU Competition Law', in Jürgen Basedow, Stéphanie Francq and Laurence Idot (eds), *International Antitrust Litigation: Conflict of Laws and Coordination* (Hart Publishing 2011).

compulsory jurisdiction.[61] Formally, there is no need to establish that recourse to cooperation instruments be anchored to the criteria used to assess whether a body may be regarded as a court within the meaning of Article 267 TFEU; a wider approach could arguably be useful in order to extend the availability of the Commission's support with regard to arbitral proceedings and awards in which issues of EU competition law are raised.

Second, the discretionary power of the Member States, and in particular that of national courts (discretion which the Court of Justice has acknowledged), necessarily implies some risk of non-uniformity in the enforcement of EU competition law. Suffice it to mention here the judgment in *Pfleiderer*,[62] where the Court held that it is for the national court to 'weigh the respective interests in favour of disclosure of the information provided voluntarily by the applicant of leniency' (para 30). As further specified in *Donau Chemie*,[63] domestic law cannot exclude the 'possibility for the national courts of weighing up the interest involved' (para 49). The role thus conferred on national courts is of great importance with regard to uniform enforcement because it implies in the substance the need to strike a balance between, on the one hand, the need for effective public enforcement of EU competition rules and, on the other hand, the need to ensure that the right to full compensation can effectively be exercised. This delicate balance may produce uncertainty with regard to a very significant aspect of competition law enforcement, as the system governing the disclosure of evidence may influence an undertaking's choice of whether or not to cooperate under a leniency programme.

---

[61] See the landmark judgments in Case 102/81 *Nordsee Deutsche Hochseefischerei GmbH v Reederei Mond Hochseefischerei Nordstern AG & Co. KG and Reederei Friedrich Busse Hochseefischerei Nordstern AG & Co. KG* [1982] ECR 1095 and Case C-126/97 *Eco Swiss China Time Ltd v Benetton International NV* [1999] ECR I-3055. Elsewhere I have discussed the pitfalls of this case law. See Adelina Adinolfi, 'Strumenti di cooperazione e di controllo riguardo all'applicazione delle norme comunitarie sulla concorrenza nei procedimenti arbitrali', in *Studi in Onore di Vincenzo Starace* (Editoriale Scientifica 2008), vol. II, 869.

[62] *Pfleiderer*, cited above, note 19.

[63] *Donau Chemie*, cited above, note 27. A further margin of discretion results from case law declaring that EU competition rules 'must be interpreted as not precluding a national competition authority from applying Article 101(1) TFEU to an agreement that may affect trade between Member States, but that not reach the thresholds specified by the Commission in its *de minimis* notice [...]'. See *Expedia v Autorité de la Concurrence,* cited above, note 18, para 38.

Besides divergences that may stem from the margin of discretion accorded to national courts, a major risk of non-uniformity arises from the application of domestic rules of procedure. Under settled case law it is for the national legal system of each Member State to lay down the procedural conditions in respect of actions aimed at ensuring the protection of rights that EU law confers on natural and legal persons. This was well clarified by the landmark judgments in *Crehan*[64] and *Manfredi*,[65] where the Court of Justice declared that any infringement of the EU competition rules gives rise to a right to seek compensation in national courts; therefore, whilst the right to compensation stems from EU law, the procedural rules applicable to the action are in principle those established under national law.

Although this scheme is currently applied for the enforcement of EU law, the actual effect of a lack of a common or harmonized procedural law seems to have negative implications with regard to the fair application of competition law.[66] In short, the strong level of convergence pursued in the enforcement of antitrust provisions is not currently combined with a parallel harmonization of procedural law.[67] Since national procedural rules differ widely across Europe, the chance of a person obtaining compensation depends greatly on the Member State in which he or she happens to bring an action. Moreover, it would be desirable for companies to enforce their competition claims all over Europe on the basis of the same procedural rules. One should also consider that the competition rules needed for the functioning of the internal market now fall within the exclusive competence of the Union; from this perspective, the gap between the significant role that EU law plays with regard to substantive regulation and, by contrast, the current very loose harmonization of national procedural rules is likely to become wider, at least absent further harmonization efforts.

---

[64] Case C-453/99 *Courage Ltd v Bernard Crehan* [2001] ECR I-6297.

[65] Case C-295/04 *Vincenzo Manfredi v Lloyd Adriatico Assicurazioni SpA* [2006] ECR I-6619.

[66] As stated in the Commission's Report on the functioning of Regulation 1/2003, cited above, note 48, 'stakeholders have pointed to what they perceive as uneven enforcement of the [EU] competition rules by national courts' (para 34).

[67] In this regard, it is significant that in its document of 9 July 2014 (COM(2014) 453, 'Ten Years of Antitrust Enforcement under Regulation 1/2003: Achievements and Future Perspectives' the Commission argues that the remaining divergences in the enforcement of competition law 'are largely due to differences in the institutional position of NCAs and in national procedures and sanctions. These issues were largely left open by Regulation 1/2003, subject to the EU law principles of effectiveness and equivalence' (para 24).

The Current Debate on the Harmonization of National Procedural Rules: From Soft-Law Convergence to Proposals for EU Legislation

For the reasons summarized above, the need to harmonize the national procedural rules that apply to the enforcement of the EU competition rules in domestic courts is at the core of the debate on the uniform application of antitrust law, and it is emerging as an important part of the Commission's agenda.[68] According to the Commission, the low rate of private enforcement of competition law is in large part due to divergences in the tort and procedural rules applied in the Member States.[69] The Commission has so far opted for a soft-law strategy to foster convergence of national procedural rules. However; it is questionable whether this approach was a true policy choice or whether in fact it was a fallback plan, possibly due to the reluctance of certain Member States to advance towards a hard law approach. In any case, the Commission has set out a series of non-binding principles for collective redress mechanisms which it considers should be adopted by the Member States so that natural and legal persons can enforce the rights conferred on them under EU law where these have been violated. A recent step in this direction was taken by the Commission in its Recommendation of 11 June 2013 on common principles for injunctive and compensatory collective redress mechanisms in the Member States concerning violations of rights granted under EU

---

[68] The need to achieve harmonization with regard to the application of competition law was considered by the Commission in its preparatory documents concerning the specific areas of consumers law and antitrust law as well as the general issue of enforcing EU law as a whole. See, *inter alia*, the Commission's Green Paper and White Paper on damages actions, each cited above, note 4; Green Paper on consumer redress, COM(2008)794 27 November 2008; Commission Staff Working Document, 'Towards a Coherent European Approach to Collective Redress', SEC(2011)173, 4 February 2011; Communication, 'Towards a European Horizontal Framework for Collective Redress', COM(2013)401, 11 June 2013. Among several reactions in the legal literature to the foregoing initiatives, see Stefano Bastianon, 'Il Risarcimento del Danno Antitrust tra Esigenze di Giustizia e Problemi di Efficienza. Prime Riflessioni sul Libro verde della Commissione', in (2006) 8 Mercato Concorrenza Regole 322; Dimitrios-Panagiotis L. Tzakas, 'Effective Collective Redress in Antitrust and Consumer Protection Matters: a Panacea or a Chimera?' (2011) 48 Common Market Law Review 1125; Rebecca Money-Kyrle and Christopher Hodges, 'European Collective Action: Towards Coherence?' (2012) 19 Maastricht Journal of European and Comparative Law 477; Bruce Wardhaugh, 'Bogeymen, Lunatics and Fanatics: Collective Actions and the Private Enforcement of European Competition Law' (2014) 34 Legal Studies 1.

[69] Green Paper of 2005 and White Paper of 2008 (each cited above, note 4).

law;[70] this Recommendation is intended to be applied in any case involving the enforcement of EU law, which is to say that its relevance is not limited to competition law.

It should be further considered that under the settled case law of the ECJ, national procedural rules have to comply with the basic principles of equivalence and effectiveness. These principles have produced a significant impact in promoting harmonization, and they may help the efforts directed at harmonizing national rules on remedy and procedures. Over time, the Court has gradually developed, in its rulings applying these principles, a set of criteria with which national procedural laws must comply;[71] this case-by-case approach, whilst imposing growing restrictions on national discretion and thereby fostering indirect harmonization, necessarily produces uncertainties as to the conformity of national rules with (judge-made) EU standards. National courts thus have the difficult task of determining whether domestic rules of procedure are consistent with the principles of equivalence and effectiveness as defined by the ECJ, and they must disapply national rules that conflict with those standards. Indeed, a violation of EU law could not only trigger an infringement procedure, it could also lead any allegedly damaged natural or legal person to lodge an action for compensation based on the *Francovich* case law.[72]

Significantly, a need for binding harmonization measures was recently underlined by the Commission, on the assumption that soft-law convergence may have only limited impact in areas where divergence is rooted in national legal traditions.[73] The fact that differences in procedural rules

---

[70] Recommendation 2013/396 [2013] OJ L201/60, discussed in Chapter 2 of this book. See also Roger van den Bergh, 'Private Enforcement of the European Competition Law and the Persisting Collective Action Problem' (2013) 20 Maastricht Journal of European and Comparative Law 12. With regard to the 'horizontal' application of the Recommendation, in other words, its application in fields outside of antitrust, see Chiara Favilli, 'I ricorsi collettivi nell'Unione Europea e la tutela antidiscriminatoria: verso un autentico approccio orizzontale' (2014) Diritto dell'Unione Europea 439.

[71] The Commission has adopted several Recommendations to promote convergence in enforcement by way of follow-up to the 2009 Report on application of Regulation 1/2003: see <http://ec.europa.eu/competition/ecn/documents.html> accessed 30 August 2014.

[72] Joined Cases C-6/90 and C-9/90 *Andrea Francovich and Daniela Bonifaci and others v Italy* [1991] ECR I-5357.

[73] Commission Staff Working Document, 'Enhancing competition enforcement by the Member States' competition authorities: institutional and procedural issues', SWD(2014) 231/2, para 86.

lead to legal costs and uncertainty for undertakings operating cross-border seems to have contributed to the momentum behind the Commission's discourse in this regard.[74] Pursuing this approach, the Commission published a draft Directive on 11 June 2013[75] which proposed rules to govern actions for damages for infringements of the competition law provisions of the Member States (in certain circumstances) and of the EU. Thus, the Commission finally opted to propose binding measures in this crucial area. On 17 April 2014, the European Parliament on first reading adopted a compromise text of the proposal. The Council adopted the proposal on 10 November 2014 and, as of this writing, the signing of the Directive by the Parliament is imminent.

Whilst the Damages Directive is discussed further in other chapters of this book (see especially Chapter 1), a few remarks may be made here in respect of this new instrument. First of all, it is noteworthy that the Directive addresses the enforcement of not only EU competition law but also, in the case of parallel application within the meaning of Article 3(1) of Regulation 1/2003, national competition law as well. It thus aims to establish, within that framework, the same pattern of judicial protection with regard to both EU law and national law claims. In that regard, although the Directive itself does not establish detailed rules concerning the quantification of damages, a working document attached to the 2013 draft version of the Directive provides substantial guidance in this area, and the principles therein may lead, to some degree, to a *de facto* harmonization of judicial approaches.[76]

Apart from its *raison d'être* of establishing procedural rules supporting legitimate claims for damages consistent with the case law of the Court of Justice, the Directive seeks to confront key issues concerning the relationship between public and private enforcement. In this context, it notably limits the disclosure of documents submitted in connection with leniency programmes in order to maintain their attractiveness. It also

---

[74] Communication, 'Ten Years of Antitrust Enforcement under Regulation 1/2003: Achievements and Future Perspectives', COM(2014)453, para 33. On the consequences of national procedural differences, see Cseres, 'Comparing Laws in the Enforcement of EU and National Competition Laws', cited above, note 32, at 32–33.

[75] Proposal for a Directive on certain rules governing actions for damages, cited above, note 4. The EU's Economic and Social Committee, giving a favourable opinion on the proposal on 16 October 2013, stressed that the differences in liability rules across Member States may 'damage competition and hinder the proper functioning of the internal market'. For an early comment on the key issues of the proposal, see Cisotta, cited above, note 6.

[76] SWD(2013)205, 11 June 2013.

establishes principles regarding limitation periods (fixing them at 5 years minimum) and regarding the moment at which limitation periods begin.

Some provisions of the Directive are not really innovative. For example, Article 4 is clearly aimed at codifying the ECJ case law, and merely reiterates the principles of effectiveness and equivalence. Article 17(1) codifies the same principles, providing merely that Member States must ensure that the burden of proof and the standard of proof required for the quantification of harm do not render the exercise of the injured party's right to damages practically impossible or excessively difficult. The loose nature of certain other provisions reveals how difficult it is to attain true harmonization of procedural rules that are strongly influenced by typically national choices. For example, Article 3(1) simply states that 'Member States shall ensure that any natural or legal person who has suffered harm caused by an infringement of competition law is able to claim and to obtain full compensation for that harm'.[77] However, a legislative codification of the principles expressed by the Court of Justice could arguably be useful – even if it necessarily leaves some room for discretion in ascertaining their actual content – and it may contribute to clarifying the meaning of those principles, especially as regards the criterion of effectiveness.

Overall, the Directive might help to resolve the paradox that arises from strongly emphasizing, on the one hand, the need for uniform enforcement of competition law, and establishing a series of instruments of control and cooperation to pursue this aim; whilst on the other hand basing the enforcement of competition law on procedural rules that diverge widely across the Union.

---

[77] The Commission acknowledges that the application of some of the rules may raise 'implementation challenges' concerning, *inter alia*, their 'prompt and coherent application [...] by national courts'. It therefore attached to the original proposal a staff working document laying down an 'implementation action plan' to facilitate the effective enforcement of the Directive.

PART II

Litigating antitrust and state aid issues before the courts of the European Union and the courts of the Member States

Section 1:

Antitrust

4. Evaluation of evidence by the European Courts in competition cases

Alexandre Geulette[*]

ABSTRACT

The evaluation of evidence is crucial in determining the outcome of competition cases brought before the Courts of the European Union. The present chapter reviews the rules governing the burden of proof, the standard of proof and the standard of review applied by the EU Courts, following which an overview is given, based on relevant case law, of how evidence is evaluated by the Courts in competition cases.

INTRODUCTION

The evaluation of evidence is crucial in determining the outcome of competition cases brought before the EU Courts. To mention only cartels, which make up most of the competition law caseload in Luxembourg, the pleas and arguments raised by the parties usually require an extensive analysis of the evidence contained in the Commission's case file.

Although one might have expected, due to the success of the Commission's leniency programme, that the evaluation of evidence would become less important in cartel litigation before the Courts, this has not been the case. On the one hand, a number of infringements are still being fiercely contested on the merits. On the other hand, even where an infringement is not contested as such, an in-depth review of the evidence in the case file may be required when reviewing the legality of the fine.

* Référendaire, European Court of Justice, Luxembourg. The views expressed in this chapter are strictly personal.

This chapter provides a brief overview of the way the EU Courts evaluate evidence in competition cases. However, before discussing evidentiary issues as such, it is worth recalling some of the issues relating to the burden and standard of proof as well as the review exercised by the Courts in competition cases.

BURDEN OF PROOF AND STANDARD OF PROOF

It is incumbent on the Commission to prove the infringements found by it and to adduce evidence capable of demonstrating to the requisite legal standard the existence of the circumstances constituting an infringement.[1] It is therefore the Commission that bears the risk of facts remaining unresolved or allegations unproven.[2] In some instances a shift of the evidential burden occurs.[3] It is then for the undertaking invoking a defence against a finding of infringement to demonstrate that the conditions for applying such a defence are satisfied, so that the authority will then have to resort to other evidence.[4]

Neither the Treaty nor the case law has set out an explicit legal standard of proof for competition cases. The case law of the EU Courts usually refers to facts being proven 'to the requisite legal standard' or, in French (the working language of the EU Courts), '*à suffisance de droit*' without, however, saying quite what that standard is.[5] In practice, the role

---

[1] Council Regulation (EC) No 1/2003 of 16 December 2002 on the implementation of the rules on competition laid down in Articles 81 and 82 of the Treaty [2003] OJ L 1/1, recital 5 and Article 5. See also *Baustahlgewebe v Commission*, C-185/95 P, EU:C:1998:608, para 58; *Commission v Anic Partecipazioni*, C-49/92 P, EU:C:1999:356, para 86; *KME and Others v Commission*, C-272/09 P, EU:C:2011:810, para 105; *E.ON Energie v Commission*, C-89/11 P, EU:C:2012:738, para 71; *Intel v Commission*, T-286/09, EU:T:2014:547, para 62.

[2] See Opinion of Advocate General Kokott in *Akzo Nobel and Others v Commission*, C-97/08 P, EU:C:2009:262, note 64.

[3] *Aalborg Portland and Others v Commission*, C-204/00 P, C-205/00 P, C-211/00 P, C-213/00 P, C-217/00 P and C-219/00 P, EU:C:2004:6, para 79; *Galp Energia España and Others v Commission*, T-462/07, EU:T:2013:459, para 240. See also Per Hellström, 'A Uniform Standard of Proof in EU Competition Proceedings', in Claus-Dieter Ehlermann and Mel Marquis (eds), *European Competition Law Annual 2009: The Evaluation of Evidence and its Judicial Review in Competition Cases* (Hart Publishing 2009) 147, note 1.

[4] *Peróxidos Orgánicos v Commission*, T-120/04, EU:T:2006:350, para 50.

[5] See Christopher Bellamy, 'Standards of Proof in Competition Cases', in OECD Policy Roundtables, Judicial Enforcement of Competition Law, OCDE/GD(97)200, 1996.

of the Courts consists of assessing whether the evidence and other information relied on by the Commission in its decision are sufficient to establish the existence of the alleged infringement.[6]

REVIEW BY THE EU COURTS

It follows from Article 263 TFEU that there is a distinction between: on the one hand, the standard of review that applies when the Courts assess the legality of Commission decisions; and on the other, the Courts' unlimited jurisdiction with regard to fines. The EU Courts review all the issues which have been raised by the applicant, whether they concern the law, the facts, the assessment of the facts or the fine.

Questions of law are subject to full judicial review. In particular, the Courts undertake a comprehensive review of the question as to whether or not the conditions for the application of the competition rules are met.[7] Despite the fact that it is well established that decisions concerning the application of Articles 101(1) TFEU and 102 TFEU to agreements or practices do not, as a general rule, involve complex economic assessments of a type that only allow for marginal review,[8] some assessments which are necessary to find an infringement (such as, for instance, the definition of the relevant markets) have arguably been found to be 'complex' by the Courts, and, as such, subject to such marginal review.

Questions of fact (and questions concerning the application of the law to the facts) are subject to full judicial review of both the Commission's substantive findings of facts and its legal appraisal of those facts. In other

6 *JFE Engineering v Commission*, T-67/00, T-68/00, T-71/00 and T-78/00, EU:T:2004:221, para 175, and case law cited therein.

7 *Microsoft v Commission*, T-201/04, EU:T:2007:289, para 87; *Galp Energia España and Others v Commission*, EU:T:2013:459, para 237; *Total Raffinage Marketing v Commission*, T-566/08, EU:T:2013:423, para 36; *Sasol and Others v Commission*, T-541/08, EU:T:2014:628, para 219.

8 See Nicholas Forwood, 'The Commission's "More Economic Approach" – Implications for the Role of EU Courts, the Treatment of Economic Evidence and the Scope of Judicial Review', in Ehlermann and Marquis (eds), *The Evaluation of Evidence and its Judicial Review in Competition Cases*, cited above, note 3, 260. See also *Amann and Söhne and Cousin Filterie v Commission*, T-446/05, EU:T:2010:165, para 136; and see, *a contrario*, *Deutsche Telekom v Commission*, C-280/08 P, EU:C:2010:603; *France Télécom v Commission*, C-202/07 P, EU:C:2009:214; *CEAHR v Commission*, T-427/08, EU:T:2010:517; *Telefónica and Telefónica de España v Commission*, T-336/07, EU:T:2012:172.

words, the Courts will verify whether the facts have been accurately stated and whether they substantiate a given claim to the requisite legal standard. However, the exact delineation between what constitutes 'facts' and what constitutes an 'assessment of facts' may not always be clear.[9] This task may be easy for basic facts (such as where a meeting took place, whether particular persons attended, and so on) but may be less so for facts of an economic nature.[10]

Matters which relate to the exercise by the Commission of its discretion or margin of appreciation are subject to *limited* review. The expression 'margin of appreciation' is often used to describe the limit placed on judicial control in relation both to the control of the exercise of discretionary powers and in relation to the control of certain types of fact-finding.[11] This margin has been recognized in the case law of the EU Courts with regard to matters of policy (for example, policies concerning enforcement priorities or the fining of undertakings)[12] as well as complex economic or technical assessments, in respect of which the Commission has sometimes been deemed to be particularly well-placed to make choices (for example, methodological choices necessary to determine the relevant market or calculate costs when analyzing pricing abuses).[13] Where the Commission has a margin of discretion, review by the EU

---

[9] See Matteo Bay and Javier Ruiz Calzado, 'Tetra Laval II: the Coming of Age of the Judicial Review of Merger Decisions', (2005) 28 World Competition 433, 450; Luca Prete and Alessandro Nucara, 'Standard of Proof and Scope of Judicial Review in EC Merger Cases: Everything Clear after Tetra Laval?' (2005) 26 European Competition Law Review 692, 693.

[10] See Damien Geradin and Nicolas Petit, 'Judicial Review in European Union Competition Law: A Quantitative and Qualitative Assessment', in Massimo Merola and Jacques Derenne (eds), *The Role of the Court of Justice of the European Union in Competition Law Cases, GCLC Annual Conferences Series* (Bruylant 2012) 49.

[11] Karol Paul Edward Lasok, 'The Nature of Judicial Control', in *Célébration des 20 ans du Tribunal de Première Instance des Communautés Européennes. De 20 Ans à l'horizon 2020. Bâtir le Tribunal de Demain sur de Solides Fondations*, Actes du Colloque du 25 Septembre 2009, 165.

[12] *Schindler Holding and Others v Commission*, T-138/07, EU:T:2011:362, para 295; *Telefónica and Telefónica de España v Commission*, C-295/12 P, EU:C:2014:2062, para 54. See also Renato Nazzini, 'Administrative Enforcement, Judicial Review and Fundamental Rights in EU Competition Law: a Comparative Contextual-functionalist Perspective', (2012) 49 Common Market Law Review 992.

[13] Heike Schweitzer, 'Judicial Review in EU Competition Law', in Damien Geradin and Ioannis Lianos (eds), *Research Handbook on EU Antitrust Law* (Edward Elgar 2013) 491, at note 83.

Courts is necessarily limited to checking whether the relevant rules on procedure and on stating reasons have been complied with, whether the facts have been accurately stated and whether there has been any manifest error of assessment or a misuse of powers. Where the Commission's decision is the result of complex technical appraisals, those appraisals are in principle subject only to limited review by the Courts. This does not mean that the Courts decline to review the Commission's interpretation of economic or technical data. Not only do they establish whether the evidence put forward is factually accurate, reliable and consistent; they also consider whether that evidence contains all the relevant data that must be taken into consideration in appraising a complex situation, and whether the evidence is capable of substantiating the conclusions drawn from it.[14] Furthermore, the EU judicature cannot use the Commission's margin of discretion as regards the assessment of that evidence as a basis for dispensing with an in-depth review of the law and of the facts.[15]

Pursuant to Article 261 TFEU and Article 31 of Regulation 1/2003, the EU Courts have 'unlimited' jurisdiction to review Commission decisions whereby the Commission has fixed fines for competition infringements. The Courts thus have the possibility to cancel, reduce or increase the amount of the fine or the periodic penalty payment imposed. That jurisdiction empowers the Courts, in addition to carrying out a mere review of the lawfulness of the penalty, to substitute their own appraisal for that of the Commission.

The issue of the intensity of review applied by the courts, from the perspective of individual rights, has drawn increasing attention in competition cases, notably in light of the judgment of the European Court of Human Rights in the *Menarini* case[16] and in light of the recent case law of the European Court of Justice (ECJ). These cases have been the subject matter of abundant legal literature.[17] According to its case law,

---

14 *Microsoft v Commission*, EU:T:2007:289, paras 87 to 89; *Commission v Tetra Laval*, C-12/03 P, EU:C:2005:87, para 39; *KME Germany and Others v Commission*, C 389/10 P, EU:C:2011:816, para 121

15 *Chalkor v Commission*, C-386/10 P, EU:C.2011.815, para 62; *Schindler Holding and Others v Commission*, EU:C:2013:522, para 155; *Telefónica and Telefónica de España v Commission*, EU:C:2014:2062, para 56.

16 *A Menarini Diagnostics SRL v Italy*, App no. 43509/08 (ECHR 27 September 2011).

17 See Anne-Lise Sibony, 'Case C 272/09P, *KME Germany and others v Commission*, Judgment of the Court of Justice (Second Chamber) of 8 December 2011', (2012) 49 Common Market Law Review 1977, at note 1.

the position of the ECJ appears to be that, since the review provided for by the Treaties involves review by the EU judicature of both the law and the facts, and since it has the power to assess the evidence, to annul the contested decision and to alter the amount of any fine imposed, the review of legality established by Article 263 TFEU, as supplemented by its unlimited jurisdiction, is not incompatible with the requirements of the principle of effective judicial protection enshrined in Article 47 of the Charter.[18]

EVALUATION OF EVIDENCE BY THE EU COURTS IN COMPETITION CASES

Jurisdiction of the General Court to Establish the Facts and Examine the Evidence

It is clear from Article 256 TFEU and from the first paragraph of Article 58 of the Statute of the Court of Justice that the General Court (GC) has exclusive jurisdiction, first, to find the facts (except where the substantive inaccuracy of its findings is apparent from the documents submitted to it) and, second, to assess those facts. When the GC has found or assessed the facts, the ECJ has jurisdiction to review the legal characterization of those facts by the GC, and to review the legal conclusions it has drawn from them.[19] The ECJ thus has no jurisdiction to establish the facts or, in principle, to call into question the evidence the GC has accepted in support of those facts. Provided that the evidence has been properly obtained, and provided the general principles of law and the rules of procedure in relation to the burden of proof and the taking of evidence have been observed, it is for the GC alone to assess the value which should be attached to the evidence submitted to it.[20]

---

[18] *Chalkor v Commission*, EU:C:2011:815, para 61; *Schindler Holding and Others v Commission*, EU:C:2013:522, para 38. See also *Telefónica and Telefónica de España v Commission*, EU:C:2014:2062, para 42.

[19] *General Motors v Commission*, C-551/03 P, EU:C:2006:229, para 51; *ThyssenKrupp Nirosta (formerly ThyssenKrupp Stainless) v Commission*, C-352/09 P, EU:C:2011:191, para 179; *Baustahlgewebe v Commission*, EU:C:1998:608, para 23; *Dow Chemical v Commission*, C-179/12 P, EU:C:2013:605, para 71.

[20] *General Motors v Commission*, EU:C:2006:229, para 52; *Moser Baer India v Council*, C-535/06 P, EU:C:2009:498, para 32; *Quinn Barlo and Others v Commission*, C-70/12 P, EU:C:2013:351, para 25.

Thus, the appraisal by the GC of the probative value of the documents submitted to it cannot be challenged before the ECJ, save where the rules on the burden of proof and the taking of evidence have not been observed or where the evidence has been distorted.[21] It follows from the above that, while the ECJ cannot entertain an appeal against the assessment of evidence by the GC, it is nevertheless incumbent on the ECJ to verify whether, in making its assessment, the GC has committed an error of law by infringing the general principles of law, such as the presumption of innocence, or by infringing the applicable rules of evidence.[22]

Furthermore, it is not for the ECJ, when ruling on questions of law in the context of an appeal, to substitute, on grounds of fairness, its own assessment for that of the GC exercising its unlimited jurisdiction to rule on the amount of fines imposed on undertakings for infringements of EU law. It is only where the ECJ considers that the level of the penalty is not merely inappropriate but also excessive to the point of being disproportionate that it would have to find that the GC erred in law due to the inappropriateness of the amount of the fine.[23]

Evidence Adduced by the Parties

When reviewing the legality of a decision imposing fines for infringement of the competition rules as well as the fine imposed, the EU judicature must carry out its review of legality on the basis of the evidence adduced by the applicant in support of the pleas in law put forward.[24] Even the exercise of unlimited jurisdiction does not amount to a review of the Court's own motion: it is thus for the applicant to raise

---

[21] *Siemens v Commission*, C-239/11 P, C-489/11 P and C-498/11 P, EU:C:2013:866, para 129; *Telefónica and Telefónica de España v Commission*, EU:C:2014:2062, para 84

[22] *Commission v Brazzelli Lualdi and Others*, C-136/92 P, EU:C:1994:211, para 66; *Deere v Commission*, C-7/95 P, EU:C:1998:256, para 22; *Baustahlgewebe v Commission*, EU:C:1998:608, para 24; *Hüls v Commission*, C-199/92 P, EU:C:1999:358, para 65.

[23] *Schindler Holding and Others v Commission*, EU:C:2013:522, paras 164 and 165; *Telefónica and Telefónica de España v Commission*, EU:C:2014:2062, para 205.

[24] *Chalkor v Commission*, EU:C:2011:815, para 62; *Schindler Holding and Others v Commission*, EU:C:2013:522, para 155; *Telefónica and Telefónica de España v Commission*, EU:C:2014:2062, para 56.

pleas in law against that decision, and to adduce evidence in support of those pleas.[25]

Under Articles 44(1)(d) and 46 of the Rules of Procedure of the General Court, the application for annulment and the statement of defence must state, where appropriate, the nature of any evidence offered in support thereof. Under Article 48 of the Rules of Procedure, a party may still offer further evidence in reply or rejoinder, but in such a case it must give reasons for the delay in submitting it. Under Articles 64 and 65 of the Rules of Procedure, the GC may decide to have measures of organization of the procedure, such as putting questions to the parties, inviting the parties to make written or oral submissions on certain aspects of the proceedings, asking the parties or third parties for information or particulars, or asking for documents or any papers relating to the case. The GC may also adopt measures of inquiry by which it requires the personal appearance of the parties or calls for information and production of documents, oral testimony, the commissioning of an expert's report, or an inspection of the place or thing in question. It must be observed that, whereas in some cases the GC has considered that a party has not provided sufficient proof of its assertions or has not provided it in a timely fashion[26] without deciding to order measures of organization of the procedure or measures of instruction, in other cases it has played a proactive role in having the parties submit certain pieces of evidence. In this respect, the ECJ has made clear that the GC is the sole judge of any need to supplement the information available to it concerning the cases before it.[27]

Unfettered Evaluation of Evidence

The activity of the EU Courts is governed by the principle of the unfettered evaluation of evidence, unconstrained by the various rules laid down in the national legal systems.[28] It results from this principle, first,

---

25 *KME Germany and Others v Commission*, EU:C:2011:816, paras 128–131.

26 *Dole Food and Dole Germany v Commission*, T-588/08, EU:T:2013:130, paras 41–48.

27 *Ufex and Others v Commission*, C-119/97 P, EU:C:1999:116, para 66; *Ismeri Europa v Court of Auditors*, C-315/99 P, EU:C:2001:391, para 19; *E.ON Energie v Commission*, EU:C:2012:738, para 115; *Deltafina v Commission*, C-578/11 P, EU:C:2014:1742, para 67.

28 *Dalmine v Commission*, T-50/00, EU:T:2004:220, para 72; *Wabco Europe and Others v Commission*, T-380/10, EU:T:2013:449, para 50; *Total Raffinage*

that, where evidence has been obtained lawfully, its admissibility cannot be contested before the GC.[29] Inadmissible evidence includes statements or documents acquired by the Commission in earlier proceedings under the same regulation, documents in respect of which the undertaking concerned has not had the opportunity to exercise its right to be heard during the course of investigation, communications between lawyers and clients of a legally protected confidential nature, evidence collected during an unlawful inspection or documents which did not fall within the scope of the inspection decision.[30] The second implication that follows from the principle of unfettered evaluation is that the only relevant criterion for the purpose of assessing the probative value of evidence lawfully adduced relates to its reliability. Apart from exceptions laid down in the EU legal order, it is only the reliability of the evidence before the Court which is decisive as regards its evaluation.[31]

The principle of the unfettered evaluation of evidence cannot jeopardize the presumption of innocence,[32] which is reaffirmed in Article 48 of the Charter. The presumption of innocence is strictly observed by EU Courts in the evaluation of evidence, and any doubt in the 'mind' of the Court must operate to the advantage of the undertaking to which the decision finding an infringement was addressed.[33] The Court therefore cannot conclude that the Commission has established the infringement at issue to the requisite legal standard if it still entertains any doubts on that

---

Marketing v Commission, EU:T:2013:423, para 42; *Intel v Commission*, EU:T:2014:547, para 718.

29 *Siemens v Commission*, EU:C:2013:866, para 128. See also Koen Lenaerts, 'Some Thoughts on Evidence and Procedure in European Community Competition Law', (2006) 30 Fordham International Law Journal 1465.

30 See Fernando Castillo de la Torre, 'Evidence, Proof and Judicial Review in Cartel Cases', (2009) 32(4) World Competition 532 and case law cited therein. A differently edited version of this paper was published in Ehlermann and Marquis (eds), *Evaluation of Evidence and its Judicial Review in Competition Cases*, cited above, note 3, 319.

31 *Siemens v Commission*, EU:C:2013:866, para 128; Opinion of Acting Advocate General Vesterdorf in *Rhône-Poulenc v Commission*, T-1/89, EU:T:1991:56; *Sasol and Others v Commission*, EU:T:2014:628, para 225; *Toshiba v Commission*, T-519/09, EU:T:2014:263, para 37; *Intel v Commission*, EU:T:2014:547, para 718.

32 *Sumitomo Chemical and Sumika Fine Chemicals v Commission*, T-22/02 and T-23/02, EU:T:2005:349, para 106; *Intel v Commission*, EU:T:2014:547, para 63. See also Lenaerts, 'Some Thoughts on Evidence and Procedure in European Community Competition Law', cited above, note 29, at 1470.

33 *JFE Engineering v Commission*, EU:T:2004:221, para 178; *Sasol and Others v Commission*, EU:T:2014:628, para 220.

point, in particular in proceedings for the annulment of a decision imposing a fine.[34]

Holistic View of Evidence

The evidence on which a contested decision is based must be considered not in isolation but as a whole. Thus, it is not necessary for every item of evidence produced by the Commission to lay doubts to rest in relation to every aspect of the infringement. It is sufficient if the body of evidence on which it relies does so when viewed as a whole.[35] That does not mean that the Commission may not rely on a single piece of evidence in order to establish an infringement of the competition provisions of the Treaty, provided that its evidential value is undoubted and provided the evidence itself definitely attests to the existence of the infringement.[36]

The GC has held that, in practice, the Commission is often obliged to prove the existence of an infringement under conditions hardly conducive to that task. Several years may have elapsed since the time of the events constituting the infringement, and a number of the undertakings may not have actively cooperated during the investigation. In that light, although it is necessarily incumbent upon the Commission to establish that an illegal agreement was concluded, it would be excessive to require it also to produce evidence of the specific mechanism by which that objective was attained.[37]

---

34 *E.ON Energie v Commission*, EU:C:2012:738, para 72; *Dresdner Bank and Others v Commission*, T-44/02 OP, T-54/02 OP, T-56/02 OP, T-60/02 OP and T-61/02 OP, EU:T:2006:271, para 60; *Galp Energia España and Others v Commission*, EU:T:2013:459, para 243; *Wabco Europe and Others v Commission*, EU:T:2013:449, para 45; *Total Raffinage Marketing v Commission*, EU:T:2013:423, para 37.

35 *Imperial Chemical Industries v Commission*, 48/69, EU:C:1972:70, para 68; *Total Raffinage Marketing v Commission*, EU:T:2013:423, para 40; *Wabco Europe and Others v Commission*, EU:T:2013:449, para 48; *Toshiba v Commission*, EU:T:2014:263, para 38; *Intel v Commission*, EU:T:2014:547, para 64.

36 *Cimenteries CBR and Others v Commission*, T-25/95, T-26/95, T-30/95 to T-32/95, T-34/95 to T-39/95, T-42/95 to T-46/95, T-48/95, T-50/95 to T-65/95, T-68/95 to T-71/95, T-87/95, T-88/95, T-103/95 and T-104/95, EU:T:2000:77, para 1838; *Galp Energia España and Others v Commission*, EU:T:2013:459, para 241; *Intel v Commission*, EU:T:2014:547, para 719.

37 *Sasol and Others v Commission*, EU:T:2014:628, para 224; *Toshiba v Commission*, EU:T:2014:263, para 39.

Value of Evidence

The function of evidence is to establish convincingly the merits of an argument or a decision.[38] Each piece of evidence has a certain probative value based on its reliability.[39] According to the general rules relating to evidence, the credibility and thus the probative value of a document depends on the person from whom it originates, the circumstances in which it came into being, the person to whom it was addressed and whether it appears sound and reliable.[40]

In the field of competition law, the Commission may not compel individuals to testify under oath. Evidence is thus mostly made up of documents. Documentary evidence can be contemporaneous with the infringement, in other words, documents drafted at anticompetitive meetings or shortly afterwards, such as formal agreements, minutes of meetings, results of meetings provided by a trade association, hand-written notes, agendas of employees involved, expense reports,[41] letters or e-mails exchanged between participants or even with third parties, and so on. Frequently, such documents will have been found at the undertakings' premises or provided in the context of a leniency application.

Pre-existing documents of the kind just described usually have a stronger probative value than documents prepared for the purpose of

---

38 *Commission v Tetra Laval*, EU:C:2005:87, para 41.

39 *Dalmine v Commission*, EU:T:2004:220, para 72; *Wabco Europe and Others v Commission*, EU:T:2013:449, para 52; *Keramag Keramische Werke and Others v Commission*, T-379/10 and T-381/10, EU:T:2013:457, para 106; *Sasol and Others v Commission*, EU:T:2014:628, para 226. See Castillo de la Torre, 'Evidence, Proof and Judicial Review in Cartel Cases', cited above, note 30, 524 and 525; Eric Gippini-Fournier, 'The Elusive Standard of Proof in EU Competition Cases', in Ehlermann and Marquis (eds), *Evaluation of Evidence and its Judicial Review in Competition Cases*, cited above, note 3, 295, 300; Ioannis Lianos and Christos Genakos, 'Econometric evidence in EU competition law: an empirical and theoretical analysis', CLES Working Paper Series, 6/2012, available at <http://ssrn.com/abstract=2184563> accessed 5 June 2014, at 79

40 *Cimenteries CBR and Others v Commission*, paras 1053 and 1838; *Esso and Others v Commission*, T-540/08, EU:T:2014:630, para 44; *Total Raffinage Marketing v Commission*, EU:T:2013:423, para 44; *Keramag Keramische Werke and Others v Commission*, EU:T:2013:457, para 107. See also the Opinion in *Rhône-Poulenc v Commission*, EU:T:1991:56.

41 See, for example, *Bavaria v Commission*, T-235/07, EU:T:2011:283, para 83. It is frequent for employees to try to destroy most written documents. However, expense reports are usually submitted to (and safely stored at) accounting departments for certain travel, fees or purchases related to the infringement.

proceedings, in view of the fact that the former were drafted *in tempore non suspecto*. Great importance is attached to the fact that a document has been drawn up in close connection with the events,[42] or that it was prepared by a direct witness of those events[43] or that it is very detailed.[44] The fact that a document may be in draft format, or found on a computer hard drive, or that it is unsigned or undated or badly written nonetheless does not impugn its evidentiary value, in particular when its origin, probable date and content can be determined with sufficient certainty.[45] Nor does the fact that the document is anonymous preclude it from being probative, provided that the rights of defence have been safeguarded.[46]

Indeed, the GC has held that the fact that a document is badly written, unsigned and undated is quite normal for a note taken during a conversation, probably over the telephone, and if the object of the note is anticompetitive, this would have been a reason for its author to leave the least trace possible.[47] Further, the GC has considered that, unlike a document that has been distributed among the undertakings concerned, a document that is purely internal to one of those undertakings cannot be controlled and corrected by the other participants and therefore can reflect only the view of the undertaking or the person who drafted it. With regard to the other participants, it therefore has a lower probative value; however, nothing prevents the Commission from relying on an internal document as an item contained in a broader body of evidence.[48]

Where the Commission has relied on documentary evidence, it is for the undertakings concerned not merely to present a plausible alternative to the Commission's theory but to show that the evidence used in the

---

42 *Empresa Nacional Siderúrgica SA (Ensidesa) v Commission*, T-157/94, EU:T:1999:54, para 312; *Nederlandse Federatieve Vereniging voor de Groothandel op Elektrotechnisch Gebied v Commission*, T-5/00 and T-6/00, EU:T:2003:342, para 181; *Sasol and Others v Commission*, EU:T:2014:628, paras 231 and 267.

43 *JFE Engineering v Commission*, EU:T:2004:221, para 207.

44 *Sasol and Others v Commission*, EU:T:2014:628, paras 231 and 267.

45 *FNCBV v Commission*, T-217/03 and T-245/03, EU:T:2006:391, para 124; *Sasol and Others v Commission*, EU:T:2014:628, para 232; *Toshiba v Commission*, EU:T:2014:263, para 94.

46 *Dalmine v Commission*, C-407/04 P, EU:C:2007:53, paras 46–50; *Salzgitter Mannesmann v Commission*, C-411/04 P, EU:C:2007:54, paras 44–53.

47 *Shell v Commission,* T-11/89, EU:T:1992:33, para 86.

48 *JFE Engineering v Commission*, EU:T:2004:221, para 231; *Toshiba v Commission*, EU:T:2014:263, paras 97 and 98.

decision is insufficient to establish the existence of an infringement.[49] Documents may of course be subject to interpretation. The Court will therefore review the Commission's interpretation of the document(s) in question, taking due account of the presumption of innocence.[50] In this respect, an applicant may propose another plausible interpretation of the document(s).[51]

Documents may also have been prepared for the purpose of proceedings, and can take various forms such as responses to requests for information, corporate statements provided in the framework of a leniency application or affidavits of employees annexed to the Court application.[52] Statements can be oral[53] (oral corporate statements, oral statements at a hearing or during an inspection) or written (written corporate statements or affidavits).

As regards statements, particularly great probative value may be attached to those which: (i) are reliable; (ii) are made on behalf of an undertaking; (iii) are made by a person under a professional obligation to act in the interests of that undertaking; (iv) go against the interests of the person making the statement; (v) are made by a direct witness of the circumstances to which they relate; and (vi) were provided in writing deliberately and after mature reflection.[54]

Corporate statements provided in the context of a leniency application usually contain a description of the anticompetitive practices based on the factual accounts provided by the employees involved and supplemented with contemporaneous evidence which the company may have gathered in support of its application. Where the contemporaneous evidence is scarce, the precision of the statement will be key in determining whether

---

49 *JFE Engineering v Commission*, EU:T:2004:221, para 187; *E.ON Energie v Commission*, T-141/08, EU:T:2010:516, para 56; *Intel v Commission*, EU:T:2014:547, paras 67 and 542.

50 Breach by the Commission of the presumption of innocence amounts to an error of law.

51 *Bavaria v Commission*, EU:T:2011:283, para 83. In this case, the GC found the evidence to be inconclusive in view of an alternative explanation provided by the applicant and in view of the isolated and laconic nature of the references made in the handwritten notes concerned.

52 *E.ON Energie v Commission*, T-141/08, EU:T:2010:516.

53 *BASF v Commission*, T-15/02, EU:T:2006:74, para 506.

54 *JFE Engineering v Commission*, EU.T:2004:221, para 231; *Toshiba v Commission*, EU:T:2014:263, paras 207, 211 and 212; *Hitachi and Others v Commission*, T-112/07, EU:T:2011:342, para 71, and case law cited therein; *Sasol and Others v Commission*, EU:T:2014:628, para 235; *Toshiba v Commission*, EU:T:2014:263, para 47.

it has probative value. Statements must be coherent and clear, although some slight inaccuracies regarding events that occurred over a long period of time are considered to be normal.[55] Statements should not be ambiguous.[56] The period of time which elapsed between the submission of the witness statement and the facts to which it relates may be relevant in the assessment of its reliability, given that witnesses may provide, as a general rule, more detailed and more reliable evidence in respect of recent events.[57]

Corporate leniency statements have a high probative value, especially where they are corroborated by other evidence. It must be recalled that no provision or any general principle of EU law prohibits the Commission from relying, as against an undertaking, on statements made by other incriminated undertakings. If that were not the case, the Commission's burden of proving anticompetitive conduct, assuming the parties deny their participation in it, would be unsustainable.[58] Nonetheless, where the accuracy of an admission by one undertaking accused of having participated in a cartel is contested by several other undertakings similarly accused, that admission cannot be regarded as constituting adequate proof of an infringement committed by those other undertakings unless it is supported by additional evidence,[59] though the degree of corroboration required may be attenuated in view of the reliability of the statements at issue.[60]

In addition, the GC has held that even if some caution as to the evidence provided voluntarily by the main participants in an unlawful cartel is generally called for (considering the possibility that they might tend to play down the importance of their contribution to the infringement and exaggerate that of the others), the fact that an undertaking has sought to benefit from leniency does not necessarily create an incentive to submit distorted evidence in relation to the participation of the other members of the cartel. Indeed, any attempt to mislead the Commission

---

55 *Siemens v Commission*, T-110/07, EU:T:2011:68, para 76.

56 *Kone and Others v Commission*, T-151/07, EU:T:2011:365, para 169.

57 *Hitachi and Others v Commission*, T-112/07, EU:T:2011:342, para 133.

58 *JFE Engineering v Commission*, EU:T:2004:221, para 50; *Sasol and Others v Commission*, EU:T:2014:628, para 234; *Toshiba v Commission*, EU:T:2014:263, para 46.

59 *JFE Engineering v Commission*, EU:T:2004:221, para 219; *Keramag Keramische Werke and Others v Commission*, EU:T:2013:457, para 104; *Intel v Commission*, EU:T:2014:547, para 720.

60 *Siemens v Commission*, EU:C:2013:866, para 135; *Sasol and Others v Commission*, EU:T:2014:628, para 236.

could call into question the sincerity and the completeness of the cooperation of the person seeking to benefit therefrom, and thereby jeopardize his chances of benefiting fully under it.[61] In addition, a finding of infringement of the competition rules may result, in particular, in regulatory implications, legal actions by private operators and damage to commercial reputation. Therefore, it is not plausible that an undertaking would admit the existence of an infringement and its own participation in it if that infringement has not been committed.[62] More generally, the Court has already had the opportunity to point out that a statement made by a person acting in the capacity of a representative of a company and admitting the existence of an infringement by that company entails considerable legal and economic risks.[63]

In the event of a contradiction between the statement of an employee and the response of a company to a Statement of Objections, the probative value of the latter is higher, having regard to the case law according to which a statement given on behalf of the undertaking as such carries more weight than that of an employee of the undertaking, whatever his individual experience or opinion.[64]

Arguably, in a recent Article 102 case, the GC held that it was inappropriate to establish a general rule according to which the statement of a third-party undertaking indicating that a firm in a dominant position has adopted a certain type of conduct can never suffice on its own to prove the facts constituting an infringement of that provision.[65]

Inferences can also be used to prove the existence of an anti-competitive practice.[66] Thus, the existence of an anticompetitive practice or agreement may be inferred from a number of coincidences and indicia which taken together can, in the absence of another plausible explanation, constitute evidence of an infringement.[67] The rationale behind this

---

61 *Sasol and Others v Commission*, EU:T:2014:628, para 237; *Toshiba v Commission*, EU:T:2014:263, para 47, and case law cited therein.

62 *Toshiba v Commission*, EU:T:2014:263, para 49.

63 *Sumitomo Metal Industries and Nippon Steel v Commission*, C-403/04 P and C-405/04 P, EU:C:2007:52, para 103; *Siemens v Commission*, EU:C:2013:866, para 140.

64 *Bavaria v Commission*, EU:T:2011:283, para 217.

65 *Intel v Commission*, EU:T:2014:547, para 724.

66 See, for example, Cases 29/83 and 30/83 *Compagnie Royale Asturienne des Mines SA (CRAM) and Rheinzink GmbH v Commission*, 29/83 and 30/83, EU:C:1984:130, paras 14–23.

67 *Aalborg Portland and Others v Commission*, EU:C:2004:6, para 57; *Esso and Others v Commission*, EU:T:2014:630, para 45; *Faci v Commission*, EU:T:2014:138, paras 49–51; *JFE Engineering v Commission*, EU:T:2004:221,

lies in the fact that, as mentioned above, anticompetitive agreements take place in a clandestine fashion: meetings are held in secret and the associated documentation is reduced to a minimum. Minutes of meetings will normally be only fragmentary and sparse, and it is therefore often necessary to reconstitute certain details by deduction.

If the evidence is circumstantial, the company concerned will be able to contest it by shedding a different light on the facts established by the Commission in the contested decision.[68]

Economic studies may prove useful where it is necessary to shed some light on a particular economic context, especially in cases involving concerted practices, abuses of dominance or merger cases.[69] Under the Commission's 1998 Fining Guidelines[70] this type of evidence also proved to be useful to demonstrate the absence of impact of an infringement in order to secure a reduction of the fine. Where companies submit economic or technical studies, these should be made comprehensible to the Court and should therefore be presented in a way that is accessible to lawyers who likely have accumulated some experience in the field of competition but who typically do not have any formal economic training.[71] Economic or technical studies cannot however take the place of legal assessment,[72] nor should they take the place of a proper legal argument. Interestingly, in one case the GC considered that an econometric analysis provided by the applicant could not be regarded as a neutral and independent expert report insofar as it was requested and paid for by the applicant and drawn up on the basis of information provided by that company, without the accuracy or the relevance of that information being subject to any kind of independent assessment. It thus held

---

para 186; *Wabco Europe and Others v Commission*, EU:T:2013:449, para 49; *Sasol and Others v Commission*, EU:T:2014:628, para 230.

68 *Compagnie Royale Asturienne des Mines and Rheinzink v Commission*, EU:C:1984:130, para 16; *Sasol and Others v Commission*, EU:T:2014:628, para 228; *Intel v Commission*, EU:T:2014:547, para 66.

69 See Lenaerts, 'Some Thoughts on Evidence and Procedure in European Community Competition Law', cited above, note 29.

70 Guidelines on the method of setting fines imposed pursuant to Article 15(2) of Regulation No 17 and Article 65(5) of the ECSC Treaty [1998] OJ C 9/3.

71 See Marc Jaeger, 'The Standard of Review in Competition Cases involving Complex Economic Assessments: Towards the Marginalisation of the Marginal Review?', (2011) 2(4) Journal of European Competition Law & Practice 295. See also Schweitzer, 'Judicial Review in EU Competition Law', cited above, note 13, at note 27.

72 See the Opinion in *Rhône-Poulenc v Commission*, EU:T:1991:56.

that it was not possible to attach thereto a level of credibility, and therefore a probative value, beyond that of a mere statement from the applicant.[73]

Presumptions constitute legitimate conclusions drawn on the basis of common experience.[74] In other words, presumptions are statements of what normally happens based on common judicial experience.[75] Even where they are difficult to rebut, presumptions remain within acceptable limits provided that: they are proportionate to the legitimate aims pursued; there is a possibility to prove the contrary; and the rights of defence are safeguarded.[76]

A number of presumptions have been recognized by the EU Courts, such as: the existence of a causal link between concertation and conduct on the market;[77] the presumption that if a company has participated in meetings at which anticompetitive agreements were concluded, without manifestly opposing them, it has in fact participated in the cartel;[78] and the presumption of liability of the parent company where it holds 100 per cent or close to 100 per cent of the share capital of its subsidiary.[79]

CONCLUDING REMARKS

Despite the principles and trends identified in this chapter, there is no unique way for the EU Courts to evaluate the evidence put before them. In other words, evidence that convinces one judge may not necessarily be

---

[73] *Siemens v Commission*, EU:T:2011:68, para 137.

[74] See the Opinion of Advocate General Kokott in *T-Mobile Netherlands and Others*, C-8/08, EU:C:2009:110, para 90 (discussing the presumption of a causal link between concertation and market conduct which the Court recognizes in relation to concerted practices).

[75] See Lianos and Genakos, 'Econometric Evidence in EU Competition Law: an Empirical and Theoretical Analysis', cited above, note 39, at 77.

[76] See *Saint-Gobain Glass France SA and Others v Commission,* T-56/09, EU:T:2014:160, para 215 and case law cited therein.

[77] *Commission v Anic Partecipazioni*, EU:C:1999:356, paras 83 and 87; *Aalborg Portland and Others v Commission*, EU:C:2004:6, paras 79 and 81 to 85. See also the Opinion of Advocate General Kokott in *T-Mobile Netherlands e.a. v Commission*, EU:C:2009:110, para 90.

[78] *Hüls v Commission*, C-199/92 P, EU:C:1999:358, para 155; *Commission v Anic Partecipazioni*, EU:C:1999:356, para 96, *Romana Tabacchi v Commission*, T 11/06, EU:T:2011:560, para 158.

[79] *Akzo Nobel and Others v Commission*, C-97/08 P, EU:C:2009:536, *Commission v Aalberts Industries and Others*, C-287/11 P, EU:C:2013:445, para 32; *Total v Commission*, T-548/08, EU:T:2013:434, paras 122 and 123.

enough to convince another. The role of the EU Courts consists in deciding, based on the pleas, arguments and evidence provided by the parties, whether the case put forward by the Commission in its decision is sufficiently robust. The role of the parties before the Courts is therefore to convince the judges of the merits of their case; in so doing, the evidence on which the parties rely, provided that it is admissible, clearly plays a decisive role.

Faced with criticism about the alleged lack of adequate judicial scrutiny of Commission decisions, the EU Courts have recently tended to provide very detailed accounts of how each piece of evidence is evaluated and interpreted in a given factual context. Invariably, the judges, sitting in chambers, assess the evidence on a case-by-case basis, in a very concrete manner. When carrying out this exercise, they are necessarily influenced to a certain extent by their own academic, professional or cultural background as well as the degree to which they adopt a proactive role in having parties submit evidence.

5. The evolution of the 'full jurisdiction' of the Union Courts in Article 101 and 102 matters

Renato Nazzini*

ABSTRACT

This chapter examines the jurisprudence of the Courts of the European Union with a view towards assessing the impact of the KME judgment of the Court of Justice. This judgment upholds the compatibility of the jurisdiction of the Union Courts to review the decisions of the European Commission applying Articles 101 and 102 TFEU and imposing fines for infringements of those provisions with the EU principle of effective judicial protection. The examination demonstrates the evolution of the standard of review in such cases to a standard of correctness. In this regard, it is argued that the standard of correctness is required as regards any issue of fact or law that bears directly on the imposition of, or the calculation of, a fine. The paper also clarifies that the standard of correctness applies where the Union Courts review the Commission's evaluation of factual evidence, except in matters of complex economic or technical assessment, where a more deferential standard persists. With regard to the more deferential approach in the latter context, it is argued that this vestige of the margin of appreciation concept is contrary to fundamental rights principles given the current institutional configuration

* Professor of Law, King's College London and Partner, LMS, Milan. I am most grateful to Pierre Pecheux for his assistance and comments.

THE PROBLEM AND THE PURPOSE OF THE INQUIRY

In recent years, it has been controversial whether the standard of judicial review of decisions of the European Commission ('Commission') applying Articles 101 and 102 of the Treaty on the Functioning of the European Union ('TFEU')[1] amounts to 'full jurisdiction' and is therefore compatible with the EU principle of effective judicial protection.[2]

Under Regulation 1/2003, the Commission enforces Articles 101 and 102 TFEU, determining whether undertakings have infringed the prohibitions set out in these Articles, and imposing remedies and fines on the undertakings concerned. The Court of Justice of the European Union, which includes the General Court, with first instance jurisdiction in Article 101 and Article 102 matters, from which an appeal lies on points of law to the Court of Justice ('ECJ'), has jurisdiction to review the Commission's decisions under two legal bases. Under Article 263 TFEU, the Union Courts exercise a review of legality of the acts of the Union

---

1 Treaty on the Functioning of the European Union (consolidated version) [2010] OJ C83/47 (TFEU).

2 The standards currently in force in the European Union are Article 47(2) of the Charter of Fundamental Rights of the European Union [2010] OJ C83/389 (the 'EU Charter') and the EU fundamental right of effective judicial protection, which is distinct from Article 47(2) of the EU Charter (see, for example, Case C-279/09 *DEB Deutsche Energiehandels- und Beratungsgesellschaft mbH v Bundesrepublik Deutschland* [2010] ECR I-13849, paras 31–40). Article 6(1) of the European Convention on Human Rights is also indirectly relevant under Union law. The Convention is not yet binding on the Union but will be so when the Union accedes to the Convention as provided in Article 6 of the Treaty on European Union (consolidated version) [2010] OJ C83/13 (TEU). However, the effect of Article 52(3) of the EU Charter, construed in the light of the Explanations Relating to the Charter of Fundamental Rights [2007] OJ C303/17, 33, which can be used as an interpretative aid to the Charter (see *DEB Deutsche Energiehandels,* cited above, para 35) is that the content of the right to an independent and impartial tribunal under Article 47(2) of the EU Charter is very likely to be the same as that of the equivalent right under Article 6(1) of the Convention; the jurisprudence of the European Court of Human Rights can thus be relied on to construe the right under Article 47(2) of the Charter. In any event, the three constitutional standards mentioned (Article 47(2) of the EU Charter, the EU general principle of effective judicial protection and Article 6(1) ECHR) are largely co-extensive and differences in their scope of application are not relevant for present purposes. Therefore, in this chapter they will be referred to collectively as the 'principle of effective judicial protection'. The Court of Justice considers that it is sufficient to refer only to Article 47(2) of the Charter: Case C-199/11 P *Europese Gemeenschap v Otis NV*, 6 November 2012, EU:C:2012:684, para 47.

institutions and have the power to set aside, in whole or in part, the impugned act 'on grounds of lack of competence, infringement of an essential procedural requirement, infringement of the Treaties or of any rule of law relating to their application, or misuse of powers'. In addition, under Article 261 TFEU and Article 31 of Regulation 1/2003, the Union Courts have 'unlimited jurisdiction to review decisions whereby the Commission has fixed a fine or periodic penalty payment' and the power to 'cancel, reduce or increase the fine or periodic penalty payment imposed'.

Historically, as has been explained in detail elsewhere,[3] the review exercised by the Union Courts has been deferential. It is true that the case law makes it clear that when the General Court reviews the legality of a decision finding an infringement of Article 101(1) or 102 TFEU, the Court undertakes 'an exhaustive review of both the Commission's substantive findings of facts and its legal appraisal of those facts'.[4] This means that the Commission's findings of facts must be correct, they must be appraised correctly and the correct legal conclusions must be drawn.[5] Therefore, the standard of review that can be exercised in law would appear to amount to full jurisdiction.[6] However, while the Union Courts have the power to review the correctness of Commission decisions, in a number of instances they refrained from doing so, deferring instead to the Commission's exercise of discretion or margin of appreciation.[7] First of all, the case law recognized that the fining system is an important

---

[3] Renato Nazzini, 'Administrative Enforcement, Judicial Review and Fundamental Rights in EU Competition Law: A Contextual-functionalist Perspective' (2012) 49 Common Market Law Review 971.

[4] Joined Cases T-25/95, etc. *Cimenteries CBR v Commission* [2000] ECR II-491, para 719; Joined Cases C-204/00 P, C-205/00 P, C-211/00 P, C-213/00 P, C-217/00 P and C-219/00 P *Aalborg Portland AS v Commission* [2004] ECR I-123, para 49; Case T-214/06 *Imperial Chemical Industries v Commission,* 5 June 2012, EU:T:2012:275, para 63; Case T-482/07 *Nynäs Petroleum AB v Commission*, 16 September 2013, EU:T:2013:437, para 181.

[5] Case C-272/09 P *KME Germany v Commission* [2011] ECR I-12789, para 106; Case T-68/89 *Società Italiana Vetro v Commission* [1992] ECR II-1403, para 160; Opinion of AG Tizzano in Case C-12/03 P *Commission v Tetra Laval BV* [2005] ECR I-987, para 86.

[6] See, for example, Wouter Wils, 'The Increased Level of EU Antitrust Fines, Judicial Review and the ECHR' (2010) 33 World Competition 5, 22–28.

[7] On the terminology and the concept of margin of discretion and margin of appreciation, see Okeoghene Odudu, 'Article 101(3), Discretion and Direct Effect' (2002) 23 European Competition Law Review 17; David Bailey, 'The Scope of Judicial Review under Article 81 EC' (2004) 41 Common Market Law Review 1327, 1355.

question of policy.[8] Therefore, the Union Courts accepted that 'the Commission has a margin of discretion when fixing fines', including 'a particularly wide discretion as regards the choice of factors to be taken into account for the purposes of determining the amount of the fines'.[9] The fact that this margin of discretion was granted in the area where the potential scrutiny of the Union Courts is the most intense demonstrates that the issue is not one relating to the abstract standard of review but to judicial restraint in individual cases. The discretion granted to the Commission extends to crucial matters such as whether to impose a fine at all,[10] the level of the fines necessary to achieve the objectives of the Treaties[11] and the imputation of an infringement to the parent company.[12] Second, in matters of complex economic or, more generally, technical[13]

[8] Policy and discretion are matters that may be legitimately left to be determined by administrative authorities subject to deferential review under the Article 6(1) ECHR. See *Bryan v United Kingdom* (1996) 21 EHRR 342, para 47, referring to 'specialised areas of the law such as the one in issue' and adding that 'the subject matter of the contested decision by the inspector was a typical example of the exercise of discretionary judgment in the regulation of citizens' conduct in the sphere of town and country planning'. See also *Zumtobel v Austria* (1993) 17 EHRR 116, para 32, a case concerning judicial review of expropriation decisions, in which the Court referred to the 'respect which must be accorded to decisions taken by the administrative authorities on grounds of expediency'.

[9] Case T-150/89 *Martinelli v Commission* [1995] ECR II-1165, para 59; Joined Cases T-213/95 and T-18/96 *SCK and FNK v Commission* [1997] ECR II-1739, para 239; Case C-137/95 P *SPO v Commission* [1996] ECR I-1611, para 54; Case C-219/95 P *Ferriere Nord v Commission* [1997] ECR I-4411, para 33; Case C-289/04 P *Showa Denko v Commission* [2006] ECR I-5859, para 36; Case C-3/06 P *Group Danone v Commission* [2007] ECR I-1331, para 37; Case T-461/07 *Visa Europe Ltd v Commission* [2011] ECR II-1729, para 212.

[10] *Visa Europe,* cited previous note, para 212; *SCK and FNK v Commission*, cited previous note, para 239.

[11] Joined Cases C-189/02 P, C-202/02 P, C-205/02 P to C-208/02 P and C-213/02 P *Dansk Rørindustri A/S v Commission* [2005] ECR I-5425, para 227, applied in *Group Danone*, cited above, note 9, para 90.

[12] Joined Cases T-204/08 and T-212/08 *Team Relocations NV v Commission* [2011] ECR II-3569, para 156, appeal dismissed: Case C-444/11 P, 11 July 2013, EU:T:2014:773; Joined Cases T-259/02 to T-264/02 and T-271/02 *Raiffeisen Zentralbank Österreich v Commission* [2006] ECR II-5169, paras 331 and 333.

[13] While the case law mainly concerns economic assessments, a number of cases refer more broadly to technical matters. See Case T-201/04 *Microsoft v Commission* [2007] ECR II-3601, paras 87–89; Case T-65/96 *Kish Glass v Commission* [2000] ECR II-1885, para 64, appeal dismissed: [2001] ECR I-7759; Case C-42/84 *Remia v Commission* [1985] ECR 2545, para 34; Joined

assessment, the Union Courts have repeatedly stated that it is not for the courts to substitute their own view for the assessment of the Commission.[14] The standard of review is limited to verifying whether the facts relied on have been accurately stated, whether there has been any manifest error of appraisal, whether the legal consequences deduced from those facts were accurate, whether the rules on procedure and on the statement of reasons have been complied with, and whether there has been any misuse of power.[15] This formula is a convoluted way to say that the standard of correctness applies only to the establishment of the facts and the respect for the law, whether substantive or procedural, whereas the appraisal of the facts is subject to the more deferential standard of 'manifest error'.[16] Third, a deferential standard of 'manifest error of appraisal' was also occasionally applied to the Commission's evaluation of the evidence when the Union Courts considered that the Commission was better placed to carry out such an assessment. In *Archer Daniels*, for instance, the General Court had to determine whether the Commission had been right to rely on certain documents in order to conclude that Archer Daniels was the ringleader of the cartel. The Court reviewed the evidence and held that 'the Commission did not commit a manifest error of assessment' in reaching its conclusion.[17] This margin of appreciation extends to issues inextricably intertwined with the evaluation of evidence

---

Cases C-142/84 and C-156/84 *BAT and Reynolds v Commission* [1987] ECR 4487, para 62. It appears that economic assessments are a species of the broader category of technical assessments.

[14] Case C-525/04 P *Spain v Lenzing* [2007] ECR I-9947, para 57; Case T-17/93 *Matra Hachette v Commission* [1994] ECR II-595, para 104; Case C-194/99 P *Thyssen Stahl AG v Commission* [2003] ECR I-10821, para 78.

[15] Case T-28/03 *Holcim (Deutschland) v Commission* [2005] ECR II-1357, para 95; *Remia,* cited above, note 13, para 34; Case C-7/95 *John Deere v Commission* [1988] ECR I-3111, para 34; *Aalborg Portland,* cited above, note 4, para 279.

[16] See, for example, Joined Cases C-56/64 and 58/64 *Etablissements Consten SàRL and Grundig-Verkaufs-GmbH v Commission* [1966] ECR 299, para 347; Case T-112/99 *Métropole Télévision (M6) v Commission* [2001] ECR II-2459, para 156, Case T-131/99 *Shaw v Commission* [2002] ECR II-2023, para 38; Joined Cases C-501/06 P, C-513/06P, C-515/06 P and C-519/06 P *GlaxoSmithKline Services Limited v Commission* [2009] ECR I-9291, paras 85 and 146; Case T-340/03 *France Télécom SA, formerly Wanadoo Interactive SA v Commission* [2007] ECR II-107, para 129, appeal dismissed: in Case C 202/07 P *France Télécom SA v Commission* [2009] ECR I-2369.

[17] Case T-59/02 *Archer Daniels Midland Co v Commission* [2006] ECR II-3627, paras 220–226. See also ibid., paras 277, 279, 290 and 299. The judgment was partly set aside by the Court of Justice in Case C-511/06 P *Archer*

such as the degree of cooperation of an undertaking during the administrative procedure. In *Archer Daniels*, the ECJ ruled that the Commission has a degree of 'discretion' in determining whether an undertaking's cooperation has been decisive for the finding that a cartel had existed and, as a consequence, the decision is set aside only if the Commission has committed a 'manifest error of appraisal'.[18] Such matters are not, strictly speaking, discretionary but the ECJ considered it appropriate to exercise judicial restraint in reviewing them. The reason for a deferential standard is probably that the evaluation of evidence is better carried out by the first instance decision-maker rather than by a court of review.

In two seminal cases, the European Court of Human Rights (ECHR) in *Menarini* and the ECJ in *KME* have apparently upheld the compatibility of the current system with, respectively, Article 6 ECHR and with the EU principle of effective judicial protection. *Menarini* preceded *KME* by a few months, and in the former case the ECHR held that the Italian system of judicial review of fining decisions adopted by the national competition authority, which is similar to, albeit not the same as, the EU system, is compatible with Article 6 of the ECHR.[19] A few months' later, the ECJ in *KME* held that the EU system of judicial review of decisions of the Commission under Articles 101 and 102 TFEU is compatible with the EU principle of effective judicial protection.[20] However, in the

---

Daniels Midland Co v Commission [2009] ECR I-5843, but not on the issue of the test of manifest error.

[18] Case C-511/06 P *Archer Daniels Midland*, cited previous note, paras 150–153.

[19] Article 6(1) ECHR applies to administrative proceedings that may result in the imposition of fines for breaches of competition law because such proceedings are deemed to involve the determination of a 'criminal' charge under the Convention. See *Menarini Diagnostics srl v Italy* [2011] ECHR 43509/08, judgment of 27 September 2011, paras 57–62. This has long been accepted by the Court of Justice. See Case C-199/92 P *Hüls AG v Commission* [1999] ECR I-4287, para 150 (citing *Öztürk v Germany* (1984) 6 EHRR 406 and *Lutz v Germany* (1987) 10 EHRR 182); *Dansk Rørindustri,* cited above, note 11, para 202; Opinion of Advocate General Sharpston in Case C-272/09 P *KME Germany AG v Commission* [2011] ECR I-12789, paras 64–66. But see *OOO Neste St Petersburg v Russia* (European Court of Human Rights, Third Section, decision on admissibility, 3 June 2004).

[20] Article 47(2) of the EU Charter applies to proceedings that may result in the imposition of a fine regardless of their characterization as 'criminal' or otherwise. This follows from the very text of the provision, which does not contain any limitation concerning the type of right, charge or dispute involved: 'Everyone is entitled to a fair and public hearing within a reasonable time by an independent and impartial tribunal previously established by law'.

characteristic judicial style that plagues the judgments of the highest court in the Union, the *KME* judgment does not make it clear whether it upholds previous case law without reservations, or whether it instead requires the Union Courts to change their standard of judicial review, from one taking a deferential approach to a more substantive standard assessing the correctness of the decision.[21] This lack of clarity is exacerbated by the fact that, even before *KME*, the precise delineation of the standard of judicial review of Commission decisions by the Union Courts was far from clear.

This chapter reviews the case law of the Union Courts that has emerged subsequent to *KME* in order to discern whether there has been a development in the standard of review of Commission decisions. The analysis focuses on the review of fining decisions, the assessment of factual evidence, and complex economic assessments. The final section draws some conclusions.

FINING DECISIONS

In the area of fining decisions, after some initial uncertainty, it seems now clear that the standard of review is correctness.[22]

The General Court began by trying to reconcile *KME*, rather clumsily, with a continuing discretion enjoyed by the Commission. In *Bolloré*, the General Court restated the principle that the Commission has discretion when determining the amount of each fine, and it understood this principle to be compatible with the judicial review standard required by the ECJ in *KME*.[23] The General Court then went on to carry out a

---

[21] See, for example, Anne-Lise Sibony, 'Case C-272/09 P, KME Germany and others v Commission' (2012) 49 Common Market Law Review 1977, 1999–2000. Sibony recognizes that certain statements of the Court sit oddly with each other and comes to the conclusion that *KME* maintains the power of the Union Courts 'to preserve the Commission's discretion'.

[22] Marco Bronckers and Anne Vallery, 'Fair and Effective Competition Policy in the EU: Which Role for Authorities and Which Role for the Courts after Menarini?' (2012) 8(2) European Competition Journal 283, 296; Rein Wesseling and Marc van der Woude, 'The Lawfulness and Acceptability of Enforcement of European Cartel Law' (2012) 35 World Competition 573, 580–582.

[23] Case T-372/10 *Bolloré v Commission*, 27 June 2012, EU:T:2012:325, para 222, appeal dismissed: Case C-414/12 P, 8 May 2014, EU:C:2014:301. See also, post-*KME*, Case T-348/06 *Total Nederland v Commission*, 27 September 2012, EU:T:2012:481, Case T-357/06 *Koninklijke v Commission*, 27 September 2012, EU:T:2012:488, appeal dismissed: Case C-586/12 P, 19 December 2014,

detailed review of the Commission's fining decision without deferring to the latter's margin of discretion.[24] Similarly, in *MRI*, the General Court agreed with the Commission's argument that it has a margin of discretion as regards the factors affecting the gravity of the infringement.[25] However, the court appears to have carried out a detailed review of the fining decision notwithstanding its reference, in paragraph 341, to the 'manifest error' standard.[26] By contrast, in *E.On Ruhrgas AG v Commission*, the General Court significantly reduced the fine imposed on the applicant by the Commission without any mention of the Commission's margin of discretion.[27]

This confusion in the application of the *KME* standard of judicial review has possibly been dispelled by the ECJ in *Schindler*.[28] In that case, the General Court had rejected the applicant's ninth plea alleging that the reduction in the fine granted by the Commission for cooperation outside the 2002 Commission notice on immunity from fines and reduction of fines in cartel cases (the '2002 Leniency Notice')[29] had been too small. The General Court had ruled that the Commission had a margin of discretion in the matter, and that only if the Commission manifestly exceeded the boundaries of that discretion could it set aside the decision.[30] The ECJ held that the General Court had misdirected itself

EU:C:2013:863; Case T-343/06 *Shell Petroleum v Commission*, 27 September 2012, EU:T:2012:478 (appeal withdrawn), para 110; Case T-352/09 *Novácke chemické závody a.s. v Commission*, 12 December 2012, EU:T:2012:673, para 43.

24 *Bolloré v Commission*, paras 221–269.

25 Case T-154/09 *MRI v Commission*, 27 May 2013, EU:T:2013:260, para 234.

26 Ibid., para 341.

27 Case T-360/09 *E.On Ruhrgas AG, E.ON AG v Commission*, 29 June 2012, EU:T:2012:332. According to Anja Wiesbrock, 'E.On/GDF: Revisiting the Standard of Judicial Review for Fines in Competition Cases' (2013) 4(1) Journal of European Competition Law & Practice 58, 59, '[t]he E.ON judgment [bears] witness to the Courts' increasingly inquisitive approach towards the exercise of the Commission's discretion in respect of calculating fines and the demands for a rigorous judicial review of such decisions by the GC'.

28 Case C-501/11 P *Schindler Holding v Commission*, 18 July 2013, EU:C:2013:522.

29 2002 Commission Notice on immunity from fines and reduction of fines in cartel cases [2002] OJ C45/3.

30 Case T-25/05 *KME Germany v Commission* [2010] ECR II-91, para 54.

in law in paragraphs 295 to 300 of its judgment.[31] The ECJ then set out the relevant test at paragraph 155, explaining that when the Union Courts review the legality of a decision imposing fines for infringement of the competition rules, they 'cannot use the Commission's margin of discretion – either as regards the choice of factors taken into account in the application of the criteria mentioned in the [2006 Fining Guidelines] or as regards the assessment of those factors – as a basis for dispensing with the conduct of an in-depth review of the law and of the facts'.[32] It appears, therefore, that any form of deference to the Commission's discretion in setting the amount of the fine is now ruled out. The 'manifest error' standard can no longer be applied to the review of the Commission's fining decisions.

What is puzzling, even in *Schindler*, is the ECJ's continuing reference to the 'Commission's margin of discretion'. This element of continuity with the previous case law is bound to give rise to further legal uncertainty. For example, in *Total Raffinage Marketing*, a case decided after *Schindler*, the General Court referred to the Commission's discretion as to fines, which was limited but not excluded by the Guidelines on the method of setting fines imposed pursuant to Article 23(2)(a) of Regulation No 1/2003 (the '2006 Fining Guidelines').[33] However, in line with *Schindler*, the Court went on to say that this margin of discretion did not curtail the unlimited jurisdiction of the Union Courts to cancel, reduce or increase the fine.[34]

The rather confused approach of the Union Courts to the relationship between the 'discretion' enjoyed by the Commission in relation to fines and the 'full jurisdiction' standard of review is not satisfactory. It is undoubtedly true that a margin of discretion enjoyed by the Commission is compatible with an unlimited jurisdiction to cancel, reduce or increase the fine. The question is when the Courts' unlimited jurisdiction can or should be exercised, and the answer that appears to flow from *Schindler*

---

31 *Schindler Holding*, cited above, note 28, para 156. See also Case C-510/11 P *Kone Oyj and Others v Commission*, 24 October 2013, EU:C:2013:696, paras 44 and 92.

32 *Schindler Holding*, cited above, note 28, para 155; *Kone Oyj*, cited previous note, paras 39–44.

33 Case T-566/08 *Total Raffinage Marketing v Commission*, 13 September 2013, EU:T:2013:423, para 543, on appeal: Case C-634/13 P *Total Marketing Services v Commission*, not yet decided. The Guidelines on the method of setting fines imposed pursuant to Article 23(2)(a) of Regulation No 1/2003 are published in [2006] OJ C210/2.

34 *Total Raffinage Marketing*, cited previous note, para 545.

is that the Courts must always exercise their unlimited jurisdiction as to fines without paying any deference to the Commission's discretion in relation to the setting of an individual fine.

What, then, of the continuing reference to the 'discretion' enjoyed by the Commission even in *Schindler*? In judicial review, the recognition of a margin of discretion to an administrative authority means that the courts show a certain degree of deference to that discretion. If judicial review is not deferential, then what is the meaning of giving the Commission a margin of discretion? In EU competition law, the answer is probably that the Commission's discretion continues to apply in the formulation of the general fining policy. Thus, one can distinguish two types of discretion. The first is a general type of discretion, which the Commission continues to enjoy, in the choice and assessment of factors relevant to the setting of the fine as a matter of general policy. This would include, for instance, the principle that an undertaking that reports certain infringements to the Commission may be given immunity from, or a reduction in the amount of, the fine, the classification of infringements according to their seriousness, the choice of ranges of percentages of turnover as the starting point for the calculation of a fine and the general level of the fines.[35] In *Dole Food*, the General Court referred to the Commission's margin of discretion 'when fixing the amount of the fines'.[36] This statement was made in the context of an argument by the applicant that the Commission had applied, in the case of the applicant, a share of sales as the starting amount for the fine, which was higher than fines imposed in previous cases. The General Court explained that the Commission may increase the amount of the fines it imposes so as to 'direct the conduct of undertakings towards compliance with the competition rules'.[37] The reference to the Commission's discretion was thus made in the context of the review of the Commission's formulation of its general fining policy rather than in relation to the imposition of a specific fine in an individual case. This point is very helpfully made by Advocate General Wathelet in *Telefónica SA v Commission*.[38] A second and distinct

[35] *Dansk Rørindustri*, cited above, note 11, paras 241–243; *Total Nederland*, cited above, note 23, para 59; Case C-511/11 P *Versalis S.p.A. v Commission*, 13 June 2013, EU:C:2013:386, paras 103–104.

[36] Case T-588/08 *Dole Food Company Inc and Dole Germany OHG v Commission*, 14 March 2014, EU:T:2013:130, para 662.

[37] Ibid.

[38] Opinion of AG Wathelet in Case C-295/12 P *Telefónica SA v Commission*, delivered 26 September 2013, EU:C:2013:619 , para 124: 'An argument which is often raised against the approach advocated in this Opinion is that the General

type of discretion is individualized discretion, which the Commission no longer enjoys or should enjoy, and which refers to the application of the general fining policy in individual cases. In this respect, it is unhelpful to continue to speak of the Commission's discretion, and even less of its margin of discretion. The Commission, as a first-instance decision-maker, obviously makes an assessment of all the relevant factors, and such an assessment naturally has a significant element of non-mechanistic judgment.[39] But both the factual basis and the assessment of the Commission are subject to full correctness review by the Union Courts; hence, there is no room left for any discretion.[40] In application of these principles, Advocate General Wathelet in *Telefónica SA v Commission* recommended that the judgment under appeal be set aside because the General Court had not exercised its unlimited jurisdiction with regard to the fine imposed on the applicants.[41] The ECJ rejected the ground of appeal, holding that it was too general; however, it did not disagree with the legal analysis of the Advocate General.[42] Nor was Advocate General Wathelet's approach contradicted by the judgment of the ECJ in *Siemens v Commission*, which upholds a judgment of the General Court in which the latter had ruled that it did not have the power to substitute its own view for that of the Commission as to whether the deterrent multiplier applied to the applicant was necessary to ensure that the fines had sufficient deterrent effect with regard to those undertakings concerned.[43] The ECJ rejected the appeal because the General Court had in fact dealt with the plea of the applicant and the ground of appeal argued that the

---

Court should not or cannot "interfere" in the setting of a fine, and hence in competition policy, which is the sole responsibility of the Commission. I do not share that reasoning since the General Court adjudicates only in individual cases. The Commission therefore retains all its powers to define and to apply its general policy in other cases'. I return to this Opinion, and the judgment of the Court of Justice, in the main text below.

[39] This is helpfully explained in *Versalis*, cited above, note 35, para 103 (relying on Joined Cases 100/80 to 103/80 *Musique Diffusion Française and Others v Commission* [1983] ECR 1825, para 121, and on *Dansk Rørindustri*, cited above, note 11, para 243).

[40] *Schindler Holding*, cited above, note 28, para 155.

[41] Opinion of AG Wathelet in *Telefónica*, cited above, note 38, paras 107–174.

[42] Case C-295/12 P *Telefónica SA v Commission*, 10 July 2014, EU:C:2014:2062, paras 230–233.

[43] Joined Cases C-239/11 P, C-489/11 P and C-498/11 P *Siemens AG, Mitsubishi Electric Corp and Toshiba Corp v Commission*, 19 December 2013, EU:C:2013:866, paras 332–341.

General Court should have substituted its view for that of the Commission on its own motion.[44]

If any deference to the Commission's discretion in relation to the setting of the individual fine is inconsistent with the principle of effective judicial protection, it seems that the same approach should extend not only to the actual calculation of the fine, but also to the attribution of liability, reductions or increases in fines depending on cooperation or lack thereof, and any other issue of fact or law that is directly relevant to the imposition or the setting of the fine. However, on such matters the General Court is still wavering. For example, in *Hansa Metellwerke v Commission*, the General Court still refers to the Commission's wide margin of discretion when assessing the utility of the evidence provided to it in a leniency application and to the manifest error standard of review.[45] This language is used despite the fact that we are reminded, in a case decided on the same day, that the General Court cannot use that margin of discretion as a basis for dispensing with a thorough review of the Commission's assessment in matters of both fact and law.[46] Similarly, in *Roca Sanitario v Commission*, the General Court considered that the Commission had a margin of appreciation as to whether to attribute liability for a cartel to the parent company of the actual participant, even though the court then adds that this margin of appreciation does not absolve the Union Courts from verifying whether the conditions for liability of the parent company are met.[47] However, in light of *KME* and *Schindler*, even in relation to the attribution of liability, any deference to the Commission's discretion is incompatible with the principle of effective judicial protection. The standard of review is full correctness, and the only discretion that the Commission continues to enjoy is in the formulation of its general fining policy.

EVIDENCE OF FACT

As regards factual evidence, the standard of review has always been, or should always have been, correctness. However, in certain cases the

---

[44] Ibid., paras 339–340. For the same approach, see Joined Cases C-247/11 P and C-253/11 P *Areva SA v Commission*, 10 April 2014, EU:C:2014:257, paras 166–182.

[45] Case T-375/10 *Hansa Metellwerke v Commission*, 16 September 2013, EU:T:2013:475, para 138, on appeal: Case C-611/13 P, not yet decided.

[46] Case T-412/10 *Roca v Commission*, judgment of 16 September 2013, EU:T:2013:444, para 188, on appeal: Case C-638/13 P, not yet decided.

[47] Ibid., para 57.

Union Courts still deferred to the Commission's assessment of the evidence.[48]

The post-*KME* case law now generally applies a full correctness judicial review standard to evidence relevant to infringement, with no reference to the 'manifest error' test. Thus, in *Dole Food Company Inc v Commission*[49] and in *Total Raffinage Marketing v Commission (Paraffin Wax)*,[50] the General Court reviewed the evidence of the infringements in question without any reference to either the 'manifest error' test or to any 'discretion' enjoyed by the Commission. In *Roca v Commission (Bathroom Fittings)*, although in the applicant's pleadings it was argued that the Commission had committed a manifest error of appreciation, the General Court reviewed the evidence without reference to the 'manifest error' standard.[51] In *Almamet GmbH Handel mit Spänen und Pulvern aus Metall v Commission (Calcium Carbide and Magnesium for the Steel and Gas Industries)*, the General Court found that the applicant's arguments challenging the existence of a single overall infringement did not tend to establish a 'manifest error' but concerned the material accuracy of the facts and the correct application of the law.[52] However, the court then proceeded to deal with the applicant's plea, thus accepting, albeit implicitly, that the applicant was indeed entitled to challenge the correctness of the Commission's findings of fact.[53] In *Intel*, the General Court reviewed the factual evidence without any reference to the 'manifest error' standard.[54] In *Kone*, the ECJ held that the General Court did not commit an error of law when it ruled that, in order to obtain immunity from fines under point 8(b) of the 2002 Leniency Notice, an undertaking had to provide to the Commission evidence which is 'sufficient in nature, precision and probative value to enable the Commission to find an

---

48 See *Archer Daniels Midland*, cited above, note 17, paras 220–226; and, on appeal, paras 150–153 of the judgment of the Court of Justice. As explained above, the Court partly set aside the judgment of the General Court, but not on the issue of the test of manifest error.

49 *Dole Food Company*, cited above, note 36.

50 *Total Raffinage Marketing*, cited above, note 33.

51 *Roca*, cited above, note 46.

52 Case T-410/09 *Almamet GmbH Handel mit Spänen und Pulvern aus Metall v Commission (Calcium Carbide and Magnesium for the Steel and Gas Industries)*, 12 December 2012, EU:T:2012:676, para 167.

53 Ibid, paras 168–179. The Court describes the plea as raising an issue of law (ibid., para 179), but clearly a number of factual issues were relevant to the legal characterization of the facts as a single infringement.

54 Case T-286/09 *Intel v Commission*, 12 June 2014, EU:T:2014:547, on appeal: Case C-413/14 P, not yet decided.

infringement of Article [101 TFEU]'.[55] The ECJ went on to say that 'the General Court assessed […] the probative value of the evidence provided by the Kone group and considered that value to be limited'.[56] The Court found it relevant that the General Court had set out the correct criterion for the assessment of the evidence and had then evaluated its probative value in the light of that criterion.

In this author's view, the current approach of the Union Courts to the assessment of factual evidence is correct. When the Courts review the Commission's assessment of such evidence, no margin of appreciation or discretion is warranted. Deferential review is now untenable after the judgment of the ECJ in *Schindler*. It is true that *Schindler*, and *KME* itself, only concerned decisions imposing a fine. But both cases also concerned the Courts' review of the legality of Commission decisions.[57] There is no principled basis on which it is possible to argue that evidence pertaining to the imposition of the fine and its level should be reviewed according to a stricter standard than evidence pertaining to the infringement. It might be thought that a decision imposing a fine has more severe consequences for the undertakings concerned. But the decision imposing a fine is the consequence of the decision finding the infringement. A more thorough review of the decision imposing a fine would therefore not afford the applicant any real guarantee because evidence relevant to the infringement is also relevant to the imposition of the fine. To limit the correctness standard of review only to the assessment of the evidence to the extent that it is relevant to the fine would be wholly artificial, as it would subject the same evidence to two different standards of review depending on the plea to which the evidence is relevant, which would be absurd.

MATTERS OF COMPLEX ECONOMIC ASSESSMENT

It is well established that judicial review of complex economic assessments by the Commission is deferential.[58] The question is whether *KME*

---

[55] Case C-510/11 P *Kone Oyj*, cited above, note 31, para 49 (quoting para 94 of the contested judgment of the General Court).

[56] Ibid., para 52.

[57] This is a point rightly made by Sibony in her case note on *KME*, cited above, note 21, at 1995–1997.

[58] *Spain v Lenzing*, cited above, note 14, para 57; *Matra Hachette*, cited above, note 14, para 104; *Tetra Laval*, cited above, note 5, para 39; *Thyssen Stahl*, cited above, note 14, para 78.

has had, or will have, any impact on the deferential standard of judicial review of such matters. On its face, *KME* is limited to decisions imposing a fine. Furthermore, it recites the formula for the deferential judicial review standard of complex economic assessments, implying that such a standard complies with the principle of effective judicial protection.[59] The post-*KME* case law appears to confirm this.

In *E.ON Ruhrgas AG v Commission*, an Article 101 case decided about six months after *KME*, two companies operating a gas pipeline for importing gas into Germany and France had agreed not to sell gas transported on the pipeline into each other's home markets. One of the issues in the case was whether the agreement, which the Commission had found to be a cartel,[60] was ancillary to the building and operation of the pipeline. The General Court considered it appropriate to apply a deferential standard of review 'inasmuch as the assessment of the ancillary nature of a particular agreement in relation to a main operation entails complex economic assessments by the Commission'.[61]

Likewise, following *KME* and *Schindler*, the ECJ itself has confirmed that deferential review survives the *KME* case law. In *Kone Oyj v Commission*, the Court explicitly upheld the limited review of matters of complex economic assessment even in the context of the review of legality of fining decisions. As the Court stated:[62]

> [...] when it falls to the European Union judicature to review the legality of Commission decisions imposing fines for infringements of the EU competition rules, it cannot encroach upon the discretion available to the Commission in the administrative proceedings by substituting its own assessment of complex economic circumstances for that of the Commission, but, where relevant, must demonstrate that the way in which the Commission reached its conclusions was not justified in law.

It is noteworthy that the Court cited, in support of the proposition set out above, *Commission v Alrosa*, a case concerning a decision accepting commitments and not a fining decision.[63] At first instance in *Telefónica SA v Commission*, an abuse of dominance case decided about four months after *KME*, the General Court confirmed that matters of complex

---

[59] *KME*, cited above, note 19, para 121.

[60] Commission Decision of 8 July 2009 in Case COMP/39.401 – *E.ON/GDF*, recitals 177–182.

[61] *E.ON Ruhrgas*, cited above, note 27, para 69.

[62] *Kone Oyj*, cited above, note 31, para 27.

[63] Case C-441/07 P *Commission v Alrosa* [2010] ECR I-5949, para 67 (cited in *Kone Oyj*, cited above, note 31, para 27).

economic and technical assessment are only subject to 'limited' review.[64] On appeal, the ECJ (relying on, among others, *Tetra Laval v Commission*, a merger case[65]) upheld the General Court's judgment and approved of the deferential standard of review that the court had applied.[66] It follows that the Courts' limited review of complex economic assessments does not change depending on whether the decision imposes a fine or not.[67] The standard is the same standard that applies in commitments and merger cases.

In conclusion, it is likely that deferential review still applies in the area of complex economic and technical assessments. The reason for this is clear. The Union Courts are reluctant to undertake a full review of matters in specialized fields of knowledge where the Commission is perceived to possess superior expertise. However, this reason is not convincing when the decision under review is a decision finding that the undertakings concerned have infringed EU competition law, from which serious consequences in terms of administrative fines and private law liability may ensue. Matters of complex economic assessment may be the central issue in a case – and often are, in cases other than those involving naked cartels. Whether a price-fixing arrangement is ancillary to a lawful operation or whether an undertaking is dominant on a given market (which includes the issue of the proper definition of the relevant market) is a matter of complex economic assessment within the meaning of the case law, but such issues are central to those types of cases. Depending on how they are decided, the undertaking(s) concerned will be acquitted or convicted of an infringement of Article 101 or Article 102. Yet judicial review continues to be deferential essentially for reasons of efficiency. It is self-evident, however, that efficiency alone cannot trump the principle of effective judicial protection. The nature of the subject matter may make deferential judicial review more appropriate but then, as in the

---

[64] Case T-336/07 *Telefónica SA v Commission*, paras 69–70, upheld in C-295/12 P *Telefónica and Telefónica de España v Commission*, cited above, note 42.

[65] *Tetra Laval*, cited above, note 5, para 39.

[66] Case C-295/12 P *Telefónica*, cited above, note 64, para 54. The Court also relied on Case C-386/10 P *Chalkor v Commission* [2011] ECR I-13085, para 54, and Case C-199/11 *Otis and Others v Commission*, cited above, note 2, para 59.

[67] The standard of review upheld in para 27 of *Kone Oyj*, cited above, note 31, and set out in para 28 of the same judgment, is the well-established deferential standard of review of matters of complex economic assessment. See, for example, *Tetra Laval*, cited above, note 5, para 39; *Spain v Lenzing*, cited above, note 14, paras 56 and 57; *Chalkor*, cited previous note, para 54; *Otis and Others*, cited previous note, para 59.

ECHR case of *Bryan*,[68] additional safeguards should be implemented that ensure that the first-instance decision-maker enjoys a sufficient degree of impartiality and independence from the investigating and prosecuting agents.[69]

CONCLUSIONS

The analysis of the case law of the Union Courts post-*KME* shows that *KME* has triggered a change in the approach of the Union Courts. There appears to be little doubt, currently, that the Commission does not, or at least should not, enjoy a margin of discretion in the setting of the fine in individual cases. Individual fining decisions are subject to a review of legality supplemented by the Courts' unlimited jurisdiction, and this results in the application of a standard of review under which no deference is due to the Commission. The continuing references in the case law to the 'discretion' or 'margin of discretion' enjoyed by the Commission are unhelpful. Such references, properly understood, mean that the Commission continues to enjoy general discretion as regards its approach to fines as a matter of competition policy, within the boundaries set by EU law. This discretion is compatible with the principle of effective judicial protection not least because it does not relate to individualized decision-making but to the design of the fining system as a whole, where primary and secondary EU law leave some room for policy formulation to the Commission as the primary enforcer of Articles 101 and 102. By contrast, reference to this type of discretion has no place when judicial review of individualized decision-making is at issue. It is also possible that references to the Commission's discretion are used in a purely non-technical way simply to describe the fact that the Commission makes an assessment of the various factors relevant to the fine in the first place, subject to the review of the Union Courts. However, referring to discretion in this way is misleading and inappropriate. Discretion, in administrative law, denotes a sphere of decision-making where deference is due to a public authority; no such privileged sphere exists in this context. The Union Courts should avoid any reference to the Commission's discretion when reviewing fining decisions in individual cases.

The correctness standard of review also applies, and in any event should apply, to the assessment of factual evidence that does not raise

68 *Bryan v United Kingdom*, cited above, note 8.

69 Nazzini, 'Administrative Enforcement, Judicial Review and Fundamental Rights', cited above, note 3, at 989–991 and 999.

complex economic or technical issues. This was probably already so even before *KME*, but it has become clearer since that case was decided. Indeed, it is difficult to maintain that the same evidence should be subject to two different standards of review depending on whether it is assessed for its relevance to the issue of infringement or for its relevance to the fine. Here too, any reference by the Union Courts to the Commission's 'discretion' should be strongly discouraged.

A deferential standard of review continues to apply to complex economic or technical assessments, regardless of whether such assessments are relevant to the issue of infringement or relevant to the propriety of the fine. This position is legally untenable under the current institutional structure,[70] as it sacrifices the guarantee of effective judicial protection to considerations of efficiency and superior expertise of the administrative authority; limited judicial review in this context is thus clearly in breach of Article 47(2) of the EU Charter. One may predict that, over time, even this last bulwark of judicial deference to the Commission will be eroded and, eventually, a standard of review that requires the Courts to examine the correctness of the Commission's individualized decision-making will apply across the board.

---

70 For an argument whereby, under a different institutional arrangement, deferential judicial review could be justified in certain cases, see Nazzini, ibid., 996–1005.

6. *Dura lex sed lex*: the parent-subsidiary relationship in EU antitrust law and the *AEG Telefunken* presumption – independence of the EU legal system, effectiveness of competition law and protection of fundamental rights

Lorenzo F. Pace*

ABSTRACT

The increasingly frequent reference to the protection of fundamental rights in the application of EU antitrust law is a trend that has grown significantly in parallel with the reforms brought about by Regulation 1/2003. The application of fundamental rights to antitrust law is explained by several factors, including for example, the increasingly harsh penalties imposed for violations of antitrust law; the tensions that arise from the Commission's multiple roles; and the introduction of Article 6(2) TEU, as amended by the Lisbon Treaty, and the binding nature of the EU Charter of Fundamental Rights. The greater attention being given to fundamental rights is evident in the development of the application of the AEG Telefunken presumption, whereby a parent company may be penalized for the antitrust infringements of its wholly-owned subsidiary on the ground that the parent and the subsidiary constitute a single economic entity, and hence a single 'undertaking'. Recently, the Court of Justice has confirmed the lawfulness of that presumption. However, increasing attention is now given to the adequacy

* Professor of Law, University of Molise and Partner, Studio Legale Pace, Rome.

of the Commission's reasoning, particularly when the Commission rejects arguments made by parent companies to rebut the presumption. These developments suggest that the growing importance of fundamental rights protection may under certain conditions temper the principle of the effectiveness of EU competition law.

INTRODUCTION

The reform of Regulation 1/2003[1] has enabled the Commission to focus its enforcement mainly against cartels. This trend in the Commission's policy has been accompanied by certain changes in the application of the EU antitrust rules, including a new and more severe fining policy with higher sanctions imposed on companies.[2] At the cornerstone of what one could call an effective and thus far successful 'war on cartels' was, *inter alia*, the so-called *AEG Telefunken* presumption. This presumption concerns the imputation of the sanctions for breach of antitrust rules to a parent company that holds 100 per cent of the shares of the subsidiary that has engaged in conduct contrary to EU competition law. Because of its features, this presumption of imputability has drawn much criticism, and it has in fact been challenged in some 50 judgments in the last few years.[3]

---

[1] Council Regulation (EC) No 1/2003 of 16 December 2002 on the implementation of the rules on competition laid down in Articles 81 and 82 of the Treaty, [2003] OJ L1/1.

[2] See Wolfgang Bosch, 'The Role of Fines in the Public Enforcement of Competition Law', in Kai Hüschelrath and Heike Schweitzer (eds), *Public and Private Enforcement of Competition Law in Europe*, (Springer Verlag 2014) 53.

[3] Opinion of Advocate General Mischo and the judgment of the ECJ in Case C-286/98 P *Stora Kopparbergs Bergslags AB v Commission* [2000] ECR I-9925; Case C-196/99 P *Siderúrgica Aristrain Madrid SL v Commission* [2003] ECR I-11005; Case T-325/01 *DaimlerChrysler AG v Commission* [2005] ECR II-3319; Case T-314/01 *Coöperatieve Verkoop- en Productievereniging van Aardappelmeel en Derivaten Avebe BA v Commission* [2006] ECR II-3085; Joined Cases T-109/02, and so on. *Bolloré SA and Others v Commission* [2007] ECR II-947; Joined Cases C-322/07 P, and so on. *Papierfabrik August Koehler AG and Others v Commission* [2009] ECR I-7191; Opinion of Advocate General Kokott and judgment of the ECJ in Case C-97/08 P *Akzo Nobel NV and Others v Commission* [2009] ECR I-8237; Case C-407/08 P Knauf Gips KG v Commission [2010] ECR I-6375; Opinion of Advocate General Mazák and judgment of the ECJ in Case C-90/09 P *General Química SA and Others v Commission* [2011] I-1; Opinion of Advocate General Bot and judgment of the ECJ in Joined Cases C-201/09 P and C-216/09 P *ArcelorMittal Luxembourg SA v Commission*

The Commission's 'war on cartels' has led to the trend of increasingly frequent complaints raised by companies subject to the Commission antitrust proceedings, according to which a number of aspects of those proceedings, including the *AEG Telefunken* presumption, infringe their fundament rights. This phenomenon – unknown to this extent in the U.S. experience – is related to the specific characteristics of the EU antitrust enforcement system.

(C-201/09 P) *and Commission v ArcelorMittal Luxembourg SA and Others* (C-216/09 P) [2011] ECR I-2239; Case T-386/06 *Pegler Ltd v Commission* [2011] ECR II-1267; Case T-382/06 *Tomkins plc v Commission* [2011] ECR II-1157; Case T-217/06 *Arkema France and Others v Commission* [2011] ECR II-2593; Case T-194/06 *SNIA SpA v Commission* [2011] ECR II-3119; Case T-185/06 *L'Air Liquide, Société Anonyme pour l'étude et l'exploitation des Procédés Georges Claude v Commission* [2011] ECR II-2809; Joined Cases T-208/08 and T-209/08 *Gosselin Group NV and Stichting Administratiekantoor Portielje v Commission* [2011] ECR II-3639; Case T-196/06 *Edison SpA v Commission* [2011] ECR II-3149; Case T-191/06 *FMC Foret, SA v Commission* [2011] ECR II-2959; Case T-138/07 *Schindler Holding Ltd and Others v Commission* [2011] ECR II-4819; Case T-59/07 *Polimeri Europa SpA v Commission* [2011] ECR II-4687; Case T-39/07 *Eni SpA v Commission* [2011] ECR II-4457; Case T-12/06 *Deltafina SpA v Commission* [2011] ECR II-5639; Case T-234/07 *Koninklijke Grolsch NV v Commission* [2011] ECR II-6169; Case C-521/09 P *Elf Aquitaine SA v Commission* [2011] ECR [2011] ECR I-8947; Case T-39/06 *Transcatab SpA v Commission* [2011] ECR II-6831; Opinion of Advocate General Kokott and judgment of the ECJ in Joined Cases C-628/10 P and C-14/11 P *Alliance One International Inc. and Standard Commercial Tobacco Co. Inc. v Commission and Commission v Alliance One International Inc. and Others*, decided 19 July 2012; Case C-286/11 P *Commission v Tomkins plc*, 22 January 2013; Case T-347/06 *Nynäs Petroleum AB and Nynas Belgium AB v Commission*, 27 September 2012; Case T-361/06 *Ballast Nedam NV v Commission*, 27 September 2012; T-362/06 *Ballast Nedam Infra BV v Commission*, 27 September 2012; Opinion of Advocate General Kokott in Case C-681/11 *Bundeswettbewerbsbehörde and Bundeskartellanwalt v Schenker & Co. AG and Others*, decided 18 June 2013; Opinion of Advocate General Kokott and judgment of the ECJ in Case C-501/11 P *Schindler Holding Ltd and Others v Commission*, decided 18 July 2013; Case C 508/11 P *ENI SpA v Commission*, 8 May 2013; Case C-511/11 P *Versalis SpA v Commission*, 13 June 2013; Case C-440/11 P *Commission v Stichting Administratiekantoor Portielje and Gosselin Group NV*, 11 July 2013; Opinion of Advocate General Mengozzi and judgment of the ECJ in Joined Cases C-231/11 P to C-233/11 P *Commission v Siemens AG Österreich and Others and Siemens Transmission & Distribution Ltd and Others v Commission*, decided 10 April 2014; Case C-179/12 P *The Dow Chemical Company v Commission*, 26 September 2013; Case C-238/12 P *FLSmidth & Co. A/S v Commission*, 30 April 2014.

Against this background, the aims of this chapter are: first, to briefly assess the evolution of the application of the protection of fundamental rights in EU antitrust law; second, to give an overview of the issue of the imputation of liability within corporate groups; third, to take into account the development of the *AEG Telefunken* presumption in the EU case law; and, last, to assess the implications that the increasing attention given to fundamental rights protection may have with respect to that presumption.

THE PROTECTION OF FUNDAMENTAL RIGHTS AND EU ANTITRUST LAW: A BRIEF OVERVIEW

Although the discussion of the relationship between competition law and the protection of fundamental rights has developed only recently,[4] the application of fundamental rights in this area began in much earlier times. In hindsight, it can be divided into three phases. The first phase began with the initial recognition of the protection of fundamental rights within the legal order of what was then the Community. As the Court of Justice (ECJ) recognized already in the *Nold* case (1974), even in the absence of any catalogue of specified rights in the Treaty, the protection of fundamental rights was part of Community law.[5] That judgment was, in fact, a competition law case. It concerned a plea against a Commission decision taken under Articles 66(1) and 66(2) of the ECSC Treaty, which established rules on, *inter alia*, the control of concentrations in the coal and steel sectors.[6]

The second phase began in the 1980s, when it was argued before the ECJ that the conduct of the Commission in the context of its competition law enforcement duties could be – and in fact was, in the case at hand – contrary to Article 6(1) ECHR (which guarantees a fair hearing by an independent and impartial tribunal).[7] In particular, this second phase arose as a consequence of the Commission's nature as a 'supranational'

---

[4] See generally Marco Bronckers and Anne Vallery, 'No Longer Presumed Guilty: The Impact of Fundamental Rights on Certain Dogmas of EU Competition Law' (2011) 34 World Competition 535.

[5] See also Case 11-70 *Internationale Handelsgesellschaft mbH v Einfuhr- und Vorratsstelle für Getreide und Futtermittel* [1970] ECR 1125.

[6] Case 4-73 *J. Nold, Kohlen- und Baustoffgrosshandlung v Commission* [1974] ECR 491, para 13. Mr. Nold had alleged the infringement of his right to property, recognized under national law, by the decision of the Commission.

[7] See Joined Cases 209 to 215 and 218/78 *Heintz van Landewyck SARL and others v Commission* [1980] ECR 3125, at page 3160 and para 79. At para 81, the Court of Justice declined to accept the arguments submitted on the ground

body, independent of the Member States (as provided today in Article 17 TEU). The Commission's independence *vis-à-vis* the Member States was necessary, according to the intentions of the draughtsmen of the Treaty of Rome, in order to create a body which, operating independently both of the States and of individuals, could protect the general interest of the Community rather than particular national or private interests.[8] On the other hand, the Commission's distinctive structure, which is designed to ensure such independence, has negative consequences with regard to investigations under Articles 101 and 102 TFEU. These are due to the double role that the Commission plays as both a 'prosecutor' (identifying possible antitrust violations) and 'judge' (verifying infringements and imposing penalties).[9] The claims put forward in the 1980s – which have not disappeared, as can be seen, for example, in the 2013 *Schindler* case[10] – is that the system described above was entirely incompatible with Article 6 ECHR[11] because, so the argument goes, the decisions taken under the antitrust rules, which are of quasi-criminal character, are issued by an authority that is neither independent nor impartial.

The arguments concerning the alleged illegality of Article 6 ECHR were based on an overly strict reading of the law, and they did not take into consideration the 'checks and balances' of the European system, as the ECJ itself has underlined in *Schindler*.[12] Nevertheless, this complaint regarding the structure of enforcement was already in 1980 a 'cry of pain' from companies which perceived an 'abuse' caused by the 'conflict

---

that the Commission was not itself a 'tribunal' within the meaning of the Convention.

[8] On the nature and role of the Commission in antitrust law enforcement, see Lorenzo Federico Pace, *European Antitrust Law* (Edward Elgar 2007) 26 and 199.

[9] See the proposal to separate the Commission's decisional power from its prosecutorial power in Massimo Merola and Denis Waelbroeck (eds), *Towards an Optimal Enforcement of Competition Rules in Europe – Time for a Review of Regulation 1/2003?* (Bruylant 2010) 237.

[10] Judgment of the ECJ in *Schindler*, cited above, note 3, para 23.

[11] A memorable incident occurred in 1996, when Claus-Dieter Ehlermann – Director General of DG IV at that time – was participating as a speaker at a conference organized by the Italian Antitrust Authority in Rome. Following an intervention in which it was alleged that the role of Commission in the European antitrust enforcement system was incompatible with Article 6 ECHR, Ehlermann, smiling, remarked that '[i]f this were true, a large part of the overall activities of the Commission would be unlawful'.

[12] Judgment of the ECJ in *Schindler*, cited above, note 3, para 30.

of interest' inherent in the Commission's multiple roles. It is no coincidence that in 1981, in order to find a partial solution to this issue, the Hearing Officer was established within the Commission as a means of better protecting the procedural rights of companies subject to investigation.[13]

The third phase of the developing relationship between competition law and fundamental rights began in the mid-2000s.[14] This phase concerns the claim of illegality for breach of fundamental rights not by the nature of the European enforcement system as such but of specific aspects of it. As suggested above, this phase is in large part a consequence of the launch of the Commission's 'war on cartels' following the adoption of Regulation 1/2003. In the context of this war, companies have sought – due, *inter alia*, to the severe monetary sanctions imposed by the Commission – new forms of protection (or rather, they have raised new grounds for claiming the unlawfulness of Commission decisions). Another factor behind this new 'climate' was the introduction of Article 6(2) TEU by the Treaty of Lisbon, which established that the EU Charter of Fundamental Rights (EUCFR) was to be legally binding. A third factor was the *Menarini* judgment of the European Court of Human Rights (ECtHR).[15] In that case, as is well known, the ECtHR, in examining the standard of review applied to a decision of the Italian Antitrust Authority, characterized the competition rules at issue – given, *inter alia*, the size of

---

[13] See Giacomo Di Federico, 'The Role of the Hearing Officer in Antitrust Cases. A Critical Assessment of the New Mandate and Practice After 2011', forthcoming, (2014) *Yearbook of Antitrust and Regulatory Studies*. As for the Court of Justice, it is proceeding to make clear in various cases that the Commission must ensure respect for the rights of the defence in performing its functions and, in particular, in administrative proceedings in which sanctions, in other words, fines or penalty payments, may be imposed. See, for example, Case 85/76 *Hoffman-La Roche & Co. AG v Commission* [1979] ECR 461, para 9); Case 322/81 *NV Nederlandsche Banden Industrie Michelin v Commission* [1983] ECR 3461, para 7; Joined Cases 46/87 and 227/88, *Hoechst AG v Commission* [1989] ECR 2859, para 15; Case 374/87 *Orkem v Commission* [1989] ECR 3283, paras 32–33).

[14] On the timing of the Commission's new policy, see the judgment of the ECJ in *ENI SpA*, cited above, note 3.

[15] *A Menarini Diagnostics SRL v Italy*, App no. 43509/08 (ECHR 27 September 2011). On this case, see, for example, Christopher Bellamy, = 'ECHR and Competition Law Post *Menarini:* An Overview of EU and National Case-Law', e-Competitions, No. 47946, 5 July 2012. See also Pascal Cardonnel, 'The European Court of Human Rights Rules on the Standard of Judicial Review on Adopted Cartel Decisions by National Competition Authorities' *Menarini Diagnostics v Italy*), (2011/4) Concurrences 166.

the financial penalties imposed for their violation – as quasi-criminal in nature, within the meaning of the ECHR. Consequently, the authorities applying that law were bound to respect the rights protected by the ECHR in quasi-criminal proceedings.

THE IMPUTABILITY OF THE INFRINGEMENT OF ARTICLES 101 AND 102 TFEU IN CORPORATE GROUPS AND THE *AEG TELEFUNKEN* PRESUMPTION

The *AEG Telefunken* presumption is closely linked to the problem of the imputability of the violation of antitrust prohibitions where corporate groups are concerned. Imputability is of particular importance for the Commission and for the companies themselves. Indeed, the concrete identification of the company liable for the breach is relevant for different aspects such as: the magnitude of the fine pursuant to Article 23(c)(2) of Regulation 1/2003 (since attribution of the infringement to the parent company enables the Commission to increase the basis for computing the penalty, and hence the value of the penalty imposed, subject to the 'ceiling' of 10 per cent of the total turnover of the corporate group); the identification of the addressee of the Commission's decision for its execution; the identification of the company that must submit a request for leniency and its consequences; and so on.

The problem of the imputation of liability in the case of corporate groups, and in particular, imputation to the parent company, raises the issue of the concept of an 'undertaking'. The TFEU indicates that the addressees of the prohibitions laid down in Articles 101 and 102 TFEU are 'undertakings'– yet the Treaty provides no specifications with regard to the meaning of that concept.[16] In its case law, the ECJ has clarified that the concept of an 'undertaking' covers any entity engaged in an economic activity, regardless of its legal status and the way it is financed.[17] The Court has also stated that, in this context, the term 'undertaking' must be understood as designating an economic unit, even if, in law, that economic unit consists of several natural or legal persons[18] – as in the case of a corporate group. Moreover, if such an economic entity infringes the competition rules, it is for that entity, consistently

[16] On the interpretation of this notion, see Wouter Wils, *The Optimal Enforcement of EC Antitrust Law: Essays in Law and Economics* (Kluwer Law International 2002) 156.

[17] Judgment of the ECJ in *Schindler*, cited above, note 3, para 53.

[18] Ibid., para 53.

with the principle of personal liability, to answer for that infringement.[19] That is to say, a legal person who is not the perpetrator of an infringement of the competition rules may nevertheless be penalized for the unlawful conduct of another legal person, if both of those persons form part of the same economic entity and thus together constitute the 'undertaking' that infringed competition law.[20] Consequently, the parent company is itself deemed to have infringed the EU competition rules, and its liability for the infringement derives entirely from that of its subsidiary.[21] The Commission will thus also be able to regard the parent company as jointly and severally liable for the payment of any fine imposed on its subsidiary.[22]

With regard to the imputability of sanctions in corporate groups, which no doubt arises when both the parent and its subsidiary are involved in the antitrust violation. In these cases, it is indisputable that the parent company shares responsibility for the infringement.[23] This may be distinguished from scenarios where the parent company is not directly involved in a violation of Article 101 or Article 102 TFEU, where such a violation is perpetrated by a subsidiary that the parent company controls. In this case, the imputation to the parent company is a consequence of the fact that both companies are part of the same 'undertaking'. In order to conclude that these companies are part of the same 'undertaking', the parent company must not only be capable of having a 'decisive influence' on its subsidiary, it must also have effectively exercised such influence. Thus, the mere possibility that the parent company could exercise a certain influence over the subsidiary is not sufficient to define the existence of an 'undertaking' within the meaning of Articles 101 and

---

[19] Case 48-69 *Imperial Chemical Industries Ltd. v Commission* [1972] ECR 619; Case 107/82 *Allgemeine Elektrizitäts- Gesellschaft AEG-Telefunken AG v Commission* [1983] ECR 3151, para 49. See also the judgments of the ECJ in *General Química*, cited above, note 3, paras 34–35; in *ArcelorMittal Luxembourg*, cited above, note 3, para 95; and in *Schindler*, cited above, note 3, para 53.

[20] Judgment of the ECJ in *Siemens AG Österreich*, cited above, note 3, para 45.

[21] See the judgment of the ECJ in *Commission v Tomkins*, cited above, note 3, paras 43 and 49; Case C-50/12 P *Kendrion NV v Commission*, 26 November 2013, EU:C:2013:771, para 55; judgment of the ECJ in *Siemens AG Österreich*, cited above, note 3, para 47.

[22] See, for example, the judgments of the ECJ in *ArcelorMittal*, cited above, note 3, para 98; and in *Siemens AG Österreich*, cited above, note 3, para 48.

[23] Case C-248/98 P *NV Koninklijke KNP BT v Commission* [2000] ECR I-9641; judgment of the CFI in *Koninklijke*, cited above, note 3.

102;[24] as is clear from the foregoing discussion, this in turn is relevant for the imputability of the penalty to the parent company. The burden of proof as concerns these two elements (decisive influence and the effective exercise thereof) is on the Commission.

The peculiarity of the case law relating to the *AEG Telefunken* presumption is related to the different situation in which the parent company has a 100 per cent (or nearly 100 per cent) shareholding in a subsidiary that has violated EU antitrust law. In this circumstance, it is clear, according to the case law, that the parent has the possibility to exercise decisive influence over its subsidiary. However, in contrast to the scenario described above, in this case the Court presumed, by way of a rebuttable presumption, that such influence was actually exercised, and that the parent and the subsidiary thus together constituted an 'undertaking'. This presumption puts the Commission, when holding the parent company responsible for a violation perpetrated by its wholly-owned subsidiary, in the 'cosy' position of having to prove only that the parent owns all or nearly all of the shares in its subsidiary. Where that is the case, the Commission will then be able to regard the parent jointly and severally liable for payment of the fine, unless the parent – which bears the burden of rebutting that presumption – adduces sufficient evidence to show that its subsidiary acts independently on the market.[25]

The *AEG Telefunken* presumption has in fact been successfully challenged by parent companies; but only in a very limited number of cases, and not in recent practice.[26]

---

[24] Joined Cases T-144/07, and so on. *ThyssenKrupp Liften Ascenseurs NV and Others v Commission* [2011] ECR II-5129; Case T-141/07 *General Technic Otis Sàrl and Others v Commission* [2011] ECR II-4977.

[25] See judgments of the ECJ in *Stora*, cited above, note 3, para 29; in *Akzo Nobel*, cited above, note 3, para 61; in *General Química*, cited above, note 3, para 40; and in *ArcelorMittal*, cited above, note 3, para 98.

[26] Commission Decision of 16 December 2003 in Case COMP/38 240 – *Industrial Tubes*, para 479; Commission Decision of 20 October 2004 in Case COMP/38.238 – *Raw Tobacco Spain*, para 251; Commission Decision of 11 June 2002 in Case COMP/36.571 – *Austrian Banks - 'Lombard Club'*, para 376.

THE *AEG TELEFUNKEN* PRESUMPTION, THE PRINCIPLE OF INDEPENDENCE OF THE EU LEGAL SYSTEM AND THE PRINCIPLE OF EFFECTIVE APPLICATION OF COMPETITION LAW

The heated discussions around the *AEG Telefunken* presumption are due to its characteristics.[27] The consequence of the presumption is that a company which has not directly perpetrated an antitrust violation may be sanctioned, on the basis of the presumption, for an amount up to 10 per cent of its worldwide turnover for the behaviour of a subsidiary, legally distinct although wholly owned by it. The level of the fine thus imposed may be quite substantial. Thus, for example, in *Schindler*, the amount of the overall fine applied to the Schindler group was more than 145 million euros.[28]

The *AEG Telefunken* presumption is a typical example (as is the term 'undertaking'[29]) of a legal notion defined in a manner designed to ensure

---

[27] See Aitor Montesa Lloreda and Angel Givaja Sanz, 'When Parents Pay for their Children's Wrongs: Attribution of Liability for EC Antitrust Infringements in Parent-subsidiary Scenarios' (2006) 29 World Competition 555; Richard Burnley, 'Group Liability for Antitrust Infringements: Responsibility and Accountability', (2010) 33 World Competition 595; Karl Hofstetter and Melanie Ludescher, 'Fines Against Parent Companies in EU Antitrust Law: Setting Incentives for "Best Practice Compliance"' (2010) 33 World Competition 55; Matteo Beretta and Patrick Marco Ferrari, 'La Presunzione di Responsabilità delle Società Madri per le Infrazioni alle Regole di Concorrenza Commesse dalle Proprie Controllate' (2010) Contratto e Impresa/Europa 1; Alexander Riesenkampff and Udo Krauthausen, 'Liability of Parent Companies for Antitrust Violations of their Subsidiaries' (2010) 31 European Competition Law Review 38; Laura La Rocca, 'The Controversial Issue of the Parent-company Liability for the Violation of EC Competition Rules by the Subsidiary' (2011) 32 European Competition Law Review 68; Laura De Sanctis, 'L'imputabilità della Responsabilità delle Violazioni Antitrust e i Gruppi di Società', in Lorenzo F. Pace (a cura di), *Dizionario Sistematico del Diritto della Concorrenza* (Jovene 2013); Bernardo Cortese, 'The Notion of Undertaking: Piercing the Corporate Veil in EU Competition Law – Parent Subsidiaries Relationship and Antitrust Liability', in Bernardo Cortese (ed), *EU Competition Law – Between Public and Private Enforcement* (Wolters Kluwer 2014) 73.

[28] Judgment of the ECJ in *Schindler*, cited above, note 3, para 13.

[29] For example, it was difficult indeed for Member States to accept that single individuals and even public bodies could fall within the definition of 'undertaking' within the meaning of EU law when, under the relevant national law, they could not be categorized in this way. See, for example, Case C-41/90 *Klaus Höfner and Fritz Elser v Macrotron GmbH* [1991] ECR I-1979.

the effective application of the Treaty rules, and in particular the competition rules, taking advantage of the principle of the independence of the European legal system.[30] Their interpretation can be understood only if one keeps in mind the specific nature of competition law, which is applied to ascertain the 'actual conduct of undertakings on the market'.[31]

Regarding the term 'undertaking', the *fictio iuris* that an 'undertaking' is a 'single economic entity' composed of different legal entities was intended from the outset to establish a common concept in Europe with reference to the addressees of the Treaty's competition rules. This approach ensured, *inter alia*, that the laws of the various Member States would not prevent or otherwise interfere with the application of the prohibitions.[32]

As seen from the foregoing discussion, the *AEG Telefunken* presumption is a consequence of the legal concept of an 'undertaking', and the *fictio iuris* of a 'single economic entity' is designed in light of the need for effective enforcement of EU competition law. In particular, the presumption ensures, in first place, that the parent company cannot exploit the legal autonomy of its wholly-owned subsidiary to (secretly) delegate to the subsidiary the concrete execution of the antitrust violation. If that tactic had been permitted, the penalty for the anticompetitive behaviour would have been calculated within the limits of 10 per cent of the turnover of the subsidiary, rather than 10 per cent of the turnover of the parent. That, in turn, would have limited or even neutralized the effectiveness of the competition rules.

The *AEG Telefunken* presumption also has an impact on the Commission's fining policy: by amplifying the possible magnitude of the fine as just described, the Commission can ensure the maximum deterrent effect of its decision establishing the infringement. In this regard, joint and several liability plays an important role, as it constitutes an additional legal device available to the Commission to strengthen the effectiveness

[30] See, for example, Case 26/62 *NV Algemene Transport en Expeditie Onderneming van Gend en Loos v Netherlands Inland Revenue Administration* [1963] ECR 1, 3 (English special edition); Case 6/64 *Flaminio Costa v ENEL*, [1964] ECR 1129; Case 106/77 *Amministrazione delle Finanze dello Stato v SpA Simmenthal* [1978] ECR 629; Case 28/67 *Molkerei – Zentrale Westfalen/Lippe GmbH v Hauptzollamt Paderborn* [1968] ECR 192; Joined Cases C-6/90 and C-9/90 *Andrea Francovich and Danila Bonifaci v Italy* [1991] ECR I-5357.

[31] Opinion of Advocate General Kokott in *Schindler*, cited above, note 3, para 66.

[32] See also Case 49/71 *Hagen OGH v Einfuhr- und Vorratsstelle für Getreide und Futtermittel* [1972] ECR 23, para 6.

of its enforcement actions. In particular, it reduces for the Commission, as creditor of the 'debt' that arises where such fines are imposed, the risk of insolvency and failure to collect the amount owed. In this way, joint and several liability promotes deterrence, a core objective of EU competition law.[33]

However, the ability of the ECJ to draw from a legal term (in this case, 'undertaking') autonomous concepts needed for the effectiveness of the competition rules is not without limits. For instance, as stated recently by the Court, the concept of joint and several liability for the payment of fines is not an autonomous concept in the EU legal system to be interpreted by reference to the objectives and system of competition law.[34] Consequently, the internal allocation of the debt for the payment of which the companies concerned are held jointly and severally liable is to be determined by applicable national law.[35]

THE *AEG TELEFUNKEN* PRESUMPTION AND THE PROTECTION OF FUNDAMENTAL RIGHTS

With regard to the Court's case law concerning the *AEG Telefunken* presumption and bearing in mind its limits, one cannot deny some aspects worthy of critique. The discussion here must begin with the most conspicuous feature of the presumption – namely, the fact that EU law (or rather, the jurisprudence of the Court) has deleted, with 'a stroke of the pen', certain traditional principles common within the Member States. Above all, it has in essence overridden the company-law principle of the separation of liability.[36]

By no coincidence, from 2011 onwards one observes, in the case law relating to the *AEG Telefunken* presumption,[37] that pleas and grounds of

---

[33] Judgment of the ECJ in *Siemens AG Österreich*, cited above, note 3, para 59.

[34] Ibid., para 67.

[35] Ibid., para 61.

[36] Opinion of Advocate General Kokott in *Schindler*, cited above, note 3, para 64.

[37] The most recent cases represent a third significant phase in the development of the jurisprudence concerning the presumption. In an initial phase, the Court limited itself to defining the content of the presumption in the *AEG Telefunken* judgment (see *AEG-Telefunken*, cited above, note 19). Later, in the *Stora* judgment (above, note 3), the Court elaborated the nature of the rebuttable presumption. Then, in a second phase, the Court was asked to clarify the obligations of the Commission regarding the presumption. In *Bollorè* (above,

appeals alleging the breach of fundamental rights are being raised regularly. These arguments have been submitted specifically with reference to decisions after 2005, when the Commission began systematically to exploit the *AEG Telefunken* presumption and when fine levels increased significantly.

Already in *General Quimica* (January 2011), the Court stated that the *AEG Telefunken* presumption, 'given its rebuttable nature, [...] does not lead to the automatic attribution of liability to the parent company holding 100 per cent of the capital of its subsidiary, [as this] would be contrary to the principle of personal responsibility on which EU competition law is based'.[38] In this way, and for the first time, reference to general principles of Union law, including the protection of fundamental rights (specifically, the principle of personal responsibility) is made in the reasoning of the Court. Keeping this in mind, the Court in that case annulled the judgment of the General Court, although it then dismissed the original appeal on other grounds.

However, it was in the *Elf Aquitaine* judgment (September 2011)[39] – two days after the *Menarini* case was handed down – that the lawfulness of the *AEG Telefunken* presumption was challenged on fundamental rights grounds. In *Elf Aquitaine*, it was argued that the *AEG Telekunken* presumption violated Article 6 ECHR, partly as a result of the 'institutional amalgamation of powers within the prosecuting authority' (para 42), in other words, in light of the above-mentioned 'conflict of interest' arising from the Commission's divided 'soul' as prosecutor and judge. In this case, other grounds for appeal related to principles protected by fundamental rights were also submitted. However, the Court considered those grounds to be raised for the first time on appeal, and thus inadmissible. This showed, on the other hand, that in the time between

---

note 3), the General Court had changed the structure of the presumption and claimed that, in order for the presumption to apply, the Commission had to prove not only that the parent had the capacity to exert decisive influence on the subsidiary but also that decisive influence had in fact been exercised. Moreover, both Advocate General Mischo in *Stora* (Opinion of 18 May 2000) and the Advocate General Bot in *Arcelor Mittal*, cited above, note 3 (Opinion of 26 October 2010) had raised criticisms regarding the presumption. The question was then resolved by the Court in its judgment in *Akzo Nobel* (above, note 3), where it clarified that, for the Commission to meet its burden of proof, it must demonstrate that the parent company holds a 100 per cent shareholding in the subsidiary (an approach also suggested by Advocate General Kokott in her Opinion of 23 April 2009 in the same case).

[38] Judgment of the ECJ in *General Química*, cited above, note 3, para 52.

[39] *Elf Aquitaine*, cited above, note 3.

the action for annulment and the appeal, the debate regarding the relationship between antitrust law and fundamental rights had led lawyers to formulate new grounds of illegality not initially identified.

In *Elf Aquitaine*, the Court resolved the issue of the legality of the *AEG Telefunken* presumption, explaining that the aim of the ground of appeal was not to secure a declaration that the presumption was unlawful as such. The objective of the parties, as construed by the Court, was to challenge the interpretation of the presumption on the ground that it violated the principle of the presumption of innocence.[40] The Court then invoked not only its own previous case law but also the jurisprudence of the ECtHR.[41] Concretely, the Court, dismissing the plea of illegality, held that 'a presumption, even where it is difficult to rebut, remains within acceptable limits so long as it is proportionate to the legitimate aim pursued, [and so long as] it is possible to adduce evidence to the contrary and the rights of the defence are safeguarded'.[42] As the Court explained, the presumption and its limits seek to strike a balance between different objectives. On the one hand, the presumption is justified by 'the objective of combating conduct contrary to the competition rules, in particular [...] Article 101 TFEU, and of preventing a repetition of such conduct'.[43] On the other hand, the Court acknowledges 'the importance of the requirements flowing from certain general principles of EU law such as the principle of the presumption of innocence, the principle that penalties should be applied solely to the offender, the principle of legal certainty and the principle of the rights of the defence, including the principle of equality of arms'.[44] It is 'for that reason, among others, that [...] the presumption is rebuttable'.[45] Moreover, in the Court's view, the 'presumption is based on the fact that, save in quite exceptional circumstances, a company holding all the capital of a subsidiary can, by dint of that shareholding alone, exercise decisive influence over that subsidiary's conduct'.[46] The need for such a presumption derives from the fact that 'it is within the sphere of operations of those entities against whom the presumption operates that evidence of the lack of actual exercise of that power to influence is generally apt to be found'.[47]

---

40 Ibid., para 52.
41 Ibid., para 62.
42 Ibid.
43 Ibid., para 59.
44 Ibid.
45 Ibid.
46 Ibid., para 60.
47 Ibid.

Up to that point in the *Elf Aquitaine* judgment, the plea asserting the illegality of the *AEG Telefunken* presumption for breach of fundamental rights seems *prima facie* destined to fail. However, the influence of that plea is revealed later in the judgment when the Court discusses the issue of the adequacy of the Commission's reasoning in rejecting the elements in fact and in law submitted by the parent company in order to rebut the presumption. As the Court states in this context, when 'a decision taken in application of the EU competition law rules relates to several addressees and raises a problem with regard to the imputability of the infringement, it must include an adequate statement of reasons with respect to each of its addressees, in particular those of them who, according to the decision, must bear the liability for the infringement' (emphasis added).[48] Referring expressly to the *AEG Telefunken* presumption, the Court adds that, 'as regards, more specifically, a Commission decision which relies exclusively, with respect to certain addressees, on the presumption that they actually exercised decisive influence, the Commission is in any event required – *if it is not to render that presumption in reality irrebuttable* – to explain adequately to those addressees the reasons why the elements of fact and of law put forward did not suffice to rebut that presumption' (emphasis added).[49] In this way, the importance of the arguments relating to the protection of fundamental rights is clearly shown. In effect, they compel the Commission to provide adequate reasons for the maintenance of the presumption, in line with the protection of fundamental rights.

The importance of the position taken by the Court in *Elf Aquitaine* is apparent in the subsequent European case law. Indeed, in the wake of that judgment, the Court has annulled a number of decisions, particularly in view of the lack of reasoning of both the Commission and the General

[48] Ibid., para 152.

[49] The Court then concludes: 'For example, owing to the formulation of recital 258, it appears very difficult – impossible even – to ascertain in particular whether the body of indicia submitted by Elf Aquitaine in an attempt to rebut the presumption applied to it by the Commission was rejected because it failed to convince or because, in the Commission's eyes, the mere fact that Elf Aquitaine held 98 per cent of Atofina's capital was sufficient for liability for Atofina's actions to be imputed to it, whatever the indicia that might have been provided by Elf Aquitaine in response to the statement of objections'. (para 168)

Court in relation to the information submitted by the parent companies in order to rebut the presumption.[50]

The plea of illegality of the *AEG Telefunken* presumption on the ground of an alleged breach of Article 6 ECHR was later presented to the Court in the *Schindler*[51] and *FLSmidth* cases.[52] In both judgments, the plea on this point was rejected.

CONCLUSIONS

The increasingly frequent reference to the protection of fundamental rights in the application of EU antitrust law is a trend that has grown significantly in parallel with the reforms brought about by Regulation 1/2003. The application of fundamental rights to antitrust law – unknown to this extent in the antitrust law experience of the United States – is due to three main reasons. The first factor is the significant increase in the level of penalties imposed by the Commission for violations of antitrust law as a consequence, *inter alia*, of the innovations contained in its Guidelines on the matter. The second factor relates to the Commission's nature as a 'supranational/independent' authority, and to its conflicted 'soul' as both 'prosecutor' and 'judge'. The increase in the level of fines

---

[50] See *L'Air liquide*, cited above, note 3; judgment of the CFI in *Koninklijke*, cited above, note 3; *Edison SpA*, cited above, note 3; judgment of the GC in *Gosselin Group NV*, cited above, note 3.

[51] Judgment of the ECJ in *Schindler*, cited above, note 3. In *Schindler*, as in the case of *Elf Aquitaine*, and unsurprisingly, Schindler's first ground of appeal related to the radical illegality of the Commission's decision for breach of Article 6 ECHR in view of the Commission's combined roles (those of prosecutor and judge). At para 24 of the judgment, the Court writes: 'The appellants contest the General Court's response to the plea concerning infringement of Article 6 of the ECHR, by which they contended that the Commission's procedure infringes the principle of the separation of powers and does not comply with the principles of the rule of law that are applicable to criminal procedures under that provision'. Later, the Court held this contention to be unfounded, recalling the *Menarini* judgment verbatim (paras 30–38). Regarding the plea of illegality of the *AEG Telefunken* presumption for violation of Article 6 ECHR, the Court expressly referred to the reasoning of *Elf Aquitaine* (paras 107–110).

[52] *FLSmidth & Co. A/S v Commission*, cited above, note 3. In this case, the Court answered succinctly in order to clarify that the issue was to be considered as settled. As the Court stated, 'it should be pointed out that that presumption results from settled case-law [...] and that it does not in any way infringe the rights conferred by Article 48 of the Charter and Article 6(2) of the ECHR' (para 25).

has made even more clear (once again) certain critical aspects of the European antitrust enforcement system. On closer inspection, the Commission as early as the 1980s sought to mitigate this issue (especially with reference to the protection of procedural rights) through the establishment of the Hearing Officer. The third relevant factor is the introduction of Article 6(2) TEU, as amended by the Lisbon Treaty, and the related binding nature of the EUCFR. With these reinforced foundations, greater importance and attention are now being given to the control of violations, by the Commission, of the rights protected by the Charter and by the ECHR.

The importance of this trend is evident in the development of the application of the *AEG Telefunken* presumption. The presumption is based on the concept of an 'undertaking' in EU competition law, and it reflects the principle of the independence of the EU legal system. The *AEG Telefunken* presumption, as well as the term 'undertaking', were both devised in order to ensure the effective application of EU competition law. The relevant consequence of the *AEG Telefunken* presumption is that a parent company, distinct from the wholly-owned subsidiary that violated antitrust, may be penalized by a fine of up to 10 per cent of its worldwide turnover for the behaviour of its subsidiary merely on the presumption that the parent and the subsidiary constitute a single economic entity, in other words, a single undertaking pursuant to Articles 101 and 102 TFEU.

The ECJ has recently confirmed the lawfulness of that presumption even under the ECHR. However, the grounds of review regarding the protection of fundamental rights have produced positive consequences for companies that have claimed this violation, especially as regards the adequacy of the Commission's reasoning. Indeed, as seen in the foregoing analysis, pleas based on the protection of fundamental rights have in effect compelled the Commission to observe a higher standard of reasoning in its decisions. This is true in particular with reference to its reasoning when it rejects elements of fact and law presented by parent companies in order to rebut the *AEG Telefunken* presumption. The fact that the Court perceives a risk, where the reasoning of the Commission or the General Court is inadequate, that the *AEG Telefunken* presumption might be transformed into a principle of strict liability – contrary to the principle of presumed innocence – is telling. It shows the importance that the Court attaches to fundamental rights, including in the form of general principles of EU law, and the check they impose on the principle of the effectiveness of EU competition law.

In this sense, the respect for principles of fundamental rights in the application of EU antitrust law may be seen as an increasingly important constraint that can rectify (to the extent possible) a conflict of interest from which the Commission cannot free itself, given the current design of the European antitrust enforcement system.

7. Judicial assessment of anticompetitive behaviour in Italy

Francesco Munari*

ABSTRACT

The central role of the Italian Competition Authority (AGCM) in the Italian competition law enforcement system, together with the civil law tradition, with no discovery mechanism and with structural difficulties in dealing with complex factual issues, has left a quite marginal role for national courts in adjudicating antitrust cases. Moreover, the attitude of the courts has proved to be unsatisfactory due to the excessive deference given to the AGCM. The decisions of the AGCM are subject merely to limited judicial scrutiny, especially in the field of 'technical discretion'. As this chapter shows, the provisions of the EU Damages Directive, including in particular Article 9 thereof, may in fact exacerbate the problem, inter alia, by making it even more difficult to secure meaningful review of ACGM decisions. The chapter also provides a critique of Article 21-bis of legge 287/1990, which empowers the AGCM to challenge the acts of other Italian administrative authorities that are contrary to competition rules. It is suggested that this provision is a significant but not unproblematic tool both in the context of the Italian constitutional system, where it gives rise to sensitive litigation within the public sphere, and in the context of the decentralized system of EU (competition) law enforcement, with which the supervisory power it confers upon the AGCM risks to overlap.

* Professor of EU Law at the University of Genoa. Founding partner of Munari Giudici Maniglio Panfili & Associati, Genoa.

INTRODUCTION

In the Italian legal system, the judicial assessment of anticompetitive behaviours is entrusted to both civil and administrative courts, first of all in the field of private antitrust enforcement and, where challenges are brought against decisions adopted by our national competition authority – the Autorità Garante della Concorrenza e del Mercato (hereinafter, the AGCM) – under the public enforcement of antitrust rules.

These different types of courts apply identical provisions, in other words, Articles 101 and 102 TFEU as well as Articles 2 and 3 of *legge* 287/1990[1] (the Italian antitrust statute), the latter being fully modelled after the EU competition rules.

However, the application of these provisions by civil and administrative courts is not identical. There is a reason for this: although they pursue the same goal of combating anticompetitive conduct, private and public enforcement have different scope and purposes, and this is reflected at the judicial level. In particular, administrative courts intervene as review judges scrutinizing the activities of the AGCM; civil courts adjudicate issues bearing on rights, such as, for example, the issue of whether a party to an agreement limiting competition has a right to enforce the agreement, or to oppose enforcement, as the case may be; or whether the behaviour of a dominant firm is compatible with the competition rules or whether it has infringed the rights of third parties; or whether persons that have suffered harm as a result of anticompetitive conduct have a right to claim compensation or damages.

Along these lines, a 'natural' complementarity between Italian civil and administrative courts has developed, yet not without inconsistencies.

In addition, a third kind of judicial assessment in the Italian legal system has recently been introduced at statutory level which is linked to the attribution of a new power to the AGCM to challenge, before the competent administrative courts, any act adopted by (other) public bodies which in its view restricts competition.

The following sections briefly examine the main problems characterizing these different types of judicial assessments.

---

[1] [1990] GURI [*Gazzetta Ufficiale della Repubblica Italiana* – Italian OJ] 240.

CIVIL COURTS AND COMPETITION RULES

The 'Direct Effect' of Articles 101 and 102 TFEU and the Consequences for National Courts

Before the enactment of the Italian antitrust statute, there was no issue of public versus private antitrust enforcement: our legal system did not have a competition authority; it did not provide for any domestic antitrust provisions; and the (timid) application of competition rules was reserved to national civil courts. In *BRT v SABAM*,[2] the European Court of Justice (ECJ) established that Articles 101 and 102 TFEU (then Articles 85 and 86EEC) had direct effect. Thus, the task of an Italian civil court with regard to the application of the Community competition rules was the ordinary one, in other words, it was obliged to ascertain whether in a given situation those rules conferred rights to individuals or firms that the court had to safeguard.

There was an obstacle to exempting 'pro-competitive' agreements caught by Article 85(1) EEC because of the exclusive powers entrusted to this end to the European Commission by Article 9 of Regulation 17/62/EEC;[3] however, this exclusive authority to grant exemptions was not a material hindrance for national courts given the existing block exemption regulations – in those years numerous – and given the simplified notification procedure to the Commission of those allegedly 'pro-competitive' agreements that did not fall directly within the scope of a block exemption.

With the adoption of Council Regulation 1/2003,[4] the Commission's 'monopoly' on the application of Article 101 TFEU (then Article 81 EC) was removed. National courts were – and are – subject to modest constraints in the interpretation and application of the EU competition rules within the cooperation schemes between them and the Commission established by Article 16(1) of Regulation 1/2003 and in light of the duty to guarantee the uniform application of competition rules. But again, this was not then, nor is it today of any consequence; in any case, it was not, nor is, specific to the Italian legal system.

---

[2] See Case 127/73 *Belgische Radio en Televisie and Société Belge des Auteurs, Compositeurs et Editeurs v SV SABAM and NV Fonior (BRT I)* [1974] ECR 51.

[3] Council Regulation 17 of 6 February 1962, First Regulation implementing Articles 81 and 82(4) of the Treaty [1962] OJ 13/204.

[4] Council Regulation (EC) 1/2003 on the implementation of the rules on competition laid down in Articles 81 and 82 of the Treaty [2003] OJ L1/1.

The Enactment of the Italian Antitrust Statute and Its Effects on Civil Courts

When *legge* 287/1990 was adopted, the Italian legislator copied our domestic antitrust provisions from the corresponding rules of the EEC Treaty. For purposes of this chapter it is worth noting that private antitrust enforcement was contemplated in Article 33(2) of this *legge*, and civil courts[5] were given the powers to assess the invalidity of agreements restricting competition, to adjudicate damages claims and to adopt all relevant interim relief measures.

Much more significant, however, was the introduction of public antitrust enforcement in our legal system. This boosted the public application of competition rules, but not private enforcement.

Indeed, putting aside some pioneering interim relief granted by civil courts using their new statutory powers established by the above-mentioned Article 33(2),[6] the entry into force of the Italian antitrust

---

[5] For a long time, only the courts of appeal; Article 2.2 of *decreto-legge* 1/2012 [2012] GURI 19, SU [Ordinary Supplement] 18 (converted with amendments by *legge* 27/2012 GURI 71, SU 53) eventually entrusted this power to the more recently established 'commercial courts' (*tribunali delle imprese*). Apart from their other features, the above measures eliminated substantial inconsistencies stemming from the fact that the EU competition rules could be – and had to be – applied by tribunals because of their direct effect, but these tribunals were prevented from applying the identical domestic provisions in those antitrust cases falling outside the scope of application of Articles 101 or 102 TFEU.

[6] See, for example, Corte d'Appello Milano [2005] *Tele 2 Italia v Telecom Italia*, *Giurisprudenza Commerciale* [2007] 1062; Corte d'Appello Milano [2005] *Petrone Farmacie v Pfizer Italia*, *Foro Italiano* [2005] 1886; Corte d'Appello di Roma [2003] *Albacom v Telecom Italia*, *Foro Italiano* [2003] 2474; Corte d'Appello Milano [1999] *Inaz Paghe v Consiglio Nazionale Ordine Consulenti Lavoro*, *Diritto Industriale* [1999] 338; Corte d'Appello Milano [1998] *Tramaplast v Macplast*, *Foro Italiano* [1999] 831; Corte d'Appello Milano, 27.9.1994, *Telesystem v SIP*, unpublished; Corte d'Appello Roma [1995] *Omnitel Pronto Italia v Telecom Italia*, *Foro Amm.* [1995] 2099. On this kind of action, see more generally Corte d'Appello Milano [2010] *Conto TV v Sky*, *Foro Italiano* [2010] 1298; Corte d'Appello Milano [2006] *Fastweb v Telecom Italia*, *Giurisprudenza Italiana* [2007] 919; Corte d'Appello Milano 10.1.2006, *Exergia v Trans Tunisian Pipeline Company Limited*, unpublished; Corte d'Appello Milano [2005] *Alice v Auditel*, *Foro Italiano* [2005] 2155; Corte d'Appello Milano [2004] *Autogrill v Moto*, *Giurisprudenza Commerciale* [2006] 448; Corte d'Appello Milano [2003] *Gemeaz Cusin v SCM*, *Diritto Industriale* [2003] 537; Tribunale Roma [2003] *Juventus v Tim Telecom*, *Giurisprudenza Romana* [2003] 222; Corte d'Appello Torino [2000] *Pagine Italia v Telecom Italia*, *Corriere Giuridico* [2001] 371; Tribunale Milano [2000], *Europa Tv v Soc. Napoli Calcio*,

regime was far from being a watershed as regards the application of competition rules by Italian courts.

On the contrary, the statutory provision entrusting civil courts with the (only) power to ascertain the invalidity of anticompetitive agreements,[7] adjudicate claims for damages and adopt interim relief implicitly functioned as a tool to push private enforcement to the sidelines; the task of developing a domestic legal system ensuring that competition in the market is not distorted was fully assumed by the AGCM, and the courts were left with a sort of ancillary role: that of assessing damages claims arising out of anticompetitive conduct, mostly in follow-on cases.

Italian Courts and Antitrust: Is There An Intrinsic Judicial Self-restraint in Applying Competition Rules?

An assessment of whether or not this limited role for the civil courts was or is a desirable development of Italian competition law falls beyond the scope of this chapter. It is, however, a fact: after more than 40 years since the ECJ's declaration concerning the direct effect of Articles 85 and 86 EEC (in other words, Articles 101 and 102 TFEU), and after almost 25 years since the entry into force of the Italian antitrust statute, there is no landmark judgment by the Italian civil courts on competition law. There

---

Contratti [2001] 127; Corte d'Appello Torino [2000] *Ass. Car v ASI Automoto-club Storico Torino*, *Diritto Industriale* [2002] 276; Corte d'Appello Ancona [1999] *Filco v Lavazza*, *Foro Padano* [2000] 189; Corte d'Appello Catanzaro [1998] *Ierullo v Enel*, *Foro Italiano* [1999] 2359; Tribunale Napoli [1998] *Espresso Uno Più v Lavazza*, *Gius* [1998] 3077; Tribunale Modena [1997] *Panini v DS*, *Diritto Industriale* [1997] 1047; Corte d'Appello Milano [1995], *Sanguinetti v Ania*, *Diritto Industriale* [1996] 304; Corte d'Appello Torino [1995], *Alitalia v Sagat*, *Giurisprudenza Italiana* [1996] 288; Corte d'Appello Roma [1993], *Cms Europa v Enel*, *Rassegna Giuridica Energia Elettrica* [1994] 718; Corte d'Appello Roma [1993], *Gruppo Sicurezza v Aeroporti Roma*, *Foro Italiano* [1993] 3377. (Where reference is made to unpublished decisions by Italian courts, the date and case number will be indicated.)

[7] To be precise, the power established by Article 33(2) of *legge* 287/1990 concerning the assessment of the invalidity of agreements restricting competition refers, in my view, (a) not only to restrictive agreements, but also (b) to downstream contracts that result from restrictive agreements as well as (c) to contracts concluded between a dominant firm and a client/supplier when their content is the result of the abuse of the former's dominant position. However, to my knowledge, Italian case law is very limited concerning this specific provision, and with limited exceptions the cases mainly refer to the first (and the second) type of case described above.

is no civil court precedent capable of guiding the AGCM in its interpretation and application of the antitrust provisions. And there is very little 'grand litigation' between large firms before an Italian civil court in an antitrust matter. We do have important cases, some of which will be considered below; but they concern procedural, not substantive issues. And they are normally linked to public, not private enforcement.

Must we conclude that there is something wrong with Italian civil courts and their role in the field of antitrust?

I have been always persuaded that the limited role of these courts was sound, and that it could not be different.

This belief of mine is based on the following reasons. First, the procedural rules governing litigation in our legal system (as well as in many other civil law systems) are not appropriate for adjudicating antitrust cases, in particular due to lack of discovery and due to the complexity of the factual issues in antitrust disputes. In other words, the problem with private antitrust enforcement in Italy was not, and is not, a problem of applying the substantive competition rules, whether Italian or European; and it was not, and is not, connected with any hypothetical inability of our judges to deal with antitrust reasoning.[8]

Another reason has to do with the efficiency of the AGCM. Over the years, this authority has been capable *de facto* of 'monopolizing' antitrust enforcement: whenever anticompetitive behaviours are perceived in the market, aggrieved parties bring the matter immediately to the attention of the AGCM; this avenue of public enforcement is their 'natural' safeguard to remove any alleged restrictions of competition. Furthermore, this solution has been quite effective, since the AGCM enjoys investigative powers that reach much further than those of a court, and since its staff includes skilled professionals who discharge their duties in the interest of the complainant. This mode of enforcement also relieves the complainant from costly proceedings, and in particular from the risk of paying the legal fees of the defendant(s) if its action is rejected by a court.

We should therefore conclude that civil courts enjoy full jurisdiction to apply EU and Italian antitrust rules, and hence full jurisdiction to examine relevant facts, assess potential anticompetitive behaviour, declare null and void agreements restricting competition and adjudicate claims for damages. But if they entertain fewer cases than one would

---

[8] On the contrary, I would consider it very strange if a court, and certainly an Italian court, declared itself 'unable' to apply legal provisions and instead delegated this activity to an administrative body, like the AGCM. A court will – and above all is bound to – discharge its duty to interpret and enforce the law, based on facts presented to it.

expect, the ultimate reason is that public antitrust enforcement is more efficient from several viewpoints. I will return later in this chapter to issues concerning the full capability of courts to assess antitrust issues.

Needless to say, damages claims cannot be addressed by the AGCM, as they are reserved to civil courts. This explains why, over the years, civil courts have gradually focused their activity on this sort of private enforcement.

The private enforcement deficit, and the correspondingly abundant reliance on agency enforcement, is not unique to Italy: the most striking evidence of the widespread nature of the problem throughout the EU is the new Directive on certain rules governing actions for damages under national law for infringements of the competition law provisions of the Member States and of the EU (the 'Damages Directive').[9] After several attempts to enhance private antitrust enforcement,[10] the Commission has finally realized that the decentralized application of competition rules works efficiently with strong decentralized public enforcement and an improved role of courts in adjudicating damages claims.

While more extensive commentary on this new Directive is provided in another chapter of this book and goes beyond the scope of the discussion here, I wish to underline that this piece of legislation – which aims at introducing 'special' procedural rules within private antitrust proceedings before domestic courts – does raise systemic problems which Member States will have to deal with very carefully when transposing the Directive in their national legislation. Some of these problems are briefly highlighted below.

---

[9] As of this writing, the Directive has not been published in the Official Journal. The available text is the one adopted by the European Parliament in accordance with the ordinary legislative procedure. However, the text of the Directive is final, as reported by the Commission on its website.

[10] See in particular the White Paper of 2 April 2008 on Damages Actions for Breach of the EC antitrust rules, COM(2008) 165, and the Green Paper of 19 December 2005, on Damages actions for breach of the EC antitrust rules, COM(2005) 672. See also Commission Notice on the cooperation between the Commission and the courts of the EU Member States in the application of Articles 81 and 82 EC [2004] OJ C101/54, and its predecessor, Commission Notice on cooperation between national courts and the Commission in applying Articles 85 and 86 of the EEC Treaty [1993] OJ C39/6.

Actions for Damages: Italian Case Law and the EU Damages Directive

As noted earlier, civil courts in Italy deal with antitrust matters particularly when hearing claims for damages, and almost invariably these are follow-on cases.

Consequently, it goes without saying that a paramount role for adjudicating such claims is the ascertainment of liability on the part of the defendant(s). In a follow-on case, this task has already been discharged by the AGCM (or, less frequently, by the European Commission). Yet, since the AGCM is not a court but an administrative authority, there is a need for guarantees that no flaws have blemished the conduct of the administrative investigation and decision. Such flaws would also tend to taint the follow-on case heard by the court.

The Italian case law has dealt with this topic, and our Supreme Court (the Corte di Cassazione) has declared that facts ascertained by the AGCM can be used as 'privileged evidence' before national courts.[11] Thus, in a follow-on case, the defendant may demonstrate, for instance, that certain conduct *vis-à-vis* a customer is not the direct consequence of, say, a cartel whose existence has been verified by the national competition authority (NCA); however, in order to overcome the privileged evidence principle referred to above, the defendant must bring before the court the specific reasons for the adoption of the contested behaviour, which obviously must be reasons distinct and independent from the implementation of the cartel.

I feel nevertheless obliged to stress that the national court should always ascertain how the evidence has been obtained and treated by the AGCM, and whether the rights of the defendant(s) have been safeguarded in the acquisition and handling of this evidence. After all, and with all due respect, I do not believe that the AGCM is really an 'impartial' institution in respect of the application of Articles 101 and 102 TFEU (or Articles 2 and 3 of *legge* 287/1990), since its mission is to prosecute antitrust infringements. Indeed, if this were not the case, then there might not be any need for judicial review of the AGCM's decisions by the Italian administrative courts.

The outcome of any AGCM decision, if it is used in follow-on actions, should therefore be closely scrutinized by the competent civil court, not only as regards the merits but also with respect to procedural rights. Only

---

[11] See, *inter alia*, Corte di Cassazione [2011] *Allianz S.p.A. v Palladino*, *Foro Italiano* [2011] 2674.

if these principles are observed will the rights of aggrieved parties to claim and obtain damages caused by antitrust infringements be properly enforced.

If courts do not apply these strict principles, I believe that uncritical trust in an AGCM decision may not be in line with our constitutional rules and our principles of civil procedure. This is all the more true when the competition infringement found by the authority stems from leniency applications, where in fact the evidence is brought before the AGCM by a competitor of the undertaking that becomes the defendant in a follow-on case, in other words, a person that has a direct interest in harming that undertaking.

However, the Damages Directive has introduced important novelties, providing that 'an infringement of competition law found by a final decision of a national competition authority or a review court is deemed to be irrefutably established for the purposes of an action for damages brought before their national courts'.[12]

The Directive thus seems to have taken an even stronger stance as regards the binding effect of a NCA decision on national courts, as although the infringement decision may have been reviewed by a competent review court (in Italy, this would be an administrative court).

I am not very sympathetic to this choice, unless: (a) the strict criteria described above for the judicial assessment of all relevant procedural and substantial issues in the AGCM decision are fully considered by the court that is called on to adjudicate damages in a follow-on action; and (b) the quality of the judicial review by the administrative courts of the NCA's decisions is improved according to criteria I propose below.[13]

Less problematic is the way the Damages Directive treats decisions adopted by an NCA of a Member State other than that where the follow-on action takes place: in this transnational scenario, the infringement decision constitutes 'at least *prima facie* evidence that an infringement of competition law has occurred and, as appropriate, may be assessed along with any other material brought by the parties' (Article 9(2) of the Directive). The foreign decision thus amounts to a factual circumstance that does not prevent the court from considering any other factual (or legal) issue submitted by the parties to the proceedings. Nonetheless, even in this case the civil court should carry out a thorough assessment concerning the way in which the foreign NCA has rendered its decision, and in particular to determine whether this *prima facie*

12 Article 9(1) of the Directive.

13 See below.

evidence is consistent with the Italian rules on the taking of evidence, with the principle of equality of arms and with the rights of defence.

The Damages Directive, however, goes further in trying to help national courts to decide claims for damages resulting from anti-competitive conduct. More precisely, it introduces special discovery rules that amplify the powers of the courts to obtain evidence, with a view to removing one of the major obstacles to private antitrust enforcement.[14] As recalled earlier,[15] one of the reasons why civil court activity in combating restrictions of competition have lagged behind is that the procedural tools available to courts have been inadequate. This attempt to introduce special rules on evidence is remarkable, and it will potentially endow the courts with 'superpowers'; but it also raises fundamental questions on a systemic level. In particular, the infringement of antitrust provisions is a tortious act: it belongs to a genus of illicit acts that are quite widespread in any legal system. This genus comprises innumerable unlawful acts that potentially cause harm to third parties and a corresponding right to claim damages for such harm.

From the European perspective of the decentralized application of competition rules, it is understandable that the legislator may wish to have a homogeneous regime for damages arising from anticompetitive behaviour. However, from the general perspective of the national legal order, all tortious acts should be addressed, and all tort victims should be protected by an adequate damages regime. The proposition that a court should have 'superpowers' to combat only one specific kind of tort cannot be persuasive. Indeed, the risk is that asymmetric procedural rules will create discrimination among tort victims. In the envisaged system, different procedural tools will be available depending on which kind of tort is at stake. That may not be so easily justifiable under constitutional principles of equality and the right of access to justice.

---

[14] The regime governing disclosure of evidence is established by Chapter II of the Directive (Articles 5 to 8). It encompasses a detailed series of provisions concerning the evidence to be obtained directly by the parties involved (in other words, mainly the defendant) in the proceedings before the court; evidence contained in case file of an NCA (including any leniency application or settlement submission, which however are not accessible); and the modalities for transferring this evidence to the file of the civil court, and the sanctions with which the court must be empowered to compel any non-compliant party. As stated above in the main text, an examination of the Directive is beyond the scope of this chapter.

[15] See above.

This is not to say that the policy underlying the rules on discovery contained in the Damages Directive is wrong. Rather, it is an invitation for the Italian legislator to consider the systemic impact of this Directive when transposing it into our national law, with a view either to: (a) considering this piece of legislation as an opportunity to establish homogeneous principles of discovery even beyond the scope of application of the directive; or (b) thoroughly justifying – if possible and if legitimate – this special regime *vis-à-vis* all other damages actions available in our legal system. Since a reform of our code of civil procedure is apparently under way, I believe this opportunity should not be missed.

Whatever the outcome will be, one thing seems certain: in the future, the judicial assessment of anticompetitive behaviour by Italian civil courts will avail itself of more effective tools. These tools will be the consequence of the quasi-binding effects for the court of final AGCM infringement decisions, and of the legal relevance that can be attached to the factual circumstances and evidence gathered in the course of public enforcement.

This prompts us to shift the focus of the analysis to the role of the courts that review the AGCM's decisions, and the way they assess or should assess anticompetitive behaviour, especially in light of the entry into force of the Damages Directive.

ASSESSMENT OF ANTITRUST ISSUES BY COURTS REVIEWING AGCM DECISIONS

The Long (and Unfinished) Task of Improving Judicial Review of AGCM Decisions by Italian Administrative Courts

It took some years for the administrative courts to realize the specific roles they enjoyed when reviewing decisions adopted by the AGCM. In compliance with the 'classical' model of review of acts adopted by public administration bodies, the earlier judgments of the *Consiglio di Stato* were adamant in declaring that the review of an AGCM decision was to be limited to 'extrinsic' scrutiny, that is to say, a check on whether the reasoning underlying the AGCM decision was logical.[16] In this way, there

[16] See, *inter alia*, T.A.R. Lazio [2001] *Foro Amministrativo* [2001] 2490; Consiglio di Stato [2001] *Foro Amministrativo* [2001] 2089; Consiglio di Stato [2001] *Foro Amministrativo* [2001] 625; Consiglio di Stato [2000] *Foro Amministrativo* [2000] 933.

was no real assessment by these courts of the competition provisions. As a consequence, the administrative courts essentially left the AGCM with full power to decide antitrust cases.

Luckily enough, a few years later this extraordinary judicial self-restraint was reduced, and the administrative courts affirmed their power to scrutinize, without limitation, the AGCM's evaluations, 'in particular those having technical nature'.[17]

This development in the intensity of judicial review was clearly also influenced by the entry into force of Regulation 1/2003, the entrustment to the AGCM of the power to fully apply the EU antitrust provisions, and the consequent need to strive towards a uniform regime not only regarding the application of Articles 101 and 102 TFEU by the NCAs but also with regard to the judicial review of agency decisions.

In this vein, the Italian administrative courts have at least apparently moved towards the same lines of reasoning adopted by the ECJ and by the General Court when the latter courts review the Commission's decisions in antitrust cases.[18]

Among the abundant Italian case law on this matter, it is worth noting a recent judgment of the *Consiglio di Stato*, which specifies that, even in the:

> 'assessment of complex facts corresponding to "indeterminate legal notions" [...] or "technical-scientific rules of uncertain nature", [the AGCM must] adopt a rigorous methodology and a coherent approach that cannot escape the checks and controls by the administrative court in their intrinsic development.

---

[17] See T.A.R. Lazio 14.4.2011, no 3252. 'Intrinsic' scrutiny was applied for the first time in Consiglio di Stato 9.4.1999, no. 601 (a case that did not deal with an AGCM decision) and was later employed in the field of antitrust. See, *inter alia*, Consiglio di Stato [2002] *Foro Amministrativo* C.d.S. [2002] 977; Consiglio di Stato [2002] *Foro Amministrativo* C.d.S. [2002] 2505; Consiglio di Stato [2004] *Foro Amministrativo* C.d.S. [2004] 890; Consiglio di Stato [2007] *Foro Amministrativo* C.d.S. [2007] 594; Consiglio di Stato 29.9.2009, no. 5864; Consiglio di Stato 16.9.2011, no. 5171 and 5172; T.A.R. Lazio 15.1.2013, no. 363; Consiglio di Stato 12.4.2013, no. 2002; Consiglio di Stato 21.5.2013, no. 2722.

[18] See, for example, Case C-12/03 P *Commission v Tetra Laval BV* [2005] ECR I-987 and the Opinion of Advocate General Tizzano in that case; Case C-289/11 *Legris Industries SA,* 3 May 2012, EU:C:2012:270; C-386/10 P *Chalkor AE Epexergasias Metallon v Commission* [2011] ECR I-13085; C-295/12 P *Telefónica SA and Telefónica de España SAU v Commission,* 10 July 2014, EU:C:2014:2062, and the Opinion of Advocate General Wathelet in that case. Similar principles have also been followed in the state aid sector. See, for example, Case C-525/04 P *Spain v Commission* [2007] ECR 9947.

This is in order to ensure that any technical discretionary evaluation does not become an arbitrary exercise of professional skills [...] [Indeed, even] those subject-matters characterized by substantial technical content are governed by rules and principles which, notwithstanding their capability of being evaluated under different ways, must nevertheless be rooted in an intrinsic logic and an intimate coherence which the AGCM must observe under sanction of an error which is challengeable as misuse of powers. [...] Therefore, the administrative court always has the power to assess whether the [AGCM] has made proper use of relevant technical rules and discretionary evaluations adopted to ascertain the existence or the discipline of complex facts, and to assess whether, in the concrete case, the application of these rules and facts underpinning the [AGCM] decision have occurred *iuxta propria principia*. This also implies the duty of the court to avail itself, if necessary, of expert witnesses.'[19]

Faced with these clear statements, one would be tempted to conclude that the long path towards a thorough assessment of antitrust provisions by the Italian administrative courts has been traversed, and that no boundaries prevent the courts from adjudicating relevant issues. This conclusion would also seem natural from a general legal point of view, and it is coherent with the approach that should apply in other fields (including, at least as a matter of principle, the field of private enforcement).

Not all decisions rendered by the Italian administrative courts as review courts exhibit the same attention to the evaluation of facts and technical matters that is given in the quoted language above.[20] Yet this is not the place to enter into a detailed analysis of specific judgments.

The Final (?) Principles of Law Expressed by the Corte di Cassazione Regarding Judicial Review of AGCM Decisions: The Issue of the Relevant Market

Notwithstanding the apparent trend described in the previous sub-section, however, it must be pointed out that this thorough assessment and full review is, in fact, not a true portrayal of the state of practice in Italy. Indeed, judicial self-restraint is still routinely exercised by the administrative courts; this is worth considering.

Reference here will be made in particular to the issue of the relevant market, which is a cornerstone notion in any antitrust assessment, and which nevertheless is still – as regards Italian judicial review – a 'hunting' area reserved to the AGCM.

---

19 Consiglio di Stato 2.4.2013, no. 1856 (free translation of the author).

20 See, for example, Consiglio di Stato 13.12.2011, no. 6525.

In a recent judgment of our Corte di Cassazione,[21] which will probably be a landmark case for the coming years, this issue was fully considered, as were the limits of judicial assessment by the administrative courts in antitrust matters. In this judgment, the *Corte* first restates the conclusions of the *Consiglio di Stato* recalled above, and then it specifies the judicial review power as follows: despite the fact that the court does not have jurisdiction to review the merits of the case, this does not imply that it is limited to scrutinizing the formal and legal aspects of the AGCM's decision. In particular, the review court has full jurisdiction to assess disputed factual circumstances when such disputed facts are relevant to verifying the legality of the AGCM's decision.[22]

That said, there may remain a sphere of evaluation reserved to the AGCM, which in our legal system is described as *discrezionalità tecnica*. This concept may be relevant where a court reviews certain technical evaluations made by the AGCM and challenged by the parties requesting annulment, if those evaluations inevitably call for a margin of appreciation.[23] The Corte di Cassazione does not affirm, in principle, that the court never has a possibility to scrutinize the choices of the authority in this context. Yet, since the AGCM is the agency entrusted with the enforcement of competition law, and since to this end it has been granted specific technical capabilities and tasks that are 'objective and neutral', the judicial assessment of its technical evaluations of complex and disputable issues, such as that of the relevant market, is limited. More precisely, the review court may only check 'whether the reasoning contained in the challenged decision is reasonable, logical and coherent, and – specifically as regards the definition of the relevant market – whether the margin of appreciation allowed to the AGCM has been

---

[21] Corte di Cassazione, Sez.Un. 20.1.2014, no. 1013.

[22] *«[L]a non estensione al merito del sindacato giurisdizionale sugli atti dell'Autorità Garante implica, certo, che il giudice non possa sostituire con un proprio provvedimento quello adottato da detta Autorità, ma non che il sindacato sia limitato ai profili giuridico-formali dell'atto amministrativo, restandone esclusa ogni eventuale verifica dei presupposti di fatto. La pienezza della tutela giurisdizionale necessariamente comporta che anche le eventuali contestazioni in punto di fatto debbano esser risolte dal giudice, quando da tali contestazioni dipenda la legittimità del provvedimento amministrativo che ha inciso su posizioni di diritto soggettivo.»*

[23] *«È su questo punto che occorre allora interrogarsi: se le valutazioni tecniche operate dall'Autorità Garante, al fine di conferire concreto significato e di dare attuazione al precetto legale, possano e debbano esser sindacate da parte del giudice amministrativo, in presenza di un'impugnazione sollevata dalla parte interessata, pur quando presentino un inevitabile margine di opinabilità.»*

surpassed. The court therefore cannot substitute its own assessment for that of the AGCM when the latter has decided within the above limits'.[24]

In the final analysis, the judicial review exercised by administrative courts in Italy is not unlimited, and it is incomplete. The courts do not enter into the merits of the case, and they leave the AGCM with substantial exclusive powers to assess technical questions virtually immune from scrutiny. In this regard it is relevant to note that the Corte di Cassazione has excluded the possibility of challenging the above-described limits on judicial review on the ground that they are unconstitutional.

The question of whether this position is satisfactory or not will be evaluated briefly in the next sub-section.

Some Tentative Remarks Regarding the Courts' Self-restraint

In the initial sections of this chapter it was highlighted that, as norms having direct effect, the EU competition rules are theoretically applied by civil courts like any other rule of law. In the case of review courts, limits are encountered in assessing the merits of a case differently from the way they were assessed in the AGCM's decision. This is rather logical and stems from the nature of the courts' jurisdiction to review such decisions. From this perspective, the position ultimately reached by the Corte di Cassazione leaves little room for further discussion.

However, I tend to believe that more systemic reflections are needed, especially in light of the entry into force of the Damages Directive. The problem lies with the fact that the definition of the relevant market is one of the most important preconditions for applying the competition rules.

---

24 Free translation of the author. The '*principio di diritto*' expressed by the Corte di Cassazione is the following: «*Il sindacato di legittimità del giudice amministrativo sui provvedimenti dell'Autorità Garante della Concorrenza e del Mercato comporta la verifica diretta dei fatti posti a fondamento del provvedimento impugnato e si estende anche ai profili tecnici, il cui esame sia necessario per giudicare della legittimità di tale provvedimento; ma quando in siffatti profili tecnici siano coinvolti valutazioni ed apprezzamenti che presentano un oggettivo margine di opinabilità – come nel caso della definizione di mercato rilevante nell'accertamento di intese restrittive della concorrenza – detto sindacato, oltre che in un controllo di ragionevolezza, logicità e coerenza della motivazione del provvedimento impugnato, è limitato alla verifica che quel medesimo provvedimento non abbia esorbitato dai margini di opinabilità sopra richiamati, non potendo il giudice sostituire il proprio apprezzamento a quello dell'Autorità Garante ove questa si sia mantenuta entro i suddetti margini.*»

This is true for cases involving restrictive agreements, and it is paramount in abuse of dominance cases. The idea that this cornerstone of antitrust enforcement cannot be reviewed by the courts leaves something to be desired, to say the least.

Like many other lawyers frequently involved in antitrust cases and disputes with the AGCM, I can testify that the definition of the relevant market for an antitrust lawyer is an exercise not unlike many other non-legal assessments that lawyers (and judges) are required to carry out. It is an evaluation of data and studies, which are normally disputed in the public enforcement stage between the AGCM and the interested firms (usually availing themselves of technical expert witnesses), where not infrequently the opinions diverge.

When this dispute comes before a review court, I personally find it odd that the court, which should be impartial *vis-à-vis* both of the litigators, in other words, the AGCM and the party challenging the infringement decision, relies on the 'technical' assessment made by the AGCM as if it were the 'technical expert witness' of the court itself.

It is true that the relevant market is not a 'fact' and is rather the result of the analysis of many facts, which implies knowledge of disciplines other than law. Nevertheless, I do not regard this as an insurmountable obstacle to sound and meaningful assessment by a court. After all, in the context of private antitrust enforcement, a civil court would be obliged to grapple with the issue of the proper definition of the market; and as noted earlier,[25] no one would question the legitimacy (and indeed mandatory nature) of this task.

If this kind of assessment is entrusted to civil courts, then the same should hold true for administrative courts. In this regard, I doubt that a different level of assessment should be accepted based on the nature of the jurisdiction exercised by civil and administrative courts. Furthermore, this doubt will grow stronger when Italian law, transposing the Damages Directive, endows the AGCM's infringement decision (as reviewed by an administrative court, but only to the extent allowed so far by the Corte di Cassazione – see above) with binding effects in civil damages cases. The same doubt emerges again in relation to the AGCM's power to challenge administrative acts under Article 21-*bis* of *legge* 287/1990, to which I return below.[26]

Before moving on, it may be noted that at European level, in reviewing Commission decisions in antitrust cases, the EU Courts have not been

---

25 See above.

26 See the next section.

prevented from analyzing whether the relevant market has been correctly defined by the Commission. Indeed, there are cases, some of them among the leading cases in competition law, where the Commission's analysis of the relevant market has been struck down without much ado.[27]

Hence, if public and private antitrust enforcement must go hand in hand, and if the assessment of antitrust issues by courts is to function as an overall coherent and consistent system, encompassing the EU and the domestic legal systems, a more refined reasoning with regard to the principles of judicial review is needed.

ADMINISTRATIVE COURTS AS REVIEW COURTS OF ADMINISTRATIVE ACTS ALLEGEDLY INFRINGING COMPETITION

The AGCM as Competition Watchdog of Italian Administrative Authorities …

In Italy, the possible scenarios of judicial assessment of anticompetitive behaviour have developed as a result of another piece of legislation, in other words, the relatively recently enacted Article 21-*bis* of *legge* 287/90. This provision empowers the AGCM to challenge before administrative courts any act, decree or regulation adopted by any administrative authority in Italy if the AGCM considers that the act in question infringes rules of competition law.

The purpose of this provision is to enhance the watchdog role of the AGCM, not only against undertakings but also *vis-à-vis* public bodies of administration, which are often seen as entities hampering the development of the competition culture in our legal and bureaucratic systems. For scholars with experience in EU law, this new power is reminiscent of the infringement procedure provided for by Article 258 TFEU and of the enforcement powers enjoyed by the Commission *vis-à-vis* the Member States – except that in the case of Article 21-*bis* this power is strictly limited to the violation of competition provisions. Whether it is right or wrong that the AGCM should be the 'controller' of all other Italian administrative authorities is a matter beyond the scope of this chapter, and will not be discussed here.

---

[27] See Case 6/72 *Europemballage Corporation and Continental Can Company Inc. v Commission* [1973] ECR 215, paras 31 et seq.; Case T-427/08 *Confédération Européenne des Associations d'horlogers-réparateurs (CEAHR) v Commission* [2010] ECR II-5865, paras 105 et seq.

Equally beyond the scope of this discussion is the debate about the nature of the power entrusted to the AGCM and of the 'interest' justifying its right to challenge other public authorities' acts, decrees or regulations. Indeed, it was debated whether this right to go to court in order to enforce a general improvement of competition was even consistent with the Italian Constitution. In any case, the legislative idea of pitting one administration against another is certainly a revolutionary step, and at most it should be used only as an extreme remedy, as it deviates from a general principle of law, specifically the loyal cooperation among public institutions. This should always be carefully considered by the AGCM before challenging an act of another authority.[28]

… or (Mere) *Amicus Curiae* for Administrative Courts? The Practical Implementation of Article 21-*bis* of *Legge* 287/90: Unresolved Issues

After some three years since the entry into force of Article 21-*bis* (as of this writing), the case practice seems to show that the AGCM has used this new power either to challenge before the courts general regimes that restrict competition on which its 'moral suasion' has gone unheeded by the relevant authorities,[29] or to strengthen – by means of an autonomous and parallel action – a claim already made by an individual before an administrative court against an act allegedly restricting competition. In this second scenario, what happens is *de facto* a joint action by the individual and the AGCM challenging the same act before the competent

[28] This view was likewise adopted in the first decision applying Article 21-*bis* of *legge* 287/90 (see T.A.R. Lazio, 15.3.2013, no. 2720). In that decision, the T.A.R. Lazio also excluded any conflict between this provision and the Italian Constitution.

[29] For the sake of precision it should be noted that Article 21-*bis* requires the AGCM first to address to the authority in question an opinion inviting the latter to remove the allegedly anticompetitive act; only if this is not done may the AGCM take the matter to court. This occurred, for example, in a case concerning the pricing regulation scheme adopted for road transport. This is a 'sickness' of our regime for hauliers that still affects Italian markets after 20 years. The claim by the AGCM was decided by the T.A.R. Lazio (cited previous note), and, in a preliminary reference from that court, the ECJ held that the Italian pricing regime for road transport, whereby prices must be maintained at a level at least equal to minimum operating costs – as determined by a body composed mainly of industry representatives – is incompatible with Article 101 TFEU read together with Article 4(3) TEU. See Joined Cases C-184/13 to C-187/13, C-194/13, C-195/13 and C-208/13 *API – Anonima Petroli Italiana SpA v Ministero delle Infrastrutture e dei Trasporti and Ministero dello Sviluppo Economico,* 4 September 2014, EU:C:2014:2147.

administrative court.[30] Needless to say, when this occurs the claim by the individual plaintiff is amplified by the AGCM, whose endorsement of the same view of the individual implies that the alleged breach of competition principles by the defendant public authority is considered particularly serious.

Whether this turns the AGCM into a sort of *amicus curiae* of the competent administrative court is not yet clear. However, this evolution in the implementation of Article 21-*bis* – with the AGCM supporting an individual claimant – was probably not the real intention of our legislator: if an administrative act infringes competition rules, in particular the EU competition rules, there is no need for our legal system to add Article 21-*bis* to the tools available to secure the removal of the act. Indeed, since the end of the 1960s, the ECJ has developed the fundamental mandatory principle of (what was then) Community law according to which Member States are prevented from introducing or maintaining any measure capable of depriving the competition rules of their *effet utile*.[31] And because national courts are obliged to cooperate in the enforcement of EU law, it goes without saying that any act, decree or regulation adopted by any public authority which can be challenged before an administrative court and which infringes EU competition law, can be, and should be, declared null and void.

---

[30] This occurred in a case decided by the T.A.R. Catania [2014], where the claim by the AGCM was however declared inadmissible for procedural reasons.

[31] See the landmark judgments in Case 14/68 *Walt Wilhelm and Others v Bundeskartellamt* [1969] ECR 1; Case 13/77 *SA G.B.-INNO-B.M. v Association des Détaillants en Tabac (ATAB)* [1977] ECR 2115; Case 229/83 *Association des Centres Distributeurs Édouard Leclerc and Others v SARL 'Au blé vert' and Others (Books)* [1985] ECR 17; Case 231/83 *Henri Cullet and Chambre Syndicale des Réparateurs Automobiles et Détaillants de Produits Pétroliers v Centre Leclerc (Fuel)* [1985] ECR 315; Case 123/83 *Bureau National Interprofessionnel du Cognac (BNIC) v Guy Clair* [1985] ECR 402; Case 41/83 *Italy v Commission (British Telecom)* [1985] ECR 873; Joined Cases 209-213/84 *Lucas Asjes and Others (Nouvelles Frontières)* [1986] ECR 1457; Case 267/86 *Pascal Van Eycke v ASPA NV* [1988] ECR 4769; Case 66/86 *Ahmed Saeed Flugreisen and Silver Line Reisebüro GmbH v Zentrale zur Bekämpfung Unlauteren Wettbewerbs e.V.* [1989] ECR 803; Case C-41/90 *Klaus Höfner and Fritz Elser v Macrotron GmbH* [1991] ECR I-1979; Case C-179/90 *Merci Convenzionali Porto di Genova SpA v Siderurgica Gabrielli SpA* [1991] ECR I-5889. Before the TFEU entered into force, this principle was construed by combining the application of Articles 3, 10, 81 and/or 82, and Article 86 EC. Now it may be construed from the principle of loyal cooperation as per Article 4(3) TEU, Articles 101 and/or 102, and Article 106 TFEU.

This is tantamount to saying that Article 21-*bis* is necessary when no individuals can challenge before a court an anticompetitive act adopted by any public authority on the ground that it breaches competition rules. When the act has already been challenged, then one would not need the AGCM's claim to have the above fundamental principle of law enforced. Here the role of the AGCM should probably be more akin to that envisaged by Article 15(3) of Regulation 1/2003, yet enhanced so that it may also address acts adopted by administrative authorities, and not only the anticompetitive conduct of undertakings. Again, such a conception may contribute to an organic system of decentralized antitrust enforcement, and may ensure that, in certain Member States such as Italy, this enforcement does not become unbalanced compared to the situation of other Member States. Such disequilibrium would be contrary to the uniform application of competition rules throughout the EU legal system, which is required by EU law and, specifically, by Regulation 1/2003.

A Modest Proposal to Read Article 21-*bis* Coherently with a Consistent Decentralized Application of Competition Rules in the Italian Legal System

Whatever the aims of the Italian legislators were, one's impression is that Article 21-*bis* was drafted with a strong domestic (or worse, parochial) approach. More precisely, it suffers from an inadequate understanding of the following principle, namely that the predominance of the EU competition rules *vis-à-vis* the Italian competition rules[32] requires a 'European' approach to antitrust enforcement, with logical consequences for the judicial assessment by our administrative courts in cases involving Article 21-*bis*.

That said, the case law developed so far pursuant to Article 21-*bis* still leaves enough room to propose the proper scope of application of this provision and the proper nature of the judicial assessment by the administrative courts, consistent with a sound systemic interpretation and interaction of the EU and national legal systems.

More precisely, my argument is that the scope of Article 21-*bis* should be construed consistently with EU legal principles governing the co-existence of the need, on the one hand, to enforce the competition

---

[32] To this end, statistics show that the AGCM is increasingly applying Articles 101 and 102 TFEU rather than the equivalent Italian antitrust provisions. This means that the AGCM has in fact fully embraced its role as a 'decentralized' authority for the enforcement of EU law. In cases where the EU rules are applied by the AGCM, it is also necessary for our courts to follow this approach.

rules and, on the other hand, to allow Member States to exclude certain sectors or circumstances from the operation of competition law. To this end, the ECJ's case law on the judicial assessment of national measures (unduly) restricting competition[33] should therefore serve as guidance for measuring the extent of the AGCM's powers under Article 21-*bis* to attack allegedly anticompetitive acts adopted by other public authorities.

This means that the AGCM may bring actions before an administrative court to challenge, for example, administrative acts setting price schemes that limit the ability of firms to freely establish the price of goods or services they sell in a competitive market.[34] Another useful (and necessary) application of Article 21-*bis* by the AGCM should be that of challenging acts favouring or strengthening cartels among firms,[35] or even requiring them, as well as acts that simply 'transpose' cartels.[36]

Other scenarios covered by Article 21-*bis* may be those involving acts that create a situation in which an undertaking to which they have conferred special or exclusive rights (or a public undertaking), merely by exercising its preferential rights, is led to abuse its dominant position; or acts granting preferential rights if they are liable to create a situation in which the undertaking is led to commit such an abuse.[37]

As can be seen, the cases where Article 21-*bis* might be applied are numerous. However, the scope of application of this provision cannot touch those sectors where the Government or other public authorities have established services of general economic interest within the meaning of Article 106(2) TFEU, and where the application of competition provisions would impede the adequate fulfilment of the public service task in question.[38] For example, any attempt by the AGCM to challenge before an administrative court an act establishing a regulated market featuring services of general economic interest, or implementing measures to be applied in such a market, should be declared inadmissible by

---

[33] See above, note 31 and accompanying text.

[34] See, for example, Joined Cases 240-242, 261-262, 268-269/82 *Stichting Sigarettenindustrie (SSI) and Others v Commission* [1985] ECR 3831.

[35] See *BNIC v Clair*, cited above, note 31.

[36] See *Van Eycke*, cited above, note 31.

[37] See, for example, *Höfner* and *Siderurgica Gabrielli*, cited above, note 31. See also Case C-323/93 *Société Civile Agricole du Centre d'Insémination de la Crespelle v Coopérative d'Elevage et d'Insémination Artificielle du Département de la Mayenne* [1994] ECR I-5077; Case C-163/96 *Silvano Raso and Others* [1998] ECR I-533.

[38] See, for example, in Case C-266/96 *Corsica Ferries France SA v Gruppo Antichi Ormeggiatori di Genova and Others* [1998] ECR I-3981.

the courts on the ground that the challenge falls beyond the scope of application of Article 21-*bis*.

Otherwise, the balance among public institutions would be upset, and the AGCM would in fact wield a power that does not seem legitimate under the principles of loyal cooperation among institutions and the power of States, recognized in Article 106(2) TFEU, to remove certain sectors from the normal play of competition. This is the role administrative courts should play in assessing alleged 'anticompetitive' acts adopted by other public authorities, and it is consistent with their role as 'watchdogs' of a constitutional equilibrium among those authorities that emerges implicitly, in my view, from Article 21-*bis*.

As a final observation, the enactment of Article 21-*bis* provides further food for thought concerning the relationship between administrative courts and the AGCM. In this regard, as a 'party' in institutional litigation against other administrative authorities, the AGCM should also be considered a party in all other litigation in which the administrative courts exercise their powers of judicial review. This evolution of the Italian legal system should therefore be considered when reflecting on the role of judges carrying out antitrust assessments; that role should be globally homogeneous, and courts should be capable of exercising their judicial powers without any restraint, as is true in all legal fields, and when EU rules with direct effect are at stake.

CONCLUDING REMARKS

In this chapter an attempt has been made to make sense of the overall judicial assessment of competition law before Italian courts.

The different roles played by civil courts and administrative courts in Italy have become increasingly evident, and the divergence will be enhanced as the Damages Directive is transposed into national law.

However, the growing interaction between the national and the EU legal systems, which is also demonstrated by the rationale embodied in Article 21-*bis* of *legge* 287/1990, calls for a judicial assessment in antitrust matters by Italian courts that is more coherent with a unified framework of decentralized enforcement of competition law in which the EU and the domestic levels work in parallel and in full consistency. This should be the compass that guides all our courts, of whatever category, when dealing with this subject matter.

Section 2:

State Aid

8. Services of general economic interest and state aid in EU law: the challenges for the Court of Justice after the 'Almunia Package'

Daniele Gallo*

ABSTRACT

This chapter reviews the principal components of the 'Almunia Package' of December 2011, which is the European Commission's latest expression of state aid policy with regard to the financing of public services. Following a detailed description of the package, several remaining open legal questions are highlighted. The Court of Justice is urged to provide clarity with regard to these issues going forward.

INTRODUCTION

When the issue at stake is that of public intervention in the economy, the problem of the scope and limits of judicial power raises the question of a fair balance between the powers of judges and those of the legislator and/or the executive. It is thus a problem of – *lato sensu* – democracy, judicial activism and the Welfare State. Moreover, when the actor vested with that balance is supranational, as is the case of the European Court of Justice (ECJ), the issue becomes even more sensitive since its jurisprudence has a strong impact on the European as well as on the national 'socio-economic constitution'.[1]

* Qualified as Associate Professor of International and EU Law/Senior Lecturer in EU Law at Luiss Guido Carli University, Rome, Italy.

[1] See, *inter alia*, Gráinne de Búrca, 'Towards European Welfare?' in Gráinne de Búrca (ed), *EU Law and the Welfare State. In Search of Solidarity* (OUP 2005) 1.

In this chapter I will deal with a specific form of public intervention in the economy, that is, the financing of services of general economic interest (SGEIs)[2] or, to be more precise, economic services of general interest,[3] as regulated and shaped by the EU institutions. Against this background, what I want to show in my contribution, in more general terms, is that the financing of SGEIs is a 'privileged' tool of analysis that can be used to investigate both the dialectical – more than merely dialogical – relationship between the EU institutions, including the ECJ, and the interplay between the spheres of the market and of the state in EU law. This will be done in light of the so-called 'Almunia Package' (hereinafter also the 'Package') inasmuch as its principal uncertainties will be carefully highlighted.[4]

---

[2] For an overview of the relationship between SGEIs and state aid, see recently Daniele Gallo, *I Servizi di Interesse Economico Generale. Stato, Mercato e Welfare nel Diritto dell'Unione Europea* (Giuffrè 2010) 631–713; Thomas von Danwitz, 'The Concept of State Aid in Liberalized Sectors' in Marise Cremona (ed), *Market Integration and Public Services in the European Union* (OUP 2011); Stéphane Bracq, 'Le Financement des Services d'intérêt Economique Général en Droit de l'Union Européenne' (2012) 1 Revue du Droit de l'Union Européenne 85; Erika Szyszczak and Johan van de Gronden (eds), *Financing Services of General Economic Interest* (TMC Asser Press 2013).

[3] Generally on SGEIs, and with regard to the concepts of economic activity and non-economic interest, see (most recently in the post-Lisbon Treaty context) Gallo, cited above, note 2, at 234–371; Leigh Hancher and Pierre Larouche, 'The Coming of Age of EU Regulation of Network Industries and Services of General Economic Interest' in Paul Craig and Grainne de Búrca (eds), *The Evolution of EU Law* (OUP 2011); Cremona (ed), cited above, note 2; Ulla Neergaard, 'Services of General Economic Interest under EU Constraints' in Dagmar Schiek, Ulrike Liebert and Hildegard Schneider (eds), *European Economic and Social Constitutionalism after the Treaty of Lisbon* (Cambridge University Press 2011); Erika Szyszczak, Jim Davies, Mads Andenaes and Tarjei Bekkedal (eds), *Developments in Services of General Interest* (TMC Asser Press 2011); José Luis Buendía Sierra, 'Writing Straight with Crooked Lines: Competition Policy and Services of General Economic Interest in the Treaty of Lisbon' in Andrea Biondi, Piet Eeckout and Stephanie Ripley (eds), *EU Law After Lisbon* (OUP 2012); Johan van de Gronden and Catalin Stefan Rusu, 'Services of General (Economic) Interest post-Lisbon' in Martin Trybus and Luca Rubini (eds), *The Treaty of Lisbon and the Future of European Law and Policy* (Edward Elgar 2012); Vassilis Hatzopoulos, *Regulating Services in the European Union* (OUP 2012) 86–96; José Luis Buendía Sierra, 'Article 106 – Exclusive Rights and Other Anti-competitive State Measures' in Jonathan Faull and Ali Nikpay (eds), *The EC Law of Competition* (OUP 2014).

[4] The Package is discussed below.

A second Section will focus on the period before the adoption of the Package, and a third Section will provide a general overview of the Package, while the fourth Section will be devoted to the new judicial challenges that have emerged since it was adopted. Finally, in the fifth Section, I will make some brief concluding remarks.

THE EUROPEAN COMMISSION, THE ECJ AND THE COMPENSATION FOR PUBLIC SERVICE OBLIGATIONS BEFORE THE ADOPTION OF THE 'ALMUNIA PACKAGE'

With regard to state aid and SGEIs, EU institutions must answer the following seminal questions: what does 'financing services of general economic interest' actually mean and what does it imply?

Since the 1970s,[5] EU institutions have always been clear in stating that Member States can compensate the costs incurred by undertakings entrusted with the operation of public services in order to ease the carrying out of their missions of general interest. The complex issue to be solved by those institutions, including above all the ECJ, was and still is another: how and to what extent such compensation may be considered admissible under EU law. In this regard there have been numerous contrasts between the ECJ and the General Court (GC) and amongst Advocates General, and between the ECJ and the Commission. The main problem has been and, in some measure, still is: whether compensation must be regarded *ex ante* as legitimate and not amounting to state aid according to Article 107(1) TFEU because no economic advantage is conferred (the so-called 'compensation criterion'); or whether the compensation does constitute aid but is nevertheless compatible with the internal market by virtue of Article 106(2) TFEU, which allows Member States and undertakings entrusted with the operation of SGEIs to derogate (not only from the Treaty's antitrust and free movement rules, but also) from state aid rules (the 'state aid criterion').

From the 1970s until 2005, in a first phase which included the famous *Altmark* judgment of 2003,[6] the EU Courts behaved as 'agents of

[5] Case 78/76 *Steinike and Weinlig v Germany* [1977] ECR 595, para 18.

[6] See, *inter alia*, Case 280/83 *A.D.B.H.U.* [1985] ECR 538, para 18; Case T-106/95 *FFSA II* [1997] ECR II-229, paras 164–172; Case T-46/97 *Sociedade Independente de Comunicação SA* [2000] ECR II-2125, paras 82–84; Case 332/98 *France v Commission* [2000] ECR I-4833, paras 27–33; Case C-53/00

change',[7] responding to the issues and needs raised by Member States, undertakings and, *lato sensu*, civil society. They acted in order to fill *lacunae* and give legal certainty, in the absence of horizontal secondary law. To be very concise, what can be inferred from those judgments is that in the great majority of cases the compensation criterion prevailed even though the ECJ, with the identification of the four *Altmark* requirements,[8] rendered it *de facto* very difficult for compensation not to be treated as state aid. This ECJ's activism pushed EU institutions, and specifically the Commission, to intervene. It thus became necessary for the EU to make normative choices.

Therefore, in a second phase, with a view to providing legal certainty, the Commission adopted the 'Monti Package',[9] named after the Commissioner responsible for competition at the time. This Package, which remained in force until November 2011, made a (more or less) clear distinction between those public measures which were not to be considered state aid *ab origine* and those which qualified as state aid but were potentially compatible with Article 106(2).

In a third phase, after a few years of judicial restraint, the GC took action, and with decisions such as *BUPA*,[10] tried to solve problems that had not been solved by the 'Monti Package'. It thus attempted to indicate

---

Ferring [2001] ECR I-9067, paras 20–29; Case C-280/00 *Altmark* [2003] ECR I-7747, paras 78–95; Cases C-34-38/01 *Enirisorse* [2003] ECR I-14243, para 31; Case T-157/01 *Danske Busvognmoed* [2004] II-917, para 98; Case T-274/01 *Valmont Nederland BV* [2004] II-3145, paras 129–139.

[7] Mauro Cappelletti, *Giudici Legislatori?* (Giuffrè 1984).

[8] See *Altmark*, cited above, note 6, paras 88–95.

[9] The 'Monti Package' was composed of the following acts: Decision of 28 November 2005 on the application of Article 86(2) of the EC Treaty to state aid in the form of public service compensation granted to certain undertakings entrusted with the operation of services of general economic interest, [2005] OJ L312/67; and Community Framework for state aid in the form of public service compensation, [2005] C297/4. On this package, see, *inter alia*, Barbara Rapp-Jung, 'State Financing of Public Services – The Commission's New Approach' (2004/2) European State Aid Law Quarterly 205; Lars Peter Svane, 'Public Service Compensation in Practice: Commission Package on State Aid for Services of General Economic Interest' (2005/3) Competition Policy Newsletter 34; José Luis Buendía Sierra, 'An Analysis of Article 86(2) EC' in Michael Sánchez Rydelski (ed), *The EU State Aid Regime* (Cameron May 2006).

[10] See, *inter alia*, Case T-266/02 *Deutsche Post* [2008] ECR II-1233; Case T-289/03 *BUPA* [2008] ECR II-81; Case T-222/04 *Commission v Italy* [2009] ECR II-1877.

more precisely when Article 106(2) was to be used, and how compensation for public service was to be evaluated in light of the universal and binding character of that service.

Besides the issue of ensuring the *effet utile* of Article 106(2) in the area of state aid, the option of applying the compensation criterion rather than the state aid criterion represents a 'burning' procedural matter with very relevant practical consequences in terms of the distribution of competences between the EU and its Member States. Indeed, if the conferral of compensation does not amount to state aid, Member States normally are neither required to notify the measure nor are they bound by the standstill obligation under Article 108(3) TFEU; by contrast, if the compensation does constitute state aid then, even though it is compatible under Article 106(2), both the notification and standstill obligations will normally apply. This presents a problem of decentralization in the field of state aid: in particular, a very broad application of the compensation criterion, by opening up the possibility of self-assessment by the Member States of financing schemes, would risk calling into question the Commission's *ex ante* powers of control in the field of state aid when public service compensation is at issue.

AN OVERVIEW OF THE 'ALMUNIA PACKAGE'

Under the overall umbrella of the Communication of 20 December 2011 on 'A Quality Framework for SGEIs in Europe',[11] and following a dialogue with Member States in 2008–2009 as well as a public consultation with stakeholders (national authorities, municipalities, big private operators, social service providers, and so on) launched in 2010 and several formal meetings with other EU institutions, in particular with the European Parliament, the Commission on 23 March 2011 adopted a Communication entitled 'Reform of the EU State Aid Rules on Services of General Economic Interest'.[12] After publishing an initial draft in September 2011,[13] the Commission then unanimously adopted a new

---

[11] COM/2011/0900.

[12] COM/2011/0146.

[13] On the different stages of this consultative process, see Georgios Kamaris, 'The Reform of EU State Aid Rules for Services of General Economic Interest in Times of Austerity' (2012) 33(2) European Competition Law Review 55, 55–58; Gianni Lo Schiavo, 'Dalla Giurisprudenza *Altmark* all'adozione del Pacchetto "Almunia"'. Chiarimenti Sulla Portata delle Compensazioni Concesse per la Prestazione dei Servizi di Interesse Economico Generale' (2012/6) Rivista

reform package on state aid rules for SGEIs. This was the above-mentioned 'Almunia Package', named after Joaquín Almunia, the Vice-President of the Commission and Commissioner responsible for competition policy as of this writing. It was Almunia who had prompted a debate in the College on the main guidelines that the draft text should follow.

The Package[14] is constituted by: two Communications; one Decision, which was adopted on 20 December 2011 and which entered into force on 31 January 2012;[15] and one Regulation, which was adopted on 25 April 2012 and which entered into force on 29 April 2012.[16]

With the adoption of the Package, the Commission provided a systematic framework in the field of SGEIs and state aid[17] and, in line with the

---

Italiana di Diritto Pubblico Comunitario 1247; Elisabetta Righini, 'The Reform of the State Aid Rules on Financing of Public Services' (2012/2) European State Aid Law Quarterly 3, 3–12.

[14] See also <http://ec.europa.eu/competition/state_aid/overview/public_services_en.html#reports> accessed 14 October 2014.

[15] Communication from the Commission on the application of the European Union state aid rules to compensation granted for the provision of services of general economic interest [2012] OJ C8/4; Commission Decision of 20 December on the application of Article 106(2) of the Treaty on the Functioning of the European Union to state aid in the form of public service compensation granted to certain undertakings entrusted with the operation of services of general economic interest [2012] OJ L7/10; Communication from the Commission, European Union framework for state aid in the form of public service compensation [2012] OJ C8/15.

[16] Commission Regulation on the application of Articles 107 and 108 of the Treaty on the Functioning of the European Union to *de minimis* aid granted to undertakings providing services of general economic interest [2012] OJ L114/8.

[17] For an overview of the Package, see José Luis Buendía Sierra and María Muñoz de Juan, 'Some Legal Reflections on the Almunia Package' (2012/2) European State Aid Law Quarterly 63; Damien Geradin, 'The New SGEI Package' (2012/3) European State Aid Law Quarterly 1; Nicola Pesaresi, Adinda Sinnaeve, Valérie Guigue-Koeppen, Joachim Wiemann and Madalina Radulescu, 'The New State Aid Rules for Services of General Economic Interest' (2012/1) Competition Policy Newsletter; Wolf Sauter, 'The *Altmark* Package Mark II: New Rules for State Aid and the Compensation of Services of General Economic Interest' (2012) 33(7) European Competition Law Review 307; Adinda Sinnaeve, 'What's New in SGEI in 2012? – An Overview of the Commission's SGEI Package' (2012/2) European State Aid Law Quarterly 347; Erika Szyszczak, 'Modernising State Aid and the Financing of SGEI' (2012) 4 *Journal of European Competition Law and Practice* 1; José Luis Buendía Sierra and María Muñoz de Juan, 'The Almunia Package: State Aid and Services of General Economic Interest' in Szyszczak and van de Gronden (eds), cited above, note 2;

'Monti Package', by re-valuating Article 106(2), thus addressing certain problems (including but not limited to procedural issues) which would have arisen if the 'compensation criterion' had been given full application. Communication 8/02 clarifies crucial concepts related to state aid and SGEIs in light of the '*Altmark* conditions', while the Decision and the Framework Communication explain when public service compensation is compatible with the TFEU. The *de minimis* Regulation establishes a threshold below which such compensation does not constitute state aid. Moreover, it must be stressed that Commission Directive 2006/111/EC of 16 November 2006 on the transparency of financial relations between Member States and public undertakings as well as on financial transparency within certain undertakings remains applicable.[18]

The Package clarifies important concepts so that national authorities and stakeholders can comply with EU law, and it simplifies the law for small local operators that are not apt to distort competition. It also provides diversified rules with the aim of ensuring diversity between SGEIs, and finally it extends the list of social economic services that are exempt from prior scrutiny by the Commission.[19] With the Package the Commission also intends to respond to the economic and financial crisis by highlighting the importance of guaranteeing access to essential high quality services as more and more people become dependent on the supply of those services; and it seeks to ensure greater economic efficiency of public spending in this area.[20] Indeed, as observed by Commissioner Almunia, 'competition policy must [...] help to guarantee accessible and affordable high-quality public services, which are fundamental to citizens' well-being and quality of life and which also contribute to social and territorial cohesion'.[21] Furthermore, Almunia has recently observed that the EU's reforms in the field of state aid in recent

---

Tim Maxian Rusche, 'The Almunia Package: Legal Constraints, Policy Procedures and Political Choices', in ibid.; Stéphane Rodrigues, 'The European Commission's Reform Strategy', in ibid.; Daniele Gallo, 'Gli Aiuti di Stato, l'art. 106 § 2 e la Compensazione di Obblighi di Servizio Pubblico' in Lorenzo Federico Pace (a cura di), *Dizionario Sistematico della Concorrenza* (Naples 2013).

[18] OJ L318/17.

[19] On this point, see Massimo Merola and Tecla Ubaldi, 'The 2011 Almunia Package and the Challenges Ahead: Are the New Rules Flexible Enough to Fit the Wide Variety of SGEI?' (2012) 2 European State Aid Law Quarterly 17, 19.

[20] See Elisabetta Righini, cited above, note 13, at 3.

[21] See the hearing of J. Almunia of 12 January 2009 before the European Parliament (http://www.europarl.europa.eu/hearings/static/commissioners/speeches/almunia speeches_en.pdf Accessed 14 October 2014).

years 'turned out to be timely as well, since the latest stages of the crisis have been putting public services and the spending capacity of governments under unusual pressure [...] Owing to these measures and to dwindling resources, public authorities struggle to cope with the increasing demands from the many European citizens who have seen their standards of living fall and are turning to them for services and support'.[22]

As concerns the legal base chosen for the adoption of the Package, the Commission decided to act autonomously. It thus decided not to propose legislation on the basis of Article 14 TFEU, which, following the Lisbon amendments, contains an explicit basis for the adoption by the Council and the Parliament under the ordinary legislative procedure of regulations setting principles and conditions for the provision of SGEIs. Although the use of this new legal base had been advocated by the Parliament[23] as well as by the Committee of the Regions[24] and the Economic and Social Committee,[25] the Commission found that: on the one hand, there was no need for a specific legal base as far as the issues covered by the two Communications were concerned; and, with regard to the two binding acts, it could base its *de minimis* Regulation on Council Regulation 994/98 of 7 May 1998, and could base its Decision on Article 106(3) TFEU.[26] Regarding the latter provision, in particular, it is recalled that Article 106(3) confers upon the Commission the competence to adopt, without the participating of its sister institutions, directives or decisions to liberalize markets and in that sense to restrict Member States' influence in the economy. It is thus clear that a problem with that choice is the marginalization of the Parliament and the Council, notwithstanding the fact that the financing of public services not only raises issues of competition law but also touches concerns that lie at the crossroads between economic and social needs.

---

22 Joachín Almunia, 'Preface' (2012) 2 European State Aid Law Quarterly 1–2.

23 EU Parliament Report of 24 October 2011 on the reform of the EU state aid rules on Services of General Economic Interest (2011/2146(INI)).

24 Opinion of the Committee of the Regions on the Reform of the EU state aid rules on Services of General Economic Interest – CdR 7/2011.

25 Opinion of the Economic and Social Committee on the Reform of the EU state aid rules on Services of General Economic Interest – TEN/455.

26 See José Luis Buendía Sierra and María Muñoz de Juan, cited above, note 17, at 67.

Communication 8/02

In Communication 8/02 the Commission clarifies the circumstances in which public compensation does not qualify as state aid, in line with the *Altmark* criteria.[27] As is well known, in *Altmark* the ECJ set out four conditions under which the funding of SGEIs escapes state aid scrutiny, as it does not qualify as aid: the recipient undertaking must have public service obligations that are clearly defined; the parameters for calculating the compensation must be objective, transparent and established in advance; the compensation must not exceed what is necessary to cover all or part of the costs incurred in the discharge of the public service obligations, taking into account the relevant receipts and the need for a reasonable profit; and, where the relevant undertaking is not chosen pursuant to a public procurement procedure allowing for the selection of a tenderer capable of providing those services at the least cost to the public, the level of compensation needed must be determined on the basis of an analysis of the costs of a typical well-run company.

In the Communication, the Commission explains first of all that Member States retain a wide margin of appreciation in defining a SGEI. Indeed, the Commission's competence in this respect is limited to checking whether a national authority has made a manifest error of assessment. Second, the public service mission should be assigned on the basis of an official act specifying the content, duration and territorial coverage of the SGEI. Third, the Commission gives detailed guidance on the definition of compensation insofar as it covers only costs directly associated with the provision of the SGEI. Fourth, it is explained that the compensation cannot exceed what is necessary to cover all or part of the costs incurred in the discharge of the public service obligations, including a reasonable profit. Fifth, the compensation may be either the result of a public procurement procedure or determined on the basis of a benchmarking exercise taking account of the costs of a typical well-run undertaking.

The main problem with the approach adopted in the Communication lies in the statement that '[t]he granting, without tendering, of licenses to occupy or use public domain, or of other special or exclusive rights having an economic value, may imply a waiver of State resources and create an advantage for the beneficiaries'.[28] As rightly noted in the

---

27 For general observations, see Nicola Pesaresi, Adinda Sinnaeve, Valérie Guigue-Koeppen, Joachim Wiemann and Madalina Radulescu, 'The SGEI Communication' (2012/1) Competition Policy Newsletter.

28 Para 33.

literature, not every case in which there is an exclusive right always entails an implicit transfer of State resources. It may well be that the protection granted through the exclusive right corresponds to what is strictly necessary to reduce the compensation granted to the SGEI operator. Indeed, this approach seems to overlap with the scope of Articles 106(1) (on public and privileged undertakings) and 107(1) inasmuch that it seems to constitute an attempt by the Commission to strengthen its control in the field of state aid by using 'a specific policy instrument (state aid control) to achieve a goal that is only partially connected with it (liberalization)'.[29]

Framework Communication 8/03

In Framework Communication 8/03 the Commission sets out the conditions according to which some compensation may be declared to be state aid compatible on the basis of Article 106(2). Such compensation is granted better treatment than aid granted for services which are not of general economic interest, but they are treated less favourably compared to measures which satisfy the *Altmark* conditions and are covered by Communication 8/02: unlike the latter, all compensation covered by the Framework Communication must be notified to the Commission, and the standstill obligation applies.

When is state aid deemed compatible according to the Framework Communication?

a) The aid must be granted for a genuine SGEI in the sense of Article 106(2): the Commission states clearly that state aid is an *extrema ratio* to be used by the State.
b) The responsible authority which entrusts the provision of the service to the undertaking must comply with EU public procurement law – with the exception of in-house situations – including the requirements of transparency, equal treatment and non-discrimination. If not, the aid must be regarded as a measure affecting the development of trade to an extent contrary to the interests of the Union within the meaning of Article 106(2). As observed below,[30] this is a very delicate issue: before the Package was adopted, Member States had no clear obligation to choose SGEI operators through competitive tenders; this is clear from the

[29] Buendía Sierra and Muñoz de Juan, cited above, note 17, at 135.
[30] See below.

fact that the vast majority of SGEIs have been entrusted so far by national authorities without any tender. Does this circumstance imply that many undertakings entrusted with the operation of SGEIs in Europe must be deemed as acting inconsistently with EU law?

c) With regard to the amount of compensation, it must not exceed what is necessary to cover the net cost of discharging the public service obligations, including a reasonable profit. Where the compensation is based, in whole or in part, on expected costs and revenues, they must be specified in the entrustment act and must be based on plausible and observable parameters concerning the economic environment in which the public service is being provided. The net cost must be calculated on the basis of two methodologies: the difference between the net cost for the provider of operating with the public service obligation and the net cost or profit for the same provider of operating without that obligation; and the difference between the costs and the revenues for a designated provider of fulfilling the public service obligations specified and estimated in the entrustment act.

d) Overcompensation should be understood as compensation that the undertaking receives in excess of the amount of aid for the whole duration of the contract. In this respect, the Commission states that, since overcompensation is not necessary for the operation of the service, it constitutes incompatible state aid.[31]

e) As observed by the Commission in paragraphs 51–59 of the Framework Communication, it may be possible that the conditions indicated therein, in some exceptional circumstances, are not sufficient; to that extent, serious competition distortions could remain unaddressed and the aid could affect trade in a manner contrary to the interests of the Union. Stricter control by the Commission would thus be necessary. Such exceptional distortions may arise where the entrustment is: of a long duration which cannot be justified by reference to objective criteria; conferred for a service that already exists as a commercial service and for which there is a less distortive manner for providing it; or connected with special or

---

[31] On this issue, and with analysis from an economic point of view, see Lorenzo Coppi, 'SGEI Compensation in the Almunia Package – An Economic View' (2012/2) European State Aid Law Quarterly 37; James Kavanagh, 'Financing Services of General Economic Interest: The European Commission's Economic Tests' in Szyszczak and van de Gronden (eds), cited above, note 2.

exclusive rights that seriously restrict competition in the internal market to an extent contrary to the interests of the Union.

The Decision

The Decision is the most contentious document in the Package. Here the Commission sets out the conditions under which state aid in the form of public service compensation is compatible according to Article 106(2), like the compensation contemplated in the Framework Communication, but with a crucial difference: while the latter are subject to the prior notification obligation laid down in Article 108(3), those covered by the Decision are exempt from this requirement. The Decision, therefore, aims at simplifying the law, and thus provides for a more flexible approach for local and social services than was the case under the 'Monti Package'. Indeed, the Decision extends the exemption so that it includes, in addition to hospital services and social housing, a wide range of categories of services ensuring the fulfilment of social needs.[32]

What are these new categories?

a) Compensation not exceeding an annual amount of EUR 15 million for the provision of the service in areas other than transport and transport infrastructure. This is an important novelty since the previous limit in the 'Monti Package' was EUR 30 million: given the development of intra-Union trade in the provision of public services, the Commission deemed it appropriate to set a lower limit for the amount of compensation which can be exempted;
b) Compensation for public service tasks performed by hospitals providing medical care, including, where applicable, emergency services;
c) Compensation for services meeting social needs as regards health and long-term care, childcare, access to and reintegration into the labour market, social housing, and the care for and social inclusion of vulnerable groups;
d) Compensation for transportation services in the form of air or maritime links to islands where the average annual traffic during

[32] See Johan van de Gronden and Catalin Stefan Rusu, 'The Altmark Update and Social Services: Toward a European Approach' in Erika Szyszczak and Johan van de Gronden (eds), cited above, note 2; Leigh Hancher and Wolf Sauter, 'This Won't Hurt a Bit: The Commission's Approach to Services of General Economic Interest and State Aid to Hospitals', in ibid.

the two financial years preceding the year the service was assigned does not exceed 300,000 passengers; and

e) Compensation for the provision of airport and port services for which the average annual traffic during the two financial years preceding the year the service was assigned does not exceed 200,000 passengers in the case of airports or 300,000 passengers in the case of ports.

Moreover, the Commission specifies, on the one hand, that the aid must respect relevant sectoral EU law; and on the other, that the Decision only applies where the period for which the undertaking is entrusted with the operation of the service does not exceed 10 years.

To sum up, it is important to stress that, according to the Commission, some compensation measures are to be considered aid that is *per se* compatible with EU law – regardless of the amount of the compensation (even where it exceeds EUR 15 million if they concern the sectors listed in letters *b* to *e* above) – and are exempt from notification, provided they meet all conditions of the Decision; while other measures concerning sectors different from those listed in letters *b* to *e* by which compensation exceeds EUR 15 million – regardless of the nature of the activity – must be notified. Since the latter are not included within the scope of the Decision, the presumption of compatibility with the Treaty does not apply.

The Regulation

The last measure included in the Package is the *de minimis* Regulation. Under this Regulation the aid granted to undertakings for the provision of a public service is deemed not to meet all criteria of Article 107(1) and is therefore exempt from notification if it fulfils a set of cumulative conditions, starting with the setting of a threshold (or 'ceiling') below which advantages granted to undertakings entrusted with the operation of public services may be deemed not to affect trade between Member States and/or not to distort or threaten to distort competition. According to the conditions established by the Regulation:

a) The total amount of aid granted to any one undertaking providing the service must not exceed EUR 500,000 over any period of three fiscal years;

b) The ceiling specified above must be expressed as a cash grant;

c) The Regulation applies only to 'transparent' aids in respect of which it is possible to calculate precisely the gross grant equivalent of the aid *ex ante* without need to undertake a risk assessment ('transparent aid'). For instance, aid comprised in loans are considered to be transparent *de minimis* aid when the gross grant equivalent has been calculated on the basis of the reference rate applicable at the time of the grant; and

d) The *de minimis* aid under the Regulation may not be cumulated with any compensation in respect of the same SGEI, regardless of whether or not it constitutes state aid.

THE 'ALMUNIA PACKAGE' AND THE QUEST FOR LEGAL CERTAINTY: WHAT ARE THE PRINCIPAL CHALLENGES FOR THE ECJ?

It can be inferred from the above that, with the Package, the Commission decided to limit Member States' autonomy *vis-à-vis* large economic operators entrusted with the performance of public services inasmuch as the procedural obligations laid down in Article 108(3) always apply, whereas undertakings entrusted with the operation of (economic) social services of general interest and small undertakings are not subject to those obligations in accordance with, respectively, the Decision and the Regulation. While under the 'Monti Package' all SGEIs were essentially treated the same way (verification for absence of overcompensation), the new Package tightens the rules for large undertakings.[33]

In light of the considerations set out in the previous sections, I will now focus on the new challenges that the EU Courts will face if and when confronted with an interpretation of the content and scope of the Package. These challenges concern above all the Framework Communication and the Decision.

With regard to the Framework Communication, a first comment relates to paragraphs 39–43 regarding efficiency incentives, where it is stated, among other things, that Member States, in devising the method of compensation, 'must introduce incentives for the efficient provision of SGEI of a high standard, unless they can duly justify that it is not feasible or appropriate to do so'. What does 'efficiency' mean in this context? Are the EU institutions the appropriate bodies to assess such efficiency? If required to rule on the matter, does the ECJ have the power to conduct such an analysis? The answer might be: not if we follow, for

[33] Erika Szyszczak, 'Introduction' in Szyszczak and van de Gronden (eds), cited above, note 2, at 27.

instance, Advocate General Tizzano's opinion in the *Ferring* case. There he says that, '[…] in the absence of any harmonized rules governing the matter, the [EU] institutions are not entitled to rule on the basis of the public service tasks assigned to the public operator […], such as the level of costs linked to that service, or the expediency of the political choices made in this regard by the national authorities or [… the] economic efficiency of the undertaking'.[34] The ECJ will therefore have to clarify this issue and elaborate the meaning of the efficiency requirement put forward by the Commission.

A second comment on the Framework Communication concerns paragraph 14, where it is affirmed that Member States, for the scope of application of the principles set out in the measure, 'should show that they have given proper consideration to the public service needs supported by way of a public consultation or other appropriate instruments to take the interests of users and providers into account'. The provision contains a final sentence according to which a prior consultation is unnecessary if it is clear that it 'will not bring any significant added value to a recent consultation'. It would be interesting to have a statement from the ECJ as regards which body (whether national authorities or the EU institutions) would be vested with the power to undertake that consultation: it can be seen that at least one consultation is required, since paragraph 14 refers to a 'recent consultation'.[35] Moreover, is this criterion in fact relevant?

A third comment regards the role attributed to public procurement by paragraph 19 of the Framework Communication. There it is established that state aid is to be considered necessarily compatible with EU law under Article 106(2) TFEU 'only where the responsible authority, when entrusting the provision of the service to the undertaking in question, has complied or commits to comply with the applicable Union rules in the area of public procurement'. The question is whether the tendering of the grant of a SGEI mission automatically entails that the state aid rules do not apply.[36] Thus far, the Commission has not clarified whether a public procurement procedure in itself ensures that no overcompensation is granted. This is an important issue for Member States that have privatized the provision of various SGEIs without such a procedure. It would be important to have a clear indication from the ECJ in this respect since

[34] See Stéphane Rodrigues, cited above, note 17, at 95–96.

[35] See comments by Adinda Sinnaeve, cited above, note 17, at 359.

[36] See generally Albert Sanchez Graells, 'The Commission's Modernisation Agenda for Procurement and SGEI' in Szyszczak and van de Gronden (eds), cited above, note 2.

the case law, or at least that of the GC, is inconsistent with regard to this redeeming conception of procurement. In *Olsen*, for example, the GC clarified that 'it is not apparent either from the wording of Article 86(2) EC or from the case-law on that provision that a general interest task may be entrusted to an operator only as a result of a tendering procedure'.[37] A flexible interpretation of the Framework Communication therefore seems necessary.[38]

A fourth comment concerns the calculation of the net cost and, in particular, paragraph 25, where the Commission emphasizes that 'the net cost calculation should assess the benefits, including intangible benefits as far as possible, to the SGEI provider'. The issue here is the meaning of 'benefits': does the term refer to all the benefits resulting from the exclusive right enjoyed by the undertaking, or does it include only those enjoyed by the provider as a direct result of the provision of the specific SGEI?[39]

As concerns the Decision, one issue that the ECJ will have to face is that of enforcement since, in the Package, 'too much rides on the Commission services'.[40] This is why more activism on the part of the Court with regard to the requirements set out for the block exemption would be welcome. Another issue is whether the list of social services covering basic needs indicated in Article 2.1(c) of the Decision is exhaustive or not. In this regard, it is remarkable that, by identifying the social services covered therein, the Commission does not seem to have drawn any inspiration from its own definition of social services of general interest. As a result, no social security scheme (having an economic character), such as supplementary pension or health care schemes, seem to benefit from the exemption. In my view, it is inevitable that in the future the Commission or the ECJ will have to clarify under which circumstances the provision of social security services ought to be legitimately financed by the State. A further issue concerns the silence implied in the Decision as to what is meant by a service meeting social needs (Article 2.1(c)) or a hospital (Article 2.1(b)). As to the latter, it would be helpful for the EU Courts to specify whether both aid granted

---

37 Case T-17/02 *Fred Olsen, SA v Commission* [2005] ECR II-2031, para 239.

38 See Damien Geradin, 'Public Compensation for Services of General Economic Interest: An Analysis of the 2011 European Commission Framework' (2012/2) European State Aid Law Quarterly 51, 54–55; José Luis Buendía Sierra and María Muñoz de Juan, cited above, note 17, at 75–76.

39 See Geradin, cited previous note, at 55–56.

40 Sauter, cited above, note 17, at 313.

to public and private hospitals could benefit from the exemption. And to what extent does the exemption apply to the pursuit of activities ancillary to hospital services, such as research? In slightly different terms, to what extent should public funding of investments in activities that are closely related to care and the curing of patients be deemed legitimate?

Finally and more broadly, onc may ask whether it is possible to establish a sort of hierarchy among the measures comprised in the Package.[41] There is an urgent need for clarity from the ECJ in this respect. The logic may be the following: if the compensation complies with the requirements contained in the Regulation, it cannot constitute state aid; if it cannot be included within the scope of the Regulation, it may nevertheless comply with the *Altmark* conditions, in which case it will not be regarded as aid; if one or more *Altmark* conditions are not fulfilled, the public financing may come under the scope of the Decision as being state aid exempt from the notification obligation; and if not, it may be subject to prior notification in accordance with the Framework Communication. In this respect, the ECJ should clarify whether, in the case of overcompensation, and if neither the *Altmark* conditions nor the Package applies, there may still be room for the application of Article 106(2).

CONCLUDING REMARKS

The Almunia Package is at once more flexible and stricter than its predecessor:[42] it is more flexible because it increases the number of situations where Member States are exempted from notification; it is stricter because it reduces the thresholds of *ex ante* legitimate aid. This means that, on the one hand, more measures – at least those which do not have a significant impact on the internal market – will probably fall within the scope of the Regulation or the Decision and, on the other, SGEIs will be subject to more stringent rules with regard to compensation where an individual notification will continue to apply, given the distortive effects on competition this public funding may produce.

It is obviously difficult to assess whether the main general objective of the reform, specifically, boosting the economy in a context of crisis, has been achieved given that the Package, including the Regulation, entered into force only recently, in other words, in April 2012. Nevertheless it is important to stress that the Commission has made considerable progress

---

[41] See also Szyszczak, cited above, note 33, at 15.

[42] Buendía Sierra and Muñoz de Juan, cited above, note 17, at 69.

in updating, modernizing and simplifying the *Altmark* jurisprudence and the 'Monti Package'. This could eventually lead to a convergence of national policies relating to the provision of SGEIs. The enhanced flexibility provided in both the Decision and the Regulation – with regard to certain social and health services, low compensation and small undertakings – must be welcomed. By providing this special treatment for welfare services, the Commission seems to have successfully consolidated the social market economy principles on which the EU is (and should always be) founded.

However, there are still some uncertainties and problems that need to be addressed, and on which the EU institutions will hopefully shed light in the future. I strongly believe that the ECJ should play an important role in this regard.

9. *Locus standi* of natural and legal persons before the European Courts in State aid cases

Edoardo Gambaro*

ABSTRACT

This chapter discusses a variety of issues concerning locus standi *in the field of State aid. Following a review of the acts that are subject to challenge, the chapter considers and provides critical remarks regarding key procedural criteria that determine whether a person is entitled to challenge State aid decisions. Specifically, these criteria are: direct concern; individual concern (in relation to actions filed by actual and potential beneficiaries of aid schemes as well as by rivals of aid beneficiaries); and the interest of a person in bringing an action. An evaluation is also provided with regard to the impact of Article 263(4) TFEU, which, following the amendments made by the Treaty of Lisbon, removes the requirement of 'individual concern' where challenges are brought against regulatory acts.*

INTRODUCTION

The peculiarity of State aid Commission decisions is that, unlike those pertaining to antitrust, the Member State's central authority is the sole addressee of the decision. This principle was established by the European Court of Justice (ECJ) in the *Sytraval* case[1] and then transposed into Article 25 of EC Regulation 659/99 (the Procedural Regulation).

* LL.M, College of Europe, Bruges and Partner, Studio Santa Maria, Milan.

[1] Case C-367/95 P *Commission v Chambre Syndicale Nationale des Entreprises de Transport de Fonds et Valeurs (Sytraval) and Brink's France* [1998] ECR I-1719, para 45.

According to this principle, the Member State concerned is the 'natural' applicant in any possible subsequent litigation, without having to prove its direct and individual concern with the matter.

It follows that the position of the addressee Member State differs from that of third parties. As far as the latter are concerned, their *locus standi* in order to bring an action for annulment has traditionally been a thorny issue, giving rise to abundant case law. Indeed, unlike an addressee Member State, third parties wishing to challenge a State aid decision must in principle satisfy the criteria of direct and individual concern and must prove an interest in bringing the action.

As regards regional and local authorities, they are deemed to be non-privileged applicants. Other typical non-privileged (private) applicants in the field of State aid are the recipients of the aid and the beneficiaries' competitors, which sometimes are also complainants. These parties have been included in the notion of 'interested parties' contained in Article 1(h) of the Procedural Regulation.

Furthermore it is worth noting that *locus standi* in State aid cases can be influenced by certain circumstances such as the scope of the decision – which can be either individual (for example, *ad hoc* recipient) or general (for example, aid scheme) – or the administrative process preceding the decision, in other words, the formal investigation pursuant to Article 108(2) TFEU, or the preliminary proceedings under to Article 108(3) TFEU.

ACTS OPEN TO CHALLENGE

With regard to the Procedural Regulation (recently amended by EU Regulation 734/2013), the following measures taken by the Commission can be deemed, *inter alia*, to be 'challengeable' under Article 263 TFEU:

- a decision to initiate the formal investigation procedure (Article 4(4));
- a decision to close the formal investigation procedure (Article 7);
- a decision whereby the Commission either finds that the measure does not constitute aid or decides not to raise objections;
- a decision revoking a prior decision (Article 9); and
- a decision requiring the Member State to provisionally suspend or recover the unlawful aid (respectively, Article 11(1) and Article 11(2)).

Recent case law provides some guidance on the concept of 'act open to challenge'. Above all, this notion has been extended with the effect of affecting complainants' access to the Courts in the so-called *Athinaïki Techniki* 'saga'[2] and in the *NDSHT* case.[3]

In the recent past, in practice, the Commission usually sent a letter to the complainant informing him that there were insufficient grounds for taking a view on the case; more than once, the Commission added that the assessment was not to be considered definitive in compliance with the second sentence of the former version of Article 20(2) of the Procedural Regulation.

Before *Athinaïki Techniki*, the case law was far from consistent: for example, in the *Sytraval* case (and in the General Court case *UPS*[4]) the ECJ regarded the letter to the complainant as an informal and therefore not a challengeable communication, while in the *Deutsche Bahn* case[5] the General Court (GC) suggested a substantive approach, according to which if the Commission takes a clear and reasoned position on the aid, it can be acting only in accordance with Article 4(2) of the Procedural Regulation.

According to the ECJ in *Athinaïki Techniki I*,[6] the transmission of a letter pursuant to Article 20(2) is a preliminary step that must lead anyway to a decision; for this reason, the Commission has a 'duty to associate' the complainant with the proceedings, while if the intention of the Commission is to close the file, the letter should be deemed equivalent to a decision under Article 4(2) and therefore open to challenge.

---

2 Case C-521/06 P *Athinaïki Techniki AE v Commission* (*Athinaïki Techniki I*) [2008] ECR I-5829; Case C-362/09 P *Athinaïki Techniki AE v Commission* (*Athinaïki Techniki II*) [2010] ECR I-13275.

3 Case C-322/09 *NDSHT Nya Destination Stockholm Hotell & Teaterpaket AB v Commission* [2010] ECR I-11911. On the *Athinaïki Techniki* and *NDSHT* cases, see Edoardo Gambaro and Francesco Mazzocchi, 'Case C-521/06 P *Athinaïki Techniki v Commission* [2008] ECR I-5829; Case C-322/09 *NDSHT v Commission* of 18 November 2010, nyr and C-362/09 P *Athinaïki Techniki v Commission* of 16 December 2010, nyr' 48 Common Market Law Review 2083 (2011). See also Küllike Jürimäe, 'Standing in State Aid Cases: What's the State of Play?' [2010] European State Aid Law Quarterly 303.

4 Case T-182/98 *UPS Europe SA v Commission* [1999] ECR II-2857.

5 Case T-351/02 *Deutsche Bahn AG v Commission* [2006] ECR II-1047.

6 *Athinaïki Techniki I*, cited above, note 2.

This result has been achieved relying on the EU law principles and 'forcing' the interpretation of the relevant provisions of the Procedural Regulation (specifically, Articles 10(1), 13(1) and 20(2)).[7]

In light of the above, one could argue that the protection to State aid complainants turns out to be even stronger than that granted in antitrust cases[8] because the margin of appreciation of the Commission, which has exclusive competence, is ruled out.

The ECJ implicitly criticized the Commission's practice of dismissing cases through administrative letters as well as its Best Practice Code of 2009 adopted after *Athinaïki Techniki I* (containing a prioritization method), according to which the Commission may opt to refrain from sending such letters.

As an outcome of those rulings, a likely significant increase in the numbers of applications for annulment against hybrid letters was registered.

Does *Athinaïki Techniki* contain too a radical solution? One may contend that in some exceptional cases the Commission should maintain the option to close the file with an unchallengeable letter; this is a discretionary margin to be left for example to situations of 'genuine insufficient grounds'.[9]

However, the Commission aimed at recapturing, in the Procedural Regulation, some of the margin of discretion it had claimed in the 2009 Best Practices;[10] examples of these attempts are paragraph 23(b) of the SAM Communication 'enabling the Commission to set priorities for complaints handling' and the proposal for a regulation (5 December 2012) according to which, 'in cases where the information received will not be classified as a complaint since it will not have passed the admissibility criteria, the Commission will no longer be under an obligation to adopt formal decisions'.[11]

---

7 Gambaro and Mazzocchi, cited above, note 3, at 2102.

8 See Case T-24/90 *Automec Srl v Commission (Automec II)* [1992] ECR II-2223, where there was no duty to commence proceedings.

9 For an endorsement of this position, see Case T-423/07 *Ryanair Ltd v Commission* [2011] ECR II-2397.

10 Hanns Peter Nehl, '2013 Reform of EU State Aid Procedures: How to Exacerbate the Imbalance Between Efficiency and Individual Protection' [2014] European State Aid Law Quarterly 235.

11 Explanatory Memorandum to the Commission's proposal for a regulation of 5 December 2012, COM(2012) 725 final, para 2.1.

Interestingly enough, in January 2013 the GC in the *Aiscat* case[12] confirmed *Athinaïki Techniki* and *NDSHT*, stating that '[t]he poor quality of information submitted in support of a complaint cannot [...] relieve the Commission of its obligation to open the preliminary examination stage or to close that examination by way of a decision under Article 4 of Regulation No 659/1999'.[13]

Although the *Athinaïki Techniki* case can be considered 'a silent revolution',[14] it remains unclear whether it might be deemed as a long-standing one as well. In this regard, we should take into account that, although *Athinaïki Techniki* was not an isolated ruling, it is uncertain whether it will survive after the new wording of Articles 10 and 20(2) of the Procedural Regulation, as amended by EU Regulation 743/2013. Indeed, the new Regulation crystallizes most of the 2009 Commission's Best Practices and partially confirms the Commission's proposal requiring: (a) an obligation to fill out a complaint form and to provide the mandatory information; (b) the dispatch of a letter to the complainant requiring comments within one month in case of an incomplete or unfounded complaint;[15] and (c) the automatic withdrawal of the complaint in case of failure of the complainant to make known its views within the prescribed period.

In conclusion, some other judicial 'mini-revolutions' widening of the notion of 'act open to challenge' deserve to be mentioned. First, an information injunction pursuant to Article 10(3) of the Procedural Regulation addressed to the Member State is challengeable by a private party, as it produces binding and independent legal effects.[16] Moreover, the Commission's 'record' under Article 19 of the Regulation of the Member

---

[12] Case T-182/10 *Associazione Italiana delle Società Concessionarie per la Costruzione e l'esercizio di Autostrade e Trafori Stradali (Aiscat) v Commission*, 15 January 2013, EU:T:2013:9.

[13] Ibid., para 30. See also Case C-615/11 P *Commission v Ryanair Ltd*, 16 May 2013, EU:C:2013:310.

[14] Hanns Peter Nehl, 'Judicial Protection of Complainants in EC State Aid Law: A Silent Revolution?' [2009] European State Aid Law Quarterly 401.

[15] According to Nehl, '2013 Reform of EU State Aid Procedures', cited above, note 10, at 240, if the complainant reacts within the deadline prescribed in the Commission's (preliminary) letter submitting fresh comments, the Commission would be obliged to react again even under the amended rules. If the Commission then wishes to close the procedure, it would be bound to inform the complainant again in writing: this should make the *Athinaiki Techniki* case law fully applicable despite the wording of the new legislative provisions.

[16] See Joined Cases C-463/10 P and C-475/10 P *Deutsche Post AG and Germany v Commission* [2011] ECR I-9639.

State's acceptance of its proposal of appropriate measures in case of existing aid is open to challenge as well;[17] finally, the (recently introduced) decision by which the Commission requests information from private parties (the so-called market information tool) is challengeable pursuant to Article 6*bis* (7) of EU Regulation 734/2013.

LOCUS STANDI OF PRIVATE PARTIES

With regard to the *locus standi* of private parties, three requirements must be fulfilled, notably direct concern, individual concern and the interest to bring the action.[18]

Locus Standi of *Private Parties*: Direct Concern

Usually, private applicants can easily establish whether they are 'directly concerned' by a Commission decision in the field of State aid.

The beneficiary of an aid in respect of which the Commission has issued a negative recovery decision must be regarded as directly concerned by that decision; in such a case, the obligation to recover is automatic and the Member State is granted no room for discretion.

Similarly, a competitor of the beneficiary might be deemed directly concerned by a positive decision if the aid is illegal. This is due to the fact that the Commission decision would leave intact all the effects of the measure, already implemented.

By contrast, in principle there would be no direct concern if the positive decision refers to a measure previously notified by the Member State. However, if the possibility for the Member State to decide not to grant the aid authorized by the Commission is theoretical, then the decision would be of direct concern to the applicant.

Locus Standi of *Private Parties*: Individual Concern (In General)

The demonstration of an 'individual concern' is more problematic. The leading case on the subject is still *Plaumann*,[19] in which the ECJ stated

---

[17] See Case T-354/05 *Télévision Française 1 SA (TF1)* [2009] ECR II-471.

[18] For an overview of *locus standi* in State aid cases, see Edoardo Gambaro, 'The Judicial Phase' in Alberto Santa Maria (ed), *Competition and State Aid – An Analysis of the EC Practice* (Kluwer Law International 2007) 221; Cristina Schepisi, *Aiuti di Stato e Tutela Giurisdizionale* (Giappichelli 2012).

[19] Case 25/62 *Plaumann & Co. v Commission* [1963] ECR 95.

that 'persons other than those to whom a decision is addressed may only claim to be individually concerned if that decision affects them by reason of certain attributes that are peculiar to them and [...] distinguishes them individually just as in the case of the persons addressed'.

It is indisputable that a decision declaring individual aid to be incompatible is an act individually concerning the undertaking (or undertakings) specified in that decision;[20] the same applies to the potential beneficiary of individual aid in respect of a decision declaring proposed aid to be incompatible.

The actual problems with the requirement of individual concern generally arise in case of aid schemes and, in general, with regard to actions brought by the competitors of the recipient.

Individual concern – the case of potential beneficiaries of aid schemes

It is traditionally argued that a distinction should be made between aid schemes that have been implemented and those which have not (in other words, aid schemes duly notified).

Early case law adopted a restrictive approach, which basically consisted in the application of the '*Plaumann* test' towards the actions brought by potential beneficiaries. Accordingly, in *Van der Kooy* the ECJ held that: 'the contested decision is of concern to the applicants solely by virtue of their objective capacity as growers established in the Netherlands and qualifying for the preferential gas tariff on the same footing as any other grower in the same circumstances. With regard to them, therefore, the decision is a measure of general application [...]'.[21]

The Court stated that a decision cannot be considered to affect operators whose number or identity was fixed and ascertainable at the time of its adoption.[22]

Subsequent case law confirmed this strict approach, and added the following additional corollaries:

(a) an undertaking cannot, as a general rule, bring an action for the annulment of a Commission decision prohibiting a sectoral aid scheme if it is concerned by that decision solely by virtue of the

---

20 See Case 323/83 *SA Intermills v Commission* [1984] ECR 3809.

21 See Joined Cases 67/85, 68/85, 70/85 *Kwekeriij Van der Kooy and Others v Commission* [1988] ECR 219. See also Case 282/85 *Comité de Développement et de Promotion du Textile et de l'habillement DEFI v Commission* [1986] ECR 2469.

22 See Case C-6/92 *Federazione Sindacale Italiana dell'Industria Estrattiva (Federmineraria) and Others v Commission* [1993] ECR I-6357.

fact that it belongs to the sector in question and it is a potential beneficiary of the scheme;[23]

(b) the applicant must prove that it is in a situation that differs from that of all the other operators;[24] and

(c) the appellant's participation in the formal investigation procedure is only one of the factors capable of establishing individual concern.[25]

Individual concern – the case of actual beneficiaries of aid schemes

A more open approach to beneficiaries was taken in case law including the GC's *Alzetta* and *CETM* judgments and in the ECJ's ruling in *Sardegna Lines*.[26] In the latter case, the applicant was concerned by the relevant Commission decision primarily not only by virtue of it being an undertaking in the shipping sector in Sardinia – and thus a potential beneficiary of the aid scheme for Sardinian shipowners – but also by virtue of the fact that it was an actual beneficiary of the individual aid granted under that scheme, recovery of which had been ordered by the Commission.[27]

According to Advocate General Alber, the decision must affect a 'closed group of persons that cannot be extended'; the aid recipients do not have to be specifically known to the Commission at the time that

---

23 See, *inter alia*, Case C-298/00 P *Italy v Commission* [2004] ECR I-4087; and see most recently the Order of the GC in Case T-400/11 *Altadis SA v Commission*, 9 September 2013, EU:T:2013:490, para 25.

24 See Case T-9/98 *Mitteldeutsche Erdöl-Raffinerie GmbH v Commission* [2001] ECR II-3367.

25 See Case T-86/96 *Arbeitsgemeinschaft Deutscher Luftfahrt-Unternehmen and Hapag Lloyd Fluggesellschaft v Commission* [1999] ECR II-179, with reference to an aid recipient. The *locus standi* of the aid recipient's competitors is discussed below.

26 Joined Cases C-15/98 and C-105/99 *Italy and Sardinia Lines v Commission* [2000] ECR I-8855.

27 Ibid., para 31. See also Case T-298/97 *Alzetta and Others v Commission* [2000] ECR II-2319; Case C-372/97 *Italy v Commission* (the '*Alzetta* appeal') [2004] ECR I-3679, para 39; and see, *inter alia*, Case T-136/05, *Salvat Père et Fils and Others v Commission* [2007] ECR II-4063, para 70; Case T-301/02 *AEM SpA v Commission* [2009] ECR II-1757, para 45. For a case of lack of evidence of any actual benefit from the scheme, see Case T-309/02 *Acegas-APS SpA v Commission* [2009] ECR-II 1809, where the applicant was not able to state the amount received and the assessment to tax was nil.

measure is adopted but it is sufficient for them to be identifiable by the national authorities called upon to implement the Commission's decision.[28]

Therefore, the crucial element appears to be the existence of a recovery order in the Commission's decision.

The order for recovery exposes the recipients, from the time of the adoption of the decision, to the risk that the advantages which they have received will be recovered, thus affecting their legal position. The possibility that, subsequently, the advantages declared illegal may not be recovered from their beneficiaries does not exclude individual concern.[29] It is irrelevant whether the recovery order has effects at national level.[30]

It is worth noting that if the Member State concerned excludes an applicant from the procedure to recover the aid, the consequence could be dismissal for lack of interest in bringing an action, rather than for lack of individual concern.[31]

Recently, the GC has issued several dismissal orders. For example, some Spanish applicants were not subject to a recovery obligation contained in a 2009 Commission decision (by virtue of the principle of legitimate expectations) but they claimed that the lack of a recovery order was not definitive.[32] According to the GC, the applicants confused the 'individual concern' requirement, which is determined only by the Commission decision, with the 'interest in bringing proceedings'. According to Advocate General Kokott in *Telefónica I*,[33] the only risk of recovery from the contested decision may be seen where the decision is modified due to a third party's initiative: in this case, the applicant can bring an action against the new decision.

---

[28] See the Opinion of Advocate General Alber in the *Alzetta* appeal, paras 80–85.

[29] See Case C-71/09 *Comitato 'Venezia vuole vivere'* [2011] ECR I-4727, para 56.

[30] See the Order of the GC in Case T-174/11 *Modelo Continente Hipermercados v Commission*, 21 March 2012, EU:T:2012:143, para 29.

[31] Case T-228/00 *Gruppo Ormeggiatori Porto Venezia v Commission* [2005] ECR II-787. For a different approach, see *Acegas*, cited above, note 27.

[32] This was due to an action brought before the GC by a competitor against the Commission's decision. See Case T-221/10 *Iberdrola SA v Commission*, 8 March 2012, EU:T:2012:112; Order of the GC in Case T-228/10 *Telefónica SA v Commission (Telefónica I) v Commission*, 21 March 2012, EU:T:2012:140.

[33] Opinion in Case C-274/12 P *Telefónica SA v Commission (Telefónica I)*, EU:C:2013:852.

As far as this topic is concerned, it is worth recalling other recent cases. In its orders of 9 September 2013, issued in *Altadis SA*[34] and *Telefónica II*,[35] the GC ruled on cases concerning actual beneficiaries (which had applied the aid scheme to acquisitions of shareholdings) but not covered by the recovery obligation provided for in the relevant Commission decision. The GC stated: 'The status of actual beneficiary of an aid scheme is not sufficient to identify that beneficiary individually, where the latter is not covered by the obligation to recover the aid paid under that scheme'.[36]

A different outcome had been reached in 2009 in *Koninklijke Friesland Campina*:[37] although there was no recovery obligation in the decision (due to legitimate expectations), the appeal was deemed admissible.

Individual concern – the case of beneficiaries of aid schemes – criticism and some tentative conclusions

According to traditional criticism, the EU case law on admissibility of aid scheme recipients leads to greater rights for actual beneficiaries of illegal aids than for potential beneficiaries; notwithstanding that the former undertakings are under a duty to ascertain that the aid has been properly notified by the Member State.

Others argue that, by consistently stating the principle that individual concern is 'determined only by the Commission decision',[38] the EU Courts might be giving unequal treatment to parties that deserve a similar (or even the same) protection, such as that of actual beneficiaries whose recovery orders have no effects at national level and that of actual beneficiaries not covered by the recovery order in the decision, for example in application of the legitimate expectation principle.

Finally, the current case law may have the effect of requiring the beneficiaries of the State aid to challenge the Commission decision immediately, even before knowing whether it would lead to a recovery order concerning them, with greater procedural burdens for the EU Courts; this argument has often been invoked by the Commission and has always been rejected in Luxembourg.

---

34 *Altadis v Commission*, cited above, note 23.

35 Case T-430/11 *Telefónica v Commission (Telefónica II)*, 9 September 2013, EU:T:2013:489; on appeal: Case C-588/13 P, not yet decided.

36 *Altadis*, cited above, note 23, para 34.

37 C-519/07 P *Commission v Koninklijke Friesland Campina* [2009] ECR I-8495.

38 *Iberdrola*, cited above, note 32, para 40. Similarly, see *Telefónica I*, cited above, note 32, para 35.

Individual concern – the case of the beneficiary's competitors – introduction

Pursuant to the ECJ's case law,[39] a distinction must be drawn between the conditions of standing that must be fulfilled by third parties in respect of: (a) the decisions adopted by the Commission after a preliminary examination of the aid pursuant to Article 108(3) TFEU; and (b) those adopted by the Commission at the end of the formal investigation procedure *ex* Article 108(2) TFEU.

Whereas, in relation to challenges brought against the decisions *sub* (a) it suffices for a claimant to demonstrate its status of 'interested party', a stricter test of standing must be met by applicants seeking to challenge decisions *sub* (b).

(a) The case of the beneficiary's competitors – decisions issued at the end of the formal investigation The leading case here is the ruling in *Cofaz*,[40] where the Court, referring to the criteria laid down in the area of anti-dumping, held that two main (seemingly cumulative) conditions must be fulfilled, in other words:

- the applicant must have been 'substantially involved' in the procedure before the Commission; and
- his position on the market must be 'substantially affected' by the aid in question.

The *Cofaz* conditions were applied by subsequent case law in different ways. As concerns the condition of the 'procedural involvement', the EU Courts quickly developed an inclination to abandon this requirement as a *condicio sine qua non*, since 'an undertaking may be in a position to demonstrate by other means […] that it is individually concerned'.[41] In 2007 the ECJ expressly acknowledged that active participation in the procedure 'is not a necessary condition' for a finding of individual concern.[42]

---

[39] See in particular Case C-198/91 *Cook plc v Commission* [1993] ECR I-2487; Case C-225/91 *Matra SA v Commission* [1993] ECR I-3203.

[40] Case 169/84 *Société CdF Chimie azote et Fertilisants SA and Société Chimique de la Grande Paroisse SA (Cofaz) v Commission* [1990] ECR I-3083.

[41] Case T-435/93 *Association of Sorbitol Producers Within the EC (ASPEC) and Others v Commission* [1995] ECR II-1281, para 64. See also Case T-11/95 *BP Chemicals Limited v Commission* [1998] ECR II-3235; Case T-149/95 *Etablissements J. Richard Ducros v Commission* [1997] ECR II-2031.

[42] Case C-260/05 P *Sniace SA v Commission* [2007] ECR I-10005, para 57.

The EU Courts did not provide a consistent definition of 'sufficient' involvement: might it be inferred from the mere submission of comments to the Commission,[43] or is it necessary for an applicant to be 'at the origin of the complaint which led to the opening of the procedure'?[44]

My view is that – although it is no longer a *condicio sine qua non* – the 'procedural involvement' requirement still remains an important feature.[45]

With regard to the 'substantially affects' condition, the EU Courts elaborated different degrees of this test in the aftermath of *Cofaz*.[46]

The following (slightly new) approach was then adopted by the ECJ, relying on the (pre-*Cofaz*) *Eridania* case:[47] an undertaking cannot rely solely on its status as a competitor of the aid recipient but must also demonstrate the magnitude of the prejudice to its position on the market.[48] This test must be conducted by reference to the beneficiaries of the aid measures in issue.[49]

A good example of the stricter approach is the *Deutsche Post/DHL Italia* case,[50] where the Court stated that neither the presence on the same market of the aid recipient, nor its identification by name in the decision,

---

[43] Joined Cases T-371/94 and T-394/94 *British Airways and Others and British Midland Airways v Commission* [1998] ECR II-2405.

[44] Case T-36/99 *Lenzing AG v Commission* [2004] ECR II-3597; *Ducros*, cited above, note 41.

[45] One may note a more lenient approach to standing (and to the 'substantially affects' criterion) where an applicant shows an active involvement in the administrative procedure. See *Cofaz* (cited above, note 40), *Lenzing* (cited previous note) and *Spanish Petrol Stations* (cited below, note 52; admissibility and active participation of the applicants), on the one hand; and *BP Chemicals* (note 41), *Sniace* (note 42) and Case C-367/04 P *Deutsche Post AG and DHL Express (Italia) v Commission* [2006] ECR I-26* (dismissal of the action and minor or no role in the procedure) on the other.

[46] A stricter test was applied in cases such as *BP Chemicals* (cited above, note 41), *Sniace* (note 42) and *Lenzing* (note 44) compared to *British Airways* (note 43), Case T-442/93 *Association des Amidonneries de Céréales de la CEE (AAC) and Others v Commission* [1995] ECR II-1329 and *Ducros* (note 41).

[47] Case 18/68 *Eridania v Commission* [1969] ECR 459.

[48] See Case C-106/98 P *Comité d'entreprise de la Société Française de Production (CIRFS) v Commission* [2000] ECR I-3659, para 41, followed by the GC in Case T-193/06 *TF1 v Commission* [2010] ECR II-4967 and in Case T-117/04 *Vereniging Werkgroep Commerciële Jachthavens Zuidelijke Randmeren and Others (Dutch Commercial Marinas)* [2006] ECR II-3861.

[49] *TF1 v Commission*, cited previous note, paras 78 and 81.

[50] Order of the GC in Case T-358/02 *Deutsche Post AG and DHL International Srl v Commission* [2004] ECR II-1565, upheld on appeal: Order of the

nor yet the mere existence of over-capacity on the market, is sufficient.[51] In addition, the market shares proving that DHL was one of the biggest competitors (in other words, the fifth, with more than 8 per cent) of the aid recipient were irrelevant.[52] The Court interestingly added that the 'substantially affects' criterion does not coincide with that of 'distortion of competition' *ex* Article 107 TFEU.

A more liberal stance was adopted in the *Lenzing* and *British Aggregates* cases. In those rulings, the ECJ held that the 'substantially affects' condition must not necessarily be inferred from factors such as a significant decline in turnover, appreciable financial losses or a significant reduction in market share following the grant of the aid in question. Indeed, the grant of State aid can have an adverse effect on the competitive situation of an operator in other ways, causing either the loss of an opportunity or a less favourable development than would have been the case without the aid.[53] Likewise, the seriousness of such an effect may vary according to a large number of factors including, in particular, the structure of the market concerned or the nature of the aid in question.[54] Moreover, the existence of an 'undefined number of other competitors' suffering similar harm was considered irrelevant as well.[55] In other words, the ECJ seems to have rejected the so-called 'unique position test', meaning that the fact that other competitors may have suffered similar harm cannot make an annulment action inadmissible.[56]

ECJ in Case C-367/04, [2006] ECR I-26. This was an appeal against a Commission decision authorizing a measure in favour of Poste Italiane.

[51] See also Case T-375/04 *Scheucher Fleisch and Others v Commission* [2009] ECR II-4155, para 59.

[52] *Contra* Case T-146/03 *Asociación de Empresarios de Estaciones de Servicio de la Comunidad Autónoma de Madrid and Federación Catalana de Estaciones de Servicio (Spanish Petrol Stations) v Commission* [2006] ECR II-98*, although the applicants affected represented less than 3 per cent of Spanish petrol stations.

[53] See Case C-525/04 P *Spain v Commission* [2007] ECR I-9947, paras 34–35.

[54] Ibid., para 35.

[55] Case C-487/06 P *British Aggregates Association v Commission* [2008] ECR I-10515, para 56. For a different approach, see *Deutsche Post/DHL Italia* (cited above, note 45) and *Dutch Commercial Marinas* (note 48), where the market share of the applicants and the lack of decline in turnover were deemed relevant.

[56] See Bart A. Creve, '*Locus Standi* Requirements for Annulment Actions by Competitors: the Resurfacing "Unique Position Test" Ought to Be Discarded' [2014] European State Aid Law Quarterly 233.

The *Aiscat* case[57] might be taken as another example of the ECJ's more liberal approach.[58]

In any case, the most recent GC Orders (rendered between 2011 and 2013) seem to have departed from the ECJ's more favourable approach in *Lenzing* and *British Aggregates* by requiring from competitors a sort of *probatio diabolica*.[59] Among them we may recall the following cases:

- *Vtesse Networks*:[60] the procedure ended with a dismissal order because: (i) there were at least 35 competing operators on the relevant markets; (ii) the applicant did not indicate its market shares; and (iii) the applicant did not prove a causal link between the aid and the loss of a contract in favour of the recipient;
- *Phoenix Reisen*:[61] although the applicants alleged that some of the aid beneficiaries would have disappeared from the market without the aid, the ECJ opted for dismissal;
- *Mojo Concerts*:[62] the GC examined the two markets affected by the aid and dismissed the action, as the applicants: (i) were unable to differentiate themselves from other competitors; and (ii) had grounded their action on 'hypothesis' or 'simple suppositions';
- *UPS*:[63] another dismissal despite the applicant's active role in the

---

[57] Cited above, note 12.

[58] This was an appeal against a Commission letter closing the file. The national measure was an award to CAV S.p.A, with no call for tender, of the concession for the construction of the Passante di Mestre. The GC carried out quite a detailed market analysis. In application of the *Lenzing* principle, the applicants showed a less favourable development of their commercial results than would have been the case without the aid (para 78 of the ruling), and this entailed the admissibility of the application on the basis of the 'substantially affects' criterion.

[59] For another example of a strict application of the 'substantially affects' criterion, see paras 43–58 of Case T-488/11 *Scheepsbouwkundig Advies- en Rekencentrum (Sarc) BV v Commission*, 12 June 2014, EU:T:2014:497. *Contra: Aiscat*, cited above, note 12.

[60] Case T-54/07 *Vtesse Networks Ltd v Commission* [2011] ECR II-6.

[61] Order of the GC in Case T-58/10 *Phoenix-Reisen GmbH and Deutscher Reiseverband eV (DRV) v Commission*, 11 January 2012, published in the electronic Reports of Cases.

[62] Order of the GC in Case T-90/09 *Mojo Concerts BV and Amsterdam Music Dome Exploitatie BV v Commission*, 26 January 2012, published in the electronic Reports of Cases.

[63] Order of the GC in Case T-344/10 *UPS Europe and United Parcel Service Deutschland v Commission*, 4 May 2012, EU:T:2012:216. As correctly argued by Creve, '*Locus Standi* Requirements', cited above, note 56, at 234, although the

procedure, despite the allegation that the applicant was the 'main direct competitor' of the recipient, and regardless of the very high amount of the aid;

- *UOP*:[64] the GC dismissed the appeal after having: (i) considered irrelevant the applicant's allegation that UOP was the 'world leader in aromatics technologies' and that it was one of the major competitors of the beneficiaries in each relevant market segment; (ii) contested the evidentiary value of the market shares; (iii) deemed the references to the applicant contained in the Commission's decision to be irrelevant; and (iv) rejected the applicant's references to the structure of the market based on invitations to tender, and its references to the nature (R&D) of the aid.

(b) The case of the beneficiary's competitors – decisions issued at the end of the preliminary procedure Another scenario must be dealt with, namely the case of an application brought by a recipient's competitor for the annulment of a decision based both on the Commission's refusal to open the formal investigation procedure and on the protection of the procedural guarantees under Article 108(2) TFEU.

In light of the principles set forth by the ECJ in the *Cook* and *Matra* cases (1993), the applicants only need to show that they qualify as 'parties concerned' for the purposes of Article 108(2); the rationale of this 'lighter' test can be found in the lack of information available to private parties in the pre-litigation phase.[65] Although this principle was confirmed by the ECJ in *ARE*,[66] there is a great degree of inconsistency in the case law.

On the other hand, if the applicant calls into question the merits of the decision, the mere fact that it may be regarded as 'concerned' cannot suffice to render the action admissible. The applicant must further demonstrate that it has a particular status within the meaning of the *Plaumann/Cofaz* case law.[67]

GC in *UPS Europe* dismissed the application brought before it, in doing so it followed an approach more consistent with *British Aggregates*, cited above, note 55.

[64] Case T-198/09 *UOP Ltd v Commission*, 7 March 2013, EU:T:2013:105.

[65] See the Opinion of Advocate General Tesauro in *Cook*, cited above, note 39.

[66] Case C-78/03 P *Commission v Aktionsgemeinschaft Recht und Eigentum eV (ARE)* [2005] ECR I 10737, para 35.

[67] Ibid., para 37.

Advocate General Jacobs stated in the *ARE* case that the jurisprudence in this regard is unsatisfactory, complex and illogical. He therefore suggested that the 'individual concern test' (in other words, a broader type of *Plaumann* test) should be applied in all cases, irrespective of the grounds on which the action is brought. The ECJ did not follow his opinion.

In the *Kronoply/Kronotex* case,[68] the Commission invited the ECJ to reconsider its case law and the compatibility with the Treaty of the *Cook* rule of standing, arguing that such a rule should be considered a sort of derogation to Article 263(4) TFEU. In *Kronoply/Kronotex*, Advocate General Jääskinen proposed the abolition of the distinction between procedural pleas and pleas related to the merits.[69] The ECJ again declined the opportunity to clarify the issue.

As a consequence, the *Cook/Matra locus standi* rule is still deemed to be an application of Article 263(4), and not an exception to it.

With time, a progressive broadening of the notion of 'interested party' under Article 1(h) of the Procedural Regulation was seen in appeals challenging a first phase decision. Thus, 'any persons, undertakings or associations whose interests might be affected by the granting of aid, that is, in particular competing undertakings and trade associations', in other words, an indeterminate group of addressees,[70] might be regarded as an interested party.

In addition, it is unnecessary to be a direct competitor of the aid beneficiary, provided that there is a 'sufficient relationship of competition'.[71]

Finally, in *Kronoply/Kronotex* the GC declared admissible an action brought by two undertakings that were not at all competitors of the aid recipient but rival purchasers of the raw material that the aid recipient also bought (for a different use).[72]

---

[68] C-83/09 P *Commission v Kronoply GmbH & Co. KG and Kronotex GmbH & Co. KG* [2011] ECR I-4441. The applicants were deemed by the GC to have standing on the basis of *Cook* cited above (note 39) but not on the basis of *Cofaz* (note 40).

[69] Opinion of the Advocate General in *Kronoply and Kronotex*, cited previous note.

[70] *Sytraval* (cited above, note 1), and *ARE* (note 66).

[71] Case T-395/04 *Air One SpA v Commission* [2006] ECR II-1343, where the applicant operated in the Italian market but not directly on the same routes as the aid recipient.

[72] Case T-388/02 *Kronoply GmbH & Co. KG and Kronotex GmbH & Co. KG v Commission* [2008] ECR II-305*, upheld on appeal: Case C-83/09 P, cited

The so-called 'explicit plea requirement' and the 'reinterpretation ban' were formally confirmed by, *inter alia*, two 2011 ECJ rulings in *Kronoply/Kronotex* and *Belgium/Deutsche Post-DHL*.[73] According to the Court, 'it is not for the EU judicature to interpret an action challenging exclusively the merits of an aid decision as seeking, in reality, to ensure the respect of the procedural rights [...], where the applicant has not expressly raised a plea to that effect. In such circumstances, the interpretation of the plea would be tantamount to re-defining the subject-matter of the action'.[74]

However, a substantial relaxation of the explicit plea requirement can easily be found in recent case law. Although the application does not contain a distinctly identifiable plea on procedural rights, the EU Courts can interpret the plea in light of the arguments underlying the plea on the merits as well as on the 'actual wording of the application'. This relaxation may be seen as a corollary of the decreasing importance of the distinction between procedural pleas and pleas on the merits.[75]

In the light of a substantial interpretation of the pleas, the applicant may invoke 'any plea' to show that the assessment of the information and of the evidence the Commission had at its disposal during the preliminary examination phase should have raised doubts as to the compatibility of the aid. Therefore, the key evidence to be adduced seems to be evidence supporting the existence of doubts about compatibility.[76]

In this sense, the *Smurfit Kappa* case[77] is noteworthy because it introduced the rule that the admissibility of each plea and of the underlying arguments must be examined on a case-by-case basis.[78] As a

---

above, note 68. According to the GC, it was possible that the interests of the applicants could be adversely affected by the aid.

[73] On these rulings, see Fernando Pastor Merchante, 'On the Rules of Standing to Challenge State Aid Decisions Adopted at the End of the Preliminary Phase' [2012] European State Aid Law Quarterly 601.

[74] Case C-148/09 P *Belgium v Deutsche Post and DHL International* [2011] ECR I-8573.

[75] A subtle distinction exists between pleas regarding the substance (inadmissible for *Cook*-based standing) and arguments alleging serious difficulties, which may be considered in support of a procedural plea. See *Kronoply and Kronotex*, cited above, note 68, at para 56.

[76] Ibid., para 59.

[77] Case T-304/08 *Smurfit Kappa Group v Commission*, 10 July 2012, EU:T:2012:351.

[78] Ibid., para 65.

consequence, a stand-alone explicit procedural plea is in practice no longer required in order to benefit from the broad standing conditions in *Cook*.[79]

In conclusion, the current standard seems to be the existence of doubts about the classification of the measure as State aid and about its compatibility, regardless of the basis of the applicant's *locus standi*.[80]

It is arguable whether the rationale of the 'two-scenario approach' is still valid.[81] First of all, the aim pursued by the applicant is the same whether it invokes the protection of procedural rights or challenges the merits of the decision: in both cases it seeks the initiation of the formal investigation procedure.[82]

Moreover, the current approach creates legal uncertainty as it is impossible both for the parties concerned and for the GC to clearly identify, from an amalgam of pleas, those aimed at protecting procedural rights and those concerning the substance.[83]

That being said, a question remains: Isn't it better to move to a single criterion? If so, the second question is: Which one? A strict *Plaumann* test or the criterion of the 'interested party' (perhaps restricted in order to avoid a proliferation of actions)?

Locus Standi of *Private Parties*: The Interest in Bringing an Action

Since the annulment of the measure must be capable of having legal consequences and of securing an advantage for the party who brought the action, the applicant's interest has to fulfil certain requirements and, notably, its interest has to be vested and present; and it must be evaluated

79 Nevertheless, in *Aiscat*, cited above, note 12, at paras 44–47, the GC was unable to infer a procedural plea from the application on the grounds of a strict applicability of the explicit plea requirement.

80 *Kronoply and Kronotex*, cited above, note 68, at para 59. A similar standard was proposed by Advocate General Mengozzi in *British Aggregates*, cited above, note 55. See also *Sarc BV*, cited above, note 59, at paras 63–65.

81 As mentioned, strong criticism of this approach has been put forward by several Advocates General (Jacobs, then Mengozzi, Bot, Sharpston and Jääskinen). See Andreas Bartosch, 'Procedural Rights Denied for Too Long: Is Legal Conservativism Finally Heading for its Götterdämmerung?' [2011] European State Aid Law Quarterly 579.

82 See the Opinion of Advocate General Bot in Joined Cases C-75/05 P and C-80/05 P *Germany and Others v Kronofrance SA* [2008] ECR I-6619.

83 See the Opinion of Advocate General Jääskinen in *Kronoply and Kronotex*, cited above, note 68.

when the action is brought and it must continue to exist until the final decision is adopted.

For instance, if the applicant is no longer subject to any legal obligation, the annulment would not bring him any advantage and therefore, he would no longer have standing to initiate proceedings.[84]

The assessment must be done case-by-case.[85] An applicant cannot rely upon future uncertain circumstances.

REGULATORY ACTS *EX* ARTICLE 263(4) TFEU AND STATE AID

A 'regulatory act which is of direct concern [to private parties] and does not entail implementing measures' is a new category of challengeable measure introduced by the Lisbon Treaty, and specifically by Article 263(4) TFEU. The notion of 'regulatory act' has in fact been interpreted by the EU Courts. The first case of application was the GC Order in *Inuit*.[86] This was an action for annulment of a regulation adopted through the ordinary legislative procedure banning trade in seal products from the EU markets. For purposes of the fourth paragraph of Article 263, the notion of a 'regulatory act' was said to include all acts of general application apart from legislative acts. Therefore, the action was declared inadmissible.

But the first case of successful application was the ruling of the GC in *Microban*.[87] The applicants sought to annul a Commission decision

---

84 See the Order of the GC in Joined Cases T-228/00, etc., *Gruppo ormeggiatori Porto Venezia and Others v Commission* [2005] ECR II-787; Case T-354/99 *Kuwait Petroleum (Holland) v Commission* [2006] ECR II-1475. These were cases concerning *ex post* exclusion of the applicants from the obligation to repay.

85 A recent application of the notion of 'advantage' by the GC is Case T-1/08 *Buczek Automotive sp. z o.o. v Commission* [2011] ECR II-2107, where the applicant was deemed to have no interest in bringing an action against the whole of the recovery order. Examples of a stricter (and rather complicated) approach can be found in the recent case law. See *Telefónica I*, cited above, note 33, para 86: according to Advocate General Kokott, the ECJ should not be too strict in the assessment of the 'advantage'.

86 Case T-18/10, upheld on appeal: C-583/11 P *Inuit Tapiriit Kanatami and Others v Parliament and Council*, 3 October 2013, EU:C:2013:625.

87 Case T-262/10 *Microban International and Microban (Europe) v Commission* [2011] ECR II-7697. In Case T-279/11 *T & L Sugars Ltd and Others v Commission*, 6 June 2013, EU:T:2013:299, at paras 54–57, the GC held that the

addressed to the Member States which required them not to include a dangerous substance in a list of additives adopted in the exercise of implementing powers. The GC stated that the contested decision was of general application in that it applied to objectively determined situations and it produced legal effects with respect to categories of persons envisaged in general and in the abstract. The action was consequently held admissible.

These diverging solutions are merely due to different legislative techniques, entailing the lack of focus on the substance (in other words, the content of the act) and on the individual qualities of the applicant.[88]

That said, the next question is whether one can classify a Commission decision on a State aid scheme addressed to the grantor Member State as a 'regulatory act' within the meaning of Article 263(4).

An affirmative answer was given by Advocate General Kokott.[89] In her view, although a regulatory act is not a legislative act[90] it is, nevertheless, of general application because, in spite of its being addressed only to the grantor Member State, it is binding on any organ of the addressee Member State and it has the peculiarity of producing legal effects with respect to potential beneficiaries, in other words, a category of persons envisaged in general and in the abstract.[91]

As for the notion of 'implementing measures', according to the GC, a negative Commission decision on an aid scheme cannot be regarded by the beneficiaries as an 'act not entailing implementing measures'. The GC dealt with the matter in *Telefónica I*, *Iberdrola*, *Altadis* and *Telefónica II*, issuing dismissal orders in 2012 and in 2013.[92] In those cases,

---

approach in *Microban* (with specific reference to the existence of measures implementing the contested regulations) could not be applied in the case before it.

[88] Arjen Meij, 'Standing in Direct Actions in the EU Courts After Lisbon', in Marjolein van Roosmalen et al. (eds), *Fundamental Rights and Principles: Liber Amicorum Pieter van Dijk* (Intersentia 2013) 141.

[89] Opinion of the Advocate General in *Telefónica I*, cited above, note 33, paras 17–29. See also, implicitly, the judgment of the ECJ in the same case, as well as Case C-132/12 P, *Stichting Woonpunt and Others v Commission,* 27 February 2014, EU:C:2014:100; and Case C-133/12 P *Stichting Woonlinie and Others v Commission*, 27 February 2014, EU:C:2014:105.

[90] Opinion in *Telefónica I*, cited above, note 33, paras 17–19.

[91] Ibid., paras 20–29. See also *Microban*, cited above, note 87, para 23.

[92] *Iberdrola*, cited above, note 32, paras 45–48; *Telefónica I*, cited above, note 32, paras 42–45; *Altadis*, cited above, note 23, paras 42–50; *Telefónica II*, cited above, note 35, paras 48–54. In the same vein, but with reference to a Commission decision not in the field of State aid, see the Order of the GC in

the contested decision itself referred not only to the existence of recovery/implementing measures (for example, tax notices) but also to 'other' implementing measures, such as all the 'measures for implementing the incompatibility decision' (for example, a rejection of the application for the tax advantage). In addition, according to the GC, these measures can be challenged by the applicants before a national court, possibly leading to a preliminary reference on validity. Finally, the Court deemed it immaterial that the grantor Member State had no discretion in implementing the Commission's decision.[93]

The concept was further developed by the Advocate General Kokott and the ECJ in *Telefónica I*,[94] where a pertinent issue was whether recovery measures and other measures implementing an incompatibility decision are 'implementing measures' for the purpose of Article 263(4). According to the Advocate General, on the one hand, the literal interpretation of the third category of Article 263(4) is not conclusive and, on the other hand, direct judicial protection is needed only when the act produces *per se* legal effects with respect to the private party (without need for implementing measures).

In light of the above, the recovery order is not a 'necessary implementing measure' because it does not stem as an automatic consequence from incompatibility; indeed, a tax notice is necessary in order to specify the juridical effects for the recipient of the decision of incompatibility. Moreover, a tax notice is challengeable before a national court by means of a preliminary reference regarding its validity.

The ECJ shared the Advocate General's opinion and added that a negative decision does not define the specific consequences of a declaration of incompatibility for each recipient/taxpayer. Those consequences

---

Case T-381/11 *Europäischer Wirtschaftsverband der Eisen- und Stahlindustrie (Eurofer) ASBL v Commission*, 4 June 2012, EU:T:2012:273, paras 41–64.

[93] Interestingly, the lack of discretion is indeed a relevant criterion for the issue of direct concern. However, according to the GC, the requirement of an act which 'does not entail implementing measures' is a condition distinct from that of the requirement of direct concern. See *Altadis*, cited above, note 23, para 47; *Telefónica II*, cited above, note 35, para 52; *Eurofer*, cited previous note, para 59. *Contra* the Opinions of Advocate General Wathelet in the two 'wocos' cases (Cases C-132/12 P at para 76 and note 28 and C-133/12 P at para 49 and note 19). As the Advocate General remarked in these cases, «*la condition liée à l'absence de mesure d'exécution n'est qu'une répétition de l'affectation directe*»

[94] See the Opinion of the Advocate General in *Telefónica I*, cited above, note 33, paras 30–56 and paras 27–39.

will be embodied in administrative documents (such as a tax notice), which constitute as such an 'implementing measure'.[95]

In conclusion, according to several GC Orders and to the ECJ, a negative Commission decision on an aid scheme should be regarded as a 'regulatory act', but one 'entailing implementing measures'. In principle, this should be true for recipients of illegal aid with or without a recovery order.

Some questions are still open: is there room for a residual application of the final limb of the fourth paragraph of Article 263 in the State aid field? What about the following cases, which do not imply a subsequent act challengeable at national level:[96]

(i) a negative decision appealed by the beneficiary of an illegal aid scheme whose specific nature does not provide for national implementing measures;
(ii) a negative decision challenged by a potential beneficiary of a notified aid scheme; or
(iii) the positive/no recovery decision appealed by competitors of the recipient of an aid scheme?[97]

With reference to category (iii), and in contrast to *Telefónica I*:

- the positive (or negative with no recovery) decision would likely to be 'self-sufficient', directly affecting the legal situation of the applicant (a competitor of the aid recipient);
- the implementing measures (if any) would be addressed to the aid recipients and not to their competitors;
- the competitor/applicant usually would not be in the position to challenge an implementing act before a national court[98] (and could prevail on the latter to request a preliminary ruling from the ECJ);

[95] *Telefónica I*, cited above, note 33, para 35.

[96] The ECJ has held that the question of whether a recovery order entails implementing measures should be addressed by reference to the position of the person pleading the right to bring proceedings. See *Telefónica I*, cited above, note 33, para 30. It is therefore irrelevant whether the act in question entails implementing measures with regard to other persons.

[97] This issue is pending before the GC in Case T-219/13 *Ferracci v Commission* and in Case T-220/13 *Scuola Elementare Maria Montessori v Commission*. For a peculiar case, see Case T-601/11 *Dansk Automat Brancheforening v Commission*, 26 September 2014, EU:T:2014:839, paras 53–61.

[98] See *Telefónica I*, cited above, note 33, para 28. For a strict approach (not regarding a State aid decision), see *T & L Sugars*, cited above, note 87, where the

- it is hard to imagine a situation where the competitor/applicant 'would have to break the law in order to have access to justice'.[99]

The category of applicants which are competitors of the aid recipient is one of the most 'neglected' according to the *Plaumann* test:[100] will the final limb of the fourth paragraph of Article 263 entail a new favourable status for this category?

---

appeal was declared inadmissible under the final limb of Article 263(4) even though it was uncertain whether the applicants had a legal remedy which allowed them to challenge the national measures in implementing the contested regulations. In *Dansk Automat Brancheforening*, cited above, previous footnote, paras 58-59, the GC held that the actual consequences of the Commission decision for the applicant materialized as "challengeable national acts" – above all in the form of the Danish Law on gaming duties, by which the aid scheme in question was introduced and whose entry into force had been postponed by the Danish authorities until the Commission had adopted a final decision.

[99] See the Order of the GC in *Eurofer*, cited above, note 92, para 59; *Telefónica I*, cited above, note 33, para 27 of the ECJ's judgment and paras 40–41 of Advocate General Kokott's Opinion. See also *Dansk Automat Brancheforening*, cited above, note 97, para 59. In any case, the fact that an individual affected by an EU measure might, in some instances, be able to raise issues as to the validity of the measure before the national courts (which might then submit a preliminary reference to the ECJ) by first violating the rules laid down by the measure would not be sufficient to secure for the applicant effective judicial protection. See the Opinion of Advocate General Jacobs in Case C-50/00 P *Unión de Pequeños Agricultores v Council* [2002] ECR I-6677, para 43; Case C-432/05 *Unibet (London) Ltd and Unibet (International) Ltd v Justitiekanslern* [2007] ECR I-2271, para 64.

[100] According to Kevin C. O'Higgins, 'Overview of the Jurisprudence in State Aid Cases: Substance and Procedure – an Update' [2011] European State Aid Law Quarterly 601, the burden imposed on a competitor of a beneficiary of State aid to demonstrate that it is individually concerned by a Commission decision 'is comparable to the Alpe d'Huez stage of the Tour de France'.

10. State aid cases before national judges

Mario Siragusa and Kostandin Peci*

ABSTRACT

This chapter briefly discusses the enforcement of State aid rules by national judges. The analysis first focuses on the main legal actions and remedies available to companies enforcing State aid rules as a 'sword', including damage claims against the issuance of unlawful aid. Then we examine the opposite scenario (in other words, State aid rules used as a 'shield'), in particular the case of a beneficiary of allegedly unlawful aid challenging the validity of the national recovery order before national courts on the ground that the recovery order implements an invalid Commission decision finding the aid to be unlawful.

STATE AID AND NATIONAL JUDGES: A GENERAL OVERVIEW

The basic EU State aid rules are contained in Articles 107 through 109 of the Treaty on the Functioning of the European Union ('TFEU'). Under Article 107(1) TFEU, a State measure is found to comprise elements of aid where the following four cumulative criteria are fulfilled:

- the measure is granted by the State or from State resources, and it is attributable to State action;
- the measure confers on the recipient an advantage (for example, a reduction in the tax base or in the amount of tax, a deferment or a cancellation) that it would not usually enjoy under normal market conditions;

* Partner, Cleary Gottlieb Steen & Hamilton LLP, Rome; Associate, Cleary Gottlieb Steen & Hamilton LLP, Rome.

- the measure is specific or selective (in other words, it favours a certain undertaking(s) or the production of certain goods); and
- the measure is capable of distorting competition and of affecting trade among Member States.

Measures that constitute State aid pursuant to Article 107(1) can be authorized under Article 107(2), Article 107(3) or Article 106(2), on the basis of a number of legitimate objectives. Any new State aid measure must be notified, in draft form, to the Commission for approval in accordance with Article 108(3) TFEU and Article 2 of Council Regulation (EC) 659/1999 (the 'Procedural Regulation').[1] This means that, under Article 108(3), aid may not be implemented by the Member State concerned until the Commission adopts a decision to authorize it (the 'standstill obligation'). Aid granted in violation of the standstill obligation constitutes unlawful aid, which is subject to recovery from the beneficiary (including compounded interest). However, the Commission can order recovery only if the aid is not only unlawful in the sense of having been improperly granted, but also incompatible with the Internal Market.[2] Member States may not rely on urgency as an excuse for infringing this obligation.[3]

The prohibition against Member States implementing aid absent Commission approval gives rise to directly effective individual rights of affected parties, which national courts are bound to safeguard.[4] Affected

---

[1] Council Regulation (EC) 659/1999 laying down detailed rules for the application of Article 93 of the EC Treaty [1999] OJ L/83/1.

[2] See, for example, Case C-142/87 *Belgium v Commission (Tubemeuse)* [1990] ECR 959. For the (exceptional) possibility of adopting a provisional recovery order, see Article 11(2) of the Procedural Regulation.

[3] Joined Cases T-239/04 and T-323/04 *Italy v Commission* [2007] ECR II-3265, para 89.

[4] As a matter of principle, see Case C-6/64 *Costa v Enel*, [1964] ECR 585, 596. See also Joined Cases C-261/01 and C-262/01 *Belgium v Van Calster et al.* [2003] ECR I-12249, para 75; Case C-368/04 *Transalpine Ölleitung in Österreich GmbH et al. v Finanzlandesdirektion für Tirol et al.* [2006] ECR I-9957, para 38. In the field of State aid, see Case C-39/94 *Syndicat Français de l'Express International (SFEI) v La Poste and Others* [1996] ECR I-3547, para 39. See also Case 120/73 *Gebrüder Lorenz GmbH v Germany and Land Rheinland-Pfalz* [1973] ECR 1471, para 8; Case C-354/90 *Fédération Nationale du Commerce Extérieur des Produits Alimentaires and Syndicat National des Négociants et Transformateurs de Saumon (FNCE) v France* [1991] ECR I 5505, para 11.

parties can enforce their rights by bringing legal actions before competent national courts against the granting Member State. Deciding on such claims 'is one of the most important roles of national courts in State aid rules'.[5]

However, 'according to settled ECJ jurisprudence[,] national courts do not have the power to declare an aid compatible with Article 107(2) or (3) of the Treaty'.[6] The assessment of the compatibility of aid measures with the Internal Market falls within the exclusive competence of the Commission, while it is for national courts to ensure that the rights of individuals are safeguarded where the notification obligation of new aid prior to its implementation is infringed.[7]

Hence, national courts and the Commission play distinct but complementary roles in the enforcement of State aid rules. The scope of action recognized for national courts may be summarized as follows.

The 'first issue facing national courts [...] is whether the measure concerned actually constitutes State aid within the meaning of the Treaty'.[8] If the national court finds that a given measure constitutes State aid, it should then scrutinize whether there has been a breach of the standstill obligation. In this context, it is important to make a distinction between new and existing aid,[9] since it is only the former that has to be notified to, and authorized by, the Commission. Therefore, in the case of existing aid, national courts would only scrutinize whether the measure at issue is realized in conformity with a scheme previously authorized by the Commission. Similarly, national courts would also have to analyze whether the measure falls within the scope of a block exemption regulation; if that is the case, the standstill obligation would not apply.[10]

If an infringement of the standstill obligation is found, the national judge is under an obligation to adopt all remedies available at the national level and necessary to establish the *status quo ante*. The legal actions and remedies before national courts are governed by domestic procedural rules, which are nevertheless subject to the (rather narrow)

---

[5] Commission Notice on the Enforcement of State Aid Law by National Courts [2009] OJ C85/01 (the '2009 Notice'), para 24.

[6] 2009 Notice, para 20.

[7] *Van Calster*, cited above, note 4, para 75; *Transalpine Ölleitung*, cited above, note 4, para 38.

[8] 2009 Notice, para 8.

[9] Existing aid is, in particular, aid that has already been approved by the Commission (see also Articles 1(b), 17 and 19 of the Procedural Regulation).

[10] See 2009 Notice, para 15(a).

boundaries drawn by the EU law principles of equivalence and effectiveness.[11] The *Lucchini* case provides a good example in this regard, as it illustrates how the principle of procedural autonomy gives way to the primacy and *effet utile* of the EU State aid rules. In that case, the Court of Justice held that the Italian legal system's principle of *res judicata* does not prevent recovery of illegal and incompatible aid.[12]

STATE AID CASES BEFORE NATIONAL JUDGES

Two main scenarios may be identified in relation to legal actions concerning State aid that may be brought before national courts. First, national judges can be called on to decide on actions claiming breach of State aid rules as a 'sword', the common scenario being that of the beneficiary's competitors seeking remedies for breach of the standstill obligation before national courts. Second, national courts can be confronted with actions using State aid rules as a 'shield': in practice, this occurs frequently, as actions are brought by beneficiaries of aid who challenge the validity of a national recovery order.

State Aid Rules as a 'Sword'

As elaborated below, the remedies claimed against a breach of the standstill obligation depend on whether the allegedly unlawful aid has already been disbursed.

Actions aimed at preventing disbursement of unlawful aid

Clearly, if the allegedly unlawful aid has not yet been disbursed, the claimant (for example, a potential beneficiary's competitor) can ask the national judge to find an infringement of the standstill obligation and to

---

[11] See Article 14(1) and (3) of the Procedural Regulation, as well as Case C-232/05 *Commission v France (Scott)* [2006] ECR I-10071, para 53; Case C-24/95 *Rheinland Pfalz v Alcan Deutschland GmbH* [1997] ECR I-1591; Case C-496/09 *Commission v Italy* [2011] ECR I-11483, para 78.

[12] Case C 119/05 *Ministero dell'Industria, del Commercio e dell'Artigianato v Lucchini SpA* [2007] ECR I-6199, para 63. However, in the most recent decision in the *Lucchini* saga, the Court of Rome held that the principle of primacy of EU law could not be invoked to challenge the national principle of *res judicata*. According to the court, primacy applies only to the relationship between sources of law and has no influence on the Italian procedural rules establishing the principle of *res judicata* (Court of Rome, 21 March 2011, no. 6039).

prevent payment of the aid. Normally, the claimant would challenge the validity of the national measures authorizing the unlawful aid. In this respect, where unlawful aid is about to be disbursed, the national court is therefore obliged to prevent this payment from taking place.[13]

Consequently, 'the national court's obligation to prevent violations of Article [108(3)] of the Treaty can require it to issue an interim order preventing the illegal disbursement until the substance of the matter is resolved'.[14] Interim measures appear to be the most appropriate remedies in cases where it is likely that the asserted unlawful aid is going to be paid before the outcome of the judicial proceedings. As far as the Italian legal order is concerned, national judges can grant interim measures if the claimant establishes the existence of both: (i) *fumus boni iuris*, in other words, a *prima facie* case that the application is well founded; and (ii) *periculum in mora*, that is, an extremely serious risk of irreparable harm which, in the absence of the order, would be caused by the disbursement of the unlawful aid.[15]

Recovery actions

By contrast, if the unlawful aid has already been paid, the claimant (for example, the aid beneficiary's competitor) may file a recovery action against the authority that granted the alleged unlawful aid. If the national court finds an infringement of the standstill obligation it must 'in principle order the full recovery of unlawful State aid from the beneficiary'.[16] Only in exceptional circumstances may the national judge decline to order recovery of the unlawful aid. According to the Commission, 'the legal standard to be applied in this context should be similar to the one applicable under Articles 14 and 15 of the Procedural Regulation'.[17] This means that any circumstances which would not stand in the way of a recovery order by the Commission cannot constitute a justification for a national court to refrain from ordering full recovery under Article 108(3) of the Treaty.

In this regard, the ECJ has clarified that 'undertakings to which aid has been granted may not, in principle, entertain a legitimate expectation that the aid is lawful unless it has been granted in compliance with the

---

[13] 2009 Notice, para 28.

[14] 2009 Notice, para 58.

[15] See *Sacbo Società per l'Aeroporto Civile di Bergamo S.p.A c. Ministero Trasporti Infrastrutture, ENAC, Alitalia S.p.A.*, (TAR Lombardia (Section of Brescia), 21 March 2006, no. 577).

[16] 2009 Notice, para 30.

[17] 2009 Notice, para 32.

procedure laid down in [Article 108(3)]'.[18] Advocate General Jacobs has summarized the state of the law, and the exceptions and limitations available to the national court in granting stay and provisional repayment orders, in the following terms:[19]

> 70 It seems to me to be clear from the judgment in *FNCE* that a finding that aid has been granted in breach of the last sentence of Article [108(3)] should in principle lead to its repayment. [...]
>
> 73 Nevertheless the Court has held that there may be exceptional cases in which it would be inappropriate to order repayment of aid. [...]
>
> 75 It seems to me that the national courts have a similar responsibility in proceedings based on the last sentence of Article [108(3)]. It is for national courts to assess whether a diligent businessman ought to have realized that the measures in question constituted aid which could be granted only in accordance with the procedure laid down by Article [108(3)].
>
> 76 In the present case it seems doubtful whether that is so. First, the measures in question are not ones which self-evidently constitute aid; whether they do depends on whether the Post Office received adequate remuneration for its services, a matter which SFMI may have found difficult, if not impossible, to verify. Secondly, the Commission, after conducting its preliminary inquiry, decided not to proceed with the matter; moreover, since re-opening its inquiry, it has failed for a period of more than three years to reach a decision. In such circumstances the national court, if it were to find that the measures constitute aid, may in my view be justified in considering it inappropriate to order repayment of the aid.

More recently, the ECJ held in *CELF II* that 'the existence of an exceptional circumstance also cannot be upheld in the light of the principle of legal certainty, since the Court has already held, essentially, that, so long as the Commission has not taken a decision approving aid, and so long as the period for bringing an action against such a decision has not expired, the recipient cannot be certain as to the lawfulness of the

---

[18] *Rheinland-Pfalz v Alcan Deutschland*, cited above, note 11, para 25; Case C-390/98 *HJ Banks & Co Ltd. v Coal Authority* [2001] ECR I-6117, para 74. In Italy, see, *inter alia*, Corte di Cassazione [2012] no. 6756, TAR Sardegna [2011] no. 41; Tar Lombardia [2009] no. 5059; and Tar Lazio [2005] no. 167.

[19] Opinion of Advocate General Jacobs in Case C-39/94 *SFEI v La Poste*, cited above, note 4, paras 70 *et seq*.

aid, with the result that neither the principle of the protection of legitimate expectations nor that of legal certainty can be relied upon'.[20]

It should also be pointed out that the obligation of national courts to order recovery of unlawful aid does not depend on whether the aid is compatible with the Internal Market. In other words, even if the Commission finds the unlawful aid to be compatible with the Internal Market, this does not regularize *ex post facto* the breach of the standstill obligation. If this were the case, the direct effect of the standstill obligation would be ineffective and the interests of individuals, whom must be protected by national courts, would be disregarded.[21] Hence, even if the Commission ultimately approves the aid, the national courts should provide a remedy for its premature and unlawful payment in order to offset any competitive advantage gained by the beneficiary from the early payment. In this case, the appropriate remedy could be – rather than a full recovery – an order requiring the beneficiary to pay interest for the period of unlawfulness.[22]

In addition, the ECJ held in *CELF II* that 'a national court before which an application has been brought, on the basis of Article [108(3)], for repayment of unlawful State aid may not stay the adoption of its decision on that application until the Commission has ruled on the compatibility of the aid with the common market following the annulment of a previous positive decision'. This is because 'a decision to stay proceedings would, *de facto*, have the same effect as a decision to refuse the application for safeguard measures' (in other words, 'it would have the effect that no decision on the merits of that application would be taken before the Commission's decision', and would thus amount 'to maintaining the benefit of aid during the period in which implementation is prohibited, which would be inconsistent with the very purpose of Article [108(3)] and would render that provision ineffective').[23]

Moreover, it follows from the rationale of the standstill obligation that national courts are obliged to order not only recovery of the original

---

[20] Case C-1/09 *Centre d'exportation du Livre Français (CELF) and Ministre de la Culture et de la Communication v Société Internationale de Diffusion et d'édition (SIDE) (CELF II)* [2010] ECR I-2099, para 53.

[21] Case C-199/06 *Centre d'exportation du Livre Français (CELF) and Ministre de la Culture et de la Communication v Société Internationale de Diffusion et d'édition (SIDE)* [2008] ECR I-469, paras 45–55; *Transalpine Ölleitung*, cited above, note 4, para 41.

[22] Case C-199/06, *CELF*, cited in previous note.

[23] Case C-1/09 *CELF II*, cited above, note 20, paras 31 and 40; 2009 Notice, para 62.

amount of the unlawful aid but also the recovery of interest from the day the unlawful aid was put at the disposal of the beneficiary to the day when it is effectively recovered.

Finally, when faced with recovery actions, national judges must order interim remedies pending the outcome of the proceedings. As suggested by the Commission in its 2009 Notice, 'the most expedient remedy will [...] be to order the unlawful aid *and* the illegality interest to be put on a blocked account until the substance of the matter is resolved. In its final judgment, the national court would then either order the funds on the blocked account to be returned to the State aid granting authority, if the unlawfulness is confirmed, or order the funds to be released to the beneficiary'.[24]

Damages actions brought by a beneficiary's competitors against the granting authority

Recovery actions may not be fully satisfactory for companies, such as the beneficiary's competitors, which have suffered significant loss as a consequence of the payment of the unlawful aid. Hence, these entities may decide to claim damages before national courts against the authority that granted the illegal aid. In this regard, it is well known that all the *Francovich*[25] criteria would have to be satisfied in order to successfully claim damages against a Member State for breach of EU rules. The *Francovich* conditions are as follows:

(i) ***the rule of law infringed must be intended to confer rights on individuals***. In State aid cases this condition is clearly fulfilled, as the Court of Justice 'has repeatedly emphasized that national courts play an important role in protecting the rights of individuals affected by unlawful implementation of State aid';[26]

(ii) ***the breach must be sufficiently serious***. This condition too is, as a matter of principle, easily fulfilled in State aid cases, as the

---

[24] 2009 Notice, para 61 (emphasis in the original).

[25] Joined Cases C-6/90 and C-9/90, *Andrea Francovich and Danila Bonifaci v Italy* [1991] ECR I-5357.

[26] Paolisa Nebbia, 'State Aid and the Role of National Courts', in Erika Szyszczak (ed), *Research Handbook on European State Aid Law* (Edward Elgar 2011) 397. More recently, see Francesco Bestagno, 'Il Risarcimento dei Danni per la Violazione delle Norme in Materia di Aiuti di Stato (Diritto UE)', in Lorenzo Federico Pace (ed), *Dizionario Sistematico del Diritto della Concorrenza* (Jovene 2013) 649.

standstill obligation does not leave any margin of discretion for national authorities; and

(iii) ***there must be a direct causal link between the breach of the Member State's obligation and the damage suffered by the injured parties***. The damage recovered should include both the *damnum emergens* and the *lucrum cessans*.

Damages claims filed against aid beneficiaries by their competitors

A more complex assessment should be made in relation to possible damages actions filed against an aid beneficiary by the beneficiary's competitors. First of all, the Court of Justice has already dealt with the question of whether EU law provides a basis for bringing damages actions against the beneficiary of unlawful State aid. The Court held in *SFEI*[27] that it does not. In particular, the Court noted that the Treaty does not impose any specific obligation on the recipient of aid. First, the prior notification requirement and the prohibition on implementing aid laid down in Article 108(3) are directed only at the Member State in question. Second, the Member State is also the sole addressee of the decision by which the Commission finds that aid is incompatible with the Internal Market and requires the Member State to recover the aid. Thus, the Court found that EU law itself does not provide a sufficient basis for the recipient of aid to incur liability where it has failed to verify that the aid received was duly notified to the Commission. The ruling of the Court in *SFEI* also confirms that EU law does not impose an obligation on the Member States to provide a basis in their national laws for such claims for damages.

Nevertheless, the Court also noted in that case that a national legal system is not prohibited from allowing such a claim for damages. Moreover, the Court and the Advocate General underscored the general principle according to which national law may not treat claims arising in connection with EU law less favourably than claims arising under national law. As a result, the Court ruled that, although EU law alone does not provide a basis for damages claims, it does not 'prejudice the possible application of national law concerning non-contractual liability. If, according to national law, the acceptance by an economic operator of unlawful assistance of a nature such as to occasion damage to other economic operators may in certain circumstances cause him to incur liability, the principle of non-discrimination may lead the national court

[27] *SFEI v La Poste*, cited above, note 4, para 75.

to find the recipient of aid paid in breach of Article [108(3)] liable'.[28] The latter principle is explained in the opinion of Advocate General Jacobs in the following manner:[29]

> I do not think that the Court should extend its case-law so as to confer on competitors a remedy in damages against recipients of aid. As the French Government points out, Article [108] lays down a procedure to be followed by the Commission and the Member States. It is upon the latter that the obligation to notify aid to the Commission rests. I do not, moreover, share SFEI's view that such a remedy is necessary in order to ensure the effectiveness of the prohibition in Article [108(3)]. The various remedies outlined above, including where appropriate an order for recovery and possibly an award of damages against the Member State, are capable of providing an effective response to a breach of that prohibition. [...] Finally, as regards the Commission's remark in its written observations that the national court must observe the principle of equal treatment for claims based on Community law, it seems to me that that principle could apply only in so far as the mere receipt of an unlawful payment could give rise in national law to liability to third parties. As the Court has consistently held, national rules must not discriminate between claims founded on national law and corresponding claims founded on Community law.

In the Italian legal system, competitors of the (actual or potential) aid beneficiary could in fact sue the beneficiary by claiming, for instance, unfair competition pursuant to Article 2598 of the Italian Civil Code. Indeed, in Decision 3397 of 23 May 1980, *Comafrica S.p.A. v Smo-Società Mercantile Oltremare*, the Italian Supreme Court (Corte di Cassazione) ruled that 'Italian courts may also assess cases of unfair competition arising from State aid'.[30] The admissibility of legal actions brought by competitors of the beneficiary on grounds of unfair competition has been confirmed by more recent cases.[31]

---

[28] Ibid.

[29] Opinion of Advocate General Jacobs in *SFEI*, ibid., paras 82–84.

[30] On State aid and unfair competition, see Valeria Falce and Aurora Muselli 'Gli Aiuti di Stato e la Concorrenza Sleale', in Pace (ed), *Dizionario Sistematico*, cited above, note 26, p. 796; Anna Genovese, 'La Tutela Inibitoria del Concorrente nei Confronti di Condotte Illecite ai Sensi delle Norme in Materia di Concorrenza Sleale dell'impresa Beneficiaria di Aiuti di Stato', in Pace, ibid., p. 804.

[31] Corte di Cassazione [2000] no. 5087, *Fallimento Traghetti Mediterraneo S.p.A., v Tirrenia di Navigazione S.p.A.*; Tribunale di Sassari, [2009] no. 3863, *AirOne S.p.A., v Ryan Air Ltd and Sogeal S.p.A*; Tribunale di Roma [2006] *AirOne v Alitalia* (overturned on appeal by Tribunale di Roma [2006], *Alitalia v*

As has been correctly pointed out, 'unlike for actions for damages brought against the granting authority/public administration, actions against the beneficiary of the unlawful aid are feasible as long as it can be proved that, thanks to the unlawful aid, the beneficiary company implemented unfair competition practices pursuant to article 2598 of the Italian civil code, which caused damage to competitors'; in other words, the national judge 'determines: (i) whether the beneficiary benefited from the unlawful State aid; (ii) whether the beneficiary acted in a way that is contrary to the fair competition rules under Italian Civil Code and jurisprudence; and (iii) evaluates the amount of damages to be granted to its competitors if they can prove and qualify their loss'.[32]

Finally, in the context of the unfair competition proceedings, the beneficiary's competitors may request (and obtain) injunctive relief aimed at prohibiting the beneficiary of the aid from taking advantage of the aid.[33]

Other damages claims

Damages claims filed by the beneficiary of unlawful aid. The chances of success for a damages action filed by the beneficiary of unlawful aid against the granting authority, though theoretically possible, are limited.[34] This is due to the following reasons: (i) Article 107 does not grant any undertaking a right to obtain State aid; (ii) the above-mentioned strict case law of the Court of Justice with regard to the (absence of) legitimate expectations of a beneficiary would make it difficult for the latter to prove that it had any legitimate expectation that the aid to be granted would be legal; and, in any case; (iii) the damage recovery could not

Airone S.p.A); Tribinale di Genova [1993], *Grandi Traghetti di Navigazione S.p.A. v Viamare di Navigazione S.p.A., and Finmare S.p.A.*

32 Gianluca Belotti, 'Italy Chapter', in Jacques Derenne, Alix Müller-Rappard and Cédric Kaczmarek (eds), *Enforcement of EU State Aid Law at National Level: Reports from the 27 Member States* (Lexxion 2010), p. 210.

33 This appears to have been the case in Tribunale di Roma, [2006] *AirOne v Alitalia* (overturned on appeal by Tribunale di Roma, [2006] *Alitalia v AirOne S.p.A*).

34 Cristina Schepisi, *Aiuti di Stato e Tutela Giurisdizionale* (Giappichelli 2012); Cristina Schepisi, 'Il Private Enforcement dell'art. 108 § 3 TFUE e i Rimedi in Capo al Giudice Nazionale', in Pace (ed), *Dizionario Sistematico*, cited above, note 26, p. 612; Andrea Perin, 'Il Private Enforcement dell'art. 108 § 3 TFUE e le Controversie sul Recupero Degli Aiuti Illegali e Incompatibili Dinnanzi al Giudice Civile Prima della Riforma della l. 234/2012', in Pace (ed), ibid., p. 760; Bestagno, 'Il Risarcimento dei Danni', cited above, note 26, p. 657.

equal the amount of the unlawful aid reimbursed, as this would undermine the effectiveness of the standstill obligation and would in itself amount to State aid.

Hence, the opportunity for the beneficiary to obtain damages from the granting authority appears to be rather limited in practice. Any damages thus recovered would amount, for instance, to the costs which the beneficiary incurred for entering into a contractual relationship that constituted unlawful State aid[35] or to the costs of securing a loan in order to reimburse the aid.[36]

Finally, a quite peculiar and exceptional damages action could be one brought by third parties (in other words, entities other than the beneficiary's competitors) against a national authority, claiming damages suffered as a consequence of the refusal by the national authority to grant aid to a given company with which the claimants had a contractual relationship. This situation gave rise to the decision of the Corte di Cassazione of 4 March 2005, no. 4769, *D.S. et al. v E.S.P.I. Ente Siciliano Promozione Industriale in liquidazione*, where former employees of the company SIRAP S.p.a. ('SIRAP'), who had terminated their relationship with SIRAP because of its bankruptcy on 1 October 1993, sued ESPI on the ground that the bankruptcy of SIRAP had been caused by ESPI's refusal to pay certain contributions to SIRAP as provided for by Article 4 of Sicilian Regional Law No. 23/1991 of 15 May 1991. The Supreme Court dismissed the action because the Commission had decided that the contributions sought by SIRAP constituted unlawful State aid. Hence, the refusal of ESPI to grant SIRAP unlawful State aid was legitimate.

Damages claims for failure to implement a recovery decision. The 2009 Notice clarifies that, 'like violations of the standstill obligation, failure by the Member State authorities to comply with a Commission recovery decision under Article 14 of the procedural Regulation can give rise to damages claims under the "Francovich" and "Brasserie du Pêcheur" jurisprudence'.[37] Therefore, according to the Commission, the principles applicable with regard to violations of the standstill obligation would also apply in relation to damages claims for failure of the Member State to implement a recovery decision.

---

35 Court of Clermont-Ferrand, SA Fontanille, 23 September 2004, Case no. 0101282, AJDA 2005, Jurisprudence, p. 385.

36 Administrative Appeal Court of Paris, 21 January 2006, no. 04PA01092, *Société Groupe Salmon Arc-en-Ciel*.

37 2009 Notice, para 69.

State Aid Rules Used as a Shield: Challenging the Validity of the Commission's Negative Decisions Before National Judges

As explained above, national courts are frequently called on to apply State aid rules in cases where the beneficiary of unlawful and incompatible aid contests the validity of the national recovery order implementing the Commission's decision that the aid must be recovered. Two kinds of claims challenging the validity of the national recovery order could be brought in such cases.

First, the beneficiary could contest the validity of the national recovery measures by relying on arguments of EU and/or national law that do not challenge the validity of the underlying Commission decision. Such claims might concern, for instance: the infringement of the beneficiary's procedural rights within the national recovery proceedings; the exact identification of the addresses of the recovery order; the correct amount that should be recovered; or the expiration of the statute of limitations pursuant to Article 15 of Regulation 659/99.[38]

Second, the beneficiary could seek annulment of the national recovery order by relying on the asserted invalidity of the Commission's negative decision. The beneficiary of the aid may argue, for instance, that the Commission's negative decision was contrary to State aid rules or contrary to general principles of EU law.

However, according to settled case law, 'the possibility for a person to argue in the context of a national proceeding the invalidity of provisions contained in acts of the Union does, it is true, presuppose that the party in question had no right of direct action under Article 230 EC [now Article 263 TFEU] by which it could challenge provisions, the consequences of which it is suffering without having been able to seek their annulment. However, that same case-law shows that such a direct action must be admissible beyond any doubt'.[39] Where it is not clear that the

---

[38] See Massimo Merola and Tecla Ubaldi, 'Il Recupero Degli Aiuti Illegali e Incompatibili e le Relative Controversie Dinnanzia ai Giudici Nazionali (Diritto UE)', in Pace (ed), *Dizionario Sistematico*, cited above, note 26, p. 628; Edoardo Gambaro, 'Le Difese dell'impresa Beneficiaria a Fronte dell'ordine di Recupero del Giudice Nazionale, ex art. 108 § 3 3 TFUE, e della Commissione e dello Stato Membro, ex art. 107 TFUE (Diritto UE)', in Pace (ed), ibid., p. 638.

[39] Joined Cases C-71/09 P, C-73/09 P and C-76/09 P, *Comitato 'Venezia Vuole Vivere' & Others v Commission* [2011] ECR I-4727, para 58 (citations omitted).

claimant can bring an annulment action under Article 263 TFEU, the national court must, in principle, offer legal protection.[40]

This implies that a company which has been identified as the beneficiary of unlawful aid by a negative decision of the Commission cannot challenge its validity before national judges if it has not lodged an appeal against the Commission's decision pursuant to Article 263. Consequently, it is frequent for such companies to challenge the Commission's negative decision before the General Court and, pending such proceedings, to file an action before national courts for the annulment of the national recovery order implementing the Commission's decision.

The existence of parallel proceedings raises a complex legal issue, namely that of the scope of protection that national courts may grant to the beneficiary of the allegedly unlawful and incompatible aid pending the outcome of the judicial proceedings at the EU level.

The case is straightforward if the national court considers that the grounds put forward to it by the aid beneficiary to assert the invalidity of the Commission's negative decision are unfounded: in this scenario, the court is free to reject the claim, concluding that the Commission's decision is completely valid.

On the other hand, as a general principle, 'national courts have no jurisdiction themselves to declare that acts of Community institutions are invalid'.[41]

Nevertheless, in *Zuckerfabrik* the ECJ held that this principle should be balanced with the right of effective judicial protection against Community (now EU) acts. In particular, the Court held that the right of effective judicial protection against Community acts 'would be compromised if, pending delivery of a judgment of the Court, which alone has jurisdiction to declare that a Community regulation is invalid, individuals were not in a position, where certain conditions are satisfied, to obtain a decision granting suspension of enforcement which would make it possible for the effects of the disputed regulation to be rendered for the time being inoperative as regards them'.[42] In other words, the ECJ implicitly accepted that national courts may carry out a limited validity control of EU acts if doing so is inherent to the granting of interim relief against national implementing measures.

---

[40] Joined Cases C-346/03 and C-529/03 *Atzeni and Others v Regione Autonoma della Sardegna* [2006] ECR I-1875, para 34.

[41] Case C-314/85 *Foto-Frost v Hauptzollamt Lübeck-Ost* [1987] ECR I-4199, para 20.

[42] Joined Cases C-143/88 and C-92/89 *Zuckerfabrik Süderdithmarschen and Zuckerfabrik Soest* [1991] ECR I-415, para 17.

It follows logically that, pending the outcome of judicial proceedings against the Commission's decision at the EU level, the battle of the beneficiary before the national courts would concentrate on obtaining interim measures – specifically, an order suspending the aid recovery proceedings until the EU Courts decided on the merits of the appeal against the Commission's negative decision. Indeed, with regard to applications for interim measures against the recovery of unlawful and incompatible aid, the EU judiciary plays a subsidiary role *vis-à-vis* that of the national courts.[43]

According to settled case law, the General Court would declare inadmissible a request for interim measures if the beneficiary does not demonstrate 'in what respect the domestic remedies available to it under [national] law allowing it to oppose immediate repayment of the aid would not enable it to avoid serious and irreparable damage'.[44] This means that, before seeking interim relief against the Commission's negative decision, the beneficiary of the allegedly unlawful and incompatible aid is obliged to apply to national courts for interim remedies against the national recovery order.

The conditions to be met in order for a national court to legitimately grant interim measures, as set out in *Zuckerfabrik*, are the following:[45]

(i) if the national court entertains serious doubts as to the validity of the contested EU measure and if the validity of the measure is not already in issue before the Court of Justice, the national court must itself refer the question to the Court of Justice;
(ii) there must be 'urgency', in the sense that the interim relief must be necessary to avoid serious and irreparable damage to the party seeking the relief;
(iii) the national court must take due account of the interests of the EU; and
(iv) in its assessment of all the above conditions, the national court must comply with any decisions of the Court of Justice or the General Court ruling on the lawfulness of the EU measure or on an

---

[43] Case T-27/13 *Elan v Commission*, 11 March 2013, EU:T:2013:122, para 24.

[44] Case T-181/02 *Neue Erba Lautex GmbH Weberei und Veredlung* [2002] ECR II-5081, para 109.

[45] See, *inter alia*, Joined Cases C-143/88 and C-92/89 *Zuckerfabrik Süderdithmarschen and Zuckerfabrik Soest* [1991] ECR I-415; Case C-465/93 *Atlanta Fruchthandelsgesellschaft and Others v Bundesamt für Ernährung und Forstwirtschaft (I)* [1995] ECR I-3761.

application for provisional measures seeking similar interim relief at the EU level.

Moreover, when suspending the effects of the domestic recovery order, 'the national court cannot restrict itself to referring the question on validity to the Court for a preliminary ruling, but must, when making the interim order, set out the reasons for which it considers that the Court should find the EU measure to be invalid'.[46]

Finally, it should be pointed out that the case law of the EU Courts is unclear as to whether, notwithstanding a pending challenge against a negative Commission decision before the General Court, a national court which has serious doubts regarding the validity of the decision and which therefore suspends the effects of the national recovery order is still under an obligation to refer the question to the Court of Justice. In this regard it seems more appropriate to endorse a broad interpretation of *Zuckerfabrik*'s exemption requirement (that is, 'the question has been already referred to the ECJ') so that it also includes appeals pending before the General Court on the same grounds against the Commission's decision. This interpretation would appear to be more respectful of the principle of the sound administration of justice and would avoid any *de facto* 'jumping' a level of judicial review against the Commission's decision.[47]

[46] Case C-304/09 *Commission v Italy* [2010] I-13903, para 46.

[47] See Case T-34/02 R *B v Commission* [2002] ECR II-2803.

PART III

EU competition law before arbitrators

11. Some considerations on arbitrability of competition law disputes and powers and duties of arbitrators in applying EU competition law

Roberto Cisotta*

ABSTRACT

The problem of defining the limits to the application of national procedural rules lies at the root of both the strands of case law of the Court of Justice of the EU regarding, respectively, EU competition law enforcement through arbitration and antitrust damages actions. Therefore, these two lines of private enforcement of competition law are characterized by the interplay of national procedural rules – which, as far as arbitration is concerned, define the attitude of the national legal order towards this 'private dispute settlement system' (see Case C-126/97 Eco Swiss *[1999]) – and the need for the uniform application of EU competition law. National judges have to juggle these two different – and often contrasting – forces, while arbitrators have to take due account of EU competition law in order to render awards which are likely to encounter no difficulties in the context of a possible review before national judges, without having the possibility to resort to the preliminary ruling procedure (Case 102/81* Nordsee *[1982]). This legal framework governs the relationship between public and private enforcement when EU competition law issues are at stake in a dispute to be settled by an arbitrator or an arbitral tribunal. This framework has implications with regard to the arbitrability of EU competition law issues and to the duties of arbitrators called on to settle disputes where such issues may arise.*

* Lecturer and Adjunct Professor, LUMSA Free University of Rome.

INTRODUCTION

One may say that EU competition law enforcement through international commercial arbitration suffers from a kind of imbalanced control mechanism, if compared with normal private enforcement. This stems from the case law of the Court of Justice of the EU (hereinafter the CJEU, or the Court of Justice, or the Court). In the first place, in *Nordsee*,[1] the Court stated that arbitrators cannot refer a question to it for a preliminary ruling. In the second place, in *Eco Swiss*,[2] two important principles were established: Article 81 EC (now Article 101 TFEU) has to be treated as a matter of public policy, and thus an arbitration award has to be annulled where it is contrary to that provision; however, Community (EU) law does not preclude national legislation according to which an interim arbitration award, enjoying the nature of a final award, acquires the force of *res judicata* – where no application for annulment has been filed within the prescribed limitation period – even if only in the context of a judicial review of a subsequent arbitration award it can be determined whether an agreement held valid by the interim award is nonetheless contrary to Article 81 EC (now Article 101 TFEU).

It is immediately evident that the picture drawn by the *Nordsee* and *Eco Swiss* judgments is quite different from ordinary judicial EU (competition) law enforcement, which is based on the respective roles of the national and EU Courts and on the preliminary reference mechanism. Moreover, the special mixture of public and private enforcement in the field of competition law should be re-shaped to fit within the boundaries set by the Court of Justice to litigation of EU (competition) law issues before arbitrators. As we will see, this point has recently become increasingly complex, as in some areas arbitration seems to be a privileged enforcement tool for competition law.

Nonetheless, in order to understand the problems related to arbitrability of EU competition law issues and the specific powers and duties of arbitrators in such disputes, a preliminary analysis of the meaning and underlying implications of the *Nordsee* and *Eco Swiss* judgments appears useful. Let us start to understand the strands of case law to which the two judgments belong.

---

[1] Case 102/81 *Nordsee Deutsche Hochseefischerei GmbH v Reederei Mond Hochseefischerei Nordstern AG & Co. KG and Reederei Friedrich Busse Hochseefischerei Nordstern AG & Co. KG* [1982] ECR 1095, paras 10–12.

[2] Case C-126/97 *Eco Swiss China Time Ltd v Benetton International NV* [1999] ECR I-3055, paras 36–40 and 44–47.

THE RELATIONSHIPS BETWEEN THE CJEU AND ARBITRATION: *NORDSEE* IN CONTEXT

It is not difficult to understand that, in the *Nordsee* case, the Court was confronted with the problem of the exact definition of the scope of Article 177 EEC Treaty (now Article 267 TFEU), and in particular the question of how to interpret the notion of 'court or tribunal of a Member State'. The problem arose from the power of the arbitrator to render an award having the same force of *res judicata* as judgments of State courts or tribunals under German law. The fundamental aim of the preliminary reference procedure, which is to ensure the uniform application of EC (EU) law, was at stake and it may be said that, by concluding that an arbitrator is not to be considered a 'court or tribunal of a Member State', the Court decided to run the risk of undermining that system.

By affirming that it lacked jurisdiction to respond to an arbitrator, the Court of Justice chose to limit the functioning of the preliminary reference mechanism, permitting only the judge entrusted to review the validity of the arbitral award to refer a preliminary reference question.[3] However, in some cases judicial review of an award might never occur, most obviously because the parties deem it unnecessary (as in the case of spontaneous compliance with the award). Furthermore, where judicial review does take place, the procedure may suffer from a number of limitations, depending on national procedural rules. In particular, such review will not cover the merits of the award.[4]

One may wonder why the Court of Justice decided to run the risk of undermining the preliminary reference mechanism, which had already proved to be an invaluable and extremely precious tool to ensure the uniformity of the application of (what was then) Community law. A series of interpretations can be formulated, but for our purposes the important point is that the aim of the Court might well have been to protect what may be called the purity of the preliminary reference mechanism by leaving to the remit of proper national judges the power to

---

[3] The Court of Justice has subsequently confirmed its position on this point. See Case C-125/04 *Guy Denuit and Betty Cordenier v Transorient-Mosaique Voyages and Culture SA* [2005] ECR I-923, para 13; Case C-555/13 *Merck Canada Inc. v Accord Healthcare Ltd and Others,* 13 February 2014, EU:C:2014:92, paras 15–25.

[4] See Giacomo Biagioni, 'Review by national courts of arbitral awards dealing with EU competition law', this volume, Chapter 13.

employ it.[5] With *Nordsee*, then, the Court chose its interlocutors. But litigation before arbitrators was (and is still nowadays) gaining growing importance in transnational dispute resolution. Therefore, the solution provided in *Nordsee* had to be completed.

Setting the Stage for Private Antitrust Enforcement by Ruling on the Limits to Application of National Procedural Rules: From *Eco Swiss* …

After 17 years, the opportunity arose with the *Eco Swiss* case. Here the perspective of the Court was rather different, as the problem was not to establish whether a crucial tool – and typically pertaining to the Community [EU] legal order – like the preliminary ruling, could be used or not, but to adjust and refine the mechanism which, as regards its relationship with arbitration, was sketched above. In other words, the interplay between the *dictum* in *Nordsee* – no jurisdiction for the CJEU to consider questions referred by arbitrators and arbitral tribunals – and the legal circumstance that arbitral awards are subject to review – which can vary in scope and intrusiveness, depending on national rules – before national judges, introduced a new element to be taken into account. The Court of Justice did not have to simply describe its relationship with a

---

[5] See Gerhard Bebr, 'Arbitration Tribunals and Article 177 of the EEC Treaty' (1985) 22(3) Common Market Law Review 489, 497. According to Bebr, the CJEU in *Nordsee* 'viewed the possible right of an arbitration tribunal to refer [questions for preliminary rulings] primarily from an institutional rather than a functional perspective'. The stance taken by the CJEU has not always been welcomed, and it has been proposed that the preliminary ruling procedure should be opened to arbitrators. According to this view, preliminary references from arbitrators would be useful with particular reference to competition law, especially given the new challenges arbitrators face because of decentralization. See Carl Baudenbacher and Imelda Higgins, 'Decentralization of EC Competition Law Enforcement and Arbitration', (2002) 8(3) Columbia Journal of European Law 1. See also Adelina Adinolfi, 'Judicial dialogues and uniformity in the multi-level application of EU competition law', this volume, Chapter 3 (critical of how the *Nordsee* concept of a 'court' has also unnecessarily limited cooperation between arbitral tribunals and the Commission); Mel Marquis, 'Perchance to Dream: Well Integrated Public and Private Antitrust Enforcement in the European Union', in Philip Lowe and Mel Marquis (eds), *European Competition Law Annual 2011: Integrating Public and Private Enforcement – Implications for Courts and Agencies* (Hart Publishing 2014) xlviii (in favour of access for arbitrators to the preliminary reference procedure, possibly subject to specialized design features); Laurence Idot, 'Arbitration and Competition', OECD background note, DAF/COMP(2010)40, 51, 67 (opposed to broader access).

body established – directly or indirectly – by private autonomy and recognized by national law, identifying whether it was a 'court or tribunal of a Member State', according to the parameters of Community (EU) law. The Court ended up defining some of the most relevant features of the relationship between national judicatures and awards rendered at the end of an international commercial arbitration procedure, thus indirectly shaping a particularly relevant element of the attitude of national legal orders towards this dispute settlement system. In doing so, the Court intervened on the limits to the application of national procedural rules, as regards (what may be generically called) acceptance of arbitral awards dealing with EU competition law issues.

It is clear that application of national procedural rules was the issue at stake in the *Eco Swiss* case; however, it is worth recalling the conclusion formulated by the Court itself:

1. A national court to which application is made for annulment of an arbitration award must grant that application if it considers that the award in question is in fact contrary to Article 81 EC (ex Article 85), where its *domestic rules of procedure* require it to grant an application for annulment founded on failure to observe national rules of public policy.
2. Community law does not require a national court to refrain from applying *domestic rules of procedure* according to which an interim arbitration award which is in the nature of a final award and in respect of which no application for annulment has been made within the prescribed time-limit acquires the force of *res judicata* and may no longer be called in question by a subsequent arbitration award, even if this is necessary in order to examine, in proceedings for annulment of a subsequent arbitration award, whether an agreement which the interim award held to be valid in law is nevertheless void under Article 81 EC (ex Article 85).[6]

The reasoning of the Court is simply based on the importance given by the EC Treaty to competition law, and namely to Article 81 (85); in particular, the Court relied on Article 3(g) [3(1)(g)] of the EC Treaty.[7] The public policy clause was the most natural way to achieve this

[6] Emphasis added.

[7] See para 36 of the judgment. After the Lisbon Treaty, competition is not considered *per se* an objective of the EU anymore. Nevertheless, it seems that competition law – in particular in the framework of the internal market – still ranks foremost, so that *Eco Swiss* should still be considered good law.

objective, and therefore the technical tool to which the Court resorted was to give (rather limited) guidance to the national judge as to when and under which conditions arbitral awards dealing with EU competition law were to be considered contrary to public policy and thus declared void.

What is more, the Court specified that questions regarding antitrust law should be open to examination by national courts (when reviewing arbitral awards), and that national courts should be able to refer questions to the Court for a preliminary ruling – thus re-entering the ordinary circuit of EU law interpretation and application.

As we have seen, the Court avoided an excessively wide intrusion, and saved the *res judicata* rule regarding arbitral awards, as it was shaped in the national legal order concerned. Doing otherwise would have completely undermined the existing framework governing the relationships between the national legal order and international commercial arbitration, thus forcing the former – and all the legal orders of EU Member States – to take an attitude which could have been considered arbitration-unfriendly.

. . . to Antitrust Damages Actions: *Crehan* and *Manfredi* and the Subsequent Case Law

It may be considered obvious that in *Eco Swiss* the limits to application of national procedural rules were the crucial point. Moreover, no more than two years later, the Court again used an argument related to the limits to the application of national procedural rules to create another milestone in the private enforcement of competition law.

Starting from the seminal judgments in *Crehan*[8] and *Manfredi*,[9] the Court first established the principle that breaches of antitrust rules give rise to a claim for damages, which may be brought even by one of the parties to an agreement liable to restrict or distort competition within the meaning of Article 85 EC (101 TFEU). However, in these two judgments, and in the others that have defined some essential features of antitrust damages actions, the focus is not on the right to obtain compensation for anticompetitive behaviour but on the national procedural rules to be

---

[8] Case C-453/99 *Courage Ltd v Bernard Crehan* [2001] ECR I-6297.

[9] Joined Cases C-295/04 to C-298/04 *Vincenzo Manfredi v Lloyd Adriatico Assicurazioni SpA* [2006] ECR I-6619.

applied to the related actions.[10] In particular, in the *Crehan* case, the question referred to the Court of Justice did not concern the existence of a right to obtain compensation for damages suffered as a result of anticompetitive behaviour but the application of the principle *nemo auditur propriam turpitudinem allegans*, as it was one of the parties to an agreement illicit under EU competition law that claimed compensation for the damages suffered.

Hence, the Court indirectly achieved what may be considered (one of) its real objective(s): affirming the right to compensation for damages suffered as a result of anticompetitive behaviour.

The private enforcement of EU competition law has different features in the two cases (before judges and arbitrators), but *mutatis mutandis* the problems to be dealt with by national judges always regard the application of their national procedural rules. When they have to directly decide a case, these rules concern the different features of the actions brought before them, while when they are asked to review an arbitral award, EU competition law has to be treated, as we have seen, as part of public policy. This means that, in the context of the private enforcement of EU law, national judges are called on to take on growing and delicate responsibilities, whether in the context of direct actions on which they have to rule, or in the context of the review of an arbitral award.[11]

As a consequence, arbitrators should take due account of EU competition law issues, as they have to deliver awards which are likely to be recognized and enforced by (in particular EU) national judges, should such a recognition and enforcement be asked. In particular, recognition may be refused if the 'subject matter of the difference is not capable of settlement by arbitration under the law of that country or [...] the recognition or enforcement of the award would be contrary to the public policy of that country'.[12]

---

[10] See Roberto Cisotta, 'The Evolving Framework for Antitrust Damages Actions and Collective Redress in the European Union: a First Assessment' (2014) 28(3) Diritto del Commercio Internazionale 709, 713-714, and references therein.

[11] This increasing responsibility of national judges seems to be a distinctive trend in the case law of the CJEU on private enforcement. See Cisotta, cited above, note 10; Adinolfi, cited above, note 5.

[12] Article V.2 (b) of the 1958 New York Convention. According to Sergio M. Carbone, 'Antitrust Commitments and Arbitration in European Law' (2013) 23(1) Rivista dell'arbitrato 1, 16, this provision 'may be considered as the international legal benchmark with respect to the recognition of the effects of arbitration awards, being such a rule a common reference to any statute adopted also by

Du reste, according to a widespread opinion amongst legal scholars, and to a series of arbitration rules, arbitrators should make every effort to ensure that their arbitration award, if necessary, can later be enforced (within the legal orders where such enforceability is likely to be asked).[13]

Therefore, the problem of *ex officio* application of EU competition law arises: arbitrators will be likely to ensure the correct application of EU competition law because, as a consequence of the described legal framework existing in the EU, doing otherwise they would run the extremely concrete risk that the award would be unenforceable. However, as we shall see, this point is still controversial.

THE ISSUE OF ARBITRABILITY

From the Impossibility to Settle Competition Issues by Arbitration to the *Mitsubishi* Case and Beyond

For a long time, the arbitrability of competition law disputes was not accepted; nowadays, a much more open attitude is prevailing. The turning point in this long story is usually considered to be the judgment by the U.S. Supreme Court in the *Mitsubishi* case.[14] Basically, before that judgment, the arbitrability of competition cases was denied because of

---

States which did not ratify it'. The extent of the review is different as regards procedures for setting aside arbitral awards. See Biagioni, cited above, note 4.

13 See, for example, Article 41 of the ICC Rules of Arbitration.

14 *Mitsubishi Motors Corp. v Soler Chrysler – Plymouth Inc.*, 473 U.S., 614 (1985). For other references to the U.S. case law, see Assimakis Komninos, 'Arbitration and EU Competition Law' (SSRN, 12 April 2009) <http://papers.ssrn.com/sol3/papers.cfm?abstract_id=1520105> accessed 28 August 2014, 8–9, note 29. This case law, starting already with *Mitsubishi*, has focused on the preservation of the parties' ability to vindicate their substantive legal rights. An arbitration clause that limits or hinders this ability can be held unenforceable. Although the *Mitsubishi* turning point took place long ago, arbitration of competition claims in the U.S. still had not become extremely popular up to quite recent times. See Peter E. Greene, Peter S. Julian and Julie Bédard, 'Arbitrability of Antitrust Claims in the United States of America' (2008) 19(1) European Business Law Review 43. However, other relevant developments have subsequently taken place in the U.S. regarding arbitration, and the U.S. Supreme Court has taken a rather restrictive approach regarding, in particular, class arbitration (see, for example, *AT&T Mobility v Concepcion*, 563 U.S. 321 (2011) and *American Express Co. et al. v Italian Colors Restaurant et al.*, 570 U.S. ___ (2013)). For discussion, see Barry E. Hawk and Yolaine Seaton, 'U.S. Antitrust Arbitration', in Lowe and Marquis (eds), cited above, note 5, at 159.

their highly technical complexity and private nature.[15] As to the latter, there was, in particular, widespread scepticism towards the capability of arbitration to play a regulatory function, which is at the core of antitrust rules. As we shall see, the regulatory function that arbitration might play in the field of competition law is still a controversial issue, although currently, as just said, in most cases the arbitrability of competition disputes is not seriously called into question anymore.

The two arguments – the first based on an assumed inaptitude to rule on highly technical issues and the second calling into question the capability of arbitration of playing a regulatory role – are connected, and a few words on both of them are useful in understanding their sense and rationale. Nevertheless, a response regarding the second argument will emerge only once the general picture has been drawn. Let us start, then, with the argument that competition law issues are too technical for arbitrators.

In principle, arbitrators can hardly be considered poorly equipped to rule on highly technical issues – in other words, economic analysis of market conditions and (effects of) undertakings' behaviours, evaluation of damages, legal issues concerning burden of proof, presumptions, and so on; on the contrary, they can normally be considered better equipped than judges to rule on such aspects. Indeed, arbitrators are chosen to perform their specific duty (concerning a particular case) from amongst professionals who are usually more familiar with economic analysis tools and international business practice than judges.

Nevertheless, this proximity to international business practice could lead to a different problem, that is, the arguable or suspected tendency to privilege, as parameters for their scrutiny over legal issues brought before them, legal tools or arrangements which are more common in business practice and with which business people are well acquainted. This could be considered natural, as arbitration is aimed at providing solutions best suited to the business world. In other words, the question arises as to whether arbitrators are more keen to apply international commercial law

---

[15] The arbitrability of competition law issues was already widely accepted in the legal literature before the *Mitsubishi* case. See Luca G. Radicati di Brozolo, 'Arbitrage Commercial International et Lois de Police. Considérations sur les Conflits de Juridictions dans le Commerce International', in *Recueil des Cours/ Collected Courses* 315 (Martinus Nijhoff, 2005) 265, 298. Some judgments, especially in Germany, had also already accepted the arbitrability of competition issues. See the case law mentioned in Carbone (cited above, note 12) and in Gordon Blanke, 'EU Competition Arbitration', in Luis Ortiz Blanco (ed), *EU Competition Procedure* (Oxford University Press 2013) 1075, 1082.

as it is shaped by business actors, rather than in the form which is incorporated in the will of national legislators (and of public enforcers), and as it stems from international and EU law sources.[16]

The criticism regarding the difficulty of arbitration to play a regulatory role might therefore be founded, *inter alia*, on this understanding of arbitration practice. Nonetheless, a good antidote may be found thanks to the great flexibility of arbitration as a legal tool: for instance, as already noted, arbitrators in cases where competition law issues are at stake should be chosen from amongst professionals who are familiar with those issues and with the needs of public enforcement. On the contrary, it might be said that an arbitrator or an arbitral tribunal tailored for competition law cannot always be a viable solution, as the relevance of competition law in a specific case can be controversial and one of the problems might concern, as we shall see, the *ex officio* application of EU competition law (by arbitrators who could have been chosen with regard to other kinds of skills and expertise).

Becoming even more suspicious, one might be concerned that arbitrators could expect to become more 'popular', and to improve their business by avoiding the *ex proprio motu* application of national (compulsory) legislation. Indeed, the intent of the parties in submitting a dispute to arbitrators could be precisely to circumvent that kind of legislation.

As has been pointed out, arbitrators had taken a quite timid approach, as they feared the nullity or non-enforceability of their awards. They therefore avoided taking competition law issues into account. Moreover, public enforcers, and in particular the European Commission, had put a series of burdens on private parties as regards the use of arbitration in the context of competition law enforcement.[17] The situation has changed over time – in the last 15 years, in particular – and today it seems there is much less distrust towards arbitrators (and vice versa).

As is widely acknowledged, arbitration provides a speedy, flexible and efficient resolution system for transnational disputes, and it has become extremely precious for the global business community: attaching too great importance to the arguments referred to above against arbitrability of competition law issues would deprive business actors of an excellent system for litigating such issues, or would lead to more frequent

---

[16] The expression *lex mercatoria* is consciously avoided. I do not intend to demonstrate analytically this criticism of arbitrators' attitudes; my intention is just to outline an effectively possible tendency.

[17] Komninos, cited above, note 14, at 5.

challenges of awards before national courts, thus losing some of the essential advantages of arbitration.

When ruling on the *Mitsubishi* case, the Justices of the U.S. Supreme Court were already perfectly aware of these facts: they relied, *inter alia*, on the liberal federal policy regarding arbitration and on the need to give the widest possible effect to private autonomy, especially when the parties had agreed to submit disputes to international commercial arbitration. This was due to a form of international comity towards international arbitral tribunals, which were becoming crucial, thanks to their trustworthiness and efficiency, for brisk international business. The latter had assumed great importance for the U.S., and the Supreme Court highlighted that the same liberal attitude, as regards in particular the arbitrability of competition law issues, was not always appropriate in the context of domestic litigation.

In short, no serious doubt can be raised anymore as regards the aptitude of arbitrators to apply competition law: arbitrators normally appear keen to examine competition law claims and, although the numbers regarding the application of competition law in arbitration practice may not appear dramatically significant, the trend is now definitely favourable to arbitration. If a suspicious attitude towards arbitration does not generally seem justifiable anymore, it is nonetheless true that its relationships with public enforcement, which remains central in EU competition law, have to be considered carefully, subtracting from arbitration some issues unsuitable for adjudication in private proceedings.[18]

Arbitration of Competition Law Issues in the EU Context

In the specific context of EU law, the arbitrability of competition law disputes (a large number of such disputes) is, at least implicitly, indicated by a series of data, or can be derived from normative elements, or from the case law. The provisions of Regulation 1/2003[19] which are applicable

[18] See below the Section on 'Limits to arbitrability of competition disputes under EU law'. For a more general analysis, see Renato Nazzini, 'International Arbitration and Public Enforcement of Competition Law' (2004) 25(3) European Competition Law Review 153; Gordon Blanke, 'The interaction between arbitration and public enforcement: clash or harmony?', Chapter 12 of this volume and references cited therein.

[19] Council Regulation (EC) 1/2003 on the implementation of the rules on competition laid down in Articles 81 and 82 of the Treaty [2003] OJ L1/1.

to national judges do not apply to arbitrators,[20] but it seems that no specific obstacle to arbitrability is envisaged. Moreover, arbitration is used as a procedural mechanism in many Article 9 decisions and merger cases.[21]

Furthermore, a presumption that EU competition law issues are generally arbitrable can be deduced from the *Eco Swiss* judgment itself, where the CJEU raised no objection as to the arbitrability of the case.[22]

Limits to Arbitrability of Competition Disputes under EU Law

What has been outlined so far does not amount to saying that the arbitrability of competition law issues has no limits under EU law. As a matter of principle, arbitration, as a private remedy, should not overlap with the activities of public enforcers.

In particular, the imposition of fines and the conduct of specific enforcement actions should always fall within the competence of public enforcers, whilst the competence of arbitrators can cover the assessment

---

[20] See Komninos, cited above, note 14, at 18.

[21] Council Regulation (EC) 139/2004 on the control of concentrations between undertakings [2004] OJ L24/1. For a critical analysis of the current use of arbitration in the context of merger control, see Gordon Blanke, 'The interaction between arbitration and public enforcement: clash or harmony?', Chapter 12 of this volume; Manuel Penadés Fons, 'Beyond the *Prima Facie* of Arbitration Commitments in EU Merger Control' (2012) 49(6) Common Market Law Review 1915. The use of arbitration commitments in merger control was endorsed by the General Court (then the CFI) in Case T-158/00 *Arbeitsgemeinschaft der Offentlich-rechtlichen Rundfunkanstalten der Bundesrepublik Deutschland (ARD) v Commission* [2003] ECR II-3825, paras 203, 211–212, 295, 297 and 352. More generally, behavioural commitments should be turned into quasi-structural ones to ensure their effects on the market (and, as one may infer, arbitration would be an effective tool to achieve this objective). See to that effect Case T-177/04 *EasyJet Airline Co Ltd v Commission* [2006] ECR II-1931, paras 182 and 186. See also Marc Blessing, *Arbitrating Antitrust and Merger Control Issues* (Helbing & Lichtenhahn 2003) 81; Herwig C.H. Hofmann, Gerard C. Rowe and Alexander Türk, *Administrative Law and Policy of the European Union* (Oxford University Press 2011) 704.

[22] See Luca G. Radicati di Brozolo, 'Arbitrato, diritto della concorrenza, diritto comunitario e regole di procedura nazionali' (1999) 9(1) Rivista dell'arbitrato 665, 670. In the aftermath of *Eco-Swiss*, the acknowledgement of the arbitrability of competition law issues has become more and more frequent in practice. In particular, an English judgment of the High Court has used wording that leaves no space for doubt. See *ET Plus SA v Welters* [2005] EWHC 2115 (Comm).

of the validity of specific clauses or agreements. Issues concerning the compensation of damages suffered as a result of anticompetitive agreements should also be arbitrable and so should, according to an authoritative opinion based on the U.S. case law, unjust enrichment actions as well as any claim connected to the contract in which an arbitration clause has been included; moreover, when it comes to merger control, a delicate assessment has to be made of any structural or behavioural commitments offered by the merging parties, and of the nature – generic or qualified – of the interests of third parties in order to assess if a dispute regarding the respect of such commitments can be subject to arbitration and who could be entitled to initiate the proceedings.[23]

With more specific reference to the single basic provisions of EU competition law, it can be recalled that, apart from some initial hesitations and with the aforementioned general exceptions, issues concerning the application of Article 101 TFEU are considered arbitrable, and it does not seem that arbitrators, after the modernization of competition law, should be precluded from applying Article 101(3) TFEU, as this would fragment their jurisdiction and undermine the effectiveness of arbitration.[24] Article 102 TFEU, as well as behavioural commitments under the latter, are normally considered arbitrable as well. As to Articles 107 and 108 TFEU, arbitrability has to be recognized, but the exclusive competence of the Commission to declare State aid compatible with the Internal Market cannot be affected.[25] Finally, Article 106 TFEU, for

[23] See Carbone, cited above, note 12, 4 and 7. For a comment on a recent case, see Luca G. Radicati di Brozolo, 'Il primo lodo in Materia di controllo delle concentrazioni comunitarie' (2013) 23(1) Rivista dell'arbitrato 227 and Laura Bergamini, 'Analysis of recent competition cases decided by arbitrators', this volume, Chapter 14. As regards commitments, a distinction has been proposed between first- and second-order obligations, the former directly connected with the implementation of the original commitments and thus falling within the exclusive jurisdiction of the Commission, the latter related to the implementation agreement, which are arbitrable. See Blanke, cited above, note 15, at 1085 and references cited therein.

[24] See Komninos, cited above, note 14, at 12; Laurence Idot, 'Arbitration and the Reform of Regulation 17/62', in Claus-Dieter Ehlermann and Isabela Atanasiu (eds), *European Competition Law Annual 2001: Effective Private Enforcement of EC Antitrust Law* (Hart Publishing 2003) 307, 317; Alexis Mourre, 'Arbitrability of Antitrust Law from the European and US Perspectives', in Gordon Blanke and Philip Landolt (eds), *EU and US Arbitration: A Handbook for Practitioners* (Kluwer Law International 2011) 3.

[25] See Leigh Hancher, 'Arbitrating EU State Aid Issues', in Blanke and Landolt (eds), cited previous note, at 965.

instance when invoked by a Member State to justify an allegedly anticompetitive action, can be applied in the context of an arbitral proceeding.[26]

EX OFFICIO APPLICATION OF EU COMPETITION LAW BY ARBITRATORS

It has been already explained that it is in the interest of arbitrators – and in doing so they also comply with a precise duty – to render awards which can be enforced (in the jurisdictions where enforcement is likely to be asked). The failure to apply EU competition law *ex officio* should in principle be considered as contrary to public policy and should lead to a refusal to recognize or enforce the award, provided that the relevant EU competition law issues were arbitrable (and if this was not the case, other consequences could be envisaged, like for instance the nullity of the arbitration clause).

After the *Eco Swiss* judgment, leading scholars endorsed this solution,[27] which, although apparently clear and simple, still leaves room for some uncertainties. According to a judgment of the *Cour d'Appel de Paris*,[28] the fact that arbitrators have not applied EU competition law *ex officio* does not necessarily amount to a violation of public policy. According to the *Cour d'Appel*, such a violation has to be 'flagrant, effective and concrete' in order to oblige the national judge to set aside an arbitral award. Here the judgment is illustrative of a minimalist approach in the review of arbitral awards,[29] which also stresses the responsibility of the parties, who had not raised any kind of claims

---

[26] For general discussion of the arbitrability of the categories of issues mentioned in the main text, see Blanke, cited above, note 15, at 1081 and references cited therein. On the possible application of the new EU Directive on Antitrust Damages Actions by arbitrators (or by national courts in the context of the review of an award), see the abstract of Renato Nazzini's presentation, 'Arbitration of Competition Law Disputes and the New EU Directive on Antitrust Damages Actions', TILEC Seminar: Enforcement of competition law, 22 May 2014, <http://www.tilburguniversity.edu/upload/9e2d2ba8-29b2-4bb9-a08f-32d7416b7f73_TILEC%20Invitation.pdf> accessed 28 August 2014, and the introductory chapter to this book.

[27] See Idot, cited above, note 24, at 314–315.

[28] *La S.A. Thalès Air Defence c. Le G.I.E. Euromissile GIE et al.*, cause 2002/19606, *Cour d'Appel de Paris*, 18 November 2004, (2005) 105(2) Journal du Droit International 357.

[29] See Biagioni, cited above, note 4.

regarding EU competition law during the arbitral proceedings (the party opposing the enforcement of the awards finally raised the argument before the national judge reviewing their validity).[30]

A different doctrine, summarized by Advocate General Saggio in his Opinion in the *Eco Swiss* case and which is, in its fundamentals, widely accepted as a basis of arbitration proceedings, could be used to achieve extreme results: arbitrators, as private individuals entrusted by the parties to a dispute with the task of resolving it, are in a passive position, and their competence is strictly bound to what the parties themselves have established (the principle of 'judicial passivity').[31] In particular, a passage of point 21 of the Opinion reads as follows:

> […] [a]rbitrators, being appointed by the parties to an agreement in order to settle a dispute, are under an even greater obligation to comply with the parties' wishes than a court would be, so it does not seem reasonable to require them as a matter of course to consider issues that are outside the ambit of the dispute as defined by the parties. As a form of private judicial procedure, albeit recognised by the law, arbitration is based on the principles of autonomy of the parties and the passive role of the tribunal, as is evident

[30] It is interesting to quote a famous statement of the U.S. Supreme Court in *Mitsubishi* where a minimalist approach is advocated for the review of awards and the focus is on the claims of the parties (which appears enlightening with reference to the parties' attitude in the case presented in the main text): 'While the efficacy of the arbitral process requires that substantive review at the award-enforcement stage remain minimal, it would not require intrusive inquiry to ascertain that the tribunal took cognizance of the antitrust claims and actually decided them'. For an analysis of this case in the framework of the protection of the finality of awards, see Alexis Mourre and Luca G. Radicati di Brozolo, 'Towards Finality of Arbitral Awards: Two Steps Forward and One Step Back' (2006) 23(2) Journal of International Arbitration 171, 176. It has been noted that the judgment in *Thalès Air Defence* does not appear to be in line with the previous case law of the *Cour d'Appel* itself, where the court had reviewed the consistency of the concrete results achieved by arbitrators or arbitral tribunals with requirements of public policy. See Emmanuel Gaillard, 'Extent of Court Review of Public Policy' (2007) 237 (No. 65) New York Law Journal, available at <http://www.shearman.com/~/media/Files/NewsInsights/Publications/2007/04/Extent of Court-Review-of-Public-Policy/Files/IA_NYLJ-Extent-of-Court-Review_040308_16/FileAttachment/IA_NYLJ-Extent-of-Court-Review_040308_16.pdf> accessed 28 August 2014.

[31] See points 20–21 of the Opinion. The question addressed by AG Saggio was quite complicated and regarded the application of the mentioned principle ('judicial passivity') – whose application to ordinary courts had already been addressed by the Court of Justice in its previous case law – to arbitrators.

from the fact that any award which exceeds the terms of the agreement may be annulled.[32]

Therefore, according to a somewhat extreme interpretation of this doctrine, private parties may decide to avoid the application of antitrust rules, but they would probably succeed in this attempt only if courts called on to review the awards rendered in these circumstances had to consider that those rules are not fundamental principles whose breach justifies a refusal to recognize or enforce the award in question, in other words, that they are part of public policy of their jurisdiction. Therefore, the focus would again be on the meaning of public policy and on the extent of the review.[33]

According to another interpretation, antitrust rules can be applied *ex officio* only when a decision founded on them can be considered 'within the legitimate expectation of the parties'.[34] This should be the case when competition law is amongst the rules applicable to the contract (because the parties have so decided, or because competition law is part of the applicable law generically indicated). This has been considered a 'halfway position'.[35] However, the parties would still probably have the choice of avoiding the application of competition law: when drafting an arbitration clause, this is the kind of consequence that their legal counsel

---

[32] It is worth noting that the Court of Justice did not rule directly on the first question, in other words, the one discussed by AG Saggio in the quoted passage. According to the Court, its response to the second question obviated the need to respond to the first. Nevertheless, the Court incidentally recognized that the preceding case law at issue, referred to above in the previous note (specifically, Joined Cases C-430/93 and C-431/93 *Jeroen van Schijndel and Johannes Nicolaas Cornelis van Veen v Stichting Pensioenfonds voor Fysiotherapeuten* [1995] ECR I-4705), was not applicable to the matter before it (see para 40 of the *Eco Swiss* judgment, cited above, note 2).

[33] Article V.2 (b) of the New York Convention. On the obligation of arbitrators to avoid ruling on questions not raised by the parties in the context of the *Eco Swiss* case, see also the position of the *Hoge Raad,* referred to at para 26 of *Eco Swiss*, cited above, note 2. James Bridgeman, 'The Arbitrability of Competition Law Disputes' (2008) 19(1) European Business Law Review 147, 154 speaks about 'a potential dilemma' that seems to arise out of the apparently opposite duties to rule on disputes as they are submitted by the parties and to render an award capable of surviving public policy control, including, in particular, respect of EU competition law.

[34] Yves Derains, 'Specific Issues Arising in the Enforcement of EC Antitrust Rules by Arbitration Courts', in Ehlermann and Atanasiu (eds), cited above, note 24, at 323.

[35] See Carbone, cited above, note 12, at 7.

would certainly take into account. Indeed, the stress on 'legitimate expectations' seems to leave the decision to the parties, in the form of a (possibly) implicit but clear choice, probably expressed by them and incorporated within, amongst other possible elements, the choice of the applicable law.

Hence, it seems this last position is closer to denying the *ex officio* application of competition law than one may think. When it comes to the application of EU competition rules by arbitrators on their own motion, the ultimate sense and effect of private autonomy is at stake. The theories just summarized provide examples of how the attitudes of legal systems towards arbitration, and the theoretical reconstruction thereof, come into play and may condition the final result, and of how delicate the issue is.

Other reconstructions have been put forward, which in particular pay more attention to the exigencies of the application of EU competition law. If the duty to apply EU competition rules *ex officio* were recognized, arbitrators would behave as protectors of the needs of public policy by which they would be actually, albeit indirectly, bound. It has to be recognized that, in principle, the public policy character of EU competition law would be completely deprived of its effect if private parties were able to circumvent its application by following a certain strategy, in particular by means of a choice of applicable law in the event of the arbitration of a dispute. Therefore, other authors consider competition law as a kind of *jus cogens*, whose application does not require the parties' consent.[36]

In practice, arbitrators will be led to carefully consider the balance between the legitimate aim of private autonomy to shape the arbitration proceeding – thus recognizing the role of the parties' responsibility – and the exigencies of the legal system where recognition and enforcement of the award might be sought. In this connection, the introduction of a 'uniform conflict rule' has been authoritatively suggested, obliging arbitrators to identify and take into account all the 'applicable mandatory rules, by balancing the claims (which may sometimes even be competing) of such rules', considering them with reference to the factual framework of the case and to its connections with the relevant legal systems.[37]

---

36 See Komninos, cited above, note 14, at 7 et seq. According to Komninos, EU competition rules 'are applicable notwithstanding the *lex causae* and irrespective of whether the parties have chosen a certain applicable law'.

37 Luca G. Radicati di Brozolo, 'Antitrust: A Paradigm of the Relations between Mandatory Rules and Arbitration – A Fresh Look at the "Second Look"' (2004) 7(1) International Arbitration Law Review 23, 30.

The greater the care of the arbitrators both in identifying those mandatory rules, where relevant, and in carrying out a serious scrutiny as to whether such mandatory rules have been respected, the greater the chances for the award to survive review by national judges.[38] The choice between the different perspectives is not merely a theoretical option; it has to be made with due regard to the context within which the arbitration procedure has been framed and, most importantly, with due regard to the possible enforcement of the award that the parties may seek at the end of the procedure: this seems to pave the way for arbitrators in quite a clear manner.

[38] See Gordon Blanke, 'The Role of EC Competition Law in International Arbitration: A *Plaidoyer*' (2005) 16(1) European Business Law Review 169, 180.

12. The interaction between arbitration and public enforcement: clash or harmony?

Gordon Blanke*

ABSTRACT

This chapter deals with the interaction between arbitration as a means of private enforcement of EU competition law on the one hand and the phenomenon of public enforcement on the other. It will be demonstrated that although there is no established practice, nor any firm regulatory guidance concerning co-operation between and co-ordination of pending arbitration proceedings and competition law investigations by the European Commission (or by the national competition authorities), sensible guidance can be provided on a case-by-case basis taking account of the supranational imperative governing relations under EU law, read together with the arbitrator's duty to render an enforceable award and the principle of party autonomy that is inherent to arbitration more generally.

INTRODUCTION

The interaction between arbitration and public enforcement is an important subject that is often overlooked, and it has equally received fairly little attention in specialist literature on EU competition arbitration to date. This subject goes to the very heart of the dichotomous nature of: (i) arbitration as a private dispute resolution mechanism on the one hand; and (ii) the public administrative mandate and regulatory functions

* Counsel and Sector Leader, International Arbitration Group, Baker & McKenzie. Habib Al Mulla, Dubai and Abu Dhabi.

performed by the European Commission and competent National Competition Authorities (NCAs) in the public enforcement of the EU competition law rules on the other. More specifically, whereas arbitration is entrusted with the resolution of the civil law consequences of any EU competition law violations, the European Commission and NCAs have exclusive competence to deal with all public-administrative aspects of such violations, including in particular the sanctioning of non-compliant undertakings and/or the dismantlement of a merger depending on the nature of the individual violation. Hence, arbitration serves the private enforcement of the EU competition law rules whereas the EU Commission and NCAs serve their public enforcement. In these terms, the arbitrator's private law mandate and the regulatory functions of the EU Commission and NCAs are natural complements and as such exist side by side in EU competition law enforcement.

PRIVATE ENFORCEMENT THROUGH ARBITRATION VERSUS PUBLIC ENFORCEMENT: CLASH OR HARMONY?

In this sense, rather than causing potential clashes between arbitration and EU competition law in the terms questioned by the title of this chapter, any forms of interaction, to the extent that they are well considered and constructive, help to promote the co-existence in harmony of arbitration as a means of private enforcement and the public enforcement of the EU competition law rules through the competent competition authorities. This is also supported by: (i) the supranational imperative of any arbitration involving EU competition law; (ii) the arbitrator's duty to render an enforceable award; and (iii) the arbitrating parties' exercise of their own party autonomy in submitting an EU competition dispute to arbitration and their legitimate expectation of obtaining an enforceable award. These three points are discussed below.

The Supranational Imperative

The supranational imperative articulates itself in a variety of ways, including in particular through a number of supranational legal principles that qualify the EU legal system as a *sui generis* legal order. These commonly include:

(i) the principle of direct effect, whereby sufficiently precise and unconditional provisions of EU law confer rights upon individuals that must be safeguarded by courts;[1]
(ii) the principle of supremacy, whereby both primary and secondary sources of EU law that are capable of producing direct effect, including EU Commission decisions, prevail over conflicting sources of Member State law and form an integral part of the domestic laws of a Member State;[2]
(iii) the principle of sincere co-operation, which requires the mutual co-operation between the EU institutions, including the European Commission, and competent Member State authorities in order to ensure the effective implementation of EU law throughout the internal market;[3]
(iv) the principle of State liability, whereby a non-compliant or defaulting Member State, including its courts as the '*juges communs du droit communautaire*' that qualify as an emanation of the State, will be subject to liability and more specifically to claims for compensation for violation of EU law, including EU competition law;[4] and
(v) the principle pursuant to which it is the European Commission as a 'guardian of the Treaties'[5] that bears ultimate responsibility for the effective enforcement of EU law, including EU competition law.[6]

Taken together, the preceding principles, which contribute to the supranational constitutional set-up of the EU legal order, foster a legal environment that requires stakeholders to comply with EU law, and more specifically with EU competition law, in the exercise of their commercial activities within the EU. According to established case law of the Court of Justice of the European Union, private parties cannot contract out of their obligations under EU law.[7] This arguably includes compliance with

---

1 Case 26/62 *NV Algemene Transport- en Expeditie Onderneming Van Gend en Loos v Nederlandse Administratie der Belastigen* [1963] ECR 1.

2 Case 6/64 *Costa v Ente Nazionale per l'Energia Elettrica (ENEL)* [1964] ECR 585; Case 106/77 *Amministrazione delle Finanze dello Stato v Simmenthal SpA (II)* [1978] ECR 629.

3 See Article 4(3) TEU.

4 Cases C-6 and C-9/90 *Francovich v Italy* [1991] ECR I-5357, para 37; Case C-224/01 *Gerhard Köbler v Republik Österreich* [2003] ECR I-10239, especially paras 31, 32, 36 and 51 et seq.

5 Case C-431/92 *Commission v Germany* [1995] ECR I-2189, para 22.

6 See Article 17(1) TEU.

7 Case 102/81 *Nordsee Deutsche Hochsee Fischerei GmbH v Reederei Mond Hochseefischerei Nordstern AG & Co. KG* [1982] ECR 1095.

relevant EU competition law provisions that arise in arbitration proceedings. In other words, in keeping with their obligations under EU law, contracting parties must not abuse their recourse to arbitration in order to circumvent the application of EU competition law to disputes between them. Nor may an arbitrator – who arguably qualifies as an 'undertaking' within the meaning of EU law[8] – enforce EU competition law violations through a non-compliant award without attracting liability for complicity in illicit cartel activities or facilitating the circumvention of the EU competition law rules more generally.[9] The EU Commission in turn, in its capacity as guardian of the Treaties, will not tolerate any infringements of EU competition law – whether resulting from a non-compliant arbitration award or otherwise. Member State courts and NCAs, subject to the principle of procedural autonomy,[10] will be equally reluctant to give force to infringing behaviour – whether by lending support to the enforcement of non-compliant awards or otherwise – at the risk of exposing themselves to actions of State liability.

The Arbitrator's Duty to Render an Enforceable Award

It is a generally recognized principle of international arbitration that the arbitrator is subject to a best efforts commitment to render an enforceable award.[11] For present purposes, this implies that an arbitrator dealing with EU competition law has to ensure that a resultant award will not fall foul of the public policy requirement in the State of enforcement.

Within the EU context more specifically, the Court of Justice of the European Union has confirmed in its ruling in *Eco Swiss*[12] that the EU competition law rules and in particular Article 101 TFEU qualify as public policy within the meaning of Article V(2)(c) of the New York Convention,[13] to which each EU Member State is a party. In the later case of *Manfredi*,[14] the Court of Justice equally elevated Article 102

---

8 Providing arbitral services to the arbitrating parties.

9 By analogy to Case COMP/E-2/37.857, Commission Decision of 10 December 2003 – *Organic Peroxides*, [2005] OJ L110/44, upheld: Case T-99/04 *AC-Treuhand AG v Commission* [2008] ECR II-1501.

10 See Joined Cases C-295/04 to C-298/04 *Vincenzo Manfredi v Lloyd Adriatico Assicurazioni SpA and Others* [2006] ECR I-6619.

11 See Platte (2003).

12 Case C-126/97 *Eco Swiss China Ltd and Benetton International NV* [1999] ECR I-3055.

13 United Nations Convention on the recognition and enforcement of foreign arbitral awards, done at New York on 10 June 1958.

14 *Manfredi*, cited above, note 10.

TFEU to public policy status. On the basis of this case law, Member State courts – acting in their capacity as supervisory courts within the EU – are generally understood to be bound to refuse enforcement of arbitration awards that violate EU competition law, depending on the intensity of review embraced by each individual Member State court in accordance with the principle of procedural autonomy. Given the extra-territorial reach of EU competition law where the conditions of the 'effects doctrine' are satisfied,[15] even tribunals seated outside the EU may have to take account of relevant EU competition law to the extent that activities performed outside the internal market may produce an appreciable anticompetitive effect within it in order to ensure the ready enforceability of their awards in the EU.

In the alternative, an award disregarding or misapplying EU competition law may face challenges on grounds of *infra petita* (in particular where the arbitrator's mandate has made express reference to the determination of the competition law issue) under the prevailing provisions of the applicable enforcement instrument such as, for example, Article V(1)(c) of the New York Convention.

Party Autonomy and Legitimate Expectations

In accordance with the principle of party autonomy, sophisticated contracting parties have been seen to make express provision for the interaction between the arbitration proceedings and the actions of competent competition authorities, especially the European Commission, in the terms of the underlying arbitration agreement. This is likely to be the case in particular in arbitration commitments within the meaning of the EU Merger Regulation[16] or under Article 9 of Regulation 1/2003.[17] This will in turn promote compliance of a granted award with the EU competition rules and its enforceability before supervisory Member State courts.

Irrespective of the foregoing considerations, it is arguable that compliance with prevailing EU competition law lies within the arbitrating parties' legitimate expectations to the extent that their initial agreement to

---

15 See Cases 89, 104, 114, 116, 117, and 125–129/85 *A. Ahlström Oy v Commission* [1988] ECR 5193.

16 Council Regulation (EC) No 139/2004 of 20 January 2004 on the control of concentrations between undertakings [2004] OJ L24/1.

17 Council Regulation (EC) No 1/2003 of 16 December 2002 on the implementation of the rules on competition laid down in Articles 81 and 82 of the Treaty [2003] OJ L1/1.

have recourse to arbitration must have been premised on a mutual intention to obtain an enforceable award.[18] In addition, the parties' obligation to comply with EU competition law *ab initio* prevents forms of agreement that seek to avoid the application of EU law in prospective or ongoing arbitration proceedings.[19]

THE NOTION OF CO-ORDINATION AND CO-OPERATION BETWEEN ARBITRATION TRIBUNALS AND COMPETITION AUTHORITIES IN THE PRIVATE ENFORCEMENT OF EU COMPETITION LAW

Taking account of the preceding developments, in practice, the purported interaction between arbitration and the public enforcement of EU competition law finds articulation in various forms of potential co-ordination and co-operation between arbitration tribunals and competent competition authorities in the enforcement of EU competition law. Forms of co-ordination commonly arise in the context of the sequence or concurrency in time of proceedings before competent competition authorities and arbitration tribunals. Forms of co-operation, by contrast, address how competent competition authorities and arbitration tribunals can actively assist each other in the conduct of their respective proceedings.

Potential Sources of Guidance

This being said, no forms of co-ordination or co-operation between arbitration and competition authorities have to date been institutionalized, nor is any official soft law guidance of this kind available from the European Commission or NCAs for use in arbitration proceedings. Regulation 1/2003 and the Commission Notice on Co-operation between the Commission and the Member State courts[20] only address the practice of co-ordination and co-operation between the European Commission and Member State courts or NCAs and do not apply to arbitration tribunals, which have been found to fall outside the EU definition of a

---

[18] See Derains in Ehlermann and Atanasiu (eds) (2003).

[19] Excepting a contractual carve-out that provides for the submission of relevant competition law issues to a competing forum.

[20] Commission Notice on the co-operation between the Commission and the courts of the EU Member States in the application of Articles 81 and 82 EC [2004] OJ C101/54.

'Member State court'.[21] Absent any soft law or other official guidance on the subject, guidance can be taken from other sources, such as the wording of individual arbitration commitments[22] or paralegal instruments that have been created in an attempt to provide some initial form of guidance.[23] These, however, have not been immune to criticism,[24] even though they have received some measure of support from the wider specialist community.[25]

In a similar vein, not qualifying as a Member State court within the meaning of EU law, an arbitration tribunal is not subject to the duty of sincere co-operation contained in Article 4(3) TEU. An arbitration tribunal is hence in any event not bound by any form of guidance provided by a competition authority, including the European Commission, in arbitration proceedings unless stated otherwise in the express terms of the arbitration agreement or the arbitration commitment, as the case may be. This conclusion is also supported by the widely-recognized delocalized nature of arbitration tribunals, which do not possess a proper forum and are hence not bound by the laws of any particular jurisdiction.

However, this does not mean that the EU instruments in place may not provide a source of inspiration on how to model and manage potential forms of co-ordination and co-operation between arbitration tribunals and competent competition authorities, including in particular the European Commission, in the private enforcement of EU competition law. Some authors have indeed encouraged such an approach[26] although there is no consensus on the form and content such mutual co-ordination or co-operation between arbitration tribunals and competition authorities should take. This being said, given that in light of the private and confidential nature of arbitration and the relative novelty of the subject, there is little accessible precedent to date, it would seem sensible to extrapolate by analogy from the existing practice of co-ordination and co-operation between the European Commission and the Member State courts under Regulation 1/2003 and the Commission Notice on

---

21 Case 102/81 *Nordsee Deutsche Hochseefischerei GmbH v Reederei Mond Hochseefischerei* [1982] ECR 1095; Case C-125/04 *Guy Denuit and Betty Cordenier v Transorient-Mosaique Voyages and Culture SA* [2005] ECR I-923.

22 See Blanke in Ortiz Blanco (ed) (2013) at para 29.103.

23 See, for example, the ICC Draft Best Practice Note on the European Commission Acting as Amicus Curiae in International Arbitration Proceedings, in Blanke (2006).

24 See, for example, Mourre in Blanke (ed) (2008).

25 See, for example, Idot (2012); Penadés Fons (2012).

26 See, for example, Penadés Fons (2012).

Co-operation in order to identify viable forms of potential co-ordination and co-operation between arbitration tribunals and competent competition authorities in order to ensure the reliable enforcement of EU competition law through arbitration.

However, the non-binding character of any existing instruments of co-ordination and co-operation leaves a considerable degree of latitude and discretion in how arbitration tribunals ultimately decide to take forward any proposed forms of co-ordination and co-operation on a case-by-case basis. This flexibility may constitute a strength in its own right of the private enforcement of the EU competition law rules through arbitration.

POTENTIAL FORMS OF CO-ORDINATION AND CO-OPERATION BETWEEN ARBITRATION AND COMPETITION AUTHORITIES

Potential forms of co-ordination and co-operation between arbitration and competition authorities, including first and foremost the European Commission, in the private enforcement of EU competition law have to remain speculative to the extent that they have been little tested in actual practice. Their effectiveness will ultimately depend on their practical operation in the relationship between the relevant competition authority and the individual arbitration tribunal, and their respective understanding of the level of integration of their respective proceedings.[27]

For ease of reference, any considerations made with respect to proposed practices of co-ordination and/or co-operation between the European Commission and arbitration tribunals apply *mutatis mutandis* to corresponding interactions between NCAs and arbitration tribunals, subject, of course, to the application of the principle of procedural autonomy.

Potential Forms of Co-ordination

As stated previously, potential forms of co-ordination bear on the sequence or concurrency in time of proceedings between competent competition authorities and arbitration tribunals. More specifically, the question of co-ordination arises in situations either: (i) where the

---

[27] For an important contribution to the debate, see also Komninos in Blanke and Landolt (eds) (2011).

competent competition authority has already decided on a related subject-matter in a previous investigation; or (ii) where it is in the process of doing so in parallel with ongoing proceedings before an arbitration tribunal.

Ultimately, the question as to whether a previous decision of – or parallel proceedings before – the European Commission or an NCA have to be taken into account in pending arbitration proceedings depends on: (i) their respective status and, more specifically, the legal effects they produce with respect to the arbitrating parties; as well as (ii) the impact they may have on arbitration-related court proceedings before supervisory Member State courts. Generally speaking, to the extent that an administrative decision produces effects *inter partes* between its addressees, it is arguable that any such decision produces the same binding effects on the parties in arbitration proceedings that address the same factual and legal issues between the same parties. In addition, any decision that produces binding effects on a supervisory Member State court in enforcement proceedings in accordance with the supranational imperative will also have to be taken into account by an arbitration tribunal that wishes to ensure the enforceability of an arbitral award within the EU. Corresponding considerations apply to the suspension of arbitration proceedings, a suspension essentially being justified if the parallel proceedings before the competent competition authority are likely to result in a decision that is capable of the previously indicated effects.

The status of previous decisions rendered by the European Commission[28]

As a general principle, given the delocalized nature of arbitration tribunals and their resulting existence outside any proper forum, technically speaking, arbitration tribunals cannot be bound by any decisions of the European Commission in a strictly legal sense (unless it is an addressee of the decision itself[29]). For the avoidance of doubt, even though a Commission decision binding on the parties may form part of the law on the merits in an arbitration by virtue of the doctrine of supremacy (provided the governing law is of EU provenance), it does not necessarily produce any tangible practical effect in an arbitration in

28 This section largely relies on Nazzini, 'Authority', in Blanke and Landolt (eds) (2011).

29 Which may conceivably be the case in, for example, a cartel investigation, the tribunal being investigated as a potential facilitator of the cartel (by assisting the enforcement of a cartel through a cartel-friendly award).

relation to the same subject between the same parties: this is because an arbitration tribunal might misapply the Commission decision in the same manner that it might misapply any other provision of substantive law and hence fail to give it the proper consideration it requires.

As a rule of thumb, it is safe to say that acts of the European Commission that are neither binding on the arbitrating parties nor on the Member State courts will only ever have persuasive evidentiary force in both law and fact in subsequent arbitration proceedings. This would be typically the case of a guidance letter issued by the European Commission pursuant to the Commission Notice on informal guidance[30] in relation to, for example, a competition-law-related enquiry. Similarly, opinions or informal advice tendered by the European Commission will typically only have precedential evidentiary value in arbitration proceedings, but will never produce binding effects on the deliberations of the tribunal. Equally non-binding in arbitration must be Commission decisions that deal with the same issues of fact and/or law but concern different parties. This must be so in particular given that Member State courts will not be bound by such decisions in supervisory court proceedings: instead, these decisions will only have evidentiary force depending on the degree of similarity of the facts and law in the arbitration.[31] In a similar vein, Commission decisions that deal with the same issue of law in a different factual context will *a fortiori* only ever have precedential value in support of an arbitrating party's pleaded case.

This being said, Commission acts that are binding on Member State courts, and thus its decisions applying EU competition law, are – by virtue of Article 288 TFEU – also bound to produce binding effects in arbitration as against the addressees of the decision. This is so in particular as a result of the logic of the CJEU's ruling in *Masterfoods*[32]

---

[30] Commission Notice on informal guidance relating to novel questions concerning [Arts 101 and 102 TFEU] that arise in individual cases (guidance letters) [2004] OJ C101/78.

[31] See also the interesting analogy created by the House of Lords' ruling in *Crehan v Inntrepreneur Pub Co. (CPC)* [2007] 1 AC 333, in which the House of Lords held that the duty of national courts not to take decisions running counter to a previous Commission decision did not extend to situations where the legal and factual context before the national court was not entirely identical to that prevailing in the relevant Commission decision. The line to be drawn by the national courts can be quite fine: to illustrate the point, the claimant in *Crehan* failed to convince the House of Lords of the binding character of three previous Commission decisions in three beer tie cases that addressed the same factual and legal issue in relation to agreements between different parties.

[32] Case C-344/98 *Masterfoods Ltd v HB Ice Cream Ltd* [2000] ECR I-11369.

and its subsequent codification in Article 16(1) of Regulation 1/2003. Essentially, within the terms of *Masterfoods* and Article 16(1), Member State courts are prohibited from 'tak[ing] decisions running counter to [a previous] Commission [decision]'. This obligation imposed on the Member State courts will also bind them in enforcement proceedings in relation to non-compliant arbitration awards and ultimately expose to potential nullification any award that violates relevant provisions of EU competition law as a result of disregarding a previous Commission decision binding on the arbitrating parties.

It is arguable that the binding effect of a Commission decision on a relevant matter of EU competition law may be extended to third parties to the extent that the third parties concerned have standing to challenge the relevant decision before the Luxembourg Courts in accordance with the *TWD*[33] line of case law. Pursuant to the ruling of the Court of Justice in that case, a third party that has standing to challenge a Commission decision 'without any doubt' is precluded from raising the invalidity of that decision in subsequent proceedings. There is no reason to believe that the Court's reasoning does not also apply by analogy to corresponding arguments of invalidity raised by arbitrating parties in relation to a previous Commission decision provided the contemplated third parties did have standing to appeal the previous Commission decision within the meaning of the CJEU's ruling in *TWD*. In other words, to the extent that a Commission decision has remained unappealed by reference to the usual channels of appeal before the Luxembourg Courts, the decision may be found to be conclusive on both fact and law in subsequent arbitration proceedings as against any parties to the arbitration that had *locus standi* to appeal any aspect of that decision before the EU Courts. To allow otherwise would open arbitration as a forum to re-litigate Commission decisions that have a *res judicata* effect and would as such arguably give rise to abuse of process.[34] In addition or in the alternative, it may be arguable that binding Commission acts, including in particular decisions relating to EU competition law, are authoritative in arbitration proceedings seated in the EU by reason of their binding effect in supervisory court proceedings before a Member State court read together with the arbitrator's duty to render an enforceable award.

Binding Commission decisions/acts for present purposes include in particular:

---

[33] Case C-188/92 *TWD Textilwerke Deggendorf GmbH v Bundesrepublik Deutschland* [1994] ECR I-833.

[34] For further comparative developments of this idea, see Nazzini, 'Authority', in Blanke and Landolt (eds) (2011).

(i) infringement decisions;
(ii) decisions to withdraw the benefit of a block exemption;
(iii) commitment decisions;
(iv) interim measures; and
(v) non-infringement decisions.

Infringement decisions in particular are capable of producing significant precedential evidentiary value in terms of the facts and law on the basis of which an infringement has been found by the European Commission and may as such form a viable basis for follow-on damages actions before an arbitration tribunal.

Apart from their status and the legal effect they may produce in arbitration, the specific relevance in arbitration of any of the above non-binding and binding Commission decisions will ultimately depend on their content and their specific findings of law and fact on a case-by-case basis. The following table provides an overview of the likely relevance in arbitration of the most common binding and non-binding Commission decisions/acts:

Table 12.1 Commission decisions and acts of potential relevance to arbitral proceedings

S/N	Decision type	Legal basis	Purpose	Arbitration relevance
1	Infringement decisions	Art. 7(1) – Reg. 1/2003 –	– Find infringement of Arts 101/102 TFEU – Order termination of infringement – Impose behavioural/ structural remedies	– Binding in fact and law on addressees of the decision and third parties within the meaning of *TWD* – Basis for follow-on damages action in arbitral forum (requirement to prove causation and quantify loss only)
2	Non-infringement decisions	Art. 10 – Reg. 1/2003 –	– Find that there is no infringement of Arts 101/102 TFEU	– Binding in fact and law on addressees of the decision and third parties within the meaning of *TWD* – Conclusive basis for rejection of any claim for damages based on a purported allegation of infringement of Arts 101/ 102 TFEU

S/N	Decision type	Legal basis	Purpose	Arbitration relevance
3	Fining decisions	Arts 3 and 24 – Reg. 1/2003	– Impose fines and periodic penalty payments – Punish intentional or negligent infringements of Arts 101/102 TFEU – Punish failure to comply with Commission investigative measures	– Largely irrelevant in arbitration (as it imposes a public law penalty) – However, may be conclusive evidence in arbitration of an infringement of Arts 101/102 TFEU (which gave rise to the public law penalty in the first place) – Findings of negligence or intention may produce factually-binding evidence of a party's intention or negligence in committing an infringement, which may form the basis for a finding of further civil law liabilities in the arbitration
4	Block exemption decisions	Art. 29(1) – Reg. 1/2003	– Withdraw benefit of a block exemption	– Binding in the arbitration to the extent that the withdrawal of the benefit may impact the validity of a commercial agreement in dispute between the arbitrating parties – Conclusive evidence in the arbitration of the withdrawal of the benefit of the block exemption
5	Commitment decisions	Art. 9 – Reg. 1/2003	– Conclude that there are no longer grounds for Commission to act – Impose behavioural/structural commitments	– Limited relevance in arbitration (no finding of infringement) – May provide conclusive evidence on certain findings of fact
6	Interim measures	Art. 8 – Reg. 1/2003	– Provide relief where a *prima facie* case has been made of infringement of Arts 101/102 TFEU and risk of serious and irreparable harm to competition	– Commission's *prima facie* assessment of potential infringements may carry significant evidentiary weight in arbitration on issues of both law and fact – May be conclusive evidence for a defence to a claim for breach of contract (at least for duration of interim measure)

Table 12.1 (continued)

7	Case closures	Art. 2(4) – Reg. 773/04[35]	– Close an investigation – Reject a complaint without commencing a formal investigation	– Non-binding – May constitute conclusive evidence that there are no grounds for any purported competition infringements and confirm vexatious nature of claims
8	Opinions and informal guidance	Third Recital – Reg. 1/2003 (Commission guidance letters)[36]	– Provide guidance on novel questions of law and fact	– Non-binding – Provide persuasive evidence of the Commission's view of a novel question of law or fact (that may arise in the same or similar terms in an arbitration)
9	Procedural decisions	Art. 13(1) – Reg. 1/2003 Other	– Reject case that is subject to investigation by an NCA – Make other procedural directions (for example, granting or denying access to file, and so on)	– Non-binding – Limited relevance in arbitration except for potential conclusive evidence on certain findings of fact and/or the *locus standi* of a party in the arbitration

The status of parallel proceedings before the European Commission[37]

The status of parallel proceedings before the European Commission and their relevance to pending arbitration proceedings on the same matter is guided by the same principles and parameters as the determination of the role of a previous Commission decision in arbitration proceedings. In particular, it is worth repeating that, unlike the Member State courts, arbitration tribunals are not subject to a duty of sincere co-operation within the meaning of Article 4(3) TEU. This means that arbitration tribunals – again unlike Member State courts, which may have to stay proceedings that are likely to conflict with a parallel Commission

[35] Commission Regulation (EC) No. 773/2004 of 7 April 2004 relating to the conduct of proceedings by the Commission pursuant to Articles [101 and 102 TFEU] [2004] OJ L123/18, as amended.

[36] Read together with Commission Notice on informal guidance relating to novel questions concerning [Arts 101 and 102 TFEU] that arise in individual cases (guidance letters) [2004] OJ C101/78.

[37] This section largely relies on Nazzini, 'Parallel Proceedings', in Blanke and Landolt (eds) (2011), in particular paras 25–30 et seq.

investigation pursuant to Article 16(1) of Regulation 1/2003 – have no obligation to suspend the reference before them in order to await and co-ordinate the arbitration process with the outcome of the administrative proceedings before the Commission.

This being said, any outcome of the Commission's investigation that would conflict with an arbitration award will bind a supervisory Member State court in enforcement proceedings and may hence ultimately result in the nullification of the award.

As a result, if an arbitration tribunal is faced with a complex and serious competition law issue that is simultaneously under parallel investigation by the European Commission, the tribunal is most probably well advised to suspend its proceedings and wait for the outcome of the Commission's investigation. This would ensure the compatibility of a resultant arbitration award with the outcome of the Commission's investigations and would more specifically allow the arbitrator to rely upon the Commission's findings of fact and law in order to draw the appropriate civil law consequences and to render an enforceable award. On the other hand, if the issues subject to the tribunal's determination and subject to parallel investigation by the European Commission are a simple and uncomplicated competition law matter, the tribunal clearly should – in accordance with the prevailing doctrine of '*acte clair*'[38] – proceed to its determination without undue delay.

In other words, whereas the tribunal has complete discretion to disregard any parallel proceedings of the European Commission, it should exercise this discretion sensibly. The sensible exercise of that discretion depends not only on the complexity and the degree of seriousness of the individual competition matter, but also on a tribunal's general obligation to manage the progress of an arbitration procedure with due expedition.[39] This also implies that an arbitration tribunal should only resolve to suspend its proceedings provided that: (i) the Commission has already commenced parallel proceedings; and (ii) there is a genuine risk that the Commission may reach a conflicting outcome if the arbitration proceedings are not stayed. No arbitration reference should be suspended if the Commission may only commence parallel investigations in the future or if the risk of conflicting outcomes in the arbitration and the Commission's investigation is no more than speculative.

---

38 To the same effect, see Blanke in Klausegger et al. (eds) (2009) at 61.

39 As codified in most leading arbitration rules as well as a number of arbitration laws, and as is in any event generally understood to be the case in arbitration.

Without prejudice to the foregoing, in order to comply with obligations of due process, prior to a potential stay in deference to a parallel investigation by the European Commission, an arbitration tribunal is well advised to consult the arbitrating parties on their procedural preferences. Nevertheless, the tribunal should suspend the arbitration – irrespective of the parties' disagreement – if the evidence before it is such that a future Commission decision is likely to conflict with, and would hence jeopardize, the enforcement of a resultant award.[40] That said, in the event that there is an irresolvable discord between the tribunal and the parties, the tribunal of course remains at liberty to resign provided that a failure to suspend may either implicate the tribunal in a violation of EU competition law or would otherwise be professionally indefensible.

There is no reason to believe that parallel proceedings before an NCA would be treated any differently in arbitration from those before the European Commission.[41]

Potential Forms of Co-operation

As stated previously, potential forms of co-operation bear on the mutual active assistance between competition authorities and arbitration tribunals in the conduct of their respective proceedings.

As follows from the previous discussions, neither Regulation 1/2003 nor the Commission Notice on Co-operation finds any application to arbitration tribunals. As a result, the practices on co-operation proposed there as applied to the relationship between the European Commission and the Member State courts in their respective endeavours to enforce the

---

40 Ultimately, the threshold test applicable to a determination of whether to suspend or not may vary from Member State to Member State in accordance with the test for the setting aside of arbitral awards on the basis of their violation of EU competition law. It would be imaginable that a test of 'likely conflict' may be sufficient in those EU jurisdictions that tend to embrace a maximalist approach to the review of arbitration awards, for example, Germany and The Netherlands, whereas a test of a 'conflict being almost certain to occur' would possibly prevail in EU jurisdictions that prefer the minimalist approach to Member State court review, such as, for example, France.

41 It is worth noting in this context that with the adoption of the new Damages Directive (see Directive of the European Parliament and of the Council on certain rules governing actions for damages under national law for infringements of the competition law provisions of the Member States and of the European Union) tribunals may also have to be sensitive to foreign NCA decisions, which serve as *prima facie* evidence in proceedings before Member State courts within the meaning of the Directive.

EU competition law provisions do not apply in arbitration. More specifically, pursuant to Article 15 of Regulation 1/2003, Member State courts are free to request from the Commission information in its possession or its opinion on questions concerning the application of EU competition law.[42] The Commission, in turn, may make written submissions to the Member State courts and, with the permission of the relevant court, oral submissions in order to ensure the coherent application of the EU competition law rules.[43] For the purpose of preparing its submissions only, the European Commission may request the relevant Member State court to transmit documents necessary for the assessment of the case.[44]

Despite the non-binding nature of the co-operation provisions contained in Regulation 1/2003, a number of proactive provisions of co-operation that even go beyond the practices advocated in Regulation 1/2003 can be found in arbitration commitments used for the private enforcement of behavioural remedies in EU merger control[45] and under Article 9 commitment decisions.[46] Without going into further detail, provisions of co-operation typical for use in this context are:

- Requests for information from the tribunal to the Commission, especially to assist in the accurate definition of geographic and product markets;
- Requests from the arbitrator to the Commission in relation to the correct interpretation of the intended regulatory objectives of individual commitments in order to ensure an accurate understanding by the tribunal of the competition-compliant operation of the commitments; and
- The Commission's role as *amicus arbitri*, including in particular the Commission's entitlement to:
  (i) receive the main submissions and procedural documentation issued over the course of the arbitration procedure;
  (ii) make submissions of its own motion to the tribunal at all stages of the arbitration procedure; and
  (iii) participate in the main evidentiary hearing as observer, expert witness or otherwise (including an entitlement to ask questions).

42 Article 15(1), Regulation 1/2003.
43 Article 15(3), Regulation 1/2003.
44 Ibid.
45 Blanke in Ortiz Blanco (ed) (2013) at para 29.103.
46 Ibid.

These provisions on the active co-operation between the European Commission and the arbitration tribunal in the context of EU commitment arbitrations are intended to ensure compliance of any resultant award with the regulatory objectives of the underlying Commission conditional merger clearance decision or the Article 9 commitment decision, as the case may be. Given the dearth of EU commitment arbitrations to date, these provisions have remained largely untested.

Even in ordinary EU competition arbitrations, there is no reason why the parties should not agree to a similar level of active co-operation between the European Commission and arbitration tribunals. It is ultimately in the parties' interest to obtain an enforceable award that is in compliance with the prevailing EU competition law provisions.

However, it is of course appreciated that any mechanism of co-operation has to defer to the requirements of confidentiality prevailing in EU competition law. This may in part be achieved by making specific provision for the required level of confidentiality in the individual arbitration agreement and in the terms of reference accompanying the arbitration process. To this effect, the Commission may also request a confidentiality undertaking from a tribunal to which it provides any particular information from its file. The safer option, from the Commission's point of view, would of course be only to disclose to an arbitration tribunal non-confidential versions of its own evidence.

Last but not least, testimony from Commission officials in arbitration may only be of very limited use, in particular given that Commission officials are subject to obligations of professional secrecy pursuant to Article 339 TFEU and will therefore not be able to disclose any information obtained during administrative investigations unless that information is already in the public domain.

CONCLUSION

By way of conclusion, arbitration tribunals are well advised to take a well-considered and constructive approach to the co-ordination of their proceedings with those of competent competition authorities. They should be alert to the fact that even though (unlike their homologues in the EU Member State courts) they are not bound by the duty of sincere co-operation under Article 4(3) TEU, the supranational imperative – which imposes strict obligations of EU competition law compliance on Member State courts in their supervisory role in actions for enforcement of arbitral awards within the EU – together with their duty to render an enforceable award and the potential engagement of their liability in the event of their proven complicity in a tangible competition violation (for example, by consciously facilitating the enforcement of a cartel through arbitration) militate in favour of a deferential approach to their co-operation with relevant competition authorities.

Furthermore, in order to ensure compliance with due process as well as the principle of party autonomy, tribunals are arguably under an obligation to consult the arbitrating parties on any forms of co-ordination and co-operation with any relevant competition authorities they have in mind provided the arbitrating parties have not made express provision for such co-ordination and co-operation in their underlying arbitration agreement or terms of reference. Failing the parties' express agreement, a tribunal will ultimately have to balance its own obligations as an 'undertaking' under EU law with those of a delocalized private judge in the reference before it. It is to be anticipated that true problems of this kind will only arise in the most serious of cases, for example, where arbitrating parties intend to instrumentalize an arbitration tribunal in order to enforce a cartel in violation of Article 101 TFEU. As a last resort, an arbitration tribunal remains, of course, at liberty to resign should the situation become intractable and jeopardize the tribunal's own integrity, possibly exposing it to liability for complicity in, for example, cartelization under the prevailing EU competition law rules.

BIBLIOGRAPHY

Gordon Blanke, *The Use and Utility of International Arbitration in EC Commission Merger Remedies: A Novel Supranational Paradigm in the Making?* (Europa Law Publishing 2006)

Gordon Blanke (ed), 'Arbitrating Competition Law Issues: a European and a US Perspective', 19(1) *European Business Law Review* Special Edition (2008)

Gordon Blanke, 'EC Competition Law Claims in International Arbitration', in Klausegger et al. (eds) (2009), cited below, 3 et seq.

Gordon Blanke and Philip Landolt (eds), *EU and US Antitrust Arbitration: A Handbook for Practitioners* (Kluwer Law International 2011)

Gordon Blanke, 'EU Competition Arbitration', in Ortiz Blanco (2013), cited below, 1075 et seq.

Yves Derains, 'Specific Issues Arising in the Enforcement of EC Antitrust Rules by Arbitration Courts', in Ehlermann and Atanasiu (eds) (2003), cited below, 323 et seq.

Claus-Dieter Ehlermann and Isabela Atanasiu (eds), *European Competition Law Annual 2001: Effective Private Enforcement of EC Antitrust Law* (Hart Publishing 2003)

Laurence Idot, 'L'arbitrage et le Contrôle des Engagements en Droit de la Concurrence' (2012/1) *Concurrences* 21

Christian Klausegger et al. (eds), *Austrian Arbitration Yearbook 2009* (Manz/Staempfli/Beck 2009)
Assmimakis P. Komninos, 'Assistance by the European Commission and Member States Authorities in Arbitration', in Blanke and Landolt (2011), cited above, 727 et seq.
Alexis Mourre, 'Dissenting Opinion on a Dangerous Project', in Blanke (ed) (2008), cited above, 219 et seq.
Renato Nazzini, 'Authority and Influence in Arbitrations of Previous Decisions on EU Competition Law', in Blanke and Landolt (eds) (2011), cited above, 699 et seq.
Renato Nazzini, 'Parallel Proceedings Before the Tribunal and the Courts/Competition Authorities', in Blanke and Landolt (eds) (2011), cited above, 881 et seq.
Luis Ortiz Blanco (ed), *EU Competition Procedure* (Oxford University Press 2013)
Manuel Penadés Fons, 'Beyond the *prima facie* Effectiveness of Arbitration Commitments in EU Merger Control' (2012) 49 *Common Market Law Review* 1915
Martin Platte, 'An Arbitrator's Duty to Render Enforceable Awards' (2003) 20(3) *Journal of International Arbitration* 307

13. Review by national courts of arbitral awards dealing with EU competition law

Giacomo Biagioni*

ABSTRACT

According to the Eco Swiss *judgment of the European Court of Justice, in the review of arbitral awards – which can be carried out in proceedings for the recognition or enforcement of such awards, or in proceedings for setting them aside – EU competition law is part of the domestic public policy that courts of the Member States must take into account. The case law of national courts shows that arbitral awards dealing with EU competition law are often reviewed with reference to public policy and, with some possible exceptions due to the specificities of national law or the attitude of the national courts, international public policy in particular should be the relevant concept. This has implications for the intensity of judicial scrutiny. If review is carried out by reference to domestic public policy, this may interfere with the pro-arbitration attitude that characterizes most jurisdictions. On the other hand, if review is by reference to international public policy only, this may potentially affect the effective application of EU competition law. The fact that the 'minimalist' approach – whereby only blatant breaches of EU competition law may entail the annulment of an arbitral award – is the approach that prevails widely amongst national courts, can be seen as reflecting the application of the international public policy concept. Nonetheless, the actual extent of the powers to be exercised by national courts under this approach is far from clear under the current practice.*

* University of Cagliari and Of Counsel, Studio Pietrangeli, Rome.

PRELIMINARY REMARKS: BACK TO *ECO SWISS*

After the *Eco Swiss* judgment of the European Court of Justice, the power of national courts to review arbitral awards dealing with EU competition law has not really been questioned. However, the extant case law concerning the subject matter is still very rare, as domestic courts often refrain from exercising this power or attach very strict conditions to it. On the other hand, the case law is far from consistent, since national courts give different interpretations of the grounds for review of arbitral awards alleged to be contrary to EU competition law and thus invalid. It is therefore useful to re-evaluate the role of domestic courts in order to determine the basis for, and the limits to, their intervention, and to outline systematically the role of the EU competition rules in the context of proceedings for review of arbitral awards.

At the outset, a general clarification is necessary. The phrase 'proceedings for review of arbitral awards' is often used to designate both proceedings for setting aside an arbitral award before the competent national court, and proceedings for recognition and enforcement of an arbitral award under the 1958 New York Convention. Although the issue of EU competition law may arise in a very similar way in both types of proceedings, one should not underestimate the differences in the scope of the power of review that a domestic court enjoys depending on which type of proceeding is before it. In particular, while in principle the effects of a refusal of recognition or enforcement are limited to the country where recognition or enforcement is sought, the annulment of an arbitral award by the competent court may have relevance in every other country (per Article V.1.*e* of the 1958 New York Convention).[1] As a consequence, the extent of the review and the relevant grounds, as enshrined in the 1958 New York Convention in one case and in national procedural rules

---

[1] However, it is well known that in some jurisdictions (especially in France), an award can be still enforced even though it has been set aside in the country of the seat of arbitration. This is because, under Article V of the New York Convention, national courts retain discretion to refuse enforcement of annulled awards. See generally William Park, 'Duty and Discretion in International Arbitration', (1999) American Journal of International Law 805. The attitude of French courts is discussed in Emmanuel Gaillard, 'Consolidation de la Jurisprudence Hilmarton sur la Reconnaissance des Sentences Annulées dans l'Etat du Siège' (2007) Revue de l'arbitrage 507.

in the other,[2] can diverge significantly depending on the type of proceeding. Nevertheless, as we shall see, domestic courts are inclined not to stress those differences and instead adopt a unitary approach to the issue, irrespective of the nature of the proceeding in which it arises.

The general attitude of domestic courts towards the review of arbitral awards for breach of EU competition law in this regard can be explained by recalling, as a starting point, the above-mentioned judgment in *Eco Swiss*,[3] in which the CJEU had its first (and so far its last) chance to deal with the issue. Notwithstanding the time that has elapsed and the case law developed by national courts, it is still worth reverting to this case in order to reassess some of the issues raised there.

Eco Swiss concerned an arbitral award granted in the Netherlands under Dutch law and according to the rules of procedure of the Netherlands Institute of Arbitrators, although it involved elements of transnationality. In the main proceedings, an application to set aside the award as contrary to Dutch public policy had been lodged with a Dutch court, which in its turn made a request for a preliminary ruling. The CJEU was thus called upon to evaluate whether a conflict with public policy, as a ground of invalidity of arbitral awards under national law, could arise where an award was contrary to EU competition law. The Court held that, in exercising their power to review arbitral awards, national courts must indeed take EU competition law into account as part of their national public policy, although this duty is not unconditional.

In reaching this conclusion, the Court attached great significance to the need for the effective application of EU law. Since arbitrators are not allowed to make a reference to the CJEU even when they deal with EU law issues, judicial review of arbitral awards also serve the purpose of ensuring that requests for interpretation can be addressed to the Court when a dispute has been submitted to arbitration. On the other hand, the Court accepted that the power to review arbitral awards, even when aimed at ascertaining their conformity with EU law, may be limited in scope and may be subject to time limits for the sake of legal certainty.

---

2 National rules concerning the grounds for setting aside arbitral awards show a high degree of uniformity in many States, since they are significantly influenced by Article 34 of UNCITRAL Model Law on International Commercial Arbitration. See Peter Binder, *International Commercial Arbitration and Conciliation in UNCITRAL Model Law Jurisdictions* (2nd edn, Sweet & Maxwell 2005) 268.

3 Case C-126/97 *Eco Swiss China Time Ltd v Benetton International NV* [1999] ECR I-3055.

The facts of the case presented to the Court played a significant role not only in shaping the principles stated in its judgment but also in setting the terms of the ensuing discussion among commentators. A revision of the key elements of the reasoning of the Court in the light of the subsequent national case law can thus help to clarify the extent to which *Eco Swiss* can still provide useful guidance.

PUBLIC POLICY AND EU COMPETITION LAW WITH REGARD TO ARBITRAL AWARDS

It was apparent from *Eco Swiss* that the Court did not consider the breach of EU competition rules to be an autonomous ground for invalidity of arbitral awards, but it did require national courts to take it into account insofar as it could correspond to one of the grounds for invalidity provided for in national laws or in the 1958 New York Convention.[4] Subsequently, the Court stressed this very point in *van der Weerd*, recalling that its aim was to ensure that 'equal treatment [be given] to pleas based on national law and those based on Community law'.[5]

However, most of the grounds for review listed in those instruments concern procedural issues completely unconnected with EU competition law. As regards procedural grounds for invalidity, one can only suggest, building on the Court's judgment in *Mostaza Claro*, that in very exceptional circumstances an arbitration clause could be regarded in itself as an abuse of a dominant position, and that its validity could be questioned for that reason. In *Mostaza Claro*, the Court held that under Directive 93/13/EC a national court seized with an action for annulment of an arbitral award can review the validity of the arbitration agreement in order to ensure that consumer protection requirements are observed.[6] The same line of reasoning should apply when the arbitration agreement contravenes EU competition law, even though it can prove much more

---

[4] It is commonly accepted that an arbitral award can be denied enforcement only on the basis of the grounds listed in Article V of the Convention. See, for example, Patricia Nacimiento, 'Article V(1)(a)' in Herbert Kronke et al. (eds), *Recognition and Enforcement of Foreign Arbitral Awards: A Global Commentary on the New York Convention* (Kluwer Law International 2010) 206.

[5] Case C-222/05 *J. van de Weerd and Others v Minister van Landbouw, Natuur en Voedselkwaliteit* [2007] ECR I-4233.

[6] Case C-168/05 *Elisa María Mostaza Claro v Centro Móvil Milenium SL* [2006] ECR I-10421.

difficult to show that (the imposition of) an arbitration agreement constitutes an abuse of dominance.

However, national case law has focused mainly on the few substantive grounds for invalidity. In particular, issues of EU competition law have arisen in connection with the issue of whether a dispute may be submitted to arbitration, and with the question of whether an award is compatible with public policy.

Although the issue of arbitrability of cases involving issues of EU competition rules has for some time proved to be controversial in the light of the mandatory character of those rules, there is now a wide consensus regarding the power of arbitrators to settle disputes connected with competition law and to deal with issues of competition law themselves. Indeed, the question has occasionally been raised before national courts and it has invariably been found that such disputes are capable of being submitted to arbitration.[7]

Accordingly, in the context of the review of arbitral awards, the issue of the breach of EU competition law arises above all in terms of a conflict between a given award and public policy, as the *Eco Swiss* precedent demonstrates.[8]

Under domestic law, public policy is in fact very often referred to as a ground for setting aside arbitral awards. This is explained by the fact that, as a consequence of a general pro-arbitration approach, and according to the scheme of Article 34 of the UNCITRAL Model Law on International Commercial Arbitration, most national legislation does not allow domestic courts any review of the merits of an award. However, while the scope of their power of review is limited, national courts are required to verify that the award does not conflict with the fundamental principles of their legal system.

Likewise, recognition or enforcement of arbitral awards can be denied on grounds of public policy under the above-mentioned New York Convention, as well as under national rules dealing with the recognition of foreign arbitral awards.[9] Therefore, it is by the recourse to the public

---

[7] See, for example, the decisions of the Corte d'Appello of Milan in *Società Lorenzini Istituto Biochimico v Madaus* (2002: Rivista dell'arbitrato, 2004, 105) and in *Terra Amata S.r.l. v Tensacciai S.r.l.* (2006: Rivista dell'arbitrato, 2006, 744).

[8] Sylvaine Poillot-Peruzzetto, 'L'ordre Public International en Droit Communautaire' (2000) Journal du Droit International 299.

[9] See, *inter alia*, Articles 839 and 840 of the Italian Code of Civil Procedure; Article 1498 of the French Code of Civil Procedure. See also Bernard Hanotiau and Olivier Caprasse 'Public Policy in International Commercial

policy clause that national courts have the chance to verify the conformity of arbitral awards with EU competition law.

However, in this context it is worth noting the peculiar position of the English courts. While the Arbitration Act 1975 incorporating the New York Convention explicitly refers to public policy in matters of recognition and enforcement of foreign arbitral awards, the Arbitration Act 1996, departing voluntarily from the UNCITRAL Model Law, does not mention public policy and provides that 'leave to appeal shall be given only if the court is satisfied [...] that the decision of the tribunal is obviously wrong' (Section 69).[10] Although the narrow 'obviously wrong' test[11] requires a very different analysis from the evaluation of possible conflicts with public policy, the two methods are not likely to lead to different outcomes in cases concerning the interplay with EU competition law, since an obviously wrong decision dealing with that subject matter normally entails a serious violation of competition rules.

However, the 'obviously wrong' test can give rise to severe difficulties when one of the parties requests leave to appeal against an arbitral award rendered in the United Kingdom under foreign law. Indeed, English courts have thus far taken the view that the right to appeal under Section 69 does not extend to errors of foreign law,[12] even if the parties agreed that review would be possible in those circumstances.[13] The rationale for the rule lies in the well-known principle according to which issues of foreign law are treated as issues of fact before English courts. As a consequence, in the frequent case where arbitration has its seat in England and Wales but is to be decided under foreign law, the parties have no right of appeal under UK law against the arbitral award. This

---

Arbitration', in Emmanuel Gaillard and Domenico Di Pietro (eds), *Enforcement of Arbitration Agreements and International Arbitral Awards: The New York Convention in Practice* (Cameron May 2008) 787.

[10] Andrew Tweeddale and Keren Tweeddale, *Arbitration of Commercial Disputes. International and English Law and Practice* (Oxford University Press 2007) 808.

[11] *HMV UK Ltd v Propinvest Friar Ltd Partnership* (2011) CA (Civ Div); *National Trust for Places of Historic Interest or Natural Beauty v Fleming* [2009] EWHC 1789 (Ch).

[12] *Egmatra v Marco Trading Corp* [1999] Lloyd's Rep 862; *Sanghi Polyesters Ltd (India) v The International Investor KCFC (Kuwait)*, [2001] CLC 748; *Reliance Industries Ltd v Enron Oil and Gas India Ltd and ONGC* [2002] 1 Lloyd's Rep 645; *Schwebel v Schwebel* [2010] EWHC 3280 (TCC) (QB). See Tweeddale and Tweeddale, *Arbitration of Commercial Disputes,* cited above, note 10, at 801.

[13] *Guangzhou Dockyards Co v ENE Aegiali* [2010] EWHC 2826 (Comm).

situation leaves some space for speculation as regards the role played by EU law (including competition law) in disputes not subject to English law. However, this can justify the conclusion that in the UK, in accordance with the general non-interventionist approach of the English courts, the right of appeal against arbitral awards for reasons of EU competition law have to be construed very narrowly. This can probably explain why, at least so far, English courts have not developed any case law relating to arbitral awards conflicting with EU competition law.

EU COMPETITION LAW AS A MATTER OF PUBLIC POLICY

The fact that public policy is now used by domestic courts as a tool for taking into account issues of EU competition law cannot come as a surprise. Public policy, whether it constitutes a ground for non-application of foreign law or a ground for non-recognition of (foreign or arbitral) decisions, is always described as changing in different countries and over time (hence the description of public policy as a 'chameleon of private international law'[14]). Those characteristics are due to the fact that public policy reflects the fundamental values of a given legal system (or of more than one when some legal systems are closely intertwined, as in the case of European countries). Since such values depend on variable social, ethical and economic considerations, public policy is bound to follow the social evolution of different legal systems. The actual capacity of public policy to adapt itself to social changes obviously varies according to the willingness of national courts to take those changes into account. Useful lessons about the increasing rapidity in the development of public policy principles can be learned from family law, since institutions deemed to be contrary to public policy have become part of the public policy itself after a relatively short period of time (examples can range from divorce in Southern European countries to recent developments with regard to same-sex marriages in Belgium or France)

The role of principles of competition law as a ground for review of the validity of arbitral awards can also fit into that scheme. Certainly, when the 1958 New York Convention was drafted, not many people would have thought of competition rules as being a matter of public policy. However,

[14] Philippe Schweizer, 'L'ordre Public: Caméléon du Droit International Privé?', in Bernard Dutoit, Joseph Hofstetter and Paul Piotet (eds), *Mélanges en l'honneur de Guy Flattet* (Payot 1985) 455.

for the first time in *Almelo*,[15] and then *expressis verbis* in *Eco Swiss*, the CJEU accepted that EU competition law can come into play as part of the rules of public policy to be applied by national courts when they review arbitral awards. Subsequently, the Court has recalled that statement several times and in different contexts, underlining that Article 101 TFEU is a matter of public policy and constitutes a fundamental provision indispensable for the proper functioning of the internal market,[16] so that it must be applied automatically by national courts.[17] Article 102 TFEU can be deemed to play a similar role, as the Court seems to suggest in *dicta*[18] and as the *SNF v Cytec* saga illustrates.[19] Some features of the prohibition on State aid that is incompatible with the internal market have also been considered relevant in this context.[20]

Therefore, it is nowadays indisputable that the EU competition law provisions enshrine fundamental principles which underpin the European legal system and complement the national legal systems of the Member States. Those principles must accordingly be granted extensive and effective application, and national courts are called upon to provide a wide range of remedies where the competition rules are violated. In other words, the general principles of EU competition law undoubtedly belong to 'EU public policy', meaning that a wide range of principles of public policy are now shared among all the Member States. It is obviously coherent with this general framework that the EU competition rules also

---

[15] Case C-393/92 *Municipality of Almelo and others v NV Energiebedrijf Ijsselmij* [1994] ECR I-1477, para 23.

[16] Case C-453/99 *Courage Ltd v Bernard Crehan* [2001] ECR I-6297, para 20.

[17] Joined Cases C-295/04 to C-298/04 *Vincenzo Manfredi v Lloyd Adriatico Assicurazioni SpA* [2006] ECR I-6619, para 31; Case C-8/08 *T-Mobile Netherlands BV and Others v Raad van bestuur van de Nederlandse Mededingingsautoriteit* [2009] ECR I-4529.

[18] See *Manfredi*, cited previous note, para 31.

[19] The case is well known: SNF challenged the validity of a Belgian arbitral award before the Belgian courts: Tribunal de grande instance de Bruxelles 8 March 2007, Revue de l'arbitrage 2008, 303; Cour d'appel de Bruxelles, 22 June 2009, Revue de l'arbitrage 2009, 574. On the other hand, Cytec successfully sought enforcement of the Belgian award in France: Cour d'appel de Paris, 23 March 2007, Revue de l'arbitrage 2007, 100; Cour de cassation, 4 June 2008, Revue de l'arbitrage 2008, 160.

[20] Luca Radicati di Brozolo, 'Arbitration and Competition Law: the Position of the Courts and of Arbitrators' (2011) 27 Arbitration International 1. See also Svea Hovrätt, *Republic of Latvia v Latvjia Gaze*, 4 May 2005, Transnational Dispute Management 2007.

have significant implications in proceedings for the judicial review of arbitral awards.

EU COMPETITION LAW AS PART OF THE INTERNATIONAL PUBLIC POLICY OF THE EU MEMBER STATES

Notwithstanding the remarks above, it is regrettable that in *Eco Swiss* the CJEU did not provide any guidance on how and to what extent competition rules have to be taken into consideration. In itself, the affirmation that EU competition law is a matter of public policy does not solve every problem. Inevitably, recourse to the public policy clause implies some limitations on the power of review: in particular, national courts are not allowed to subject the reasoning of the arbitral tribunal to an entire re-examination,[21] and they cannot rely on every conceivable kind of breach of competition law in order to annul or to refuse recognition and enforcement of the award. Again, however, the level of control that national courts may actually exercise when they scrutinize arbitral awards remains unclear.

In this regard, it is common ground that, in private international law, two different notions of public policy can be envisaged: domestic public policy and international public policy.[22]

Domestic public policy is a broader notion than international public policy. The domestic concept of public policy may even cover every mandatory national provision, in other words, every national provision from which parties may not derogate by way of private contract. Given the broad sweep of this concept, recourse to domestic public policy would ensure the maximum level of coherence within the national legal system and would prevent arbitral awards from affecting its internal harmony.

By contrast, international public policy includes only the most fundamental principles reflecting the core values of a legal system – principles

---

[21] Luca Radicati di Brozolo, 'Antitrust: A Paradigm of the Relations between Mandatory Rules and Arbitration – A Fresh Look at the Second Look' (2004) International Arbitration Law Review 31.

[22] The distinction is clearly outlined, as regards Article V of the New York Convention, in Dirk Otto and Omaia Elwan, 'Art. V(2)' in Kronke et al. (eds), *Recognition and Enforcement of Foreign Arbitral Awards,* cited above, note 4, 345, at 366.

that can never be renounced,[23] even when foreign law is applicable or when the recognition and enforcement of foreign judgments is at stake. Sometimes, national courts stress that deference to certain fundamental principles stems from the fact that the country in question belongs to a supranational legal tradition; but the point of view of the State concerned also carries weight.

One can take for granted that, according to the CJEU's case law, EU competition law is part of the domestic public policy in the legal systems of the Member States. However, it is necessary to investigate whether EU competition law qualifies as part of their international public policy as well. In *Tensacciai*, the Swiss Federal Tribunal was confronted with precisely this question:[24] yet it held that, from the point of view of the Swiss legal system, the principles of EU competition law do not belong to the set of essential values whose observance is always mandatory. In its reasoning the Swiss Federal Tribunal underlined, *inter alia*, that competition law differs so greatly between States, depending on their economic system, that it cannot be conceived as part of a transnational public policy.

However, what holds true for the Swiss legal system does not necessarily correspond to the position in the legal systems of the EU Member States. In particular, while international public policy attaches particular importance to principles accepted by a large number of States, it always stems from a given legal system.[25]

In *Eco Swiss*, the CJEU did not clarify the nature of EU competition rules as part of public policy. It merely recalled the distinction already made in *Nordsee* between appeal proceedings against an arbitral award and proceedings for recognition and enforcement under the New York Convention.[26] Nonetheless, it held that the distinction between those types of proceedings does not entail any real difference as concerns the relevance of EU competition law because, in both scenarios, national courts must ensure that the arbitral award is not contrary to EU

---

[23] Gary Born, *International Commercial Arbitration* (2nd edn, Kluwer Law International 2009) 2621.

[24] Swiss Federal Tribunal, 8 March 2006, Revue de l'arbitrage, 2006, 763.

[25] James D. Fry, 'Désordre Public International Under the New York Convention: [Whither] Truly International Public Policy' (2009) 8 Chinese Journal of International Law 81.

[26] Case 102/81 *Nordsee Deutsche Hochseefischerei GmbH v Reederei Mond Hochseefischerei Nordstern AG & Co. KG and Reederei Friedrich Busse Hochseefischerei Nordstern AG & Co. KG* [1982] ECR 1095, para 14.

competition law rules – at least insofar as they are required under national law to take national rules of public policy into account.

At first glance, the general reasoning that underlies the judgment may seem very puzzling. Indeed, there was really no point in mentioning the New York Convention in *Eco Swiss*: the main proceedings did not concern the recognition or the enforcement of the arbitral award but originated from an application to set the award aside according to the Dutch Code of Civil Procedure.

The reference to the New York system can therefore be understood only if one considers that, in the Court's opinion, EU competition law can play a role as part of the notion of 'public policy' recalled in Article V.2 of the Convention. However, that provision, as a result of the so-called 'pro-enforcement bias', can justify a refusal of recognition only in exceptional circumstances where the arbitral award embodies a flagrant violation of fundamental principles of international public policy (even though in some countries the exception is applied in far more liberal terms).[27] Accordingly, EU competition law can be deemed to form part of international public policy within the meaning of Article V.2 of the New York Convention.

This line of reasoning was followed in the judgment of the Gerechtshof of The Hague in *Marketing Displays International*, where the Dutch court refused enforcement of an arbitral award granted in the U.S. against a Benelux distributor under the aegis of the American Arbitration Association. Specifically, the Gerechtshof relied on principles embodied in Article 101 TFEU as a basis for applying the public policy exception under the New York Convention.[28]

In other cases, that conclusion has not as such been questioned: only the judgment of the Corte d'Appello of Florence in *Nuovo Pignone* appeared to cast some doubts,[29] while the reference to domestic public policy in matters of competition law in the judgment of the Corte d'Appello of Milan in *Tensacciai* was only *ad abundantiam*.[30] In general, national courts have not engaged in a thorough consideration of the issue. Instead, they tend to make a general reference to international public policy and then devote their attention mainly to the possible existence of a serious violation of the principles of EU competition law. In a nutshell,

[27] Otto and Elwan, 'Art. V(2)', cited above, note 22.

[28] Gerechtshof Den Haag, 24 March 2005, Yearbook Commercial Arbitration 2006, 808.

[29] Corte d'Appello di Firenze, 21 March 2006, Rivista dell'arbitrato 2006, 741.

[30] Corte d'Appello di Milano, 15 July 2006, Rivista dell'arbitrato 2006, 744.

the relevance of those principles to the international public policy of the Member State where the court sits has been deemed self-evident, requiring no particular justification.

However, some critical remarks in this regard may be useful. First of all, it is obvious that a principle that is so fundamental as to be considered a matter of international public policy is also (and *a fortiori*) relevant with respect to the domestic public policy of the State concerned.

Furthermore, in proceedings for the recognition or enforcement of an arbitral award under the New York Convention, national courts are bound to refer to international public policy as a ground of non-recognition. By contrast, in proceedings for setting aside an arbitral award, national courts may regard the award as 'domestic' (for example because the seat of arbitration was in their country).

Such a qualification may also entail the application of a domestic (and thus, as seen above, a broader) notion of public policy. Accordingly, in those purely internal disputes, EU competition law can play a more prominent role in the review of the validity of the (domestic) award in the national proceedings for setting it aside. Indeed, domestic public policy covers not only the basic principles of competition law but also more detailed provisions; and the degree of seriousness required for conduct to be found contrary to domestic public policy is less intense.

In those circumstances, the review of arbitral awards in the light of EU competition law may certainly be carried out taking domestic public policy into account. For example, the *Tensacciai* case concerned two Italian companies that had undertaken to tender joint offers for the construction of two bridges on the high-speed railway in the Italian territory. If they had submitted the dispute to arbitration in Italy, the dispute would have been purely internal but the EU competition rules would have been applicable nonetheless. Hypothetically, in an Italian proceeding for setting aside the (domestic) award, the national court would have had no reason to confine itself to an examination of the breach of international public policy.

To the extent that this entails more intensive review by national courts, one may query whether such an approach is compatible with the framework of international commercial arbitration. Indeed, this concern is reflected in certain domestic laws which provide that an 'international' arbitral award can be challenged only when it conflicts with international public policy. Such a solution is envisaged, for instance, in Article 1502 of the French Code of Civil Procedure and it is to be welcomed: it clarifies the extent of the review of arbitral awards when they involve transnational elements, and it safeguards the finality of international commercial arbitration. The lack of such provisions leaves proceedings for setting aside an arbitral award open to the risk that national courts will simply make use of the domestic notion of public policy, in particular where issues of EU competition law arise.

That remark may to some degree explain the approaches taken by French courts (although most of the cases presented to them, such as *Thalès v Euromissile*[31] and *SNF v Cytec*, were actually enforcement cases, *Linde AG v Halyvourgiki* involved an application to set aside an award[32]) and by Belgian courts (in proceedings for setting aside an award in *SNF v Cytec*).

However, even where national courts seized in a proceeding for setting aside an 'international' arbitral award refrain from applying scrutiny on the basis of domestic public policy, another doubt may arise in that connection. In particular, it can be argued that EU competition law is intended to apply precisely to transnational situations (where trade between Member States may be affected); thus, restricting the review of arbitral awards to international public policy may have the practical effect of hampering the effective application of principles essential to the functioning of the internal market.

Of course, that does not mean that national courts are always empowered to have a 'second look' at issues of competition law already settled by arbitrators. However, the effective application of EU law constitutes a major concern for the CJEU: if a request for a preliminary ruling on this point is ever submitted, the Court would probably attach great importance to the role of national courts in ensuring the primacy and the full effect of EU competition law. This role is especially crucial with regard to arbitration proceedings, since arbitrators may be called upon to apply EU law but are not allowed to request a preliminary ruling. In that context, the control permitted on the ground of international public policy ('l'illicéité qui crève les yeux', as the Cour d'appel of Paris put it in *Thalès v Euromissile*) may prove to be insufficient to ensure the uniform and consistent application of EU competition law, at least when the dispute does not exceed the borders of the EU.

---

[31] Cour d'appel de Paris, 18 November 2004, Revue de l'arbitrage 2005, 751.
[32] Cour d'appel de Paris, 22 October 2009, Revue de l'arbitrage 2010, 114.

THE EXISTENCE OF A BLATANT VIOLATION OF EU COMPETITION LAW

When the international dimension of public policy is at issue, the national court must persuade itself that a violation of a fundamental principle took place and that it attained a certain degree of seriousness.

As far as violations of EU competition law are concerned, national courts developed two different approaches: the so-called maximalist approach, which calls for an in-depth review of an arbitral award in order to ensure the effective and complete application of the competition rules even in disputes submitted to arbitration; and the minimalist approach, which underlines the prohibition of any review of the award's merits and the importance of showing broad deference to the solution reached by the arbitrators when applying competition law. Under the minimalist approach, the task of national courts is confined to ascertaining manifest violations of fundamental principles of EU competition law.[33]

The maximalist approach builds on an extensive interpretation of the CJEU's judgment in *Eco Swiss*. It found initial support in the judgment of the Tribunal de grande instance of Brussels in *SNF v Cytec* and in the above-mentioned decision of the Gerechtshof of The Hague in *Marketing Displays International*. However, it is the minimalist approach that is now widely accepted by national courts;[34] one may now conclude that Belgian courts too have aligned themselves with the majority view, as the decision of the Tribunal de grande instance of Brussels in *SNF v Cytec* was reversed by the appellate court (although the latter court did engage in an in-depth re-examination of the issues relating to EU competition law that were settled by the arbitral tribunal).

This convergence shows that the minimalist approach represents the prevailing tendency, at least in national case law;[35] on the other hand, it can be seen as the logical consequence of the application of principles of

---

33 The two approaches have been widely discussed. See, *inter alia*, Assimakis P. Komninos 'Arbitration and EU Competition Law', in Jürgen Basedow et al. (eds), *International Antitrust Litigation: Conflict of Laws and Coordination* (Hart Publishing 2012) 214; Luca Radicati di Brozolo, 'L'illicéité 'qui Crève les Yeux': Critère de Contrôle des Sentences au Regard de l'ordre Public International' (2005) Revue de l'arbitrage 529; Simon Vande Walle, *Private Antitrust Litigation in the European Union and in Japan* (Maklu 2013) 215.

34 See, for example, Svea Hovrätt, 23 October 2013, *Systembolaget v The Absolut Company* (unpublished).

35 See Luca Radicati di Brozolo, 'Arbitrage et Droit de la Concurrence: vers un Consensus' (2010) Cahiers de l'arbitrage 181.

EU competition law in the proceedings for review of arbitral awards as part of the international public policy of the Member States. The minimalist approach is also in line with the position of the CJEU in the application of the public policy clause under the 1968 Brussels Convention: in *Renault* the Court held that, in matters of recognition of foreign judgments, an error in law can amount to an infringement of public policy only when it leads to a 'manifest breach of a rule of law regarded as essential in the legal order of the State in which enforcement is sought'.[36] This statement is especially interesting, since in *Renault* an alleged violation of EU competition law (the prohibition of abuse of a dominant position) was at stake, and the Court clearly established that the violation did not attain a sufficient degree of gravity to impede recognition and enforcement of a foreign judgment.

Accordingly, when reviewing an arbitral award in the light of the principles of EU competition law, a national court will confine itself to examine whether it contains or entails a 'flagrant, effective and concrete'[37] breach of those principles. However, it is far more difficult to detect any wide consensus as to what kind of competition law infringement meets those criteria.

In that regard, one may hazard to say that the public policy clause could be invoked when an arbitral award has completely disregarded EU competition law, that is, when it has refused or failed to take Article 101 or Article 102 into account in a situation in which they ought to apply. This was in fact the case in *Eco Swiss*. Outside of those circumstances, it is very difficult to conceive of other clear-cut cases where principles of competition law might be relevant under the public policy clause.

In this connection, it may be useful to stress that, in evaluating whether the arbitral award infringes fundamental principles of EU competition law, regard must be had to the effects of the award. If these effects result in an actual infringement of the general principles enshrined in Articles 101 and 102 – for example, because the award enforces an anticompetitive agreement – the arbitral award can be set aside, or it can be denied recognition or enforcement.

Similarly, when an arbitral tribunal has recognized the existence of anticompetitive behaviour but has refused to draw the consequences of

---

[36] Case C 38/98 *Régie Nationale des Usines Renault SA v Maxicar SpA and Orazio Formento* [2000] ECR I-2973, para 30. See Paul Beaumont 'Abolition of *Exequatur* under the Brussels I Regulation as it Affects Competition Law', in Mihail Danov et al. (eds), *Cross-Border EU Competition Law Actions* (Hart Publishing 2013) 380.

[37] The quotation is from the Cour de cassation, 4 June 2008, *SNF v Cytec*.

that finding under the relevant provisions (and thus has failed, for instance, to declare void an illegal agreement), a national court would be able to conclude that a serious infringement of public policy has occurred. However, as *SNF v Cytec* illustrates, national courts will usually show deference to the formal content of the award without reviewing the substance of the proviso.

In addition, the reviewing court will face the issue of characterization. It must be borne in mind that the application of EU competition law often entails an in-depth examination of the characteristics of the legal transactions concerned and thorough economic analysis. It can therefore prove difficult to find such a manifest and unequivocal infringement of public policy. Consequently, when the arbitral tribunal has dealt with the relevant issues of competition law, either affirming or denying the existence of anticompetitive behaviour, it is possible to contest that finding only through a re-examination of the available data; yet this very re-examination will be usually regarded as an unacceptable review of the merits of the case.

Thus, one can conclude that in most cases the minimalist approach, relying on the international notion of public policy, will lead national courts to show deference to the solution reached by the arbitrators. Regrettably, that solution appears to be founded on *a priori* reasoning, insofar as it makes clear the goal to be pursued (in other words, the finality of arbitration) but neither sets forth a determined threshold for the courts' power of review nor elucidates the actual values of EU competition law to be safeguarded.

PROCEDURAL ISSUES

As a final matter, procedural issues may also interfere with the evaluation of issues of EU competition law in proceedings for the review of arbitral awards. First of all, the capacity of national courts to address issues of EU competition law not raised in the arbitration proceedings must be assessed. Of course, it is beyond doubt that arbitrators too are entitled to apply the EU competition rules, but one should not take for granted that the issue will always be raised by the parties, or raised *ex officio*, in the course of the arbitral proceedings. National courts have often been confronted with cases where competition law issues had not been addressed by the arbitral tribunal; nevertheless, they have not declined to take those issues into consideration at the review stage.

This can be seen as a logical outcome of the premise that national courts must examine the conformity of arbitral awards with EU competition law from the standpoint of public policy. Since a breach of public policy amounts to a serious infringement of the essential principles of a legal system, the existence of such an infringement can always be scrutinised by the court *ex officio*. Accordingly, national courts will be called upon to verify the consistency of the arbitral award with EU competition law irrespective of whether the arbitral tribunal actually dealt with the issue and irrespective of whether the parties raised the question before the arbitrators, or even in their pleadings before the court.

However, when the issue of competition law has actually been raised and analyzed in the course of the arbitral proceedings, it can be very difficult to persuade national courts to review the actual solution adopted in the arbitral award. If the arbitrators have addressed the relevant issues and have settled them reaching one among a series of reasonably possible solutions, the reviewing court will normally not second-guess the arbitrator and rather will be deferential to the award (as happened in *Tensacciai* before the Corte d'Appello of Milan, and in *Cytec v SNF* before the Cour d'appel of Brussels).

On the other hand, if the issue has not been raised before the arbitral tribunal, this can again lead the national court to find against the party advocating a review of the arbitral award on the ground of a breach of EU competition law. For instance, in *SNF v Cytec* and in *Linde AG v Halyvourgiki*, the Cour d'appel of Paris held that the alleged violation of competition rules could not be considered flagrant, as the parties themselves had failed to raise the issue before the arbitral tribunal. As cynical as the argument may appear, it can certainly be expected that national courts will normally disapprove the strategy of raising the issue only at the review stage in order to avoid the enforcement of the arbitral award.

A second issue often discussed in connection with the role played by EU competition law in judicial review proceedings concerns the principle of *res judicata*. National law often provides that arbitral awards can be challenged before national courts only within strict time limits; once the given period has elapsed, awards become final and from that moment no challenge as to their validity can be mounted. It has been argued that this bar is incompatible with the nature of EU competition law as a set of essential principles for the functioning of the internal market.

However, in *Eco Swiss* the CJEU accepted that such time limits can be prescribed, at least when they are not so short that they 'render excessively difficult or virtually impossible the exercise of rights conferred by Community law'. That statement seems to be consistent with the deferential attitude of the Court toward the principle of *res judicata*, whose application has been deemed incompatible with EU law only in very exceptional circumstances[38] or when a specific derogation was provided for in national law.[39]

On the other hand, even when international public policy is at stake, time limits can nonetheless be set, as the measures adopted by the EU on the basis of (current) Article 81 TFEU concerning recognition and enforcement of judgments clearly show.[40] It must be added that choosing not to file an application to set aside the arbitral award before the competent court will of course not prevent the losing party from raising the question before the courts of the country where recognition or enforcement is sought, invoking Article V.2.*b* of the New York Convention.

---

38 Case C-119/05 *Ministero dell'Industria, del Commercio e dell'Artigianato v Lucchini SpA* [2007] ECR I-6199.

39 Case C-453/00 *Kühne and Heitz NV v Produktschap voor Pluimvee en Eieren* [2004] ECR I-837.

40 See, for example, Article 33 of EC Regulation 2201/2003 and Article 50 of EU Regulation 650/2012.

14. Analysis of recent competition cases decided by arbitrators

Laura Bergamini*

ABSTRACT

In recent years an increasing number of arbitral tribunals have been asked to interpret and apply competition law decisions by the European Commission. This new trend has emerged in the context of both international commercial arbitration and public international arbitration, and may grow stronger. This chapter examines two cases reflecting these developments: Reti Televisive Italiane v Sky Italia, *and* Electrabel S.A. v Hungary. *Taken together, these cases illustrate some of the changes that can explain this new trend. They make it possible to start assessing how arbitral tribunals operating in different contexts have approached the same task, and how the Commission has approached arbitral proceedings where the implementation of its decisions was under scrutiny.*

INTRODUCTION

Competition law issues are customarily raised in international commercial arbitration because parties often argue that a contract (or a clause thereof) is invalid on the ground that it runs counter to antitrust laws (for example, Articles 101 and 102 of the Treaty on the Functioning of the European Union, or 'TFEU').[1] Until recently, arbitrators have generally

* Associate, Cleary Gottlieb Steen & Hamilton LLP, Rome.

[1] Competition law issues are typically raised as a defence (see, for example, ICC Case No. 6475, Final Award (1994), (1995) 6(1) ICC International Court Arbitration Bulletin 52; ICC Case No. 7357, Final Award (May 1995), (2003) 14(2) ICC International Court Arbitration Bulletin 53; ICC Case No. 8626, Award, (2003) 14(2) ICC International Court Arbitration Bulletin 55; ICC Case No. 10704, Partial Award (2000/2001), (2003) 14(2) ICC International Court Arbitration Bulletin 66). More rarely they are raised as a claim (for instance, as

addressed these issues before the European Commission ('Commission') issued a decision on the same facts.[2]

By contrast, public international tribunals have not traditionally dealt with competition law because disputes between States do not typically raise issues of this kind.

This scenario seems to have evolved in the past 15 years. Specifically, an increasing number of arbitral tribunals are now being requested to interpret and apply Commission decisions.[3] The two cases that will be discussed in this chapter (both concluded in 2012) – *Reti Televisive Italiane v Sky Italia* and *Electrabel S.A. v The Republic of Hungary* – reflect the emergence of this new trend.

Although these cases differ as to their nature, subject matter, procedures, parties and arbitrators involved,[4] the combined reading of these two cases may:

---

a claim of abuse of dominance: see, for example, ICC Case No. 7673, Partial Award (1993), (1995) 6(1) ICC International Court Arbitration Bulletin 57).

[2] See the other chapters in Part III of the book for an analysis of the main issues raised by 'Ordinary EC Antitrust Arbitrations' (a term used in Carl Nisser and Gordon Blanke, 'ICC Draft Best Practice Note on the European Commission Acting as Amicus Curiae in International Proceedings – The Text' (2008) 19(1) European Business Law Review 198, 202 ('ICC Draft Best Practice Note').

[3] Ordinary EU Antitrust Arbitrations are still frequent (possibly even more common than in the past due to the increasing integration of markets in the EU). For instance, one may refer to the *Linde* case (on which see, for example, Jennifer Kirby and Denis Bensaude, 'A View From Paris' (March 2010) 25(3) Mealey's International Arbitration Report 2, or to *Siemens v Areva*, which is particularly interesting because the arbitration (brought by Areva) proceeded in parallel with the Commission investigation of the same facts (triggered by a complaint by Siemens). In *Siemens v Areva*, the arbitrators issued their award before the Commission issued its preliminary assessment. The Commission later found that the scope and duration of certain non-compete and confidentiality obligations established by the arbitrators violated EU law; accordingly, it required the parties to terminate those obligations. The ICC award is not public. For the Commission's Article 9 decision, see Case Comp/39736 of 18 June 2012 – *Siemens/Areva*, C(2012) 4028 final.

[4] *Reti Televisive Italiane v Sky Italia* is a private commercial arbitration, administered by a private organization (the International Chamber of Commerce, or 'ICC'), governed by the law of the State of the arbitration seat (Milan) and subject to the jurisdiction of the Italian courts. The *Electrabel v Hungary* case is a public international arbitration, administered by a public institution (the International Centre for the Settlement of Investment Disputes, or 'ICSID') and governed by the Washington Convention (which establishes an *ad hoc* international annulment procedure against the award).

(i) illustrate some of the changes that can explain the new trend mentioned above; and
(ii) allow us the opportunity to start assessing how: (a) arbitral tribunals (operating in different contexts) have approached the same task; and (b) the Commission has approached arbitral proceedings where the implementation of its decisions was under scrutiny.

This analysis also seems useful because it is probable that, in the near future, arbitrators will be entrusted, on an increasing basis, with the task of assessing whether obligations imposed by Commission decisions have been respected.

A GROWING TREND: COMMISSION DECISIONS UNDER ARBITRAL SCRUTINY? THE CASES OF *RETI TELEVISIVE ITALIANE v SKY ITALIA* AND *ELECTRABEL S.A. v HUNGARY*

Since 2000, several changes have occurred in both the arbitration and competition sectors. As a result of these changes, arbitral tribunals have been entrusted with the delicate new task of interpreting and applying European Commission decisions.

First, arbitration has gradually become one of the most commonly used methods to resolve international commercial disputes between private parties. Furthermore:

(i) follow-on actions[5] have increasingly been brought before arbitral tribunals;[6] and

---

[5] See the ECJ's seminal judgment in Case C-453/99 *Courage Ltd v Crehan* [2001] ECR I-6297. Although this was not a proper follow-on case, the judgment opened the door to private claims for compensation of damages suffered as a result of anticompetitive behaviour. It is widely accepted that the relevant terms of Article 16 of Regulation 1/2003 are binding upon arbitrators as much as they are upon the courts. Thus, arbitrators are precluded from adopting decisions running counter to prior decisions of the Commission.

[6] The EU Directive on certain rules governing actions for damages under national law for infringements of the competition law provisions of the Member States and of the European Union (the 'Damages Directive'), approved by the European Parliament on 17 April 2014, is expected to increase the number of follow-on actions in Europe as well as, potentially, the use of arbitration to seek damages due to breaches of competition law. On the relevance of the Damages Directive for arbitration, see Renato Nazzini, 'Arbitration of Competition Law

(ii) unilateral offers to arbitrate disputes relating to the implementation of merger remedies packages[7] have been increasingly included in commitments[8] presented to the Commission.[9]

Reti Televisive Italiane v Sky Italia arbitration clearly illustrates this latter trend.[10] On 17 February 2012, an ICC tribunal issued a final award in a dispute brought under an arbitration offer included in the commitments undertaken in a package of merger remedies offered to and accepted by the Commission. To date, this is the only reported merger remedy arbitration culminating in an award.

Disputes and the New EU Directive on Antitrust Damages Actions', TILEC Seminar: Enforcement of Competition Law held on 22 May 2014, <https://www.tilburguniversity.edu> accessed 23 August 2014.

[7] A great deal of debate surrounds the nature and effects of these arbitrations. According to one view, remedy arbitration is a sort of a regulatory or 'supranational' arbitration (Gordon Blanke, 'The Case for Supranational Arbitration – Ideas and Prospects' (2008) 19(1) European Business Law Review 17) that allows the Commission to monitor compliance with commitments; according to another view, remedy arbitration is an ordinary form of international commercial arbitration (Luca G. Radicati di Brozolo, 'Arbitration and EU Merger Control: Old Wine in a New Bottle' (2008) 19(1) European Business Law Review 7).

[8] Pursuant to the EU Merger Regulation, the Commission may require 'modifications' of a proposed concentration with a 'Community dimension' which raises 'serious doubts' as to the transaction's 'compatibility with the common market'. These 'modifications' ('remedies' or 'commitments') are presented by the acquiring party to address the competition concerns identified by the Commission. If the Commission finds that the remedies are proportionate and eliminate its competition concerns, it issues a merger clearance decision.

[9] For a review of the clauses contained in EU merger clearance decisions, see Gordon Blanke, 'International Arbitration and ADR in Conditional EU Merger Clearance Decisions: EU and US Antitrust Arbitration', in Gordon Blanke and Phillip Landolt (eds), *EU and US Antitrust Arbitration. A Handbook for Practitioners* (Wolters Kluwer 2011) 1605. The wording of the commitments is negotiated with the Commission (and the Commission has often pressed the undertaking to grant it the right to intervene and control the arbitration). See Alexis Mourre, 'Dissenting Opinion on a Dangerous Project' (2008) 19(1) European Business Law Review 217.

[10] ICC Case No. 16974/FM/GZ, *Reti Televisive Italiane v Sky Italia*, Award, 17 February 2012 ('RTI Award'). Cleary Gottlieb Steen & Hamilton LLP represented one of the parties in the arbitration. The award was not made public in its entirety, but several extracts have been published. See, for example, Luca G. Radicati di Brozolo, 'EU Merger Control Commitments and Arbitration: *Reti Televisive Italiane v Sky Italia*' (2013) 29(2) Arbitration International 223.

More specifically, the dispute arose in connection with the remedies ('Commitments') that The News Corporation Limited ('Newscorp') offered the Commission in 2003 in connection with its proposed acquisition of Telepiù SpA. and subsequent merger with Stream SpA.

In the course of its investigation, the Commission had found that the merger would create 'or strengthen a dominant position with regard to the demand-side (the acquisition of the rights)' in some markets, including the 'exclusive rights to football events that take place every year where national teams participate' and 'exclusive rights to other sport events'.

To address the Commission's concerns, Newscorp undertook, *inter alia*: (i) not to acquire exclusive broadcasting rights 'concerning world-wide sports rights'; and (ii) to resolve 'any dispute that may arise regarding the implementation' of the Commitments through ICC arbitration (Articles 8(1) and 15(1)(b) of the Commitments). Pursuant to Article 3 of Part I, the Commitments were to be 'governed by and construed in accordance with Italian law and European Community law'.

The Commission found, in its Decision of 2 April 2003, that the Commitments 'address[ed] and resolve[d] in a satisfactory manner the competition concerns raised by the concentration'. It therefore authorized the merger.

On February 2010, RTI Italia SpA. ('RTI')[11] filed an ICC arbitration against SKY Italia Srl., ('Sky', one of Newscorp's wholly-owned subsidiaries), claiming that the latter had breached the Commitments by acquiring (on an exclusive basis) the 2010 FIFA World Cup broadcasting rights ('FIFA Rights') even though they qualified as 'world-wide sports rights'. On the basis of this alleged breach, RTI sought declaratory and compensatory relief.

In order to render a decision on RTI's claims, the tribunal had to assess whether Sky had correctly implemented the Commitments and whether the FIFA Rights fell within their scope. The Commission did not participate in the ICC proceedings. Ultimately, the tribunal found that Sky had not breached the Commitments (since the FIFA Rights corresponded to a market different from those markets affected by the concentration), thus rejecting RTI's claims.

The second change that has taken place in the past few years is that competition issues have also been raised in the context of public international law arbitrations.

---

[11] RTI is SKY Italia's largest competitor in the Italian pay-TV sector.

This change seems to be mainly due to the fact that private parties have been granted access to international tribunals in order to seek redress for breaches of international obligations by States as regards foreign investments (investment treaty arbitrations). In these arbitrations, States have begun to argue that their actions were legal (and even necessary) because they were required to implement EU competition law or a Commission decision.

Electrabel v Hungary is a textbook example of this trend.[12] On 10 October 1995, the Hungarian State-owned electricity supply company (Magyar Villamos Müvek Zrt, or 'MVM') and a company named Dunamenti entered into a Power Purchase Agreement ('PPA') under which Dunamenti was to supply MVM with capacity in return for payment of a capacity fee (originally until December 2010, a date later extended to December 2015).[13] Subsequently, in 2001, Electrabel (the Belgian energy company) acquired 74.8 per cent of Dunamenti's shares.[14]

On 1 May 2004, Hungary joined the European Union. On 24 May 2005, the Commission launched an investigation into the Hungarian electricity market to determine whether PPAs involved the grant of State aid in breach of EU competition law. On 9 November 2005, the Commission opened a formal investigation (under Article 88(2) EC, now Article 108(2) TFEU) of Hungarian PPAs.[15] A few months' later, Hungary reintroduced regulated pricing and forced a 40 per cent reduction of the prices under the PPA with Dunamenti.

On 4 June 2008, the Commission issued a final decision ('Final Decision') finding that MVM's purchasing obligations under the PPAs did indeed involve State aid in breach of the competition rules. Hence, the Commission required Hungary: (i) to stop providing such aid (within a six-month deadline); and (ii) to recover the aid already granted.[16]

---

[12] ICSID Case No. ARB/07/19, *Electrabel S.A. v The Republic of Hungary*, Decision on jurisdiction, applicable law and liability, 30 November 2012 ('Electrabel Award'), available at http://italaw.com accessed 23 October 2014.

[13] At that time, MVM was acting as a single purchaser exercising a state monopoly, with regulated pricing established by Hungary. See Electrabel Award, para 6.2.

[14] Electrabel Award, para 6.3.

[15] Electrabel Award, para 6.4.

[16] The State aid was calculated as the difference between each generator's actual revenues under its PPA and the revenues that could have been obtained on the spot market, without any PPA, in a simulated counterfactual scenario. See Electrabel Award, para 6.5.

Hungary did not challenge the Final Decision, and communicated it to Dunamenti.[17]

On 10 November 2008, Hungary's Parliament ordered that the State's PPAs (including the PPA with Dunamenti) be terminated.

On 27 April 2010, the Commission approved Hungary's scheme to compensate 'stranded costs' incurred by Dunamenti ('Compensation Decision').[18]

In 2007 (with the Commission's investigation pending), Electrabel filed a claim with ICSID under Article 26(3) of the Energy Charter Treaty ('ECT'). Electrabel claimed that Hungary's actions (for example, the termination of the PPA with Dunamenti and the compensation scheme adopted by the State in Dunamenti's favour) constituted an unlawful expropriation of its investment as well as a breach of its right to fair and equitable treatment and a breach of other standards of protection under the ECT.

In order to decide on Electrabel's claims, the tribunal had, *inter alia*, to assess whether the Commission had actually required Hungary to terminate (early) Dunamenti's PPA. It therefore had to interpret the meaning and scope of the Commission's Final Decision. In this case the Commission did participate in the proceedings as *amicus curiae*, and it filed a brief addressing specific issues of EU law.[19]

By an award dated 30 November 2012, the ICSID tribunal found, *inter alia*, that the Final Decision had required Hungary to terminate the PPAs[20] and thus partially denied Electrabel's claims. However, the tribunal found that Dunamenti's compensation scheme (adopted by Hungary and accepted by the Commission) lacked 'symmetry' and that, under this scheme, Dunamenti might not be able to recover proper compensation for its net stranded costs.[21] However, the tribunal decided to postpone a determination as to whether this scheme was capable of

---

[17] Electrabel Award, para 6.7. On 29 April 2009, Dunamenti challenged the Final Decision before the European Court of First Instance pursuant to Article 230 EC (Electrabel Award, para 6.8). Only Dunamenti (in other words, neither Electrabel nor Hungary) is a party to these proceedings.

[18] Electrabel Award, para 6.9 (stranded costs in this context are defined as the difference between Dunamenti's investment costs and operating revenues generated in the past and to be generated in the future up to the notional end of the PPA's term, in other words, December 2015).

[19] Electrabel Award, paras 4.89 et seq.

[20] Electrabel Award, paras 6.72 et seq.

[21] Electrabel Award, para 6.109.

breaching the principle of fair and equitable treatment until such time as Hungary fixed the amount of Dunamenti's stranded costs.

The *Electrabel v Hungary* case is not an isolated one. Since 2005, States have relied on EU competition law and Commission decisions to defend their actions in at least three other investment treaty cases. Two cases were brought against Hungary between 2007 and 2009,[22] and one case was filed against Romania in 2005.[23]

ARBITRATORS' APPROACH TO THE TASK OF INTERPRETING AND APPLYING COMMISSION DECISIONS

As noted above, in both *Reti Televisive Italiane v Sky Italia* and *Electrabel S.A. v Hungary* the tribunals were entrusted with the task of interpreting Commission decisions. In both cases the tribunals approached their task similarly.

In *Reti Televisive Italiane v Sky Italia*, the ICC tribunal first set about determining which law governed the interpretation of the Commitments, and found that the Commitments: (i) formed an 'integral part' of the Decision (and that 'different parts of the same act should be read together');[24] (ii) had to be read in light of the Decision and, specifically with regard to the Commission's competition concerns ('as their very

---

[22] ICSID Case ARB/07/22, *AES Summit Generation Limited and AES-Tisza Erdma Kft. v Republic of Hungary* and UNCITRAL Case, *EDF International S.A. v Republic of Hungary*, registered in May 2009, <http://www.encharter.org/index.php?id=213&L=0#EDF> accessed 23 August 2014.

[23] ICSID Case No. ARB/05/20, *Ioan Micula, Viorel Micula, S.C. European Food S.A, S.C. Starmill S.R.L. and S.C. Multipack S.R.L. v Romania*. In the three arbitrations against Hungary, investors sought compensation for State breaches. However, in *Micula v Romania*, investors also sought restitution, in other words, they sought an order from the tribunal requiring Romania to restore the legislation allegedly providing for State aid in breach of EU law (ICSID Case No. ARB/05/20, *Ioan Micula, Viorel Micula, S.C. European Food S.A, S.C. Starmill S.R.L. and S.C. Multipack S.R.L. v Romania*, Decision on Jurisdiction and Admissibility, 24 September 2008, paras 158 et seq.). In the merits phase, investors withdrew their request for restitution of the former legal framework (abrogated upon a request by the Commission), and only maintained their claims for damages (ICSID Case No. ARB/05/20, *Ioan Micula, Viorel Micula, S.C. European Food S.A, S.C. Starmill S.R.L. and S.C. Multipack S.R.L. v Romania*, Award, 11 December 2013, para 55 'Micula Award').

[24] RTI Award, para 414.

purpose is to meet such concerns as identified in the [d]ecision');[25] and (iii) 'belong[ed] to the EU legal system' and had to be interpreted 'in compliance with the hierarchy of EU sources of law', since the Decision was a 'form of legislation'.[26]

The tribunal then scrutinized whether the FIFA Rights fell within the scope of Article 8(1) of the Commitments by analyzing the text of the Decision and the competition concerns raised in the Commission's Statement of Objections. In doing so the tribunal proceeded autonomously, without requesting (or authorizing) comments from the Commission. Moreover, while former officials of the Commission were heard as witnesses (upon request of one of the parties), the tribunal did not refer to their statements when interpreting the Decision.

Finally, the tribunal held that it had no 'power to change the Commission's Decision'.[27] Specifically, it found that it could not extend the Commitments to markets not originally affected by the concentration (but potentially affected by it due to changes in the competitive situation), 'as this would undermine the Commission's exclusive decision making power'.[28]

In a nutshell, the ICC tribunal: (i) did not question its own power to interpret and apply the Decision; (ii) interpreted the Decision autonomously (in other words, apparently without being influenced by the statements made by the Commission or the Commission's former officials); (iii) interpreted the Decision in the light of EU law (with no reference to domestic law) by exploring the Decision's underlying rationale; and (iv) did not entertain a re-litigation of the issues decided by the Commission. By doing so, the tribunal has seemingly acknowledged both that its task was the private enforcement of the Commission's decision (not that of acting as the Commission's agent for the 'monitoring' of the Commitments),[29] and that the Commission lacks the power to provide definitive interpretations of its decisions (a power within the sphere of the courts, national or EU,[30] and thus within the sphere of the arbitrators themselves).

Similarly, in *Electrabel S.A. v Hungary*, the tribunal first stated that EU law governed the interpretation of the Final Decision and that, according

25 RTI Award, para 413 (also stating that a 'literal reading of an excerpt of the Commitments [is] not sufficient', RTI Award, para 409).

26 RTI Award, para 413.

27 RTI Award, para 445 and paras 436 et seq.

28 RTI Award, para 436.

29 See Radicati di Brozolo, cited above, note 10, at 231.

30 Ibid., 226.

to the European Court of Justice, the *dispositif* of a decision must be read together with its recitals.[31]

Second, the tribunal examined whether the Final Decision (when 'read as a whole') required Hungary to terminate the PPAs, and concluded that it did.[32] In reaching this finding, the tribunal took no account of 'extraneous circumstances', including the Commission's press releases or the pleadings the Commission had filed in the proceedings that Dunamenti brought before the then-Court of First Instance ('CFI').[33] Nor did the tribunal request or authorize the Commission to comment on the meaning or scope of its Decision (though it did hear the Commission's observations on general issues relating to EU law).[34]

Finally, the tribunal examined whether EU law or the Commission's decisions precluded Hungary from compensating Electrabel for the stranded costs that it had incurred.[35] Once again, the tribunal carried out its own assessment of EU law and found that, 'as regards EU law and the Commission, there does not appear to be any insuperable obstacle to a cash payment for Net Stranded Costs in appropriate circumstances'.[36] According to the tribunal, 'in new circumstances' (for example, in the event of an annulment of the Final Decision by the CFI), the Commission might 'look again at a cash payment for Net Stranded Costs to Dunamenti'.[37] The tribunal reached this conclusion even though the Commission had stated (before the CFI) that it had approved cash payments only in cases factually and chronologically different from the circumstances concerning Dunamenti.[38]

---

[31] Electrabel Award, paras 6.84 et seq. (also refusing to interpret the Final Decision by merely relying on the literal reading of its *dispositif* – see para 6.82).

[32] Electrabel Award, paras 6.86 et seq.

[33] See above, note 17 and Electrabel Award, para 6.89 ('[H]aving reached its own interpretation, the Tribunal takes comfort from the fact that the European Commission has consistently maintained that the Final Decision did indeed require Hungary to terminate the PPA').

[34] See the next section of this chapter. The Tribunal invited the Commission to address three issues: (a) European Community law and its connection with the ECT; (b) Community law and the State aid investigation concerning the PPAs; and (c) the effect of Community decisions on the Members States, particularly Hungary (see Procedural Order dated 28 April 2009, cited in Electrabel Award, para 4.89).

[35] Electrabel Award, paras 6.94 et seq.

[36] Electrabel Award, para 6.115.

[37] Ibid.

[38] Electrabel Award, para 6.116.

Therefore, the ICSID tribunal, for its part too: (i) did not doubt its own power to interpret the scope of the Final Decision (despite the fact that the lawfulness of the Final Decision was subject to challenge before a European Court); (ii) interpreted the Final Decision autonomously (without requiring the support of the Commission and even, seemingly, against statements made by the Commission); and (iii) found that the Final Decision was a form of EU law that had to be interpreted in accordance with EU law. Hence, the tribunal acted as if it had full power to interpret and decide autonomously the scope of the State's international obligations established by the Commission.

THE COMMISSION'S APPROACH TO ARBITRATIONS DEALING WITH THE INTERPRETATION OF ITS DECISIONS

The conduct of the Commission in *Reti Televisive Italiane v Sky Italia* and *Electrabel S.A. v Hungary* differed significantly.

As already noted, the Commission did not participate in the arbitration between Reti Televisive Italiane and Sky Italia. Specifically, the award reports: (i) no attempts by the parties or by the tribunal to seek the Commission's assistance or cooperation; and (ii) no attempts by the Commission to influence or interfere with the proceedings or the arbitrators' decision.

One may be tempted to interpret this abstention as if the Commission were not interested in monitoring the enforcement of the Commitments or the decisions of the arbitral tribunal. The reason for this 'indifference' might be seen in the fact that, in any case, the Commission can (at any time) investigate the way the Commitments are implemented and, if necessary, adopt measures ensuring compliance with them.[39]

However, it seems doubtful that the Commission would adopt the same approach taken in *Reti Televisive Italiane v Sky Italia* in any future remedy arbitrations. Indeed, the arbitration clause in the latter case did not expressly provide for the Commission's participation in the arbitration, while clauses included in more recent EU merger commitments provide for the significant involvement of the Commission in any related arbitration.

---

[39] The Commission can furthermore decide the issue differently from the arbitral tribunal (or the national court), although its decision would not affect the *res judicata* effect of the award or judgment. See Radicati di Brozolo, cited above note 10, at note 20).

For instance, Article 6(16) of the commitments approved in the US Airways/American Airlines merger[40] provides that the 'Commission shall be allowed and enabled to participate in all stages of the procedure', and that it will:

(i) receive all written submissions made by the parties and all orders, awards and documents exchanged by the arbitral tribunal and the parties (including terms of reference and procedural timetable) (letters a and b);
(ii) be given the 'opportunity to file *amicus curiae* briefs' (letter c); and
(iii) be 'present at the hearing(s)' and be 'allowed to ask questions to parties, witnesses and experts' (letter d).

By approving these types of commitments, the Commission clearly reserves its right to intervene in the arbitral proceedings and to monitor the implementation of both the commitments and its decisions.[41] This intention is made even clearer by a provision (frequently included in recent commitments) according to which, in 'the event of disagreement between the parties [...] regarding the interpretation of the Commitments, the Arbitral Tribunal may seek the Commission's interpretation of the Commitments before finding in favor of any party [...] and shall be bound by the interpretation'.[42] Indeed, under this provision, arbitrators can even defer to the Commission the task of interpreting the commitments with a binding effect over the parties and the tribunal itself.[43]

---

[40] Appended to the decision dated 5 August 2013.

[41] As regards the participation of the Commission as *amicus curiae* in ICC arbitration, see, for example, 'ICC Draft Best Practice Note' cited above, note 2, at 198; Carl Nisser and Gordon Blanke, 'ICC Draft Best Practice Note on the European Commission Acting as Amicus Curiae in International Arbitration Proceedings – An Explanatory Note' (2008) 19(1) European Business Law Review 193; Assimakis Komninos, 'Assistance by the European Commission and Member States' Authorities in Arbitrations', in Blanke and Landolt (eds), cited above, note 9, at 727.

[42] See Article 6(18) of the US Airways/American Airlines commitments. See also, for example, Article 7 of Commitments approved by the Commission in the case of International Consolidated Airlines Group/British Midlands Limited, dated 30 March 2012.

[43] It is arguable whether a decision exclusively based on the Commission's interpretation would be qualified as an award by national courts, at least when, in light of the circumstances, it may appear that the 'arbitrators' have not themselves 'adjudicated' the dispute.

In contrast to *Reti Televisive Italiane v Sky Italia*, the Commission did request leave (and was authorized) to intervene in *Electrabel S.A. v Hungary* as a non-disputing party (*amicus curiae*).

Specifically, after issuing the Final Decision, the Commission applied for permission to make a written submission under Article 37(2) of the ICSID Arbitration Rules.[44] The tribunal granted this request (noting that the 'European Commission is an expert commentator on European Community law and [can] accordingly assist the tribunal by addressing several issues')[45] and identified three specific issues on which it wished the Commission to comment.[46] The tribunal did not authorize the Commission to submit written comments on the meaning of the Final Decision. The Commission was then granted access to some of the parties' pleadings (in redacted form),[47] but it was not authorized to attend the hearing. However, as noted above, the tribunal found that the Commission's views were not binding upon it,[48] and it reached conclusions partially different from those the Commission had advanced.[49]

The Commission adopted a similar approach in three other investment cases where the measures allegedly taken to comply with EU competition law were contested: *AES v Hungary; EDF v Hungary*; and *Micula v Romania*. In each case, the Commission filed a request to intervene as *amicus curiae*,[50] and in each case it was authorized to intervene as a non-disputing party (although the Commission's right to intervene in each proceedings took a different form).[51]

---

44 Electrabel Award, paras 1.6 and 1.18. The content of the Commission's application is not publicly known.

45 Electrabel Award, para 4.89.

46 See also note 41, above.

47 Electrabel Award, para 5.6. The Commission went beyond the tribunal's requests and brought arguments, based on EU law, against the jurisdiction of the tribunal (Electrabel Award, para 4.90).

48 However, the tribunal conveyed 'its thanks and appreciation to the European Commission for its Submission, as regards both applicable law and jurisdiction' which is a 'lengthy, scholarly and important document for these arbitration proceedings' (Electrabel Award, para 4.91)

49 See the previous section.

50 Unfortunately, none of the applications filed by the Commission was made public.

51 For instance, in *AES v Hungary* the tribunal allowed the Commission to file a written submission but it denied the Commission's request for copies of the parties' written submissions (in light of the fact that the parties had not reached an agreement on the issue – ICSID Case No. ARB/07/22, *Aes Summit Generation Limited Aes-Tisza Erömü Kft v The Republic of Hungary*, Award, 23

The Commission has thus shown a clear interest in participating in investment treaty arbitrations in order to influence a tribunal's interpretation of EU (competition) law. This tendency probably reflects a general inclination that most likely will be adopted in future cases, particularly in light of the serious consequences that could flow from conflicting interpretations of EU competition law (by investment arbitral tribunals and by the Commission itself).

An illustrative case is *Micula v Romania*. Indeed, on the one hand, an ICSID tribunal ordered Romania to pay to investors more than RON 376,433,229 plus interest (more than EUR 85.4 million plus interest) as damages for breach of its obligations under the EC Treaty (by an award enforceable in all Member States pursuant to Article 53 of the Washington Convention). On the other hand, the Commission issued a 'suspension injunction' forbidding Romania from honouring the ICSID award and paying the amounts awarded, as they would constitute State aid in breach of EU competition law.[52] Thus, due to different interpretations of EU law, Romania is currently bound by two conflicting international obligations.[53]

By the same token, *Micula v Romania* shows that the direct participation of the Commission in investment treaty arbitrations as a non-disputing party may not suffice to avoid conflicting interpretations of EU law. As seen above, Romania was caught in an impasse even though the Commission did participate in the proceedings and expressly stated that payment of an ICSID award for damages would constitute unlawful State aid incompatible with EU law.[54]

September 2010, para 3.22). By contrast, in *Micula v Romania*, the Commission was granted full access to the parties' briefs and was allowed to submit a written submission 'focused on assisting the Tribunal in the determination of [the] factual or legal issues at stake'. The tribunal added that the Commission could 'within this scope decide which facts and laws are relevant to the dispute' (Micula Award, para 36). Furthermore, in *Micula v Romania* (but not in *AES v Hungary*), the Commission's representatives were heard at the hearing (Micula Award, para 80).

[52] Decision dated 26 May 2014. See http://ec.europa.eu accessed 23 October 2014.

[53] See Séverine Menétrey, 'La Participation "amicale" de la Commission Européenne dans les Arbitrages Liés aux Investissments Intracommunautaires' (2010/4) Journal du Droit International 1147, stating that Romania was in a 'trap' since, if it were to fulfil the arbitral award, it would violate European law and could be sanctioned by the Commission.

[54] Award, 11 December 2013, paras 330 et seq.

CONCLUSIONS

In light of the changes occurring in the arbitration and competition sectors, arbitrators have been (and possibly will be) increasingly exposed to the delicate task of interpreting and applying decisions issued by the European Commission.

Notwithstanding the different nature of the proceedings examined in this chapter, arbitrators have seemingly dealt with this task similarly. Specifically, both tribunals: (i) found that they could interpret and apply Commission decisions to the same extent that they could interpret and apply EU law; (ii) interpreted the Commission's decisions by applying criteria drawn from EU law (and not from domestic or international law); and (iii) interpreted the Commission decisions as a whole, without making reference to other provisions of EU law (not even those that the Commission had applied). Furthermore, none of the tribunals: (iv) found that it should defer to the Commission's own interpretation of its decisions, or that the Commission's interpretation of its decisions could bind the tribunal; or (v) reviewed the correctness of the Commission's decisions in light of EU law.

By contrast, the approach adopted by the Commission towards the two arbitrations seemingly differs. Specifically, in the ICSID arbitration the Commission requested leave (and was allowed) to intervene as *amicus curiae*, while the Commission made no such request in the remedy arbitration. However, this circumstance does not conclusively suggest that the Commission intends to participate only in investment treaty arbitrations. Indeed, some of the most recent remedy packages approved as part of the EU merger clearance process grant the Commission an extensive right to intervene in any related remedy arbitrations.

Case law further shows that there are risks of potentially conflicting interpretations on EU law and Commission decisions. Specifically, the Commission can (at any time) activate an administrative procedure relating to the same facts already examined by arbitrators, without being bound by the arbitrators' decision (and thus it can impose fines for behaviour that the arbitrators have found to be lawful). However, such a conflict has different consequences in remedy arbitrations and in investment treaty proceedings, and it may raise particularly delicate issues in the context of the latter.

Index